JACOB BURCKHARDT AND THE CRISIS OF MODERNITY

WITH THE VALUES OF WESTERN CIVILIZATION increasingly under siege, economic crises, political unrest, and environmental degradation oblige us to reassess the assumptions of modern mass society. *Jacob Burckhardt and the Crisis of Modernity,* the first major study in English dedicated entirely to Burckhardt, offers a compelling and timely interpretative and synthetic analysis of Burckhardt's unique challenge to the values and assumptions of modern society, placing his work in the context of his political ideology and work in history and art history. John Hinde provides a new assessment of Burckhardt's position, focusing on his lesser known writings.

As a historian of the Renaissance and the rise of Christianity, Burckhardt was concerned with periods of social, political, and cultural transformation. Writing in the aftermath of the 1848 Revolution and in the long shadow cast by the French Revolution of 1789, he observed the rise of industrial capitalism and mass politics with trepidation. He especially lamented the fate of the individual, whose creativity had shaped the glories of the Renaissance and ancient Greece but who was increasingly domesticated and commodified in modern society.

Unlike conventional accounts, which characterize Burckhardt as an apolitical aesthete, Hinde shows us Burckhardt as a thinker of profound importance, whose conservative anti-modernism ranks him with his colleague Friedrich Nietzsche.

JOHN R. HINDE teaches at the University of Victoria.

McGill-Queen's Studies in the History of Ideas

JACOB BURCKHARDT AND THE CRISIS OF MODERNITY

John R. Hinde

McGill-Queen's University Press
Montreal & Kingston · London · Ithaca

Legal deposit third quarter 2000
Bibliothèque nationale du Québec

Printed in Canada on acid-free paper

This book has been published with the help of a grant
from the Humanities and Social Sciences Federation of
Canada, using funds provided by the Social Sciences and
Humanities Research Council of Canada.

McGill-Queen's University Press acknowledges the
financial support of the Government of Canada through
the Book Publishing Industry Development Program
(BPIDP) for its activities. We also acknowledge the support
of the Canada Council for the Arts for our publishing
program.

Canadian Cataloguing in Publication Data

Hinde, John Roderick, 1964-
    Jacob Burckhardt and the crisis of modernity
    (McGill-Queen's studies in the history of ideas; 29)
    Includes bibliographical references and index.
    ISBN 0-7735-1027-3
    1. Burckhardt, Jacob, 1818-1897. I. Title. II. Series.
    D15.B8H56 2000   907'.202   C99-901445-5

This book was typeset by Typo Litho Composition Inc.
in 10/12 Baskerville.

Contents

Acknowledgments

THIS WORK HAS PROFITTED from the assistance of numerous individuals and institutions over the course of the last few years. In particular, I would like to express my gratitude to three of my former instructors: Thomas Saunders, at the University of Victoria; Harold Mah, at Queen's University; and Georg G. Iggers, for whom this work was originally written as a doctoral dissertation at the State University of New York at Buffalo. Not only have these scholars helped shape my ideas about history, but they have continued to support my career and have never denied my all-too-frequent requests for letters of recommendation. I would also like to thank Dr Christian Simon, who led the stimulating seminar on Burckhardt at the University of Basel, 1992–93, and the Jacob Burckhardt-Stiftung for assisting my work. That I was able to research in Basel was due to a generous scholarship from the Swiss federal government. The federal government in Ottawa provided me with support as well, and not just via unemployment benefits. A SSHRC postdoctoral fellowship at the University of Victoria enabled me to pursue my research interests further and provided me with the opportunity to teach. The congenial atmosphere at the University of Victoria was more than matched by that at Malaspina University-College, where I was fortunate enough to receive a temporary teaching assignment in 1998–99. I would also like to thank Wendy Dayton, whose thoughtful and thorough editing greatly improved this manuscript, and Joan McGilvray. It's shortcomings, of course, remain my responsibility.

In addition, my wife, Kristine, and son, Anthony, have been a source of great strength. Ted, Gail, and my brother Stephen have also stood by me and provided encouragement. This book is dedicated to my mother,

Brenda, and my late father, Ken, without whose love and support this work would never have been possible. Although my father did not live to see it completed, I know he would be proud.

Abbreviations

AfKg	*Archiv für Kulturgeschichte*
AHR	*American Historical Review*
AInB	*Allgemeines Intelligenzblatt der Stadt Basel*
Briefe	*Jacob Burckhardt Briefe*, Max Burckhardt, ed., 10 vols., Basel: Benno Schwabe 1949–86
BZ	*Basler Zeitung*
BZFGA	*Basler Zeitschrift für Geschichte und Altertumskunde*
Constantine	Jacob Burckhardt, *The Age of Constantine the Great*, New York: Dorset 1949
CRI	Jacob Burckhardt, *The Civilization of the Renaissance in Italy*, Harmondsworth: Penguin Books 1990
DVLG	*Deutsche Vierteljahrsschrift für Literaturwissenschaft und Geistesgeschichte*
GA	Jacob Burckhardt, *Gesamtausgabe*, Emil Dürr et al., eds., 14 vols., Basel: Benno Schwabe 1929–34
HT	*History and Theory*
HZ	*Historische Zeitschrift*
JES	*Journal of European Studies*
JHH	Jacob Burckhardt, *Judgements on History and Historians*, Harry Zohn, trans., Boston: Beacon Press 1958
JHI	*Journal of the History of Ideas*
Kaegi	Werner Kaegi, *Jacob Burckhardt: Eine Biographie*, 7 vols., Basel: Benno Schwabe 1947–82

NZ   *Schweizerische National-Zeitung*
SdS   *Storia della Storiografia*
WB   Jacob Burckhardt, *Über das Studium der*
            Geschichte: Der Text der Weltgeschichtlichen
            Betrachtungen, Peter Ganz, ed., Munich:
            C.H. Beck Verlag 1982

JACOB BURCKHARDT AND THE CRISIS OF MODERNITY

Introduction

DURING HIS LIFETIME, the Swiss scholar Jacob Burckhardt (1818–97) gained international recognition for his path-breaking work in the fields of cultural history and art history. Over a span of ten years he published his three most important books: *The Age of Constantine the Great* (1853), his first cultural history; *Der Cicerone* (1855), his popular guidebook to the art treasures of the Italian Renaissance; and his most famous work, *The Civilization of the Renaissance in Italy* (1860).[1] Burckhardt continued to write a great deal after 1860, but published with extreme reluctance. In fact, he always considered teaching his primary responsibility and, over time, grew to dislike intensely the "business of scholarship."[2] In a characteristic understatement, written shortly before his death, he stated that he "gladly did without literary success."[3] He turned down a number of prestigious positions at German universities, including the chair of history at the university of Berlin; the lure of greater fame could not tempt him to leave his post in Basel.

1 In 1867, under considerable pressure, Burckhardt published his promised work on the art of the Italian Renaissance, *Die Geschichte der neueren Baukunst,* as the architecture volume of Franz Kugler's series, *Geschichte der Baukunst.* This was later republished under the title *Die Geschichte der Renaissance in Italien* (1878). A number of important works were published posthumously, including *Erinnerungen aus Rubens* (1898), *Griechische Kulturgeschichte* (1898), and the *Weltgeschichtliche Betrachtungen* (1905). To facilitate access to Burckhardt's work, I have chosen to use the best available English editions. Where translations are unavailable or inadequate, I shall use the *Gesamtausgabe.* There are numerous editions of the *Weltgeschichtliche Betrachtungen.* I have chosen to use the recent authoritative edition *Über das Studium der Geschichte: Der Text der Weltgeschichtlichen Betrachtungen,* edited by Ganz, hereafter cited as WB. All translations, unless indicated, are my own.

2 Ganz, introduction to WB, 58.

3 Burckhardt, *Gesamtausgabe,* 1: ix. Hereafter cited as GA.

Burckhardt's works are still read and studied, although his reputation today rests more on his cultural criticism and his pessimistic view of modernity. With a certain pride, he cultivated the image of an outsider who stood in opposition to his age; indeed, he remained outside the mainstream European historical and intellectual community on ideological, political, and historiographical grounds. This became especially clear in 1905 with the posthumous publication of his now famous lectures on the study of history, *Weltgeschichtliche Betrachtungen,* known in the English-speaking world as *Reflections on History.*[4] The reception of this work was mixed. In the wake of the intense controversy surrounding the publication of Karl Lamprecht's cultural history, Friedrich Meinecke, one of the leading historians in Germany, expressed his admiration of Burckhardt's originality in a review for the *Historische Zeitschrift.* Meinecke, however, could not come to terms with the fact that Burckhardt's unique understanding of cultural history presented an alternative vision of history to that predominant in German academic circles.[5] Meinecke felt that Burckhardt demonstrated indifference not just to the value of traditional political history, but to the theory and methods of German historicism. Consequently, he criticized Burckhardt's work for being unsystematic and adversely dilettantish. Burckhardt, "untroubled" by the concerns for "strict scholarship" – or the opinions of his colleagues in Germany – was happy to go his own way.

The publication of *Reflections on History* confirmed what many contemporaries had long suspected: Burckhardt, the self-proclaimed dilettante and outsider, was a sceptic who, from his perch on the upper Rhine, cast a critical glance not just at contemporary historiography, but at the modern world in general. From Basel, his "Archimedean point outside events," Burckhardt did not share the optimism of his Berlin colleagues, whose voluminous works celebrated Germany's rise to political, economic, and military greatness. According to Meinecke, this was a result of provincialism, of isolation from the great political events that

4 This work was first published in English in 1943 under the title *Force and Freedom: Reflections on History* (New York: Pantheon Books 1943), and has subsequently been issued as *Reflections on History* (Indianapolis: Liberty Fund 1979). The original text consists of fragmented lecture notes, aphorisms, and glosses. Against Burckhardt's wishes, his nephew, Jacob Oeri, organized, edited, and transcribed these notes into a readable narrative, which he then published in 1905 as *Weltgeschichtliche Betrachtungen.*

5 Meinecke, "Jacob Burckhardt: die deutsche Geschichtsschreibung und der nationale Staat," 557–62. Reprinted in Meinecke, *Werke,* 7: 83–7.

had shaped modern Germany and the modern German historical profession. Instead of embracing political power, as his colleagues in Germany had done, Burckhardt expressed deep reservations about the growing dominance of the nation-state and refused to see in it an ethical force. Indeed, Burckhardt, who viewed Bismarck's aggressive wars of unification with alarm, continued to support the small state, condemning power as evil. From Basel, referred to as the "sulking corner of Europe" by the ultranationalist historian Heinrich von Treitschke,[6] the process of modernization looked decidedly less glamorous and much more destructive.

This book examines the confrontation between history and modernity, as played out in Burckhardt's life, and its shaping of his conception of history and historiography. My starting point is Meinecke's conclusion that Burckhardt's cultural critique and unique approach to history derived in large part from his experience as a citizen of Switzerland and of the city-republic of Basel.[7] Burckhardt's political thought, his critique of modernity, and, ultimately, his distinguished form of cultural history cannot be properly understood without examining his response to local experiences and to Basel's particular intellectual and cultural heritage.Unlike Meinecke, however, I do not view Burckhardt's heritage as a political or historical liability, but as a force that shaped his understanding of, and reaction to, the process of modernization. His ideology emerged in response to cultural, social, and psychological strains, when "neither a society's most general cultural orientations nor its most down-to-earth, 'pragmatic' ones suffice any longer to provide an adequate image of political process."[8] Only by examining the impact of local experiences and his relationship to the culture and traditions of his homeland, can we hope to reconstruct the precise contours of the political thought and ideology that underpinned his historical work. Thus, any discussion of Burckhardt's critique of modernity requires an examination of the social, political, and cultural strains that shaped his

6 Cornelius, ed. *Heinrich von Treitschkes Briefe*, 3:375.

7 Meinecke, "Jacob Burckhardt: die deutsche Geschichtsschreibung und der nationale Staat," 86–7; See also Meinecke, "Ranke und Burckhardt," in *Werke*, 7:93–121; and Herkless, "Meinecke and the Ranke-Burckhardt Problem," 290–321. While Burckhardt certainly did not have the same vested interest in German unification that Meinecke did, he was definitely involved in the century's "political strife" and was in no way isolated from the "great political struggles of his day."

8 By ideology I mean a cultural system, an "intricate structure of interrelated meanings," as articulated by Geertz, *The Interpretation of Cultures*, 219.

thought and gave meaning to his lived experience. Only then will those elusive "webs of significance" that make up his ideological system be understood.

In the first part of this book, I attempt to situate Burckhardt's thought and work within the context of local experiences by examining three crucial episodes in his early life that defined his mature political thought. Central to this is the understanding that Burckhardt was first and foremost a Basler. While this point may seem obvious, it requires emphasis because it is rarely, if ever, taken into consideration; indeed, his political thought and historical work have seldom been examined from this perspective. For the most part, the fact that Burckhardt was a citizen of Basel and Switzerland, not Germany, is conveniently ignored. For many historians, Basel is nothing more than the place where Burckhardt, by some strange twist of fate or sheer stubbornness, lived and worked, a sort of intellectual bedroom community for a Greater German Intellectual/Cultural Empire. When Alan Kahan, in his search for the "dialect of political discourse" that is aristocratic liberalism, argues that Burckhardt belonged to a German intellectual tradition or, specifically, to a German liberal tradition, he perpetuates this intellectual imperialism. Although Kahan is correct when he points out that the German intellectual tradition (liberal or otherwise) consisted of many dialects, Burckhardt's "dialect," linguistic or political, was most manifestly a Basel dialect.[9]

This unique Basel dialect influenced Burckhardt's thought in many ways. In effect, a number of traditions were particularly important in shaping his world view. They included Basel's orthodox Protestant heritage; the ideal of civic-republicanism, that eccentric but pragmatic mixture of cosmopolitanism and particularism that often served to make "pious Basel" more palatable; and the city's reputation as a trade and commercial centre. These traditions were reinforced, not undermined, by Burckhardt's experience of modernity and political change. In addition, key components of his political thought emerged over time in response to historical developments in Basel and Switzerland. These included his fear of centralized political power; the revolutionary potential of the masses; the social impact of industrialization and materialism;

---

9 Kahan, *Aristocratic Liberalism*, 3–7. This tendency is manifest throughout the literature. The exceptions are Meinecke (although he does not elaborate and sees it negatively) and the work of Lionel Gossman and Thomas Howard, both of whom emphasize the importance of Basel's unique heritage on the development of Burckhardt's thought.

the commodification of art and culture in the hands of the bourgeoisie; as well as his praise of the small state (the *Kleinstaat*) and his ultimate faith in the redemptive effects of education, culture, and tradition. These components provided important continuities between his work, and the traditionalist, conservative political culture and anti-modernist, orthodox Protestant Christianity of the Basel intelligentsia. In addition, they represented a coherent ideological counterbalance to the tendencies emanating from Berlin.

Against this background, the final part of this work shows how Burckhardt's confrontation with modernity found consummate expression in his work as an historian. Contrary to what some scholars have persistently maintained, his numerous books, lectures, and essays reflected ideological commitments that did grant a "genuine political function to historical knowledge,"[10] albeit one that generally, but not always, reflected the conservative ideals of the Basel elite, while being hopelessly out of tune with the optimistic views of his more famous contemporary German nationalist historians. By examining Burckhardt's lesser-known works – his major books have been extensively studied – I hope to trace how these ideological commitments shaped his understanding of cultural history and determined his approach to the study of art. The peculiarities of Burckhardt's approach to history and of Basel's cultural and political traditions notwithstanding, it is important to repeat that Burckhardt was not an isolated, provincial scholar with little interest in the outside world. On the contrary, his very cosmopolitanism, in sharp contrast to the narrowly nationalistic and ultimately parochial thought of many contemporary German historians, stemmed in no small part from the richness and diversity of the unique cultural and intellectual heritage of Basel. The point is that in a world of rapid social, political, and economic transformation, filled with uncertainty and concern about the present and the future development of the "age of revolution," there was neither a single, preordained path to modernity, nor a prescribed response to the numerous issues it raised. Each individual and nation assessed, and responded to, the dilemma of modernization in its own way, according to its own perceived interests.

· · ·

10 Rüsen, "Jacob Burckhardt: Political Standpoint and Historical Insight," 241.

Like so many of his generation, Burckhardt's understanding of modernity and history was shaped by his experience of the violence and chaos of revolution. As a youth in Basel, he witnessed first hand the impact of the July Revolution of 1830 and the subsequent political strife that tore apart his homeland during the next three years. The trauma of the separation of the rural districts of the canton of Basel in 1833 was repeated on a national scale a decade later, when Burckhardt, as a newspaper editor, reported on a series of violent political crises that eventually led to the 1847 civil war in Switzerland, the *Sonderbundkrieg*, thereby inaugurating the year of revolutions in 1848. In an attempt to avoid unrest at home and in Germany, as well as to indulge his passion for art, Burckhardt spent a large part of 1848 in Italy. But revolution caught up with him there as well; he ended up filing reports on the revolutionary upheavals in Italy for the *Basler Zeitung*, his old employer. Finally, he followed with great trepidation the progress of Bismarck's "revolution from above," finding in his colleague Friedrich Nietzsche a sympathetic audience for his fears and anxieties about Germany's future.

For Burckhardt, the most significant and formative experience of the modern age was not the revolution of 1830 or 1848, or even 1870, but rather the French Revolution of 1789. France held special meaning for Burckhardt and other intellectuals wrestling with the problems of modernity. As Kahan has pointed out, "France, not England, was the paradigmatic case for modern history,"[11] and the French Revolution the origin of modernity. At the level referred to by historians of the French *Annales*' school of historical thought as "*histoire événementielle*," Burckhardt interpreted the Revolution of 1789 as representative of the culmination of specific developments originating in the eighteenth century. "The Revolution was prepared long in advance," he pointed out, and in his lectures he consequently sought to outline precisely those elements of continuity that had converged with such force in the Revolution.[12] In particular, he emphasized four factors, originating in the powerful modernizing impulses of the Enlightenment and the trend towards the centralization of state power that had transformed the structures of European society in the nineteenth century: the rise of a new concept of the state, the idea of the nation and nationalism, the growing influence

---

11 Kahan, *Aristocratic Liberalism*, 11.

12 Nachschrift Herzog (1869–70), in Ziegler, ed. *Jacob Burckhardts Vorlesung über die Geschichte des Revolutionszeitalters in den Nachschriften seiner Zuhörer*, 455. Hereafter cited as *Geschichte des Revolutionszeitalters*.

of public opinion, and the radical increase in "trade and traffic."[13] These factors – Werner Kaegi refers to them as the "driving forces" of the age of revolution – dictated the shape of modernity. Here were the origins of those monumental, epoch-making ideas and historical forces, the "principles of 1789" that had forged the nineteenth century. Their impact was decisive and enduring; they had not ended with the final defeat of Napoleon. On the contrary, Burckhardt fully recognized that these forces were "still active and will continue to be so with that world age whose further development we do not know as yet ... Above all, the revolution has had results which now completely shape us and constitute an integral part of our feeling for justice and our conscience – things, therefore, that we can no longer separate from ourselves."[14] The continued presence of the revolution, and its impact on modern society, inspired Burckhardt to study it. As he surveyed the European political and economic situation in January 1868 from his vantage point on the upper Rhine, he felt justified in examining, once again, the events of the French Revolution as the source of all current disruptions and crises.[15]

However, at the level of the *longue durée*, Burckhardt argued that the Revolution marked a break of epochal proportions with the traditions and culture of "old Europe": "the French Revolution separates two ages from one another; that which existed before from that which has existed since."[16] The success of the revolutionary impulses of 1789 shattered the political and social order of the old regime, exposing the inadequacy of the centuries-old suppositions and concepts that governed human life and behaviour, and ushering in a new era in the history of humankind. It was impossible to turn back the clock, no matter how hard politicians tried: "Restorations, however well meant, and however much they seem to offer the only way out," he confidently wrote to

---

13 Burckhardt, *Judgments on History and Historians*, 217–24. Hereafter cited as JHH. See also Kaegi, 5:260–71. We might add a fifth development to the list: secularization. Although Burckhardt did not discuss secularization at length, he recognized its significance, writing: "[A]n essentially materialistic explanation of the world, an equally irreligious doctrine of man's nature, a hatred of Christianity (and not just for its external embodiment of power, the Catholic Church) combine with a growing criticism and scorn of the particular French state system, with the ideal of the constitutional state, with new views of national economy, and cross and coincide in part with a doctrine of the goodness of human nature in its supposed natural state, with the drive toward a radical change in mores as well as in the state," JHH, 241. See also Jaeger, *Bürgerliche Modernisierungskrise*, 142.

14 JHH, 217.

15 *Geschichte des Revolutionszeitalters*, 235.

16 Ibid., 455.

his friend Gottfried Kinkel in 1842, "cannot hide the fact that the nineteenth century began with a *tabula rasa* in relation to everything."[17] This
description of modernity's beginning as a *tabula rasa*, or blank slate, is
significant. According to Burckhardt, modernity represented not so
much the transformation of social and political structures, the roots of
which could be traced back to the eighteenth century and beyond, thus
making the Revolution so monumental to the history of humankind.
Rather, its importance was that it signified a revolution of the spirit: it
represented the creation of a new historical context, a radical, unprecedented break in the continuity of Western culture, a complete intellectual and cultural reorientation, and the emergence of a new spirit or
consciousness.[18]

The metaphor of the blank slate provides clues to the two most important features of the new spirit of modernity. First, it suggests that
modern consciousness was characterized by a new awareness of contemporary time. With the Revolution, wrote Burckhardt, "almost all European people have had what might be called the historical ground pulled
from under their feet ... The complete negation in the state, church, art
and life, that occurred at the end of the last century has unleashed
(among better people: developed) in all the relatively alert minds such
an enormous measure of objective consciousness that a restoration of
the old level of immaturity is quite unthinkable."[19] That the historical
ground could be pulled from under the feet of people suggested the
present's discontinuity with the past and a new consciousness of the
modern individual's existence in the present.

Second, it points to a new awareness of the ability to change and modify things, which Burckhardt felt was a hallmark of modernity. Modernity is constantly reforming, reshaping, and redefining itself; everything
is malleable and can be created and recreated, changed and exchanged.
Burckhardt argued that this constant redefinition originated in the
Enlightenment's meliorist vision of the world, which presupposed that
human history was governed by rationality and progress, and that this
led inevitably to moral perfection and happiness. The revolution of the
spirit was, in effect, the triumph of "objective consciousness" and universal rationality, the driving force of which was the "great *optimistic will*
which has suffused times since the middle of the eighteenth century.

17 Max Burckhardt, ed. *Jacob Burckhardt Briefe*, 1:201. Hereafter cited as *Briefe*.
18 See also Jaeger, *Bürgerliche Modernisierungskrise*, 136.
19 *Briefe*, 1:201.

The premise is the *goodness* of human nature, which, however, is a mixture of good and evil. That optimistic will hopes that changes will bring about an increasing and definitive well-being." Burckhardt singled out Rousseau for promoting this ideal, the fulfilment of which was impossible because "the overwhelming majority of the desires are material in nature," and hence insatiable, "no matter how they may disguise themselves as ideal."[20]

This "optimistic will" – the belief in progress, reason, and change – became the dominant feature of modern thought: in many respects it encapsulated for Burckhardt the spirit or *Geist* of the nineteenth-century world. However, for Burckhardt, the "blind will to change (which prevalent optimism superficially terms 'progress', as well as culture, civilization, enlightenment, development, morality, and other things),"[21] created the central dilemma of modernity. As the philosopher Jürgen Habermas explains, "A present that understands itself from the horizon of the modern age as the actuality of the most recent period has to recapitulate the break brought about with the past as a *continuous renewal*."[22] The legacy of the French Revolution was precisely that it created a society based on the need for such "continuous renewal," or what Burckhardt referred to as "eternal revision,"[23] an understanding of the world that was embodied in the portentous words attributed to Napoleon, the first of the new Caesars, who believed that he had temporarily mastered events when he claimed: *"J'ai conjuré le terrible esprit de nouveauté qui parcourait le monde."*[24]

Judgments based on this premise were dangerous because they distorted understanding of the past and fed popular myth. They became the enemy of true historical insight because they were situated fully in the present; displayed a lack of piety and a blatant disregard for tradition and culture; and considered change and progress to be the fundamental characteristic of history, rather than continuity in the past.[25] All

20 JHH, 230. Emphasis in original.
21 JHH, 231.
22 Habermas, *The Philosophical Discourse of Modernity*, 7. Emphasis in original.
23 JHH, 229.
24 "I have conjured up the terrible spirit of change which is traversing the world." Quoted in ibid.
25 *"On the Progressive Way of Thinking*: 'This or that hallway would have to be the most beautiful if only because it leads to our room'. What coldness and heartlessness there is in this attitude, the ignoring of the silenced moans of all the vanquished, who, as a rule, had wanted nothing else but *parta tueri* [to preserve what had come into being]. How *much* must perish so that *something* new may arise!" JHH, 75. Emphasis in original.

this is encapsulated, as well, in Burckhardt's use of the *tabula rasa* meta-phor. The crisis of modernity was precisely the belief in a "new start" and the rejection of the past and prior knowledge. Modernist thinkers embraced presentism and opened themselves up to the future. This was a fundamental paradox: in becoming historicized (this was, after all, the age of historicism), modern thought, with its view of the present as dis-continuous with the past, was expressing an ambivalence towards the past. This tension between history and the present is characteristic of modernist thought, as Habermas has pointed out. "Modernity can and will no longer borrow the criteria by which it takes its orientation from the models supplied by another epoch," he writes. Rather "it has to cre-ate its normativity out of itself. Modernity sees itself cast back upon itself without any possibility of escape."[26] Any society founded upon continual change, which has to create and renew its norms, standards, and values "out of itself," has no need for history and tradition.

Consequently, Burckhardt regarded the *esprit de nouveauté* not as a sign of visible progress but as proof that civilization was in a state of pro-found crisis.[27] By defining itself according to the forces of change and progress, rather than according to its relationship to the past, society can only exist in a state of constant flux, uncertainty, and instability. De-spite being the age of historicism – Burckhardt began his study of his-tory by proclaiming that "history and historical observation of the world and time has begun to penetrate our entire culture"[28] – modernity was characterized by Burckhardt as an age of disturbing "historylessness" and "barbarism."[29] This "loss of the human capacity for history" pointed to the central dilemma of modernity.[30] It brought into question the very continuity of culture and produced an "inward crisis in men's minds." In effect, it suggested that history, and indeed human existence, no longer had form, structure, or coherence; there was no longer truth, only fictions and myths.

According to Burckhardt, the idea that the historical and spiritual continuum could be broken, and that traditional institutions and forms of experience were ineffective and could be shaped and changed at will,

26 Habermas, *The Philosophical Discourse of Modernity*, 6–7.

27 The concept of crisis occupies a central role in Burckhardt's historical thought and his understanding of modernity. See especially Schieder, "Die historischen Krisen im Geschichtsdenken Jacob Burckhardts," 132. See also WB, 205–16 and 342–76.

28 WB, 83.

29 Ibid., 229.

30 This phrase comes from Jaeger, *Bürgerliche Modernisierungskrise*, 136.

demonstrated indifference towards the past; it also pointed to a basic rift between essence and experience. The individual, in effect, was the principal victim of modernity. Jeffrey Herf, in his study of "reactionary modernism" in Weimar Germany, has argued that one of the main problems for critics of modernity was how to defend the sovereignty of the individual in a society that "reduced him to the status of a means."[31] This was a primary concern for many nineteenth-century cultural critics, Burckhardt included. Although Burckhardt rejected the notion that history and human behaviour were governed by rationality, he did share with Enlightenment theorists the belief in the autonomy and sovereignty of the individual. But the forces unleashed by the Revolution – in essence, liberalism and market culture – did not liberate the subject, as modernists argued. According to Burckhardt, modern, mass society, governed by the belief in progress, science, and "moneymaking," raised the spectre of the complete abdication of individual will and the subjective side of human nature in favour of material gain, national power, and technological advance.[32] In contrast to modernist thought, which maintained that "objectifying science ... disenchants nature at the same time that it liberates the knowing subject,"[33] Burckhardt viewed rationality and the discourse of "objectifying science" (i.e., the triumph of reason or the French Revolution) as forces that threatened to destroy rather than liberate the subject, reducing the individual to the "status of a means."

This was in marked contrast to the spirit of the Renaissance, a time Burckhardt often referred to as the "leader of modern ages."[34] A brief examination of Burckhardt's survey of the history of Western Europe from the Middle Ages to modern times reveals the following general pattern. In the medieval world, which was dominated by the Church, "both sides of human consciousness – that which was turned within as that which was turned without – lay dreaming or half awake beneath a common veil. The veil was woven of faith, illusion and childish prepossession, through which the world and history were seen clad in strange hues." The Renaissance marked a break with this civilization. In a famous passage from the *Civilization of the Renaissance in Italy*, Burckhardt described how "in Italy this veil first melted into air; an *objective* treatment and

31 Herf, *Reactionary Modernism*, 123.

32 WB, 282. See also Jaeger, *Bürgerliche Modernisierungskrise*, 136ff.

33 Habermas, *The Philosophical Discourse of Modernity*, 16–18. The quote from Hegel, 16.

34 For example, Burckhardt, *The Civilization of the Renaissance in Italy*, 351. Hereafter cited as CRI.

consideration of the state and of all the things of this world became possible. The *subjective* side at the same time asserted itself with corresponding emphasis; man became a spiritual *individual*."[35] While this harmonious balance between subjectivity and objectivity characterized the Renaissance individual – thus making the period one of great cultural and historical significance – the next three centuries were characterized by disharmony. There was incessant conflict between the Church and the state, between the forces of secularization and religion; "now there takes place a truly endless crossing and entangling of all these strands."[36] The Age of Enlightenment witnessed the epic clash between the "objective" forces of reason and the "subjective" forces of faith, superstition, and myth, with reason emerging triumphant during the climax of the French Revolution and the eighteenth century. Since the French Revolution, however, a new veil had descended on mankind, a veil that was likewise woven of faith and illusion. This was the veil of reason, the blind, optimistic faith in progress and "objectifying science" that enslaved the individual because it destroyed subjectivity and imprisoned human instinct and creativity. Burckhardt compared the philosophy of the Enlightenment to a religion or a sect that had its "zealous, convinced adherents and even martyrs and which transformed the spiritual world although nobody swore allegiance to it."[37]

While the French Revolution may have liberated the people from the tyranny of the *ancien régime*, its promise of *liberté* and *égalité*, a relic of Enlightenment optimism, only imprisoned them in the depths of their own unrealistic desires, ambitions, and hopes. Materialism, egalitarianism, and the "commercial spirit" not only threatened to reduce *Kultur* to *Zivilisation*; it also destroyed the subject's organic bond with nature and the state, objectifying and atomizing individuals to the point where they were nothing more than a spiritual void, a cog in the machine of modern society. The metaphysical security and stability of the past no longer existed for the modern individual whose new objective, rational consciousness, was based on the myth of infinite progress, the premise of the eternal "goodness of human nature," and the optimistic hope that "changes will bring about an increased and definite well-being."[38] For most people, the rapidity of historical change in the age of revolution

35 Ibid., 98.
36 JHH, 157.
37 WB, 274.
38 JHH, 224, 230.

created serious inner turmoil and crisis. "Faced with such historical forces," Burckhardt wrote, "the contemporary individual feels completely powerless ... and few can overcome things spiritually."[39]

. . .

Scholars who have examined Burckhardt's critique of modernity and historiography often argue that while he had no reservations about condemning the evils of modern society, he came up lamentably short in providing answers and solutions to the contemporary crises he described and the future crises he predicted. This criticism follows a cliché formula, most commonly characterized according to the following equation: pessimism and antimodernism equal flight from reality and descent into irrationalism. Scholars have consistently argued that his poetry, correspondence, and academic work reveal an intense fear of the future, and that he consequently sought to escape from the "saeculum" into the safety of the past, in order to avoid the responsibilities of the present. Thus, Hayden White has written that Burckhardt "secluded himself in Basel ... From his vantage point on the Upper Rhine he looked down upon Europe rushing to its doom, surveyed the failure of Liberalism, diagnosed its causes, and predicted the results as Nihilism. But he refused to enter the struggle himself. Out of his disillusionment he forged a theory of society and history which was [as] accurate in predicting the crises of the future as it was symptomatic of the illnesses that would bring them on." Withdrawing from a world he did not like, Burckhardt adopted an apolitical stance that "absolved him from any further responsibility for the coming chaos."[40] This argument has been repeated by Jörn Rüsen, who claims that Burckhardt negated a "genuine political function of historical knowledge ... a function [that] was customary in the historicist concept of historical studies" by

39 WB, 229.
40 White, *Metahistory*, 235–6. Paul West, for instance, claimed that Burckhardt was a fanatic, "a romantic: self-obsessed and incapable of the middle way," whose "main shortcoming is that he abdicates from the kind of responsibility which we feel intellectuals ought to assume gladly and which only they are fitted to discharge." A "civic monk," he was "pathetic" and "enfeebled by snobbery," and led a lifestyle that was "gratuitously medieval" because he chose to live "austerely in two rooms above a baker's shop," and there dream about an heroic, epic past, all the while "sketching out his own Waste Land" of the nineteenth century. West, "Jacob Burckhardt and the 'Ideal Past'," 335–46.

"aestheticizing" history, and granted it an "apolitical function of contemplation." Rüsen goes on to warn us that "Burckhardt's attempt to reinforce the cultural values of Old Europe by an aesthetic remembrance of their role in the past has led to an apolitical attitude of educated people. Thomas Mann described this attitude as that of an 'inwardness protected by power' (*machtgeschützte Innerlichkeit*)! We have to learn that the culture critique from this point of view is the hidden ally of the disaster it laments."[41]

But was Burckhardt apolitical? To a large extent it depends upon one's definition of the term. Burckhardt certainly refused to participate in party politics and did not write traditional political history. Likewise, his work did not pay lip service to the contemporary liberal political agenda of reform and democratization; nor did it constitute an uncritical confirmation of the values of progress, modernization, and nationalism that characterized most of the work of his contemporaries. In fact, as a number of recent works assessing and categorizing Burckhardt's political thought have shown, while Burckhardt may have avoided partisan politics, he was by no means apolitical.[42] Despite these arguments, no consensus exists as to the exact nature of Burckhardt's political ideology or program: opinion places him across the political spectrum. For some he is an "enlightened conservative," or representative of a "high conservatism" that "converged with extreme leftist views about the nature of the capitalist system which allegedly subjected mankind to a new servitude."[43] Some scholars have seen more extreme tendencies in his work

41 Rüsen seems to implicate Burckhardt in the rise of National Socialism by including him within the "apolitical" German intellectual elite, while ignoring the extreme nationalism, militarism, and anti-Semitism of some of Germany's very political intellectuals. Besides the fact that there was little that was apolitical about Germany's intellectual elite, it is difficult to imagine how a Swiss scholar, who spent relatively little time in Germany and was openly hostile to Bismarck's *Realpolitik*, demagoguery, and militarism, can be implicated in events which took place in that country. Rüsen, "Jacob Burckhardt: Political Standpoint and Historical Insight," 241 and 246.

42 See for example, Hinde, "The Development of Jacob Burckhardt's Political Thought"; O'Brien, "Jacob Burckhardt: The Historian as Socratic Humanist"; Kahan, *Aristocratic Liberalism*; Sax, "State and Culture in the Thought of Jacob Burckhardt"; Sigurdson, "Jacob Burckhardt's Liberal-Conservatism," and "Jacob Burckhardt: The Cultural Historian as Political Thinker"; Mommsen, "Jacob Burckhardt – Defender of Culture and Prophet of Doom"; Gross, "Jacob Burckhardt and the Critique of Mass Society."

43 Mommsen, "Jacob Burckhardt: Defender of Culture and Prophet of Doom," 473. Mali, "Jacob Burckhardt: Myth, History and Mythistory," 109, describes Burckhardt as an "enlightened conservative."

and ideas. Lionel Gossman, for instance, writes that "many elements of a radical right-wing ideology seem to be already in place in Burckhardt, including anti-Semitism, endemic until recently in Basel as in many other parts of Switzerland."[44] According to others, Burckhardt must be seen, along with Goethe and Wilhelm von Humboldt, as representative of the "German liberal tradition" of Weimar humanism,[45] or as an "aristocratic liberal" more akin to Alexis de Tocqueville and John Stuart Mill.[46] Finally, Richard Sigurdson bridges both political worlds when he claims that Burckhardt was in fact a "liberal-conservative."[47]

Despite the confusion, these studies mark an important shift in Burckhardt scholarship: they attempt to situate his critique of modernity within a political context, in a sense reversing Rüsen's claim that "Burckhardt's political thought is culture-critique in its essence."[48] Nevertheless, those who have attempted "to outline a Burckhardtian political philosophy" still invariably find this philosophy lacking. Thus, in one of the most compelling analyses of Burckhardt's political thought, Richard Sigurdson concludes that Burckhardt "offers a unique but not entirely satisfying liberal-conservative point of view."[49] This interpretation raises several problems and begs the question, satisfying to whom? More significantly, it threatens to decontextualize or dehistoricize Burckhardt once more. Whereas previously he was considered apolitical because of the nature of his cultural critique and his refusal to participate in the political marketplace, now he has been found guilty of not fully appreciating the long-term implications of his thought; of not forming politically correct conclusions suitable for our "liberal," democratic sensibilities; and, in short, of not being the political theorist he never claimed, or wanted, to be.

But can we expect Burckhardt to have articulated a political philosophy that would have presented the world with a concrete political agenda, or solution, to the problems he believed plagued the modern world? That he ultimately did not was not because he was unable to think systematically as he often claimed, but because he was a cultural and art

---

44 Gossman, "Basel," 97, note 44.

45 Sax, "State and Culture in the Thought of Jacob Burckhardt," 27.

46 Kahan, *Aristocratic Liberalism.*

47 Sigurdson, "Jacob Burckhardt's Liberal-Conservatism."

48 Rüsen, "Jacob Burckhardt: Political Standpoint and Historical Insight," 239; See also Sigurdson, "Jacob Burckhardt's Liberal-Conservatism," 487.

49 Ibid., 511.

historian, not a political theorist.[50] He did not write political history, never mind political tracts; what we have, instead, are groupings of discernible intellectual associations of varying political attitudes scattered throughout his correspondence and lectures. Although these attitudes are expressed with general consistency throughout his lifetime and work, the only political philosophy is ultimately that which has been reconstructed by the historian. Nor was he a politician. His healthy scepticism and distrust of political parties and politicians of all colours was legendary; he had no illusions about the "evil" of power and the potentially devastating impact of powerful states on the lives of individuals and culture. This prevented him from celebrating the evolution of the modern nation-state as an ethical force and the culmination of historical development. He also believed that scholars should not become involved in political affairs. As he wrote in 1867 to his friend, the Freiburg historian Heinrich Schreiber, "The viri doctissimi should leave politics alone because they never contribute anything sensible."[51] Burckhardt had learned this lesson the hard way, more than twenty-five years earlier, when he flirted briefly with political journalism as editor of the conservative newspaper, the *Basler Zeitung*. He hated being the subject of intense political controversy and found the incessant jockeying and squabbling for power distasteful. When he did quit this job, he vowed never again to participate directly in politics, a promise he kept with little difficulty.

In one sense, therefore, the present-day critics are correct. Burckhardt did not offer a political solution to the crisis of the individual in modern society. But this was because he did not believe the crisis could be overcome by politics or politicians, whose concern was with power, not the individual. Unlike later nineteenth-century and early twentieth-century critics of modernity, Fritz Stern's "illiberals," and Jeffrey Herf's "revolutionary conservatives," Burckhardt privileged *Kultur* over politics and economics in his battle against the corrupting influence of materialism, and refused to respond to the crisis of modernity with a call to political action. This does not mean that he could not see a solution or that he sank into pessimism and nihilism. Rather, Burckhardt's antidote to the alienation of the individual in modern society demanded personal regeneration (in and of itself by no means apolitical), a regeneration based on the cultivation of the individual's spiritual and creative

50 This is not to suggest that Burckhardt is not accountable for his opinions.
51 *Briefe*, 4:253.

capacities. The goal of this regeneration was the reconstitution of the subjective and objective realms of human experience. The redemption of the fragmented individual in modern society preoccupied not only the conservative revolutionaries of the Weimar Republic, but also early nineteenth-century Weimar humanists and German Idealists. It finds a parallel in the work of such philosophers as Hegel, Johann Gottlieb Fichte, Friedrich Schlegel, and Friedrich Schelling and such poets as Friedrich Schiller and Johann Wolfgang von Goethe. All these men cultivated "a philosophical sensibility that began to look for wholeness and synthesis, not in the immediately lived realities of the everyday, but in the ideal realms of the mind and natural order" in an attempt to overcome the atomized, mechanized, and spiritless nature of modern society and the modern individual.[52]

At the centre of Burckhardt's own holistic effort was the discourse of classical *Bildung* as it manifested itself in the German tradition of Weimar humanism and Basel's neohumanist heritage.[53] The concept or ideal of *Bildung* is notoriously difficult to translate accurately into English. It entails much more than just education or cultivation. The object of *Bildung* was not practical, technical learning as an instrument of social advancement or general social welfare. Its goal, in the words of Fritz Ringer, was a "vision of learning as personal self-fulfilment through interpretative interaction with venerated texts."[54] Implicit in *Bildung*, therefore, was both a secular asceticism – a "holistic self-realization" achieved through the selfless devotion to *Kultur* – and a form of aestheticism – expressed in the intense need to cultivate the instinctive, creative energies of the human spirit. Spiritual regeneration thoroughly grounded in knowledge of the "spiritual continuum" of civilization, not opportunistic politicking, was the true task of the intellectual.

This is not to suggest that the ideology of classical *Bildung* was somehow apolitical. In fact, *Bildung* represented a philosophy of life that served as a legitimizing, authenticating ideology of the emerging intellectual elite (*Bildungsbürgertum*). As such, it had far-reaching political and social implications. Based on the study of classical texts, *Bildung*, or

---

52 This philosophical sensibility would give rise to holistic science. See, for instance, Harrington, *Reenchanted Science*, 4.

53 On *Bildung* in general, see Bruford, *The German Tradition of Self-Cultivation*, and La Vopa, *Grace, Talent, and Merit*. See also Ringer, *The Decline of the German Mandarins*, and Ringer, *Fields of Knowledge*.

54 Ringer, *Fields of Knowledge*, 2.

holistic self-realization, was essentially antimodern, elitist, and conservative. It privileged scholarship and the role of the intellectual in society,
placed specific emphasis on the spiritual cultivation of the individual,
and, as Gossman has persuasively argued, helped preserve social privilege and the political status quo in Basel.[55] Indeed, as an ideology,
Bildung was especially suitable to the elites of Basel. In effect, the concept
of *Bildung* rejects aristocratic birth as a prerequisite for participation in
political and social discourse (hence its accord with Basel's tradition of
republican self-government), and rejects meritocracy (hence its opposition to modern, revolutionary democracy which threatened to dethrone
the elite). As another author has argued, albeit in a different context:

Ultimately the new idiom [*Bildung*] was so appealing because, in the conflict between the corporatism of the old regime and the rationalist version of modernity, it declared a plague on both houses. At the same time that its fusion of
ethical idealism and aestheticism became the vital alternative to an atrophied
corporate ideal of elegance, contemptuous of the merely utilitarian, it also attested to a mounting sense that the cult of utility, for all its concern with "welfare" and "happiness," portended a dehumanizing efficiency.[56]

For Burckhardt and other neohumanists, *Bildung* represented an alternative middle path between the oppressive, corporatist structures of the old
regime and the uncertainties of rationalist, modernist thought. In practical political terms, this meant for Burckhardt the rejection of both the
"screaming radicalism" of the liberals and the absolutism of the reaction-
aries; for him, revolution and reaction were two sides of the same coin.[57]

However ill-suited this ideal was to the concrete, everyday problems of
modernity, however many "problematic ethical and political shortcomings" or "disquietingly elitist and illiberal associations" are implicit in
Burckhardt's work and in the concept of classical *Bildung*, and however
untimely these thoughts are for contemporary scholars,[58] this ideal was
the message Burckhardt gave to his students and the general public.
Bildung was a source of individual and intellectual freedom, and
Burckhardt's devotion to it enabled him to stave off pessimism and to ex-

55 Gossman, "The 'Two Cultures' in Nineteenth-Century Basle," 95–133.
56 La Vopa, *Grace, Talent, and Merit,* 387.
57 *Briefe,* 2:86.
58 Howard, "Historicist Thought in the Shadow of Theology," 393.

press his hope for future regenerations.[59] Without it there could be no possible escape from the "barbarism" of the age of money-making. Burckhardt's solution to the crisis of modernity was spiritual, not necessarily in the religious sense, although there are definite religious associations, but in the sense of individual cultivation of the mind and its creative energies. "If in misfortune," he wrote in his lectures on the age of Revolution, "there is to be some fortune as well, it can only be a spiritual one, facing backward to the rescue of the culture of earlier times, facing forward to the serene and unwearied representation of the spirit in a time which could otherwise be given up entirely to things mundane."[60]

. . .

Burckhardt saw this ideal anticipated in the Italian Renaissance. In his discussion of the revival of antiquity in *The Civilization of the Renaissance in Italy,* he told an anecdote. At once "nowhere yet everywhere true," this anecdote was from a work entitled *On the Infelicity of the Scholar* (*De infelicitate literatorum*) by a certain Pierio Valeriano. Pierio, who did not write with that "special power, which plagued the men of genius on account of their genius," nevertheless related, with charming simplicity, the facts and events that constituted everyday life during a period of grave crisis, in this case the sack of Rome. Burckhardt's attention was drawn to a story in which Pierio described a mendicant friar. In contrast to a worldly Venetian scholar, who undoubtedly had more free will and subjectivity, the friar "had lived from his boyhood in the monastery, and never eaten or slept except by rule, [and hence had] ceased to feel the compulsion under which he lived. Through the power of this habit he led, amid all outward hardships, a life of inward peace, by which he impressed his hearers far more than by his teaching. Looking at him, they

59 La Vopa, *Grace, Talent, and Merit,* 390, writes: "To define freedom as self-cultivation was to offer a liberating alternative to both the harsh constrictions of the traditional *Brotstudium* and the kind of self-denial required in the utilitarian ethic. This kind of individualism not only refused to recognize the constraints of corporate membership; it also rejected flatly the rationalist quid pro quo, which made social ascent contingent on the restriction of individual growth to the state-defined requirements of service."

60 JHH, 224. See also Sigurdson, "Jacob Burckhardt: The Cultural Historian as Political Thinker," 420.

could believe that it depends on ourselves whether we bear up against misfortune or surrender to it."[61]

While his Basel colleague, the philosopher Friedrich Nietzsche, may have regarded the Christian ascetic's renunciation of the natural impulses to be a grotesque perversion and disembodiment of the human body and soul – the ultimate, ironic triumph of Christianity – Burckhardt found much that was praiseworthy and revealing in the story of the ascetic's life. Given that Burckhardt was an apostate from the church and argued that the rise of Christianity was responsible for "the suppression of aesthetic creativity,"[62] his praise of the Christian ascetic appears unusual in a book that celebrates the rise of the individual and the glories of Renaissance humanism. At first glance, asceticism seems to contradict, even negate, the very notion of individualism, as for instance in Burckhardt's portrayal of the *quattrocento*, where we witness the wholesale rejection of the ascetic principles of self-denial and subjugation of desire. But Burckhardt's admiration of the humble friar is not out of place. As he pointed out in *The Age of Constantine the Great*, and as he demonstrates in the *Civilization of the Renaissance*, asceticism must be understood as the product of rapid historical change and crisis. "It is in the nature of man," he maintained, "when he feels lost in the large and busy external world, that he should seek to find his proper self in solitude … The anchorite way of life premises a not wholly healthy state of society and the individual, but belongs rather to periods of crisis, when many crushed spirits seek quiet, and at the same time many strong hearts are puzzled by the whole apparatus of life and must wage their struggle with God remote from the world."[63]

Burckhardt's history of the Italian Renaissance recounts not just the story of the emergence of the modern individual. As he vividly reminds us, it is also the story of "a not wholly healthy state of society and the individual," a state of profoundly disturbing historical flux and crisis. Indeed, the great cultural and intellectual force of Renaissance humanism, in its famous celebration of both human desire and temporality, emerges under Burckhardt's guidance not just in contrast to, but in confrontation with, the principles of Christian asceticism in particular and of Christianity in general. His discussion of the rise of the indi-

61 CRI, 31 and 181–2.

62 On Burckhardt's apostasy, his secular world view, and their impact on his interpretation of the Renaissance, see Howard, "Historicist Thought in the Shadow of Theology," 357.

63 Burckhardt, *The Age of Constantine the Great*, 323–4. Hereafter cited as *Constantine.*

vidual is contingent upon the process of secularization and the (largely untold) story of the decline of Christian asceticism. According to Burckhardt, the Renaissance individual, whether in politics or in art, was liberated from this self-imposed torture, that enormous burden of internalized guilt and bad conscience that had previously enslaved mankind in the form of the Christian ascetic.

Thus, argued Burckhardt, the psychological void left by the decline of the Christian ideal is filled by an almost primordial outpouring of animal energies, at times monstrous, at times brilliant, but always unique, instinctive, and natural. Burckhardt may have lamented the demise of the ascetic spirit from the monasteries at the end of the Middle Ages, but he knew that asceticism had not disappeared altogether. The story of the Renaissance is also about the emergence of a new form of asceticism, secular or pagan as opposed to Christian, which arose to challenge the vice, violence, and immorality of the new age. Burckhardt's general inference seems to be that secular asceticism emerged not during the Reformation with Luther and the concept of the "calling," as Max Weber would argue half a century later, but rather during the Renaissance. Signs of this new secular asceticism appear in the form of the cultured individual, the Italian humanist, who, when confronted with political, social, and spiritual chaos, practises a zealous devotion not to God but to arts and letters, scientific discovery, and the wonders of the natural world. But while the eremitic way of life may have become increasingly rare, asceticism itself did not disappear. Instead, the ascetic's focus shifted from the ephemeral world of the afterlife to the concrete world of the present. Mastery of the self was no longer sought in the name of religious redemption, but in the name of spiritual enrichment of the self. Even though important differences could be seen between Christian and secular asceticism, both shared the fundamental quality of being a "self-forming activity" and were focused on the subject, the self. Geoffrey Harpham, who has articulated the principal difference between the two forms writes that Christian asceticism "concentrates exclusively on the self, which is predicated to be corrupt in body and deceitful in thought." Secular or pagan asceticism, in contrast, "is founded on the idea of self-mastery and self-possession, a form of control available only to a few, and gained only through extensive learning, discipline, and culture."[64]

64 Harpham, *The Ascetic Imperative*, 27.

The ideal of the secular ascetic fascinated Burckhardt and in many ways guided his own life. Lacking the prerequisite religious zeal of the medieval eremite, he nonetheless consciously cultivated the self-image of the pagan, secular ascetic, emulating and defending the qualities of the ascetic lifestyle and philosophy. In them he found a personal antidote to the violence and discontent of the modern world, that "not wholly healthy state of society and the individual," of the nineteenth century.[65] He sought personal legitimacy and self-mastery through dedication to his work and his responsibilities as a teacher. Through learning, discipline, and culture (*Bildung*), rather than devotion to God, Burckhardt sought a form of transcendence in a world from which he felt increasingly alienated. His life was by no means devoid of personal pleasure, and he does not appear to have subjected his desires to the rigorous self-examination of the eremite. But in his quest for knowledge and his love of art, he found the goal of his devotions and the source of his freedom. Compare this with Nietzsche's approach, in which the quest for knowledge and beauty seemed inevitably to lead towards disillusionment, nihilism, and degeneration.

A number of people have discussed the importance of Burckhardt's asceticism. Wolfgang Hardtwig argues that scholarship and the pursuit of knowledge became, for Burckhardt, an ascetic enterprise designed to overcome the impulse for power. It was never "work" in the conventional sense, but the reflection of an existential need, and it was sought not for worldly progress or material gain, but rather for inner spiritual enrichment. For Hardtwig, Burckhardt's asceticism is essentially passive: he strove "less for an action-oriented external effect than a knowledge-oriented turn inwards."[66] But one might well ask whether asceticism, while reflecting a pessimistic outlook towards the world and originating in the conviction that the world is in a state of crisis,[67] must necessarily signify, especially in its secular form, passive withdrawal from the world.

---

65 "But if any man possessed by the modern preoccupation with activity and its immoderately subjective view of life would therefore wish to place the anchorites in some institution for forced labour, let him not regard himself as particularly healthy-minded," *Constantine*, 324. See also Hardtwig, *Geschichtskultur und Wissenschaft*, 177. Whether Burckhardt's asceticism emerged as a consequence of his early religious crisis or as form of compensation for his apostasy is difficult to say with any certainty, although it is quite possible.

66 Hardtwig, *Geschichtskultur und Wissenschaft*, 179.

67 Asceticism "is the authentic expression of the genuine pessimism inherent in Christianity. Entirely consistent with this is celibacy – not by any means solely as a denial of sensuality … but because the survival of mankind is not at all desirable," JHH, 37.

Harpham does not think so and concludes that "pagan asceticism is a public and even a civic practice."[68] In Burckhardt's case, asceticism was a strategic manoeuvre, an expression of protest, an ideological and political statement; it was far from being a passive withdrawal. On the contrary, Burckhardt proclaimed the principles of asceticism not only "as a man who *lived* his values independent of all the blandishments of a faithless civilization,"[69] but in his university courses and public lectures, attended by generations of Basel's cultural and political elite. Burckhardt's asceticism was consequently an active, public renunciation of the practices of a society in a state of crisis, as well as a symbolic, rebellious determination to live one's life in defiance of the dominant values and conventions of that society.

The civic or political dimension of Burckhardt's asceticism is often neglected by scholars. In much of the literature, his asceticism (and by extension his critique of modernity) is viewed negatively, taken as a sign of resignation and withdrawal from a world about which he had profound misgivings and about which he understood little. This was often the impression he gave of himself. He considered himself an outsider, unable to face the stress of modern-day life. He was, he once proclaimed, in a "motus contrarius" against his own times: "the more the world behaves as if it were raving mad, the more burning my longing becomes for the beautiful that is not of this world."[70] He did not feel that he was enough of a poet to overcome these tribulations; consequently, he sought and found solace in the dignified contemplation and observation of the past.

But Burckhardt – using his asceticism, firmly rooted in his experience of modernity, as a vehicle in the process – was able to overcome these trials. His asceticism opened up new dimensions of cultural criticism and provided a means of translating this criticism into a constructive, life-affirming statement. Hence, he avoided Nietzsche's despair and found solace and inner strength in the contemplation of the past and the cultural heritage of Western civilization. Furthermore, through asceticism, he was able to give expression to his subjective, spiritual self. For asceticism is not just an ideological act; most importantly, it is also an aesthetic act, through which Burckhardt was able to reconstruct the

68 Harpham, *The Ascetic Imperative*, 27–8.

69 Nichols, introduction to *Force and Freedom*, 21. This remains one of the best introductions to Burckhardt.

70 *Briefe*, 3:109.

world. Moreover, the ascetic's preoccupation with the control and/or the enrichment of the subject reveals that the ascetic experience, in its various dimensions, is based on an explicit relationship with the aesthetic. Asceticism is at once an aesthetic strategy and counter-strategy, a cultivation and consumption of instincts at the same time. Asceticism and aestheticism consequently are two sides of the same coin, that coin being temptation and transgression, power and freedom. They share the same source or inspiration, namely crisis, and they have the same ultimate end, the cultivation of the subject and transcendence.

Asceticism, the notion of the mastery of the self, is thus the ultimate aesthetic expression. It becomes, in both its Christian and secular forms, an aesthetics of existence. Despite the ascetic's attempt to control desire and the body, the body remains the primary intellectual and spiritual focus. In Harpham's words, asceticism is "a mediation on, even an enactment of, desire,"[71] if only in a sublimated fashion. While asceticism establishes boundaries through the manipulation of temptation – for example, between innocence and guilt, between want and denial – aestheticism epitomizes the boundary-transgressing experience; it is temptation itself. "The eremite went to the desert to achieve a self constituted entirely by transcendence-of-self," writes Harpham.[72] The ascetic achieves a state of transcendence through rigid self-discipline, the process of controlling temptation and transgression. The aestheticist, in contrast, taps the energy of transcendence precisely through the experience of temptation and transgression. Although the establishing of limits, rules, and laws through the manipulation of guilt and temptation creates structures and oppositions that mediate and marginalize, it also, ironically, presents unlimited possibilities for transgression. In the historical context of the Renaissance created by Burckhardt, the rise of the modern individual results not just in the creation of the state as a work of art, but also in the creation of the self as a work of art; new strategic boundaries are tested in a process that ultimately gives way to the expression of an untamed subjectivity, what Michel Foucault would call a "system of the transgressive."

. . .

71 Harpham, *The Ascetic Imperative*, 45.
72 Ibid., 28.

Although it can be argued that Burckhardt's political thought was based on nostalgic traditionalism, especially if one ignores the Basel perspective, his historical work has also been categorized by recent scholars as postmodern or "proto-postmodern."[73] This is the case not just because he explicitly rejected the discourse of the German historical school, which in many respects provided the historiographical and ideological underpinning of modernity.[74] It is also because his scepticism and the demystifying, ironic function of his historiography, legitimized and justified through his ideology, enabled him to aestheticize historical discourse. He could then offer the reader a new way of accounting for historical "reality" – in effect, new criteria for attributing value and meaning to "reality" and an alternate form of historical representation – that was self-reflective and self-referential. Burckhardt does give way to temptation. His rejection of "canonical" forms of historical representation, which he judged to be inadequate for modern historians, and his aestheticist view of the world and understanding of history were the ultimate transgression, and repudiation, of modernity. Burckhardt's aesthetics of existence – by which I mean neither the traditional usage of the term (which, according to the Greek *aisthesis*, focuses on art and beauty as opposed to the world of concrete reality), nor a philosophy of aesthetics or beauty, but rather the entire sensate life, the entire realm of human experience and perception and how this experience is interpreted and represented – assumes metahistorical qualities in his work and provides the basis of his prefigurement of reality within a certain discursive framework. Aestheticism is consequently understood as being fundamentally opposed to rational, conceptual thought; indeed, the possibility of rational thought can exist only as part of an instinctive desire for order and coherence, rather than in and of itself.

In Burckhardt's work, the vocabulary of aesthetics consists of the language of the senses and sensibilities; of perception and visualization; of affections, passions, and tastes; and of the imagination and the body. The sense of living in a time of profound spiritual crisis – the idea of crisis as a precondition of both asceticism and aestheticism – and the belief that the dominant modes of discourse can no longer account for "reality" provided the basis for Burckhardt's aesthetic understanding of the

73 Rüsen, "Jacob Burckhardt: Political Standpoint and Historical Insight on the Border of Postmodernism;" and Ankersmit, "Historiography and Postmodernism," 141.

74 See for example, White, *The Content of the Form*, 83–103, who writes that "Droysen's *Historik* provides nothing less than an explication of the theoretical principles of bourgeois ideology in its national-industrial phase," 86.

world and inspired his unique approach to history. Aesthetic contemplation (*Anschauung*) of history, his dominant metaphor, was a means of re-establishing the harmony destroyed by the "fragmented times"; a way of bridging the gulf between representation and explanation, the text and the reader, the subject and the object. It signalled a rebellion against the crisis of modernity and the dilemma of rational thought that objectified and colonized the individual and commodified culture; it was the poet's attempt to break through those imprisoning forces that cause the ascetic to suffer.[75] As such, Burckhardt's thought must not be seen as the work of an eccentric, but rather as an attempt to create a new language of aesthetics. His poetic vision of the world sought to reconcile and reassociate knowledge, politics, and desire, all of which had become dissociated in the modern, bourgeois world of liberal capitalism. It was a necessary counterweight to the cruelty inherent in the ascetic's unrelenting pursuit of the ideal and to the suffering caused by such commitment. As Allan Megill has astutely observed, "The notion that the present is null opens the way to an aesthetic recreation. The world's giving birth to itself as a work of art presupposes that its present existence is derelict, that it indeed needs to be reborn."[76]

75 Gossman has compared the attitude of the Basel critics with that expressed by the French poet Mallarmé, who in 1885 declared that the poet was "en grève devant la société." In the age of industrial capitalism, and perhaps one can add the age of revolution, the only appropriate stand to take is that of "heroic abstentionism." Gossman, "Basle, Bachofen and the Critique of Modernity," 141.

76 Megill, *Prophets of Extremity*, 265.

Part 1   Burckhardt and Basel

1

Basel and Revolution

JACOB BURCKHARDT was born in 1818 into one of Basel's most distinguished families. For generations the name Burckhardt had been synonymous with loyal service to the Basel *patria*. No less than eleven ancestors had served the city as *Bürgermeister*; many others had become wealthy merchants or famous scholars at the local university, the oldest in Switzerland. The same was true of his mother's family, the Schorndorffs, whose roots in Basel went back even further than the Burckhardts. Although Burckhardt was part of the city's elite, his world was that of the *Bildungsbürgertum*, the educated middle class, not that of the rich and powerful merchant families. Indeed, his branch of the family was far from wealthy, and even though he eventually held the two chairs of history and art history at the university and became a well-known figure in the city, his was a very unpretentious and modest existence. He devoted most of his time to his studies and duties at the university, although whenever he could afford the time and the money, he would indulge in his two great passions: the arts and travel.

Burckhardt was a life-long bachelor and remained very close to his immediate family. He seems to have given up the idea of marriage after an unsuccessful and unrequited courtship in 1848, which may have provided the inspiration for his short volumes of poetry, *Ferien, Eine Herbstgabe* and *E Hämpfeli Lieder*. For most of his life, he lived alone in a few rooms above a bakery in a predominantly working-class section of the city, just a short walk from the cathedral and the university, both of which overlooked the river Rhine. His dedication to his students and the small university in Basel was legendary, and his stature in the community was further enhanced by his commitment to the general cultural education of Basel's citizens. Over the course of his lifetime, the enormous number of public lectures he gave on such diverse topics as art history, literature, and even ancient Greek cuisine transformed him into a sort of hometown intellectual celebrity.[1] Although he eshewed personal fame and literary success, he was held in such esteem by his peers that, in 1858, the city authorities spared no effort to entice him back to Basel after his acceptance, in 1855, of the art history chair at the newly established Polytechnical University in Zürich. They deeply regretted that the lack of a suitable opening at the local university had obliged him to take the position in Zürich. According to the philologist Johann Jacob Bachofen, who as a member of the university board of governors had tried to persuade Burckhardt to return to Basel, he was not just the "favourite of the public," but also the desired choice of his future colleagues. Bachofen wisely appealed to Burckhardt's strong sense of civic pride and responsibility, impressing upon him the urgent need to improve the spiritual and intellectual life of the city.[2] This deep-rooted civic consciousness and local patriotism contributed to Burckhardt's decision to return to Basel in 1858. It was also one of the main reasons why he consistently refused to leave the university when offered positions in Germany. In 1871, when Ernst Curtius, on behalf of the Prussian Ministry of Culture, tried to enter into negotiations with Burckhardt to fill the chair of history being vacated by his old mentor, Leopold von Ranke, at the prestigious university in Berlin, Burckhardt decisively turned down the offer, claiming "that as a Basler at the local university he felt bound by a sense of honour and duty."[3]

Burckhardt's loyalty to his *patria* had not always been so evident and unconditional. In fact, as a young man he had often found Basel to be narrow-minded, quarrelsome, and stifling; at such times the urge to escape would become overwhelming. At no time was this need more pressing than during the months following his return to Basel in the autumn of 1843, after his studies in Berlin. He found the atmosphere in his

1 Although not everyone felt the same way; Johann Jacob Bachofen once wrote to a friend about Burckhardt's public lectures: "I find it simply impossible to have aesthetic outpourings about the beauty of buildings and landscapes flowing all over me." Quoted in Gossman, *Orpheus Philologus*, 19.

2 Bachofen to Burckhardt, 24 Jan 1858, in "Aktenstücke zur Laufbahn Jacob Burckhardts," 65.

3 Quoted in Simon, *Staat und Geschichtswissenschaft*, 82. See also *Briefe*, 5:162 and 170. Ranke's chair was filled by the ultranationalist Heinrich von Treitschke. He also refused the offer of the chair of history at Tübingen in 1867 (*Briefe*, 4:253) and the chair of art history at the university in Strassburg (*Briefe*, 5:222) for similar reasons.

home town intolerable and his future prospects uncertain. Although he anticipated a position as lecturer (*Privat Dozent*) at the university, where the following summer he was to begin his long and distinguished teaching career lecturing on art history before an audience of six, a full-time university position did not materialize.[4] Instead, he was forced to take a job with the local newspaper, the *Basler Zeitung*, during an unprecedented period of violence and political turmoil, when Switzerland was the scene of a bloody internal conflict that pitted radicals and liberals against conservatives, canton against canton, and Protestant against Catholic.

Despite his family's reassurances that life at home would be pleasant, Burckhardt had difficulties readjusting to Basel society. The lack of a suitable job at the university, his growing dislike of journalism, and the deterioration of the political situation in Switzerland weighed heavily upon him. Moreover, he was lonely. Although he tried to immerse himself in a daily routine of study and research, he missed the company and intellectual stimulation of his close German friends and, no doubt, the freedom of his student days. Basel was extremely boring, he complained, and he longed to escape from the stultifying town. In contrast, Bonn and Berlin seemed to belong to the world of his dreams. Whereas Germany, he sighed, was "a beautiful, green oasis" in his life that was now gone forever,[5] Basel was especially petty and provincial: it was "so small and narrow, lacking the free and powerful stimulation which made Bonn for me a great city," and would remain "eternally unbearable." He consequently anticipated the day when he would be able to leave.[6] When Burckhardt finally resigned his position at the newspaper and managed to get to Italy in March 1846, his relief was palpable. This longing to escape Basel's excessively pious atmosphere surfaced frequently over the course of his life; his solution was to go for long walks in the surrounding countryside or take trips abroad, visiting galleries and museums throughout Europe. With the maturity of middle age he was finally able to shake off the feeling of oppression he had felt as a young man in Basel. "Only in recent years," he wrote in 1877 to his German friend Friedrich von Preen, "have I felt really at home here."[7]

---

4 "I have an audience of exactly 6!" *Briefe*, 2:91. He also planned to teach a class on German history, but it fell through due to a lack of interest.

5 See *Briefe*, 2:47, 75, 93.

6 *Briefe*, 2:54, 50.

7 *Briefe*, 6:133.

If Burckhardt felt stifled in the city in 1843, it was certainly not because Basel was standing still. Indeed, Burckhardt remarked shortly after his return from Germany that so much had been built and planned
in his absence that he hardly recognized the city.[8] Although this was
clearly an exaggeration, there was nonetheless an element of truth in
his statement. Beginning in the 1840s, Basel was transformed over the
next half-century from a small, provincial centre with modest commercial pretensions, into a modern, industrial city. The growth of factory
production in the city's primary industry, the manufacture of silk ribbon, had a profound impact on the ancient city, as Burckhardt understood only too well. Gradually, the urban landscape was transformed as
the old city wall was torn down, new roads and railway lines were constructed, and factories and slums sprang up to employ and house the
growing number of regional labourers who flocked to the city in search
of work and a better life. Mass migration and the steady growth of factories resulted in the emergence of opposition groups and the transformation of traditional political culture. Disenfranchised labourers soon
outnumbered the city's citizens and provided a base of support for the
liberal, and later socialist, opposition determined to wrestle power from
the hands of the guilds and the commercial elite that had dominated
Basel for centuries.[9] The growth of political opposition, however, did
not result in the immediate reform of either the political system or the
constitution. The conservative ruling class of merchants and artisans,
the "traditional elite" of Basel society, successfully warded off encroach-
ments on their political power monopoly until 1875, when the city-
canton finally adopted a liberal-democratic constitution in line with the
federal constitution of the previous year. Only then were the last rem-
nants of the antiquated guild system dismantled and the centuries-old
oligarchy replaced by a modern, democratic system of government. By
1897, as the century and Burckhardt's life drew to a close, the city, now
a thriving industrial and financial centre with a population of almost
110,000, had been transformed almost beyond recognition.

. . .

8 *Briefe*, 2:47.
9 Sarasin, *Stadt der Bürger*, 20–1.

The Basel of Burckhardt's youth was a small, provincial city of less than 25,000 inhabitants.[10] Until 1832, it was the administrative seat of the canton of Basel; as such, it dominated the surrounding country districts (*Landschaft*), although these subject lands had twice the population. During the first quarter of the nineteenth century the city still retained many features typical of the early-modern "hometowns" of central Europe, and was a relatively cohesive, self-contained, and inward-looking community. Its citizens were historically wary of outsiders – despite the fact that Basel had often been a refuge for dissidents – and were fiercely proud of the city's traditional independence, its humanist heritage and commercial prowess, and its particular form of republican self-government. Basel's location at a strategically important junction on the river Rhine – where France, Germany, and Switzerland meet – was a mixed blessing. Over the centuries, the city's vulnerability made it a tempting target for hostile, expansionist neighbours: Baslers often had to fight to preserve their liberty and identity. During the conflict-ridden years of the late fifteenth century, this struggle reached a momentous climax. As an Imperial Free City of the Holy Roman Empire, Basel was caught in the middle of a conflict between the Hapsburg monarchy, which was trying to centralize its authority over the free-cities of southern Germany, and the rebellious cantons of the Swiss Confederation, which were trying to preserve their independence. Despite efforts to remain neutral, many Baslers supported the Swiss cause and looked to the Confederation for protection. The defeat of Emperor Maximilian's forces in the Swabian, or Swiss, War of 1499 determined the future of the city. The victory of the Swiss Confederation, a strong but very loose defensive alliance between the rural, mountain cantons and the various city-states, with practically no central political or economic authority, convinced the practical Baslers where their real interests lay. In 1501, unable to resist the lure of the victorious confederates any longer, Basel "turned Swiss" and joined the Confederation.[11]

The newly found security within the Swiss Confederation contributed greatly to the city's prosperity during the sixteenth century, as did its renown as a centre of refuge for dissidents and persecuted Protestants. Many individuals fleeing religious persecution in France, Italy, and the

10 The best general history of Basel remains P. Burckhardt, *Geschichte der Stadt Basel.* For Basel prior to the Reformation, the most comprehensive study remains Wackernagel, *Geschichte der Stadt Basel.* See also Berchtold, *Bâle et l'Europe.*
11 The phrase is from Brady, *Turning Swiss.*

Spanish Netherlands, arrived as refugees in the early decades of the century, including some of Basel's most famous families. Since it was the policy of the city administration to admit only the wealthy, "those who would bring profit, honour, and fame to the city," and the desire of the artisans that the refugees not enter into competition with them, the emigrants were forced to introduce new economic activities, the most important of which was the silk-ribbon industry. Ironically, as a result of their success, they quickly became the city's new economic and social elite.[12]

Basel's geographic location now proved to be of great benefit to the city's economic growth and prosperity. The economic fortunes of most cities in early-modern Europe were often connected to geography. A city's relationship with the immediate hinterland as a market for its goods and as a secure source of food and other resources was especially crucial, and Basel, like many cities in central Europe and Switzerland, dominated the surrounding rural districts politically. Unlike most home towns, however, Basel's fortunate location on the Rhine, a major north-south trade route, enabled it to break the insularity and dependence upon the countryside that had resulted in the decline of many small cities. Thus, while the city was somewhat isolated from major centres, it was connected by the Rhine to the outside world. This meant that Basel's merchants could enjoy access to international markets for both goods and ideas, while participating in a regional economic system that extended beyond the confines of the city walls and its more immediate hinterland to include Alsace, Baden, and the more distant cantons of the Swiss Confederation.

Economic prosperity enabled the city to blossom as a cultural centre in the sixteenth century, often called Basel's "golden age". Intellectual life was focused on two institutions: the university, the oldest in Switzerland, which was founded in 1460 by Pope Pius II (Aeneas Silvius Picco-lomini), and the vibrant printing and book industry. The publishing industry quickly gained an international reputation and, during the first decades of the century, about seventy printers and dozens of illustrators flourished in the small city. Its leading publishing houses included Amerbach, Petri, and Froben, the quality of which, in combination with the city's reputation for tolerance, had enticed Erasmus to Basel in 1514. Erasmus's presence in Basel attracted numerous other humanists, including Glareanus; Beatus Rhenanus, the reformer and close friend

---

12 Stolz, "Technischer Wandel in der Wirtschaftsgeschichte Basels," 72–3.

of Erasmus; Johannes Oecolampadius; Sebastian Franck; Sebastian Castellio; and a number of celebrated artists, such as Hans Holbein the Younger, who arrived in 1515 to work for Froben, as well as the famous illustrator, Urs Graf.

In comparison with its arrival in other cities, the introduction of the Protestant Reformation in Basel in 1529 was relatively peaceful. As elsewhere, the movement for reform, which grew steadily, originated at least partly in clerical abuses. Basel was the see of a bishopric (only in 1501 did the political administration of the city become the soul domain of the citizens and guilds), and the city's high clergy were mostly absentee nobles who had no contact with the population. Caught between a hated, but powerful, clergy and a popular evangelical movement, the city council adopted a policy of moderate reform. This did not satisfy the more determined evangelicals and, in February 1529, during the frenzy of Carnival, their anger exploded in the wholesale destruction of the city's treasured religious icons. Fearing more violence and disorder, the town council agreed to reform the city's religious life. By 1534, the theological reforms had been consolidated into the "Basel Confession," a synthesis of the work of Luther and Zwingli by the Basel Reformer and humanist, Oecolampadius. Arguably the high point of Reformation humanism in the city, the document became the cornerstone of Basel's reformed church.[13]

Over the course of the next centuries, the orthodox theological legacy of the Reformation remained an intellectual and spiritual pillar of fundamental importance to Basel's elite. By the early eighteenth century, Basel had experienced a revival of religious sentiment, due in large part to the spread of pietism and the work of the influential pastor, Hieronymus d'Annoni, and the community of *Herrenhuter*. One consequence of the influence of pietism on the town's religious leadership was its facilitation of a steady offensive by the religious orthodoxy against the incursions of rationalism and the "perceived threat of 'modern scientific consciousness'" that was embodied in Enlightenment thought.[14] By the end of the eighteenth century, pietism, under the auspices of the German Christian Society – in 1784 it was unflatteringly described by *Berlinische Monatsschrift* as "a true Protestant form of

13 See Bietenholz, *Basle and France in the Sixteenth Century*, and the brief survey by Guggisberg, *Basel in the Sixteenth Century*. On iconoclasm in Basel during the Reformation, see Wandel, *Voracious Idols and Violent Hands*.

14 Howard, "Historicist Thought in the Shadow of Theology," 264.

Jesuitism" – dominated religious life in Basel, numbering among its prominent followers theologians, businessmen, and local clergymen, including Jacob Burckhardt's grandfather and father.[15]

Although Basel remained "a centre of the Old Faith" and "the hub of the German Christian Society, which everywhere led the fight against rationalism in Switzerland and Germany,"[16] it would be a mistake to minimize the influence of enlightened French and German thought on Basel and Swiss intellectual life in the late eighteenth century. The Genevan, Jean Jacques Rousseau, is the most famous representative of the Swiss Enlightenment. But other men such as education reformer Heinrich Pestalozzi, political theorist and philosopher Johann Caspar Lavater, and historian Johannes von Müller also gained international reputations and set the standard in their respective fields.[17] Even in "pious Basel" the Enlightenment sank strong roots, especially among the merchant class, and managed to co-exist, however uneasily, with Basel's orthodox Protestantism. Although in decline, the university at Basel became famous during the eighteenth century as a centre of mathematics, largely through the path-breaking work of the brothers Jakob and Johann Bernoulli, and the latter's son, Daniel. The most famous Enlightenment figure in Basel, however, was Isaak Iselin (1728–82). Active in many spheres, he was a founder of the patriotic "Helvetic Society" (1761) and the philanthropic organization "Die Gesellschaft zur Beförderung des Guten und Gemeinnützigen" (1777), as well as the author of numerous works, the most important of which was his highly influential cultural history, the *Geschichte der Menschheit* (1764).[18]

Yet another Basler, Peter Ochs (1752–1821), played a crucial role in the history of Switzerland, when, in 1798, he appealed to Napoleon Bonaparte for military intervention to overthrow the old regime in Switzerland. The constitution of "La République Helvétique, une et indivisible," written by Ochs, was a monument to the ideas of the French Revolution. It abolished the abuses and privileges of the old regime; introduced economic reform; and created, for the first time, a modern unitary and centralized state in Switzerland, based upon the principles of democratic representation and universal civil liberties. The principles of the Revolution were by no means universally rejected by the city's elite. In 1797, Johann Rudolf Burckhardt, Jacob Burckhardt's grandfa-

15 Quoted in ibid., 272.
16 Quoted in ibid., 273.
17 On the Swiss Enlightenment in general, see Im Hof, *Aufklärung in der Schweiz.*
18 On Iselin, see Im Hof, *Isaak Iselin: Sein Leben und die Entwicklung seines Denkens*; and Im Hof, *Isaak Iselin und die Spätaufklärung.*

ther, recognized the need for political reform, but hoped that it could be achieved by the Swiss themselves. Like many, his greatest fear was French invasion and the loss of independence. He predicted: "Since our Citoyens are in collusion with France and France supports them, we will have to dance to their piper if we don't want to feel their heavy iron fist. And consequently our 300-year-old happy Republic must be ruled by a six-year-old daughter."[19] He was correct in his prognostication. Between 1798 and 1815, the Swiss unwillingly danced to Napoleon's unpleasant and discordant tunes. Characterized by extreme exploitation and violence, the French invasion and occupation created enormous hostility towards the French. Worse was still to come, though, as Switzerland eventually became a principal battlefield in Napoleon's Second Coalition War.

The Helvetic Republic, the product of the ideas of an "enlightened" minority within the Swiss elite, was imposed by Napoleon's "iron fist," in gross contradiction to centuries-old traditions of local self-government and independence, and was generally despised by the traditional ruling elites as well as the peasants and artisans. While many realized the need for political reforms, the concepts of liberty and equality – the bywords of the events of 1789 – held little meaning for the Swiss. Their conceptions of liberty and equality, deeply rooted in local, more popular and concrete freedoms and rights at the level of the commune, were best symbolized by the original treaty of confederation of 1291 between the cantons of Uri, Schwyz, and Nidwalden. The ideas of 1789 were consequently alien to many and resistance to the new order was extremely intense. In 1803, Napoleon dissolved the new state, imposed the "Act of Mediation," installed himself as "Mediator of the Helvetic Republic," and restored to the cantons many of their traditional rights, albeit under strict French hegemony. Following Napoleon's final defeat and the dissolution of the Act of Mediation in 1815, Swiss independence was once more established, guaranteed by the signatory powers of the Congress of Vienna. In August 1815, with the signing of the Federal Treaty, which essentially restored the pre-1798 status quo, the cantons agreed to a new form of political union. The experiment in centralized government had been deemed a failure; once more Switzerland was reduced to a "bundle of states," a loose confederation of sovereign cantons.

· · ·

19 Kaegi, 1:92–3.

Despite connections with distant markets, cultures, and political institutions, Basel's social and political structures remained essentially unchanged well into the second half of the nineteenth century. Indeed, the experience of the French Revolution – the imposition of the Helvetic Republic and the Act of Mediation – did not loosen the oligarchy's stranglehold on political life for long. Following the negotiation of the Federal Treaty of 1815, Basel's elite moved quickly to restore its traditional political institutions. As a result, the struggle for political and social change during the nineteenth century was long and arduous. Despite being challenged internally and externally by the forces of reform, the *ancien régime* in Basel was not easily dislodged from power after 1815. Moreover, despite political division and occasional mismanagement, the traditionalist, conservative ruling elite – the class of *marchands-fabricants-banquiers* – fought an extremely effective rearguard action against all opposition to its continued political hegemony.

This traditional ruling class, to which Jacob Burckhardt belonged through family connections, academic status, and, to an extent, shared convictions but not wealth, had ruled the prosperous city-republic for centuries. As the self-proclaimed guardian of the city's civic republican virtues, its cultural and religious heritage, and the liberties of its citizens, and despite constitutional changes in 1831, 1833, and 1848 and almost perpetual internal and external opposition, it managed to preserve both its dominant position within government and the guild system that sustained it in power. As with most corporatist societies, political representation was reserved for a select, highly regulated group of citizens. Of the total population of the city, only approximately one-third were citizens – the rest either came from other cantons or were foreigners – and of this one-third, only approximately 1,750 were considered *Aktivbürger*; that is, men who met the stringent property requirements enabling them to vote and participate in political life.[20] These *Aktivbürger* came primarily from economically independent and well-established merchant families. The vast majority of the population – women, servants, labourers, newcomers, and even Swiss from other cantons – were effectively excluded from political life. People were also restricted from political participation on religious grounds. For example, only a few Catholics had the right to vote, while Jews were excluded altogether, their right to settlement being strictly limited.

20 Schaffner, "Geschichte des politischen Systems," 40 and 42. See also P. Burckhardt, *Geschichte der Stadt Basel*, 202.

The patriciate maintained its grip on political power through a restrictive, guild-based system of representation, enshrined in tradition and law. All male citizens twenty-four years of age and over had to belong to one of the city's sixteen guilds.[21] This did not mean that artisans played the leading role in political life. Indeed, since the early sixteenth century, the guild system had been dominated by four "gentlemen's guilds," whose membership spanned the bourgeoisie with its wealthy businessmen, professionals, and members of the middle and lower-middle classes, and whose influence determined the form of government and the nature of administration.[22] The cantonal government consisted of a legislative body, the Grand Council (*Grosser Rat*), which was elected by both *Aktivbürger* and the guilds, and the fifteen-member Small or Executive Council (*Kleiner Rat*), which was elected by the Grand Council. At the head of the executive branch were two mayors (*Bürgermeister*). After 1833, the Grand Council consisted of 119 members; approximately two-thirds of these were elected by the *Aktivbürger*, in six district assemblies, with the remaining one-third elected by the guilds, each of which nominated two representatives. Because this body elected the powerful Executive Council, the elite dominated both levels of government. One recent study has shown that, between 1814 and 1846, nearly one-half of all members of both branches of government were either industrialists, bankers, or merchants; a quarter were artisans; and the rest were professionals.[23] Members of the rapidly expanding working class were effectively excluded from political office. Not until 1868 was the first worker elected into the Grand Council.[24]

The cantonal authorities, especially the Executive Council, had sweeping powers. The latter presided over legislative and executive matters in addition to the courts, the constitution, taxation, and, most importantly, relations with the Swiss Confederation; for instance, it chose and strictly controlled Basel's representatives to the federal diet (*Tagsatzung*). The system of administration in Basel was complicated by the ex-

21 An academic guild was established in 1836 as the sixteenth, to which Burckhardt later belonged.

22 The four gentlemen's guilds were the "Saffran" guild (small shopkeepers, grocers, stationers, bookprinters), the "Weinleute" guild (wine merchants, notaries), the "Hausgenossen" guild (bankers and moneychangers), and the "Schlüssel" guild (large merchants, manufacturers, and retailers). The *grande bougeoisie* belonged to the Schlüssel guild; the Saffran guild was the guild of the petty bourgeoisie. See generally Sarasin, *Stadt der Bürger*, 161. See also Guggisberg, *Basel in the Sixteenth Century*, 6.

23 Schaffner, "Geschichte des politischen Systems," 42–3.

24 P. Burckhardt, *Geschichte der Stadt Basel*, 203.

istence of the cantonal authorities along side a distinct city or municipal government despite the reduction of the canton to the status of a city-state in 1833.[25] In contrast to the cantonal government, the eighty members of the City Council (*Stadtrat*) were elected by the guilds; because this council had no property restrictions on its members, artisans tended to exert more influence in the City Council than in the cantonal administration. The areas of competence of the City Council differed substantially from those of the cantonal government. In existence since the days of the Helvetic Republic, the City Council had as its primary responsibility the policing of the city, which meant maintenance of law and order; regulation of the guilds, economic competition, and the procurement of foodstuffs; enforcement of the strict residency and citizenship laws; general provision of welfare and health care; and maintenance of the city's infrastructure and public buildings. An occasional overlap in jurisdiction occurred, resulting in some conflict and inefficient administration. Throughout the 1830s and 1840s, however, the cantonal government gradually assumed greater authority over the City Council.

As Basel's population grew through successive waves of immigration – non-citizens came from neighbouring cantons and southern Germany in search of employment – campaigns for the reform of the political system and extension of political rights intensified. Liberals and other reformers in Basel and throughout Switzerland took particular aim at the patrician system of rule, which they condemned as a closed caste, a *Geschlechterherrschaft*, that dominated government positions and made the important political decisions without consulting the rest of the population. Although the ruling class was not an aristocracy in the technical and constitutional sense – its members' authority and privilege were derived not from birth, but from their wealth and status within society – it had, over the centuries, become a relatively homogeneous group that behaved like a "de facto patriciate."[26] The Grand Council and the Execu-

25 Only in 1875 were these competing levels of government consolidated into one government administration.

26 Kaegi emphasizes that Burckhardt was not a patrician and that it is incorrect to speak of a Basel patriciate in the sense of a closed governing class, as was the case in Bern, Solothurn, and Fribourg. While Burckhardt did not have the economic means and lived in a working-class quarter of the city, he was nonetheless part of the elite through family origins. There is still some debate as to whether or not the ruling families of Basel constituted a closed elite. See Kaegi, 5:623 and Gossman, "Basel," 71. Still, the "*marchands-fabricants-banquiers*" continued to dominate Basel politics until 1875, and this remained a relatively homogeneous group. See Sarasin, *Stadt der Bürger*; P. Burckhardt, *Geschichte der Stadt Basel*, 205; and Schaffner, "Geschichte des politischen Systems."

tive Council were invariably dominated by men whose families had had citizenship for at least one hundred years, and family connections often determined the composition of government. Even if the regime was not technically or legally an aristocracy, the ruling class often assumed the airs of a closed elite, and appeared as such to the political opposition. Entry into the ranks of the governing class was exceedingly difficult for outsiders, not to say extremely rare. Between 1831 and 1846, only twenty "new" citizens became members of the Grand Council, and none became mayor.[27] This homogeneity was reinforced by legal and political privileges; by generations of judicious marriages within the old families of the upper bourgeoisie; and by codes of behaviour and social rules designed not only to separate the leading families from outsiders, noncitizens, and others below them on the social scale, but also to exclude them from political power. Families such as the Burckhardts, Bernouillis, Debarys, Merians, and Sarasins, to name just a few, whose dominant presence in Basel could be traced back to the late Middle Ages, continued to exercise power throughout the nineteenth century. Only in 1875, when the city adopted a new liberal and democratic constitution, did the oligarchy come to an official end. However, the post-1875 liberal era of representative democracy did not significantly reduce the patriciate's political or social influence, which lasted well into the early twentieth century.[28]

Despite this castelike homogeneity, the oligarchy was far from reactionary or authoritarian in the Prussian tradition. It tried to steer a moderate, albeit conservative, course while preserving its privileged position, and had little sympathy for either absolute monarchies or the new forms of despotism that had emerged during the French Revolution. On the contrary, the citizens of Basel viewed the long and stable traditions of their republican system of government as one of the few remaining bulwarks against both the tyranny of the dictator/monarch and the new-style tyranny of the masses. At the same time, the patriciate considered itself progressive. The constitution of 1833, for instance, was considered by many to be one of the most liberal in the Confederation, even though it explicitly rejected the principles of popular sovereignty. In the important realms of commerce, industry, and finance, the regime also advocated laissez-faire economic policies, the major exception being their refusal to support the abolition of the guild laws. But

27 Schaffner, "Geschichte des politischen Systems," 43.

28 See Schaffner, "Geschichte des politischen Systems," 49 and 50; Roth, *Die Politik der Liberal-Konservativen*; and Sarasin, "Domination, Gender Difference and National Myths."

this was the result less of economic, than political and social, concerns. Indeed, the old regime in Basel, as one recent historian has pointed out, was characterized by the "paradoxical contradiction between modernity and a longing for the old,"[29] a trait typical of much of conservatism. Yet this paradox – the regime's embrace of certain aspects of economic modernization and its unwavering desire to preserve the traditional structures that guaranteed its continued hegemony – did not substantially weaken or undermine the elite's stranglehold on political power. As Philipp Sarasin has effectively demonstrated, recourse to tradition and moral codes, especially in the decades following the Revolution of 1830 and the division of the canton (the *Kantonstrennung*) of 1833, helped legitimize the political discourse of the old regime in Basel, enabling the political elite to adapt quite easily and quickly to the changed political culture of the city and to reshape and restructure public life according to its own agenda.[30] By providing relatively few barriers to the expansion of certain industries and by actively participating in the restructuring of the public sphere to its advantage, the party of the *juste milieu* was able to embark on a program of preventive, defensive compromise when dealing with the growing demands of the liberal political opposition.

The guild system, the one particularly important institution that critics argued was most in need of reform, was the subject of considerable political debate in the city during the 1830s and 1840s. Liberals and other opponents of the system recognized the guilds as an obstacle to both economic and political modernization. An integral element of premodern power structures, guilds had once played a vital economic, political, and social role in early modern cities. They dominated urban political life; organized and maintained the urban economy, regulating the supply of goods to ensure fair competition and the quality of merchandise; set limits to the expansion of small producers, maintaining the general economic viability of the artisanal class; and established rigid codes of social, sexual, and moral behaviour, thereby helping to maintain the integrity of the family as the most important social and productive unit and the wellspring of social order. In short, the artisan class constituted a secure middle class, a buffer between the rich and the poor that was essential to the smooth functioning and continued well-being of urban societies.

29 Sarasin, "Basel – Zur Sozialgeschichte der Stadt Bachofens," 30.
30 See Sarasin, "Sittlichkeit, Nationalgefühl und frühe Ängste vor dem Proletariat."

As was the case in Basel and the rest of western and central Europe, by the early nineteenth century guilds had ceased to be the real motor of the economy and were under attack. With the growth and mechanization of industry, the spread of rail networks, and the steady influx of cheap labour and goods into Basel, artisans realized that their social status and political position were by no means secure. As the most susceptible of all the premodern institutions to economic and political change, the guilds continuously fought any attempt at reform – many citizens realized that the weakening position of the artisan class represented a potential source of social unrest. As Basel gradually industrialized, many citizens criticized the traditional guild restrictions on production and competition as unnecessary for the maintenance of social order and as an obstacle to economic growth and prosperity. One early commentator, the economist and engineer Christoph Bernoulli, wrote in 1822 that the guilds were unfairly limiting economic productivity and growth. He held up the example of the prosperity of the silk-ribbon industry, which since the mid-seventeenth century had avoided guild restrictions and had steadily increased its production and profits by expanding its "putting-out" system in the countryside, as proof of the benefits to be gained by the elimination of the anachronistic guild laws.[31] Indeed, one of the long-term consequences of the guild laws was the distortion of the local economy, as characterized by the large-scale, export-oriented businesses, manufactures, and financal firms owned by the patriciate, and by the small-scale, artisanal production.

The most important issues surrounding the guild question, however, were not economic, but political. Basel's economic structure was mirrored in the political authority of the artisans (the small-scale producers) and the patriciate (the large-scale commercial and financial sector operating outside of the guild laws). The guilds, despite declining economic fortunes, still formed the backbone of the oligarchical political system. The guild-based system of political representation not only empowered the artisans, but also sustained the elite in power; artisans and the wealthy patriciate consequently spared no effort to maintain this mutually beneficial political system, knowing that if one element of the structure was eliminated, so was the other. The artisans fought tooth and nail to preserve the political and economic privileges guaranteed by

31 Sarasin, *Stadt der Bürger,* 75. Bernoulli's criticism of the guild system evoked considerable opposition, including that of some butchers who smeared the front of his house with blood. See also Stolz, "Technischer Wandel in der Wirtschaftsgeschichte Basels."

the guild restrictions – as one contemporary claimed, they feared freedom of occupation more than cholera[32] – and consequently found erst-
while allies in the ranks of the patriciate, whose business activities were
not significantly affected by the guilds. The government was therefore
extremely reluctant to tinker with the existing political system, despite
the fact that it was anachronistic and inequitable. During the social unrest of the 1840s, the artisans and patriciate successfully warded off liberal demands to broaden representation, to abolish the privileges of the
guilds, and to establish freedom of occupation. One commentator articulated the corporatist agenda and the narrow interests of the two
groups when he explained the common bond uniting them: "Mutual interests require that we always protect each other ... It is the desire of no
one that Basel consist only of rich and poor. The wealthy estate is only
secure and protected by a solid *Mittelstand*. This old belief will always
prevail and the artisans will never cease to occupy, as has been the case
since time immemorial, a position of considerable importance in our
community."[33] As the twin pillars of the oligarchy, these two had the
most to lose in a reformed constitution.

But the most important sectors of the industrial economy in Basel
proper and in the surrounding countryside, as Bernoulli clearly understood, were controlled not by guilds, but by the small number of
wealthy families belonging to the closely-knit commercial elite. Their
factories and capital provided the basis for Basel's rapid industrial and
commercial growth in the second half of the nineteenth century, and
they employed vast numbers in their factories as well as in their opu-
lent homes. It is estimated that about 4,000 people were employed in
household service in the city during the 1830s, far more than were employed in the factories or the trades.[34] The silk-ribbon industry, which
began to mechanize production in the 1820s, beginning the process of
industrialization in Basel, employed a high proportion of the region's
workers, and generated an estimated twenty percent of the city's taxation revenues. An 1843 report from the prominent philanthropic organization, the "Gesellschaft zur Beförderung des Guten und
Gemeinnützigen" (GGG), claimed that within the walls of the city there

32 Quoted in P. Burckhardt, *Geschichte der Stadt Basel*, 207.

33 Quoted in Sarasin, *Stadt der Bürger*, 75. See also Sarasin, "Sittlichkeit, Nationalgefühl
und frühe Ängste vor dem Proletariat," 105–23.

34 M. Burckhardt, "Politische, soziale und kirchliche Spannungen," 49. There were approximately 3000 artisans enumerated in 1847. See P. Burckhardt, *Geschichte der Stadt Basel*,
206.

were at least 1,500 men and women working in the mechanized factories and another 10,000 employed directly or indirectly through the putting-out system in the countryside, where agriculture had long ceased to be sustainable.[35]

Less labour-intensive, but far more lucrative for those involved – especially for city coffers – were the financial and commercial sectors. Based on the enormous fortunes accumulated over the centuries by the *Bändelherren*, as the silk-ribbon manufacturers were called, the Basel merchants and bankers had connections stretching across the globe – Burckhardt's younger brother Lucas Gottlieb, for example, entered into business with his uncle in Moscow [36] – as well as a reputation for solid credit and investment resources. However, only a small portion of the wealth generated by these sectors was reinvested in production in the city. Sarasin points to two reasons for this. In the first place, the bourgeoisie had a long tradition of capital export. Second, because local business could not possibly absorb the enormous sums available for investment, a large percentage of Basel capital ended up in the international money market. Although the city gained a reputation as the "capital reservoir of Switzerland and upper Germany," its bankers had a far longer reach, investing not just in industrial development in Switzerland, France, and Germany, but also in business ventures much further afield, such as in New Orleans and Sydney. During Burckhardt's youth, the financial sector had already become prominent: sixteen private banking houses existed in a city of only 25,000 people.[37]

If the future of the guild system was the subject of almost perennial debate, public discussion about the situation of the growing population of labouring poor was somewhat slower to crystalize. Although there was some concern about the terrible condition of working-class living quarters and the employment of children and women in the factories, the state not only refused to become involved in the "social question" but refused to endorse legislation that would, in any way, impede the economic freedom of the industrialists and merchants. Workers'

35 Sarasin, *Stadt der Bürger*, 76–7. In 1847 the census recorded approximately 2,200 workers (men and women) in the ribbon industry and another 380 in tabacco and paper factories and in the silk-spinning industry.

36 "Basel merchants had always traveled far beyond the narrow confines of their Lilliputian state on business, and the city owed much to loyal citizens who preferred to be somewhere else," Gossman, "Basel," 87–8. Lucas Gottlieb Burckhardt (1821–1889), in contrast to Jacob, was very involved in Basel politics. See Kaegi, 1:297ff.

37 Quoted in Sarasin, *Stadt der Bürger*, 85, and Kaegi, 5:268.

associations and threats of work stoppages, although relatively common, were not generally tolerated by the authorities, and all forms of social assistance were left to charity organizations, such as the *Gemeinnützige Gesellschaft* and other church relief agencies, or to generous private individuals. In the late 1840s, however, the social question became more urgent as workers and artisans started to organize more effectively in the fight for their political and economic interests. The elite's fear of the proletariat and social revolution now became an important component of its public political discourse and private anxieties. Given the deep economic divide that separated the elite from the masses and the tremendous growth of radicalism during this decade, both in Basel and in the thoroughly regenerated canton of Basel-Landschaft, one can understand why the ribbon manufacturers, the *Bändelherren*, feared the development of mass movements and political institutions. As the country lurched towards civil and religious war in the 1840s, many, including Jacob Burckhardt, expressed the fear common in government circles: that the political and confessional strife plaguing Switzerland would degenerate into a bloody social revolution leading to the "despotism of the masses."[38]

Such a fear spread through Basel's elite in October 1846, following the *coup d'état* that overthrew the conservative regime in the canton of Geneva. In contrast to the many other coup attempts in Switzerland during the 1830s and 1840s or the ever-present threat of radical partisan incursions, the Genevan coup seemed to signal the beginning of something unprecedented and ominous to the *Ratsherren* in Basel, who had always identified with the southern city republic. Andreas Heusler, politician, professor of law, and editor of the *Basler Zeitung*, captured the ruling classes' sense of panic and near hysteria following the Genevan Revolution when he wrote that "news from Geneva has had such an effect on us as if the events had happened here. We have been knocked dead on the Rhône."[39] This was not the first time that a government had been overthrown in Switzerland during the 1840s; however, it was the first time that social issues figured prominently. In a further commentary in the *Basler Zeitung*, Heusler wrote that the coup in Geneva was "the first decisive victory that the working people, the so-called proletariat of a state, had carried over the other classes, over the so-called haute société, bourgeoisie and country people ... The revolution is not just po-

---

38 See for example, *Briefe*, 2:158.
39 Quoted in Roth, "Zur Vorgeschichte der liberal-konservativen Partei in Basel," 179.

litical but also social." He therefore appealed to the "thinking reader" to help defeat political radicalism before the country fell into the "abyss of social confusion." Conservatives like Heusler and Burckhardt were united in the belief that "socialism was the consequence of radicalism"; that a glimpse at cantons ruled by liberals and radicals would reveal the rule of the masses.[40] Many years later, Burckhardt echoed a common sentiment of the ruling classes when he pondered what would happen if one day the masses, hitherto surprisingly unsuccessful, were to become aware of their potential power. Although he saw this as happening some time in the future, his contemporary Johann Jacob Bachofen, one of the city's wealthiest and most reactionary citizens, was even more pessimistic than Burckhardt. In 1868, just one year before the Fourth Socialist International was held in Basel, Bachofen experienced apocalyptic visions during a strike against the ribbon manufacturers and believed that the end of "bourgeois society" was at hand. "Without chassepots," he wrote to a friend, "peace and security of person and property stand on shaky ground."[41]

. . .

The ruling classes' fear of revolution was not simply a paranoid response to growing working-class discontent; it also reflected anxieties about a possible repetition of the rebellion that had torn the canton apart in the early 1830s. The Basler *Wirren*, or "Troubles," of 1830–33 – the final outcome of which was the separation of the country districts of the canton (*Kantonstrennung*) from city jurisdiction and administration and the formation of two half cantons, Basel-Stadt and Basel-Landschaft – had posed a serious threat to the authority of the patriciate. Arguably, the *Kantonstrennung* was the most disruptive break in Basel's history since the crisis of the late Middle Ages and the Reformation. Its severanced of the rural hinterland from city control and destruction of the canton's territorial integrity was nothing short of a catastrophe for many leading citizens, who now believed that the era of stability, prosperity, and independence, which had lasted more or less since the sixteenth century, was now over. It soured relations with the rest of Switzerland

40 BZ, 10.10.1846.

41 *Briefe*, 7:203; Bachofen quote in Sarasin, "Basel – Zur Sozialgeschichte der Stadt Bachofens," 38.

and also substantially reduced Basel's influence within the federal government. While little talk of secession from the federation occurred, one consequence of the division of the canton and Basel's subsequent political isolation from the rest of Switzerland was the ruling conservatives' conviction that they and Basel's humanist heritage and civic-republican traditions were under siege. Increasingly, a bunker mentality prevailed, especially with regard to federal relations and demands for reform. Increasingly, the ruling class became more committed, in both parliament and the press, to the fight against liberalism and for the traditional rights and autonomy of the cantons. Vociferously hostile towards any reforms that might weaken the autonomy and sovereignty of the cantons and create a strong unitary state, Basel became the leading voice of Swiss conservatism and federalism. More than any other event, the *Kantonstrennung* set the tone of the political discourse in Basel during the 1830s and 1840s, providing the patriciate with an initially unassailable source of legitimacy and authority.

The unrest in Basel and elsewhere in Switzerland was unleashed by the French Revolution of 1830. News of the July Revolution in Paris caught most Swiss by surprise. It caused considerable anxiety, and even panic, among many conservatives, who feared a repetition of 1789. However, for a generation of liberals and radicals determined to bring an end to the policies of reaction that had followed the defeat of the French and the restoration of Swiss independence, the Revolution of 1830 served as a lightning rod, igniting passions and inspiring the hope that a new age of progress and reform was dawning.

A source of particular discontent and disappointment for opposition groups was the Federal Treaty of 1815. Intended as a compromise between "the reactionary aims of the Conservatives and the more moderate demands of the Centralists," the treaty in fact represented a victory for the conservatives and the forces of reaction that dominated post-Napoleonic Europe; moreover, it was guaranteed by the Great Powers. Although it restored Swiss independence from the French, established the principles of neutrality, and ensured Switzerland's territorial integrity, the Federal Treaty was a throwback to the pre-1798 order and proved unsuited to the needs of a modern nation-state.[42] As its name indicates, it was not a constitution in the traditional sense, but an alliance or "diplo-

---

42 See Biaudet, "Der modernen Schweiz entgegen," 871–986; Gruner, "Die Schweizerische Eidgenossenschaft von der Französische Revolution bis zur Reform der Verfassung," 112–37. See also Gordon A. Craig, *The Triumph of Liberalism*, and Remak, *A Very Civil War*.

matic transaction" between sovereign states.[43] It consisted of fifteen articles that bound the cantons in a loose federation, effectively dismantling the centralized state apparatus. The most important institution in the new system was the federal diet, or *Tagsatzung*, in which each canton received one vote, regardless of size and importance. Whereas the federal government remained in overall charge of the military and external relations, the cantons were granted almost unlimited authority and autonomy in internal affairs. They were allowed to form alliances with each other; conclude trade agreements with other countries, provided this did not undermine the confederation; and maintain their own militias – provisions which proved disastrous in the coming years. The principal accomplishment of the Federal Treaty, after the experiment in unitary government and the Act of Mediation, was the radical devolution of the central government's power and the re-establishment of the (now twenty-two) cantons' sovereign authority, as the conservatives had wished.

Ultimately, the treaty was important less for what it contained, than for what it omitted. In and of itself, it was not a repressive document. However, its omissions and inadequacies enabled individual cantons to proceed with the reconstitution of reactionary, unrepresentative forms of government without fear of federal interference. This was possible primarily because the treaty did not mention the rights of citizens, which were left up to the individual cantons. As a consequence, in many cantons, including Basel, many important political and economic rights granted to ordinary men and women after the French invasion of 1798 were once more severely restricted and recently abolished privileges were granted to the elite. Popular sovereignty was practically non-existent. Although all cantons were required by the treaty to have constitutions, in only two cantons, Geneva and Grisons, were new constitutions put before the people; in the others, supreme authority rested with the councils, which operated in secret and out of the eye of the public. In the patrician cantons of Bern, Solothurn, Fribourg, and Lucerne, opposition was suppressed and the old ruling class became once more firmly entrenched in power. The same was true in the so-called guild cantons (*Zunftkantone*) of Basel, Zürich, and Schaffhausen.[44]

The abrogation of political and civil rights was most drastically felt in the subject rural districts. The city/country dichotomy, always tendentious in early modern Europe, had been particularly so in Switzerland,

43 Rappard, *La constitution fédérale de la Suisse*, 35.
44 Biaudet, "Der modernen Schweiz entgegen," 900.

where rural and urban districts did not enjoy political or social equality. Although serfdom had been abolished in 1790 and rural residents had been granted equal rights of citizenship in 1798, the restoration of the old regime in 1815 did away with these recently won political rights. In cantons with major urban centres, such as Zürich, Bern, and Basel, political representation was once more strictly limited to the advantage of the citizens of the principal cities, while inhabitants of the countryside were once again reduced to subordinate status.[45] The authority of the cantons was also enhanced by a number of other measures and omissions, including the abolition of Swiss citizenship and the lack of any guarantee of freedom of settlement. Moreover, individual cantons maintained internal customs and tolls, a highly visible and important symbol of their sovereignty and authority, but a crucial hindrance to trade and economic modernization. Finally, freedom of religion was no longer guaranteed by the federal government, an omission of singular importance in regions with a mix of Catholics and Protestants, such as Aargau, and in a country with a history of confessional strife.

The thoroughness of the restoration had far-reaching social and political consequences, and the Federal Treaty quickly became a focal point of political opposition. In the early 1820s, liberals and other reform-minded citizens began to organize in most cantons, advocating both the implementation of more representative and democratic political institutions and far-reaching economic reforms, including the abolition of guilds, the creation of uniform weights and measures and a single currency, and the elimination of the many internal tolls and duties that restricted the free flow of goods. The driving force behind the early form of liberal opposition in Switzerland, as elsewhere in Europe, was the small group of intellectuals, professionals, and business leaders whose primary objectives were the modernization of the national economy and the state. Although still ill-defined and unrepresented by a political party in the 1820s, liberalism had become, by the end of the decade, a rallying point for most opposition groups and was gradually transformed into a mass movement of political and social liberation. Consequently, when traditionally conservative peasants, farmers, and rural labourers began to participate in a sometimes violent and explosive dialogue with their political masters for greater political rights, they proved responsive to the organizational efforts of liberal landowners, village leaders, and urban intellectuals. Attracted by the promise of an end to

45 See ibid., 894ff.

the inequities in the political system, they soon formed an important base of support for the liberal, and later the more radical, democratic movements. By the beginning of the 1830s, the liberal opposition movement had gathered significant momentum throughout the country and had won important victories in the cantons of Geneva, Vaud, and Lucerne, where a number of economic and political reforms were introduced. Finally, on 4 July 1830, on the eve of revolution, the majority of citizens in the southern, Italian-speaking canton of Ticino accepted a revised, democratic constitution.

Although liberalism was gaining momentum, especially in the urban cantons, the impetus for its explosive growth came from the July Revolution. Within a year, liberals had formed the government in eleven cantons – Aargau, Bern, Freiburg, Lucerne, Schaffhausen, Solothurn, St. Gall, Thurgau, Ticino, Vaud, and Zürich – and had introduced new constitutions, based on the ideals of popular sovereignty and representative democracy as articulated by the Vaud native, Benjamin Constant. Led by men such as Paul Usteri and Friedrich Ludwig Keller in Zürich, Gallus Jacob Baumgartner in St. Gall, and Kasimir Pfyffer in Lucerne, the new regimes introduced sweeping reforms in an attempt to liberalize and modernize – in the vocabulary of the day, "to regenerate," – the cantons. In these regions, the system of representation was reformed, civil rights became enshrined in new constitutions, existing privileges of the guilds and patriciate were systematically dismantled, and laws were introduced to liberalize the economy and facilitate trade.

Reformers were not content to see their accomplishments restricted to their individual cantons; they also looked beyond the borders of their cantons to the biggest prize, the federal government, in the hope of reforming the Confederation as well. Proceeding from the principles of popular sovereignty and representative democracy, liberals were able to exploit the national question in the name of their cause, proclaiming the unity of the Swiss *Volk* and nation. This, it was hoped, would destroy the traditional *Kantönligeist* (cantonal nationalism), legitimize their system of rule, and provide a theoretical and practical basis for a new Swiss state and nation. The new Swiss union envisioned by the liberals would confirm the achievements of the regenerated cantons and, more importantly, lead to the regeneration of the conservative ones.

Despite initial success in the cantons, the liberal movement stalled at the federal level: it was unable to achieve a majority in the *Tagsatzung* with its system of representation in which each canton, regardless of its size or importance, had the same number of votes. The liberals simply could not break conservative domination in the *Tagsatzung*. Moreover, the liberal challenge to the authority of the country's traditional regimes did not proceed without resistance. In Valais, Schwyz, and Neuchâtel, for example, the liberal movement was quickly suppressed; elsewhere, violence and bloodshed occurred as *Freischärler*, or partisans, recruited from the liberal regions, made incursions into conservative regions. But the most serious conflict between the liberals and conservatives took place in the canton of Basel, where in 1831 a brief civil war erupted, resulting in the division of the canton and the occupation of the city by federal government troops.[46]

Ironically, the initiative for political reform in Basel came not from the liberals outside the canton or from opposition politicians in the countryside, but from within the canton government during the months prior to the July Revolution. Under pressure from liberals and fully recognizing the need for some type of reform, the government council drafted a constitution to be put before a referendum in February 1831. The proposed constitution contained a number of progressive elements, including in principle the guarantee of certain basic rights and freedoms of the canton's citizens; it was far from democratic, however, and only liberalized the franchise to include all men over twenty-four years of age who met certain property requirements. Both the power of the guilds and the guild-based system of representation – the latter a target of liberal reformers and the backbone of the conservative regime – remained intact; freedom of occupation, moreover, was not extended.

The real stumbling block was not the guild question but the sensitive issue of representation. The attempt by the Basel regime to head off the liberals by a revolution from above failed. From the outset of the constitutional negotiations, the liberals in the country districts – led by rural landowners – demanded that the constitutional committee be formed on the basis of direct representation and that all subsequent elections follow the same procedure. With direct representation, the country districts, with two-thirds of the canton's population, would have an absolute majority. While the patriciate was willing to broaden the base of representation to include rural landowners, they were unwilling to give the countryside an absolute majority in the Grand Council. The city's representatives argued that since the urban residents provided well over ninety percent of the canton's tax revenue and the city was the commer-

---

46 On the *Kantonstrennung* see P. Burckhardt, *Geschichte der Stadt Basel*, 159ff; Sieber, *Basler Trennungswirren*.

cial and cultural centre of the region, they, as representatives, should retain the dominant position in the canton's government. The authorities consequently drew the line at direct representation.

With negotiations still under way in early January 1831, radical liberals in the countryside led an uprising against the cantonal government. The city militia, after quickly putting down this revolt, proceeded to occupy the small town of Liestal, the main centre of the rebellion. Although the leaders of the uprising fled, the crisis was by no means over. Despite pressure from the federal diet, which was attempting to mediate the crisis, Basel refused to grant a general amnesty; instead, it tried to arrest the rebellious countryside leaders, thereby creating further antagonism. None of this stopped the government from proceeding with the now reformed constitution and, on the last day of February 1831, it was placed before the citizens of the entire canton for ratification. In spite of some discontent in the countryside, it was accepted by almost two-thirds of the citizens. If the government had pursued a more conciliatory, less aggressive policy, the crisis might have ended at this point. But the politicians, realizing that the radicals in the countryside would not support the constitution, voted in the spring of 1832 to withdraw government administration from the forty-six rural communes that had not given their support to the new constitution. The leaders of the country districts responded by proclaiming their independence and the creation of the canton Basel-Landschaft, which in May 1832 was placed under the protection of the federal government. Although Basel had the support of five of the conservative cantons (Schwyz, Uri, Unterwalden, Valais, and Neuchâtel), the majority in the *Tagsatzung* believed that only the division of the canton would put an end to the ongoing crisis.[47] In September, after a final attempt by the *Tagsatzung* to mediate the conflict came to nought, the division of the old canton of Basel and the creation of a new half-canton of Basel-Landschaft was officially recognized.

The government and the majority of the people of Basel were profoundly shocked by the amputation of the canton's territory; they were angered, too, by what they considered the federal government's cavalier treatment of the city. In the immediate aftermath of the crisis, the city government took steps to secure Basel's weak position in the Confederation, by forming an alliance with the other conservative cantons. In November, using the division of the canton as a pretext, Basel-Stadt,

47 On Basel's relations with the rest of Switzerland during the *Wirren* and the formation of the Sarnerbund, see Gelzer, *Beziehungen Basels zur Innerschweiz.*

along with Uri, Schwyz, Unterwalden, and Neuchâtel, resolved not to send any more representatives to the federal *Tagsatzung* and formed the *Sarnerbund*, in an attempt to prevent the reform of the federal structure and to defend themselves against the growing liberal threat. This was not the first alliance concluded by the cantons; nor would it be the last. Nevertheless, although established in part to counter an earlier alliance between the liberal cantons, the so-called *Siebnerkonkordat*,[48] it was an ominous sign of the rapid deterioration of the internal political situation in Switzerland. The formation of the *Sarnerbund* did not immediately prevent constitutional negotiations from taking place. In the summer of 1832, the *Tagsatzung* established a constitutional committee with a mandate to revise the Federal Treaty so that the rights and sovereignty of the cantons would not be unduly restricted. Led by the Genevan respresentative Pellegrino Rossi, it then presented, in March 1833, the extraordinary session of the *Tagsatzung* in Zürich with a "Federal Charter of the Swiss Confederation" (*Bundesurkunde der Schweizerischen Eidgenossenschaft*) that sought not only to strike a balance between the conservatives' demands for cantonal sovereignty and the liberals' demands for a stronger central state, but also to guarantee civil rights and abolish internal custom duties and other impediments to commerce and trade. It was rejected by both the conservatives and liberals. A new committee was established and, in May, a second, less progressive and much more decentralized constitutional proposal was presented to the cantons for ratification. As expected, the cantons of the *Sarnerbund* rejected the proposed constitution; a number of liberal cantons including Lucerne, Vaud, and Ticino also failed to ratify the new constitution. The result was a disaster for the liberals, the defeat of the *Bundesurkunde*, and the continuation of the increasingly unstable status quo.[49]

The conservative cantons interpreted the defeat of the *Bundesurkunde* as a sign of their growing strength and of the collapse of liberal support within the confederation. The stage was now set for the final act in the long, drawn out spectacle of the so-called Basel *Wirren*. The Basel government, inspired by military action taken against the radicals by the reactionary regime in the central canton of Schwyz, decided as well on a policy of direct action. On 3 August 1833, the Grand Council dispatched troops to the countryside to overthrow the government of the *Landschaft* and to restore, by force, the unity of the canton. However, the

48 They were Zürich, Bern, Lucerne, Solothurn, Aargau, Thurgau, and St. Gall.
49 Biaudet, "Der modernen Schweiz entgegen," 922ff.

troops from Basel suffered a humiliating defeat at the village of Pratteln. Not only did the city militia lose sixty-five men in the battle – compared to five men killed from the *Landschaft* – but, during the retreat, it plundered and set the village alight.

Lionel Gossman has written that in comparison with contemporary "troubles," the Basel *Wirren* "might seem a ridiculous, mock-epic affair, in the style of war between Picrochole and Gargantua over the rival claims of their respective bannock-bakers in Rabalais."[50] Yet, as he also points out, the events of 1830–33 were of profound significance for the city's inhabitants. The defeat of its army at the village of Pratteln did not end the saga. In contrast to 1832, the federal diet now responded with uncommon swiftness and severity. It argued that the city government had not acted in self-defence, but as the aggressors. Blamed for breaking the peace, Basel was heavily sanctioned by the federal government. Now occupied by the federal army, the city was obliged to pay not just for the damage its troops had caused, but also for the costs of the military occupation. The final blow came when the assets of the canton were divided, not according to tax rolls, as the city had hoped, but according to population. The *Landschaft*, with twice the population of the city, received two-thirds of the total assets of the state. As a consequence, institutions founded and supported by the city and the pride of Basel's elite, such as the university and the art collection, were threatened with ruin. Only by agreeing to pay the *Landschaft* its share of the assessed value of the property, could the city keep its art collections intact and the various institutions, including the university, remain open.

With hindsight, the division of the canton was probably the only possible solution to the ongoing crisis. Neither side was willing to give in as neither wanted to be dominated by the other. Even Basel liberals, like their conservative opponents, were extremely reluctant to see any diminution of the city's traditional hegemony over the *Landschäftler.* But while the countryside liberals accused the Basel government of wanting to subjugate them, the fact that the government had been willing to reform the constitution to the benefit of the citizens of the countryside suggests that this was not necessarily the case. In fact, members of certain prominent circles of the city elite quite possibly viewed separation as a positive alternative to continued violence and unrest. Apparently, the confident citizens of Basel had long been convinced of their city's particular urban and commercial destiny; moreover, in late 1830, before the

50 Gossman, "Basel," 74.

idea of separation was seriously discussed by country liberals, Chief Justice N. Bernoulli, a man from the government side and one predisposed towards mediation of the conflict, had suggested the possibility of separate administrations. The liberal newspaper, the *Schweizerische Nationalzeitung*, later argued that this had been the secret goal of the government all along.[51]

Whether or not the *Kantonstrennung* was a revolution in the strictest sense is not entirely clear. For the people of the countryside it was a fight for the political equality of all citizens and, ultimately, for liberation against the rule of the urban patriciate. For the *Landschäftler*, it was definitely a question of political revolution. In the city itself, however, conservatives and liberals, artisans and industrialists, and citizens and non-citizens all rallied against the uprising in the rural areas, supporting the government. But while the city may have lost its political "empire," it did not experience political or social revolution. On the contrary, by being forcibly separated from the countryside, the city was spared internal upheaval. The separation of the canton thus did not mean the end of the *ancien régime* in the city, although the elite regarded the events as catastrophic and revolutionary. In effect, the elite lost direct political power in the rural hinterland, but maintained significant economic influence over a labour force that was still dependent upon its enterprises for employment. In the city, the political and social structures remained intact. The result was not the liberalization of the government of Basel-Stadt.

Of course, the political culture of the city did change. The conservative oligarchy was strengthened with the removal of the most vocal liberal opposition, and its legitimacy was renewed in its fight to preserve the traditions and customs of the city. This, along with its members' enormous wealth, was one of the main reasons why the elite was able to maintain its hegemony for the next fifty years. Of note, in the new constitution of 1833 demanded by the federal government, the political authority of the patriciate was not reduced significantly. The right to participate in elections was still restricted, and the concept of popular sovereignty – the most important element in the constitutions of the regenerated cantons – was not mentioned in Basel's constitution. As Martin Schaffner has written, "There was no talk of political equality."[52]

---

51 See P. Burckhardt, *Geschichte der Stadt Basel*, 164; Gossman, "Basle, Bachofen and the Critique of Modernity," 143.

52 Schaffner, "Geschichte des politischen Systems," 42.

While the *Kantonstrennung* did effect the course of economic development in the city, it did not prove as disasterous as many had predicted.
Although it placed the city under an increased burden of debt – in 1830
the canton had been debt free – the wealthy citizens remained largely
untouched by the crisis and city revenue continued to grow, to the point
where, in 1835, income rose moderately above expenditures.[53] In the
long run, the division of the canton had a positive impact on local industry, especially the manufacture of silk-ribbon, inasmuch as the process of mechanization was accelerated and the putting-out system was
gradually subordinated to factory production within the city boundaries. Even though the putting-out system did not end altogether, factory production began to account for a greater proportion of the wealth
generated, and soon dominated the economy.[54]

Industrialization of the city's principal manufacturing base and the ac-
companying structural changes to the economy did not result in a collapse of the guild system. On the contrary, in the years immediately
following the division of the canton, a new and stronger bond was created between the two pillars of the old regime, the patricians and the artisans. As Gossman has written: "After the *Kantonstrennung* or division of
the canton, the artisans found that they were more dependent on the
Herren than ever. They were dependent on them as their principal em-
ployers and customers, and they were dependent on them to maintain
traditional restrictions on the immigrant workers who threatened their
livelihood. The artisans were thus a conservative force, in most respects
more conservative than the *Herren* themselves."[55] In fact, the authority of
the patriciate was preserved more or less intact because it could count on
support from the artisans, who stood to lose not just their political privileges, but also their economic livelihood and social status. While the
guild system gave artisans a political voice that the growing working class
did not have, they remained unimpressed with liberal demands for economic and social reform, freedom of occupation, and greater political
representation. Thus not only did the *Kantonstrennung* not lead to the
liberalization of Basel's political system, it in reality slowed down the process. Ironically, political rebellion and the amputation of the country districts from the old body politic had sustained and strengthened, rather
than undermined, Basel's traditional political order.

53 P. Burckhardt, *Geschichte der Stadt Basel*, 212–13.
54 See Sarasin, *Stadt der Bürger*, 76.
55 Gossman, "Basel," 75.

Despite all of this, attitudes did change and many citizens felt isolated within the Confederation. While the canton of Basel may indeed have broken a "*Landfrieden*," the federal government had done little to solve the crisis and to prevent military action. Despite the forced division of the canton and its occupation by the army, Baslers nonetheless remained loyal to the Confederation. City officials called upon citizens to remember that, even with the destruction of the old canton, Basel's original prosperity and good fortune over the centuries had been a result of its ties with the rest of Switzerland. But Basel was now more alienated from the federal regime and the liberal cantons than ever before, and the city government was forced to follow a cautious policy. Over the course of the next decade, the regime in Basel remained hostile to liberalism and highly suspicious of the policies and actions of the federal government; it continued to fight vigorously against any encroachment on existing cantonal rights.

. . .

It is difficult to gauge with any accuracy Burckhardt's personal response to this unfolding crisis. As a boy he was aware of the death and destruction caused by the fighting and felt the impact of the disaster on Basel. He must also have been aware of his father's great unease. Indeed, despite his loyalty to the city, Jacob Burckhardt Sr, who had once been the pastor of the rural community of Lausen, had many strong ties to the countryside. For him, the radicals' incessant attacks on the church during the *Wirren* must have been a source of great personal anxiety. As representatives of the state church, the clergy in the countryside were bound to abide by the laws of the government of Basel. As official opponents of the actions of the radicals in the countryside, they were constantly vilified by radical *Landschäftler*.[56]

There are few direct references by Burckhardt to the crisis of the *Kantonstrennung*. Many years later he discussed, in general terms, the significance of the July Revolution as a European crisis and as a time of widespread radicalism. Never, though, did he discuss it, or its impact on Basel, in any great detail. The calm and detached assessment of his mature years provides an interesting contrast to a youthful source of infor-

56 Kaegi, 1:213–14.

mation concerning the division of the canton, namely a series of musical compositions. According to Kaegi: The "destruction of the state and of an era of national history, the Last Judgement, and the splendour of a higher world are the themes which dominate his [Burckhardt's] imagination and find their first expression in his music."[57] In fact, Burckhardt's youthful images of the apocalypse and the last judgment reflected the general mood of impending doom that swept through Basel during these turbulent years. Many of the city's more pious citizens believed that the rebellion was God's punishment for past sins.

As a boy, Burckhardt followed the intense controversy surrounding the assessment and division of the canton's assets and the consequences of this for the city's cultural life. In one of the few surviving letters to his father, who in the summer of 1834 was travelling in Italy, the young Burckhardt described the progress of the evaluation, complaining that the value of the university's property, including the library and its collection of paintings and coins, was being inflated by the assessors for the *Landschaft*.[58] Likewise, two years after the crisis, Burckhardt mentioned the confused state of the city archives following the "unfortunate division" of the canton in a letter to the Freiburg historian Heinrich Schreiber, for whom he was doing research.[59]

The archives, and perhaps more significantly, the university itself, was seriously jeopardized by the division of the canton. In some pietist circles, the university was blamed for the crisis because liberal theologians such as Wilhelm de Wette – a political refugee from Prussia – had rebelled "against the heavenly sovereignty of Jesus Christ."[60] The university certainly bore the brunt of the division of the canton's assets. The symbol of Basel's humanist heritage, it had been in decline for a number of decades and was a constant target of liberals and radicals, who argued that the education system's emphasis on the classical curriculum at the expense of practical, technical education was a waste of scarce

57 Kaegi, 1:216. The last judgment and the "dance of death" are prominent themes in Burckhardt's early poetry as well. See "Nach dem Weltgericht" and "Zu einem Totentanz," in Burckhardt, *Gedichte*, and Kaegi, 1:269ff.

58 *Briefe*, 2:219. Of course, it was in the interests of the city to have a low assessment so as not to pay too much in compensation to the canton of Basel-Landschaft. The final assessment of the paintings was Fr. 22,000 and of the library and coin collection, Fr. 44,000. The city payed two-thirds of this total to keep the collections in tact. See *Briefe*, 2, "Anmerkungen zum Brieftext," 317.

59 *Briefe*, 1:48.

60 Kaegi, 1:214, and Howard, "Historicist Thought in the Shadow of Theology," 287.

funds, privileged only the sons of the ruling class, and did not meet the demands of the modern age.[61] That the university's small faculty supported the city's cause during the *Wirren* – largely because the cantonal authorities and the patriciate were committed to the continued existence of the university – only accerbated the liberals' hostility. Starved of funds and on the brink of collapse, the university managed to survive through the efforts of a few dedicated individuals such as Councillor Peter Merian, Andreas Heusler, and Wilhelm de Wette.

But their untiring work on behalf of the university did not stop the attacks.[62] During the early 1840s, its fate once again became a matter of heated political debate. Liberal newspapers spared no ink or rhetorical excess in their assaults on the venerable institution. In 1841, the radical newspaper, the *Basellandschaftliches Volksblatt*, called the university an old stump on which no green shoots grew, "a nursing home for an invalid inteligentsia, a sinecure for burned out brains," and a "totally useless, money-eating institution." The hostility towards the university was not restricted to the radicals from the newly separated canton, but was a staple of liberals in the city as well. The more moderate *Schweizerische Nationalzeitung*, a newspaper published within the city walls, labelled the university a "crippled institution for dwarves and hermaphrodites" and a "satire on the concept of a universitas litterarum."[63] Although the university had survived the *Wirren*, there were serious doubts about it surviving the next decade. Burckhardt reported that in 1843 only twenty-eight students had enrolled, over half of whom were receiving scholarships. Naturally, people were demanding an end to this "luxury." If this number dropped to fifteen or twenty students, he worried that the call for its abolition would certainly be successful.[64]

Images of the apocalypse notwithstanding, the division of the canton certainly had a lasting impact on Burckhardt. In many respects, the lessons learned during the years of the crisis would stay with him for the rest of his life. For instance, the belief that radical democracy was a potentially destructive force, bringing chaos in its wake, never entirely left him; moreover, like many Baslers, he became imbued with an intense distrust of liberalism and longed for order and the rule of law. Furthermore, the

61 For a detailed examination, see Gossman, "The 'two cultures' in Nineteenth-century Basle."

62 Staehlin, *Geschichte der Universität Basel*, and Bonjour, *Die Universität Basel*.

63 Quotes from Kaegi, 2:399.

64 *Briefe*, 2:51 and 55. The actual number of students appears to have been higher with 45 in 1843, *Briefe*, 2, "Anmerkungen zum Brieftext," 240.

crisis revealed how vulnerable the liberties and culture of small states were when confronted by greater demagogic powers, instilling in him an instinctive fear of the power of strong, centralized states. These attitudes did not entirely disappear when he was student in Berlin, a time often referred to as his liberal phase. On the contrary, the political crisis in his *patria* was to form the basis of his conservative *Weltanschauung*.

2

Student Years

IN SEPTEMBER 1839 Burckhardt left Basel for Germany, where he began his formal training as an historian. As a teenager he had developed a keen interest in the study of the past and had demonstrated a passion for art and architecture – in fact, at the age of eighteen he published a series of articles on the cathedrals of Lausanne, Geneva, Zürich, and Basel.[1] After finishing school in the spring of 1836 and spending a number of preparatory semesters in Neuchâtel, he entered the university in Basel. Like so many other famous nineteenth-century historians, Burckhardt originally pursued a theological career according to the wishes of his father, who in 1838 became the seventeenth *Antistes*, or head minister, of Basel's Reformed Church.[2] Burckhardt studied under two prominent theologians, Wilhelm de Wette and Karl Rudolf Hagenbach, but he soon discovered that he was not meant for the church. De Wette's teachings had a particularly profound impact on the young theology student.[3] One of the leading liberal, "enlightened" theologians of the day, de Wette's appointment had provoked criticism from orthodox pietists in Basel who were extremely suspicious of his attempt to apply the current methods of historical criticism to the texts of the Old and New

1 Burckhardt, *Bemerkungen über schweizerische Kathedralen.*

2 During the Reformation, the office of antistes replaced that of bishop in the Reformed Church. Burckhardt's father held the highest ecclesiastical office in Basel until his death in 1858. On Jacob Burckhardt Sr, see Kaegi, 1:121–94, and Howard, "Historicist Thought in the Shadow of Theology," 291–304.

3 De Wette had been appointed professor of theology at the university in 1822, following his dismissal from the University of Berlin after authorities learned of his contacts with Karl Ludwig Sand, the man who murdered the reactionary publicist August von Kotzebue in 1819. On de Wette, see Howard, "Historicist Thought in the Shadow of Theology."

Testaments. His controversial views raised inevitable questions about the relationship between piety and modern "scientific" (*wissenschaftliche*) criticism. These questions were to play a fundamental role in Burckhardt's decision to abandon theology for history.

Although de Wette believed that one could apply the principles of historical criticism to the study of the Gospels without endangering one's faith, his "system" nonetheless raised considerable doubts in Burckhardt's mind. In fact, he appears to have taken de Wette's historical-critical understanding of the Scriptures to their logical extreme, something even his teacher was unwilling to do; as a consequence, he developed over the course of his theological studies an intense scepticism regarding "revelation-based Protestant orthodoxy, the faith of his youth."[4] The more he listened to de Wette, whose system of historical criticism became "daily more colossal before my very eyes," the greater his reservations grew about the veracity of the Scriptures and the legitimacy of the Christian *Weltanschauung*. As he told his friend Johannes Riggenbach, then a theology student at Berlin, he had come to regard the "birth of Christ simply as a myth," a revelation that resulted in a profound, personal crisis of faith. Confused and bewildered, he sank into deep despair, claiming that "for the moment I cannot look the ruins of my convictions in the face."[5]

It took many months for Burckhardt to come to terms with this crisis of faith. He ultimately concluded that, in good conscience, he could no longer continue to study theology. Ironically, as far as he was concerned, de Wette's "critical theology, by exposing the mythic nature of early Christianity, had more or less put itself out of business."[6] Whether or not this resulted in complete alienation from his faith and from the humanist, orthodox heritage of his father remains unclear. Burckhardt's biographer maintains that he did not reject the message of Christ or the core principles of Christianity, that he remained the "child of his parents," and that "his break with theology was more of a personal and biographical break than a fundamental and general one."[7] In contrast, Thomas A. Howard has recently argued that Burckhardt's crisis of faith resulted in a fundamental break with the principles of Christianity as well as with the "pious, humanist sensibilities that his father and generations of Basel's

4 Howard, "Historicist Thought in the Shadow of Theology," 310–11.
5 *Briefe*, 1:84 and 86.
6 Howard, "Historicist Thought in the Shadow of Theology," 305.
7 Kaegi, 1:151 and Kaegi, 2:22.

elites had cultivated."[8] Although certainly the role that organized religion played in his life diminished considerably, as Howard also argues,
an important "religious residuum" and "theological undercurrent" continued to exist in Burckhardt's thought and work.[9] Despite a great deal
of "inward anguish" and "melancholy sadness," he never abandoned altogether his faith in providence, which he believed guided the world
and conferred meaning on human history. As he stressed in a letter to
his sister: "My faith in eternal providence certainly stands as firm as a
rock. This providence is not blind fate, but a personal God. This belief
will never leave me, however much my view of religion and confessions
may change."[10]

Burckhardt's crisis of faith led him to reject theological studies and
his plans to become a pastor. Instead, he decided to devote his time to
the study of history and art. This choice was made at the cost of a great
deal of personal anguish and soul searching. He feared not just his father's displeasure – he came to a final decision only after he had made
peace with his father and obtained his permission – but also the consequences of his doubts about the truth of the Gospels. Over time, however, Burckhardt overcame this crisis and developed a secularized view
of history, in which he redefined the "sacred truths of religion in new
terms, not metaphysical but historical."[11] This had a decisive impact on
his approach to history, enabling him to overcome his depression and
doubt. While it might be an exaggeration to suggest that the study of art
and history became a substitute religion for him, he nonetheless found
in the study of past cultures an important source of spiritual comfort. Indeed, shortly after he began his studies in Berlin, he wrote that, from the
vantage point of the "ruin" of his previous convictions and of his standing before the "abyss," the only "salvation I have found against this is in
my main field of study, history, which also unseated my fatalism and my
way of viewing the world that was based on it."[12] From this early point
onwards, the study of history assumed great meaning for Burckhardt.
History provided him with a solution to his immediate crisis of faith and

8 Howard, "Historicist Thought in the Shadow of Theology," 317.

9 For example, ibid., 323 and 369.

10 *Briefe*, 1:155. Burckhardt's melancholy in this particular instance might not have
been the result of his ongoing crisis of faith, but rather due to the fact that he had just
learned from his sister that Maria Oser, with whom Burckhardt was in love, had become
engaged to another man.

11 Mali, "Jacob Burckhardt: Myth, History, and Mythistory," 96.

12 *Briefe*, 1:130–1.

became a form of long-term therapy for the crises that he believed characterized the modern world. History was now his "calling," a "religious quest," and the object of his "life's destiny." As such, it "forged a link between self and world and provided a means for self-transformation and self-justification."[13]

· · ·

With the exception of a semester of study in Bonn during the summer of 1841, Burckhardt's formal training as an historian took place in Berlin. The university was still a relatively young institution when he began his student career in the Prussian capital. It had been founded in 1810, in large part due to the initiative of Wilhelm von Humboldt, as part of the extensive administrative reforms that followed in the wake of Prussia's defeat at the hands of Napoleon. In the words of the historian Fritz Ringer, the university in Berlin was "the crowning achievement of the Prussian reform period in the field of education."[14] Under the guidance of Humboldt, head of the education section of the Prussian interior ministry, and Johann Gottlieb Fichte, the university's first rector, it became a world-renowned centre of neohumanist and Idealist scholarship and a model for the modern university. The new institution broke ground in many ways. With its emphasis on independent scholarly research, it managed to attract some of the greatest intellectuals of the day, including Georg Wilhelm Friedrich Hegel, Friedrich Karl von Savigny, Karl Friedrich Eichhorn, Friedrich Schleiermacher, and Bartold Georg Niebuhr. The Prussian state, however, still exercised considerable influence over the appointment and supervision of faculty, as well as over financial management. As officials of the state, scholars were expected to demonstrate not just loyalty, but also political and ideological conformity. Following the proclamation of the Carlsbad Decrees in 1819 and the onset of the Reaction in Prussia, the power of the state was increasingly employed against those whose independent views conflicted with the agenda of the authorities. Many scholars were dismissed,

13 Ibid., 1:233–4; ibid., 1:122. Howard, "Historicist Thought in the Shadow of Theology," 331.
14 Ringer, *The Decline of the German Mandarins*, 25.

and some, such as the prominent theological dissident Wilhelm de Wette, found refuge in Basel.

Burckhardt's student years (1839–43) were arguably the most important and formative of his life. When he arrived in Berlin, the university was the leading centre of historical research in Germany, if not the world, and he was taught by some of the greatest historical minds in Europe, including Leopold von Ranke, Johann Gustav Droysen, August Boeckh, and the art historian Franz Kugler. The impact of these men on Burckhardt's intellectual and personal development should not be underestimated, although it varied in degree and intensity. Under the tutelage of these luminaries, his understanding of the past and the discipline of history was radically transformed. His description of his first experiences in their classes recalls a religious awakening. "My eyes opened wide during the first lectures with Ranke, Droysen and Boeckh," he wrote a few months after his arrival in Berlin. "I saw that I had been like the knights with their ladies in Don Quixote: I had loved my field of study only by hearsay, and now it appeared before me suddenly in gigantic proportions, and I had to lower my eyes. Only now am I really determined to devote my life to it."[15]

Of his teachers, Ranke and Kugler played the most prominent roles in his development as a scholar. The influence of Droysen and Boeckh, in contrast, was more peripheral. Although he attended Droysen's course on ancient history during the winter of 1839–40, and was able to visit and consult him often, a close intellectual and personal relationship never developed. This was due as much to the nature of Droysen's position in Berlin, as it was to personal differences.[16] Unable to secure a permanent position at the university, Droysen was forced to teach between thirty and forty hours a week at a Berlin Gymnasium (as well as eight hours a week at the university); moreover, during the same period he was researching and writing some of his most important work.[17] Unfortunately, Droysen could not secure permanent employment at the university in Berlin at this time, and, the year after Burckhardt's arrival, was obliged to take a position at Kiel, a situation which the young student described as "fatal" to his own studies. Correctly predicting that Droysen was "very important and in ten years will be considered one of the great-

15 *Briefe*, 1:131.
16 Ibid., 1:136.
17 Kaegi, 2:36. The first volume of Droysen's *Geschichte des Hellenismus* appeared in 1836.

est,"[18] Burckhardt termed it a great shame that the Berlin university had lost Droysen: "Now in Europe's premier university, as Berlin likes to call itself, there is no one with a name to teach ancient history."[19]

Ranke's influence on Burckhardt's development as an historian was far greater than Droysen's, and their relationship much more complex. Burckhardt decided to study history in Berlin in part because of Ranke's presence there and his reputation as one of Europe's foremost historians. However, in Ranke, considered by many to be the founder of the modern discipline of history, Burckhardt again failed to find the "fatherly friend" he sought.[20] Indeed, Burckhardt found Ranke's personality disagreeable. Nor did he like Ranke's "civil-service" attitude, and in a number of early letters he gleefully repeated malicious gossip and mocked the famous scholar. In particular, he seemed to take pleasure in Ranke's various attempts to ingratiate himself with the court and Berlin's fashionable salon society, referring to him a few times as "the petty Ranke."[21]

Burckhardt's assessment of his scholarly work was also somewhat ambivalent. He presented a copy of Ranke's *German History in the Age of the Reformation* to his close friend, Gottfried Kinkel, as a birthday present.[22] Also, in 1874, in one of his only critical evaluations of his teacher's historiography, he characterized Ranke's *History of the Popes* and the first volume of his study of the German Reformation as masterpieces. He even recalled that as a student he had devoured the *History of the Popes* and knew some parts of it by heart. In spite of Ranke's age, Burckhardt found his later works to be "highly astonishing achievements," although he detected a certain political bias and did not trust him on certain issues.[23]

Over the course of his lifetime of scholarship, Burckhardt was to distance himself from Ranke's approach to history and understanding of the past. Nonetheless, Burckhardt remained inspired by the seriousness and reverence with which Ranke approached the study of the past. Clearly, Burckhardt sympathized: "One has never heard a frivolous word

18 *Briefe*, 1:145.

19 Ibid., 1:157.

20 See *Briefe*, 1:136.

21 See Gilbert, *History: Politics or Culture?*, 95. See also *Briefe*, 1:160; *Briefe*, 2:20 and 25. Quite possibly this was a reason for the low attendence in Ranke's courses, although 1841–42 saw a notable increase in his popularity. See Ranke, *The Theory and Practice of History*, xxxii.

22 See Gilbert, "Jacob Burckhardt's Student Years," 257.

23 *Briefe*, 5:263–4.

pass his lips; he often tells jokes, good ones at that, but when he speaks
of great moments, the seriousness with which he approaches history becomes clear, indeed, eerily so with his deeply furrowed expressions."[24]
More importantly, however, Ranke taught Burckhardt the craft of the
historian. In courses he took with Ranke on German, medieval, and
modern history, Burckhardt "first got to know something about historical method";[25] listening to his lectures and reading his works, he also
learned something about the art of historical representation. "If I'm unable to learn anything else [in Ranke's courses]," he wrote to Heinrich
Schreiber in early 1840, "then I'll at least learn about *representation*."[26]
In fact, Burckhardt appeared to admire and respect mainly the literary
qualities of Ranke's work, not his claim to scientific objectivity.

This, however, was only qualified praise. Burckhardt expressed general disapproval of Ranke's archconservatism and his "less than solid
opinions" in political and social matters. Although Ranke had learned
the "art of writing history" from the great contemporary French historians, whom Burckhardt especially admired, the young student suggested
that Ranke's "dazzling" and "splendid" presentation was actually trendy,
serving to camoflage his political agenda. Ranke, he wrote, "has sacrificed very much for his splendid presentation; the totality of *Anschauung*
that his writings seem to give at first glance is an illusion. Since he is unable to capture his readers through his (conservative) opinions, he gets
it done through his dazzling presentation."[27]

Despite these criticisms, their actual intellectual relationship during
his student years seems to have been generally quite positive. Ranke
was always extremely supportive of his student, clearly recognizing
Burckhardt's talent and ability as an historian. He had high praise for
Burckhardt's performance in his courses and commended him highly,
as "especially worth recommendation," to King Maximilian II of
Bavaria for a new position in Munich in 1852 and again in 1854. Ranke
also had nothing but praise for Burckhardt's first major work of cultural history, the *Age of Constantine the Great*, writing that he had demonstrated "to an unusual degree a mind for research and the gift of
presentation," the two qualities he most admired. "The extensive studies he has made in the history of art," he continued, "would especially

24 Ibid., 1:160.
25 Ibid., 1:157–8.
26 Ibid., 1:132.
27 Ibid., 1:197. See also Gilbert, *History: Politics or Culture?*, 99, and *Briefe*, 1:217.

recommend him for Munich."[28] This, and his recommendation that Burckhardt publish his work on Conrad von Hochstaden, suggest that Burckhardt may have been ungrateful and even opportunistic. However, while sometimes harsh in his criticism of Ranke in his private correspondence, Burckhardt was full of approbation in public. In a curriculum vitae presented to the faculty of the university in Basel upon the defence of his dissertation, Burckhardt wrote: "It was my great good luck that I had as my teacher in history Leopold Ranke, a scholar who can never be praised enough. He was kind enough to further my studies not only by his teachings but also by his always helpful advice."[29] This sentiment was repeated half a century later in a final tribute to Ranke: he had had, he recalled with a certain pride, "the good fortune to write two substantial works for Ranke's seminar and to receive the approval of the great teacher."[30] It would seem that no matter how hard he tried, Burckhardt could never entirely escape Ranke's long shadow.

Despite the obvious enthusiasm and seriousness with which he approached history, Burckhardt did not neglect his other great passion: the study of art. As he wrote to his friend, the Freiburg historian Heinrich Schreiber, art history "would always maintain a hold on me;" even on the journey to Berlin he had collected all sorts of material on art and architecture.[31] Burckhardt taught and studied art history throughout his professional career; it greatly broadened his cultural historical perspective and provided him with a lifelong joy. For this, Burckhardt owed a great debt to his mentor and good friend, the Berlin art historian Franz Kugler (1808–58). As Felix Gilbert has written, "attendance at Kugler's course on the history of architecture was almost a necessity" for anyone with a serious interest in the history of art.[32] Significantly, during his first semester of study in Berlin, Burckhardt chose to attend Kugler's class over Ranke's seminar, which was held at the same time.

Kugler was one of the most important and renowed art historians of the *Vormärz*. A man of considerable talent and energy, he became professor of art history at the Royal Academy of Art and the university in

28 Quoted in Kaegi, 2:73. The fact that Maximillian was trying to lure Ranke to Munich may very well have had some influence on Ranke's letters of recommendation.

29 Quoted in Gilbert, "Jacob Burckhardt's Student Years," 257.

30 GA, 1:viii.

31 *Briefe*, 1:133.

32 Gilbert, "Jacob Burckhardt's Student Years," 259.

Berlin in 1835. He produced a prodigious amount of scholarship during his short lifetime. Besides his most famous books, the two volume
Handbuch der Geschichte der Malerei seit Constantin dem Grossen (1837) and
the *Handbuch der Kunstgeschichte* (1842), he wrote a history of Frederick
the Great, which was richly illustrated by Adolph Menzel, and a lengthy
study of Brandenburg-Prussia. In addition, he was the editor of the art
journal *Kunstblatt* and the author of numerous articles and reviews,
many of which were published in 1853 in the three-volume *Kleine
Schriften und Studien zur Kunstgeschichte*, which he dedicated to his former
student Jacob Burckhardt. A firm believer in the use of art for the "education of the people," he also devoted much energy to the preservation
of national monuments and the creation of a national art curriculum,
eventually becoming an important official in the Prussian ministry of
culture.

Kugler's prominent position in the historiography of art history was
ensured by his ground-breaking handbooks. Influenced by the latest developments in historical studies, in particular the work of Ranke, Kugler
was instrumental in historicizing the study of art and emancipating it
from Hegel's speculative aesthetic philosophy. Believing that art history
was an integral part of general cultural history, Kugler stressed the need
to study art within the broader historical context, tracing its development from the perspective of universal history and emphasizing the
connections between art and society. A significant break from the standard biographies of artists and the division of art according to national
schools, this opened up new ground for the young discipline. Kugler
further expanded the boundaries of art history by examining not just
European art, but prehistoric and primitive art.[33] Burckhardt was most
impressed by the breadth and scope of Kugler's vision of art history,
which, as in Ranke's best work, was characterized by an unrivaled universal perspective and "panoramic view." Many years after Kugler's
death, he continued to recommend his handbooks for his own students
of art history.[34]

In sharp contrast to his personal relationship with Ranke, Burckhardt found in Kugler the fatherly friend he had been searching for in
Berlin. More than any other individual, Kugler was a continual source
of inspiration and stimulation for the young man. Burckhardt became

---

33 On Kugler see Waetzold, *Deutsche Kunsthistoriker*, 2:143–172, and Treue, "Franz Theodor Kugler: Kulturhistoriker und Kulturpolitiker," 483–526; Rehm, "Jacob Burckhardt
und Franz Kugler," 155–252; See also the relevant chapter in Paret, *Art as History*.

34 *Briefe*, 4:75.

an intimate guest in his household; was introduced by him to many important individuals; and, during his second extended stay in Berlin in 1846–47, collaborated with him on extensive revisions of the second edition of Kugler's handbooks, work that may have inspired Burckhardt's conception of *Der Cicerone*.[35] Following Kugler's premature death, Burckhardt remained in close contact with Kugler's son Bernhard, and his son-in-law, the poet and novelist Paul Heyse, and, on two occasions, publicly acknowledged his intellectual debt and his debt of friendship. Burckhardt dedicated his first major work of art history, *Die Kunstwerke der belgischen Städte*, to Kugler, as well as *Der Cicerone*.[36] Towards the end of his life, Burckhardt once more expressed his gratitude to Kugler for the intellectual direction he had taken: "A noble personality had opened up horizons for [me] far beyond art history."[37]

. . .

During his first three semesters of study in Berlin, Burckhardt was part of what Kaegi has described as a "milieu highly loyal to the government" that included not only his Berlin friends, but also his teachers.[38] The influence of Ranke, Droysen, and the conservative German historical school was especially strong during his first semesters of study, as can be seen in the two major essays on Carl Martell and Conrad von Hochstaden that Burckhardt wrote for Ranke's seminar. At the same time, these works reflected in subtle ways Burckhardt's own special interests and political concerns. Gilbert has written that "the factors which Burckhardt sees at work in German medieval history" – most notably the emergence of a national *Volksgeist* and the creation of a unified, Christian Europe – "are those which gave coherence and unity to Ranke's interpretation of the European past."[39] These factors also gave coherence and unity to the conservative, nationalist vision of Germany's past that dominated most historical scholarship in the early nineteenth century, a vision that

---

35 Rehm, "Jacob Burckhardt und Franz Kugler," 157; See also Kaphahn, "Jacob Burckhardts Neubearbeitung von Kuglers Malereigeschichte," 24–56. Unfortunately, at Burckhardt's request, all his letters to Kugler were destroyed by Paul Heyse, his son-in-law, after Kugler's death.
36 GA, 3:xxvii.
37 GA, 1:viii.
38 Kaegi, 2:204.
39 Gilbert, "Jacob Burckhardt's Student Years," 258.

found an echo in Burckhardt's early understanding of medieval history, in his growing enthusiasm for Germany's past, and in his hopes for Germany's present and future.

Given Burckhardt's later condemnation of the unbridled nationalism and militarism that swept across Germany following unification in 1871, his enthusiasm for Germany during the 1840s seems to strike a discordant note. It seems incongruous with his mature thought and his anti-modernism, a product of youthful romanticism, perhaps, or his early optimism and idealism. As a result, it is sometimes considered to be evidence of his close affinity with liberalism and even his adoption of the liberal cause of German national unity. However, his affection for Germany while a student in Berlin and Bonn stemmed from his recognition of the cultural and spiritual bonds that, he believed, united the German-speaking lands of central Europe. Not only was he uninterested in the creation of a strong nation-state in Germany – he distanced himself from Germany later in life primarily on ideological grounds – he also did not consider political union between Germany and Switzerland to be valid or desirable. This he made clear in a letter to his sister in 1841. Commenting upon the protracted unrest in Switzerland, he claimed it was time that the Swiss finally recognized that they were German: "Only a strong – although not a political – connection with Germany can save Switzerland. I am not being disloyal, dear Louise, when I say that only he who tries in his heart to further the interests of German *Bildung* can be of any use in Switzerland, because there is only one remedy against the threatening decline of a nation, and that is to return to one's origins."[40] Besides recognizing early on the palliative effect of *Bildung* as a solution to crisis, Burckhardt was clearly not motivated by political nationalism; rather he advocated a form of cultural nationalism that celebrated German-speaking Switzerland's shared intellectual, artistic, and historical heritage with Germany. His was a recognition of the spiritual and intellectual unity of the German-speaking population, a unity that had once existed in the Middle Ages.

His conviction that the Swiss and Germans had a common past was a view not necessarily shared by most Baslers or Swiss; hence the defensive posture in his letter to his sister. Shortly after his arrival in Berlin, he wrote that he had disdained and rejected the notion of a common German fatherland, as was usual amongst transplanted Swiss in Germany; as he put it, "With what infamous coldness does the Swiss stu-

40 *Briefe*, 1:182–3.

dent care to talk about Germany."[41] But by 1841, he knew differently. This was a revelation; he realized that his life's ambition was now "to show the Swiss that they are German."[42]

In the context of Swiss politics, such a statement was not a rejection of Switzerland as a nation or state. It did, however, imply a rejection of Swiss nationalism, which, during this time of heightened national consciousness, was a vital component of the growing liberal movement. Although this may have struck a sour note among many of his countrymen, for Burckhardt it was a confirmation of traditional Swiss particularism and federalism. The bonds that created the German *Kulturnation*, of which Switzerland was part, were cultural, not political. It is therefore not surprising or inconsistent that he recognized in the artistic and intellectual achievements of the German Middle Ages a significant and highly influential source of German-Swiss unity. For many conservative scholars, not just Romantics, this heritage represented the wellspring of German liberty and the guarantee of Germany's future greatness. The same was true for the traditional rights and sovereignty of the Swiss cantons, which had roots in the same past, although they owed a more recent debt to their northern neighbours, as Burckhardt pointed out to his sceptical sister. Germany and Prussia, after all, and not revolutionary France, had preserved Swiss independence in the long run; this was the lesson of the French Revolution and the occupation of Switzerland. "Where would all our freedom be, if Germany had not overthrown Napoleon?" he argued in April 1841, as he was travelling to the Rhineland. In the culture of Germany, he had found his roots and spiritual home. "I am like Saul," Burckhardt raptured to Louise, "who went out to look for lost asses and found a king's crown. I often want to sink on my knees before this holy German ground and thank God that I speak the German language. I thank Germany *for everything*! My best teachers have been German and I have been nurtured at the breast of German culture and scholarship. From this land I shall always draw my best powers. And this people, this glorious German youth, this country, this garden of God! Am I worthy of standing on this earth that has been soaked in the blood of Martyrs?"[43]

41 Ibid., 1:165.
42 Ibid., 1:183–4. See also the similar comments in a newspaper article Burckhardt wrote for the *Kölnische Zeitung*, in *Jacob Burckhardt als Politischer Publizist*, Dürr, ed., 116.
43 *Briefe*, 1:165.

As excessive as this highly charged outburst may seem, this cultural nationalism echoed a strain of the conservative nationalism and patriotism that was sweeping through Prussia in the early 1840s.[44] Burckhardt was conscious of the fact that his enthusiasm for Germany was the articulation of a conservative *Weltanschauung*. He made this clear in a letter to his sister, in which he related an intense and emotional evening spent in Leipzig with his friend Hermann Schauenburg. Burckhardt, who described Schauenburg as "ultraliberal," spent part of the night discussing the political situation in Germany and ended up defending his conservatism with such force and determination that even he was surprised. In one of the most quoted passages from his vast correspondence, he claimed that:

[I]n this moment, certainly one of the noblest of my life, the future of the glorious German fatherland came alive before my eyes. I saw Prussia's coming constitutional battles before me and thought, *now* you must do your part, if only to enlighten one important, noble person about these wild, confused pursuits of freedom. I was now able to begin from a newer, higher point of view; I had the courage to be conservative and not to give in (to be a liberal is the easiest thing). We spoke with intense emotion, and I do not recall ever being so eloquent. He fell about my neck and kissed me. I was the first person he had heard speak from conviction in a conservative vein. Then I made a silent vow never to be ashamed of my convictions. He acknowledged that because of my studies I had considered these questions more thoroughly than he ... He promised me that he would never be unduly contemptuous of royalists and conservatives in the future.[45]

This discussion with Hermann Schauenburg was an important moment in Burckhardt's life. According to Kaegi, it represented nothing less than the "birth of Burckhardt's political consciousness."[46] Among his liberal acquaintances, given the potentially confrontational environment, Burckhardt needed courage to defend his conservative political convictions. Significantly, he based his political conservatism on lessons learned from his study of the past, as well as his experience of contem-

---

44 See Sperber, *Rhineland Radicals*, 114–15.
45 *Briefe*, 1:164.
46 Kaegi, 2:103. Gilbert, "Jacob Burckhardt's Student Years," 255, note 22, does not agree and argues that Kaegi overemphasizes its importance.

porary politics. His conservatism was a reflection of a consciousness moulded by his experience of events in his hometown of Basel; the atmosphere at the university of Berlin, where he was surrounded by state officials; and, equally as important, the conservative views of Leopold von Ranke.

Ironically, however, once away from Berlin, Burckhardt's commitment to conservatism diminished considerably and he did not keep his silent vow. The contrast between Bonn and Berlin could not have been greater for the young man. Berlin, which he described a few months after his arrival as an "objectionable place, a boring, large city on an endless sandy plain,"[47] was the conservative capital of authoritarian, reactionary Prussia. At its university, Ranke towered over historical scholarship and presided over the reconstruction of official historical memory. Bonn, in contrast, was decidedly provincial and by no means committed to a vision of the world dominated by power politics and Great Powers. Although the Prussians had ruled this part of the Rhineland since 1814, their presence was not generally welcomed and strong particularist sentiments still prevailed. In the Rhineland, Burckhardt witnessed a different picture of Prussian rule. With its large Catholic population, separate legal traditions, and different social structures, the Rhineland was fertile ground for the liberal opposition movement that was in perpetual conflict with the Prussian authorities during the *Vormärz*. The move from the centre of Prussia to the periphery in Bonn consequently brought Burckhardt into intimate contact with this political opposition for the first time. He began to see the world from a new political and historical perspective and to sympathize with the Rhinelanders' struggle for political reform, greater personal liberties, and increased popular participation in public life. Certainly, the complexities of the Rhineland's political situation bore a resemblance to the situation in Basel. In particular, it illustrated the threat posed by the power of larger states and the ominous forces of political centralization to the precarious existence of the *Kleinstaat*, which Burckhardt would soon argue was the best possible political entity for maintaining true freedom and individual liberty. For a time, at least, he ceased being the courageous defender of the Prussian monarchy and conservatism.

Burckhardt first encountered the political opposition in Bonn when he became involved in the activities of a close-knit circle of friends at a

47 *Briefe*, 1:147.

literary and music club called the *Maikäferbund*. The Protestant theologian, pastor, poet, and historian, Gottfried Kinkel (1815–82), the group's leading light, influenced Burckhardt the most.[48] They met at the university in Bonn, where Kinkel taught church history, and for the next few years were close friends. Kinkel is best remembered today not for his literary or historical writings, but rather for his participation in the Revolution of 1848. Kinkel developed the ideological foundations of his radicalism early in life. Soon after his appointment to the theology faculty at Bonn in late 1837, he gained a reputation for unorthodox theological views. People soon began to complain about his liberal sermons, which brought him to the attention of the Prussian authorities. While his sermons were generally tolerated, at least by the university administration, his engagement, and later marriage, to the divorced Catholic Johanna Matthieux, whom Burckhardt affectionately called "Frau Directrix," brought him into open conflict with the Bonn Protestant establishment. As a consequence, he lost his position as a pastor. He managed to save his academic career, however, by switching from the theological faculty to the philosophy faculty, a move Burckhardt described as, given the lack of academic freedom in Prussia, the best thing a "negative" theologian could do.[49]

In Kinkel, Burckhardt believed he had found a kindred spirit. While they shared a common interest in art, literature, and history, it is quite likely that Kinkel's unorthodox theological views provided the initial bond of friendship between the two men. Like Burckhardt, Kinkel had absorbed the recent debates and controversies surrounding the new critical theology and now approached it from an historical perspective, rather than from faith alone. This produced an inner turmoil in Kinkel as well, and he, too, began to demonstrate a growing indifference towards his theological career.[50] While Burckhardt encouraged his friend to finish his work on a history of paganism in late antiquity, he also tried to pursuade him to stop participating in controversial theological debates and to give up theology altogether. Having accurately assessed Kinkel's tempestuous personality, Burckhardt argued in a letter of 1842 that "in the long run theology cannot be your thing," something he had discovered for himself a few years earlier. He encouraged Kinkel to

48 See Kaegi, 2:115ff and 3:205ff. A number of older works are also useful. Bollert, *Gottfried Kinkels Kämpfe*, and De Jonge, *Gottfried Kinkel as Political and Social Thinker*. See also Kinkel, *Selbstbiographie, 1838–1848*.
49 *Briefe*, 2:62–3.
50 Bollert, *Gottfried Kinkels Kämpfe*, 47ff.

devote his energies to the study of history instead. He advised Kinkel that, unlike theology, history "will remain true to you."[51]

Like Burckhardt, Kinkel tried to overcome his crisis of faith by indulging in art and poetry. The vehicle for his creative energy was the *Maikäferbund*, which Burckhardt enthusiastically joined. As a member of this select group, Burckhardt enjoyed a high degree of personal and creative liberty, uncompromised by political and ideological differences; meanwhile, he contributed poems, composed music, and wrote short historical pieces. The two friends may not have agreed on all political matters – in a letter written many years later, Burckhardt recalled that in his youth he had learned how to deal with people of opposing political views in a manner that allowed him to keep his life as pleasant as possible[52] – but they had mutual respect and admiration for each other's creative talents. After Kinkel's abortive revolutionary activities in 1848–49, by which time they had gone their separate ways, Kinkel described the loss of Burckhardt's friendship as the worst of the many he had suffered because of his revolutionary zeal.[53]

When Burckhardt returned to Berlin in the autumn of 1841 to begin his final year as a student, his attitude towards politics and the study of history had changed. Foremost, perhaps, was a renewed, extremely intense interest in the history of art. Inspired by both Kugler and Kinkel, this passion bore fruit almost immediately in the shape of his first guidebook, *Die Kunstwerke der belgischen Städte* (1842), which was based on notes taken on a two-week excursion to Belgium in September 1841. Just as significant was the influence of a new set of friends and a fresh appreciation of the political situation in Germany. It is surely no coincidence that after his experiences in the Rhineland and the liberalism of Kinkel, Burckhardt began to distance himself from Ranke's conservatism and his vision of history; he also began to broaden his historical perspective, however, to include the constituent elements of cultural history.

Once back in Berlin in the autumn of 1841, Burckhardt was introduced by Kinkel and Johanna Matthieux to a new set of acquaintances, the most famous being the liberal socialite Bettina von Arnim. The sister of Clemens Brentano, Bettina was married to the poet Achim von Arnim and had been a friend of Goethe. Her salon in Berlin, which attracted many prominent literary figures and scholars, among them the historian

51 *Briefe*, 1:226.
52 Ibid., 4:238.
53 Kaegi, 2:126.

Friedrich Dahlmann and the brothers Grimm, had gained notoriety as a focal point of liberal opposition, even though she had relatively close contacts with the Prussian king and the royal family.

Burckhardt's brief acquaintance with Bettina is usually considered evidence that he was, or had become, a confirmed liberal.[54] But this seems to be an exaggeration. He was naturally delighted to participate in her prestigious salon and, in a letter to his sister, excitedly described his first meeting with Bettina. Clearly he was clearly in awe of the great woman. The main reason, though, was most certainly intellectual – she had a famous literary past, a prestigious salon, and provided a living connection to Goethe – rather than political and ideological. However, even if we accept Burckhardt's moderate liberalism as sincere – which it undoubtedly was – and even if he did enjoy Bettina's flaunting of convention in the staid and stifling atmosphere of Prussia's reactionary conservative capital, Burckhardt cannot have agreed with her more extreme political program, described by Kaegi as "pre-socialist."[55] Although Burckhardt pointed out that "the powerful woman deals with everything from a great, noble perspective," he qualified this by adding, "even if she may also be somewhat ultraliberal." He then recalled an embarrassing moment, which revealed just how conscious he was of the political gulf dividing them. Evidently, Bettina had told a story about a man who had been arrested for slandering the king, to which Burckhardt had replied that such a thing must have harmed his good reputation. " 'Look here,' Bettina said with a stabbing look in her eyes, 'that is precisely the thing I could bitterly hate you for'," at which point Burckhardt backtracked furiously, so as not to cause undue offence or appear disagreeable.[56] Bettina clearly doubted Burckhardt's commitment to liberalism, and this bothered Burckhardt. When he became the tutor in the home of a Prussian nobleman, Bettina objected on the grounds that Burckhardt might not remain true to his liberal principles. "As if a historian could change his convictions from one day to the next!" he protested.[57]

. . .

54 See for example, Kahan, *Aristocratic Liberalism*, 7; Gilbert, "Jacob Burckhardt's Student Years," 255.

55 Kaegi, 2:205.

56 *Briefe*, 1:189–90.

57 Ibid., 1:210.

Despite this pronouncement, Burckhardt did not feel truly at home in the liberal camp. While he may have sympathized with liberalism on an intellectual level, his experience of the realities of social and political conflict during these years reinforced his conservative instincts, not his liberal convictions. In the authoritarian political environment of Prussia, he undoubtedly viewed himself as a moderate liberal. At times he was very critical of Prussian conservatism; in sharp contrast to the traditional conservatism of the Basel city-state, it held no pretenses as to democratic participation and representation in government, had no constitution, and guaranteed no civil liberties. When Hermann Schauenburg was arrested for belonging to a secret reading society, for example, Burckhardt was outraged at the arbitrariness and reactionary policies of the authorities. But as social and political tensions mounted in Europe in the early 1840s, he became more concerned with maintaining social and political order than with ensuring political rights and liberties. Although he never abandoned his belief in the necessity of the rule of law, he increasingly feared the rise of mass politics and political revolution. His experience in Basel had taught him to be wary of extremes. Overall, despite rebelling against the pietism of his father – and in a certain sense against the conservatism of Ranke – he followed a moderate political course, although always instinctively erring on the side of caution. As a result, he never became a true convert to liberalism and grew to abhor its more radical extremes. This is especially true when one examines his political thought within the Swiss context – with its much more violent liberalism so threatening to the established order, and its much less reactionary and authoritarian (at least in Basel) conservatism – where he had much more at stake. In effect, the greater the deterioration of the political situation in Switzerland, the greater became his fear of the masses, social unrest, and liberal extremism. After his return to Switzerland, where violent social tension and political unrest were more endemic than in Germany, he openly supported the political status quo, preferring order, stability, and rule of law to the uncertainties and extremism of liberalism and the more radical forces of popular democracy. Not surprisingly, his relationship with his radical German friends gradually at this time ended.

An interesting example of the subtle shifts in Burckhardt's political opinions can be found in his reading of the Prussian situation. The ascension of Friedrich Wilhelm IV to the throne in 1840 had given intellectuals throughout Germany hope that a new age of liberalization would emerge, continuing the belief of many moderate liberals that the state and government should be the leading proponents of reform.[58] In particular, the king had indicated that press censorship would be eased; that the provincial estates would evince greater political involvement; and, finally, that the constitutional question would be reopened. These hopes, however, were soon dashed, only underlining the emptiness of the king's promises. The outlines of the deception became evident during a political crisis in March 1843, when the diet of the Prussian province of Posen, which had a Polish majority, petitioned the king for an expansion of its political rights and the alleviation of the most recent censorship laws. Friedrich Wilhelm's refusal to grant its wishes sparked considerable controversy and refocused political debate. Both issues were central to the liberal agenda, because censorship and the Prussian system of provincial diets had effectively prevented the emergence of a politically mature public life. Created in 1820 by reactionary court officials, the provincial diets were not representative assemblies; rather they were dominated by the nobility. Their proceedings were secret – censorship prevented their publication – and public participation and debate were almost nil. This was a particular cause of political frustration in the Prussian Rhineland, where there existed different social structures, political institutions, and traditions.[59]

Burckhardt, like so many of his contemporaries, recognized the need for a politically mature public life in Prussia. He knew how effectively the regime stifled political participation and public debate and was unhesitating in his criticism of the Prussian government's heavy-handed actions. He compared them during the March 1843 crisis with those of the regime in Hanover six years earlier, when the suspension of the constitution resulted in the infamous expulsion of the seven Göttingen professors.[60] But his criticism seemed to be motivated less by ideological considerations than by an understanding of the practical political consequences of the Prussian government's policies. By refusing to make constitutional concessions, he noted, Friedrich Wilhelm was demonstrating a profound lack of judgment and knowledge about the real situation in the country, not to mention a politically dangerous disregard for the mood of the people. From the enchanted windows of his Berlin palace, "the surroundings appear to be thriving, wealthy and peaceful."[61] Burckhardt saw that, in reality, the people in Prussia were suffering

58 See most recently, Barclay, *Frederick William IV and the Prussian Monarchy.*
59 See Sperber, *Rhineland Radicals,* 39–40.
60 *Briefe,* 1:242.
61 Ibid., 1:243.

under the authoritarian yoke, engendering a set of circumstances that, if not competently addressed, would lead to revolution. For all his dislike of absolutism, however, he was careful not to lay blame directly on the king and was even somewhat sympathetic to the latter's plight. His criticism focused, instead, on the activities of the king's advisors, who were trying to protect their own interests, he felt, rather than the interests of the monarchy or nation.[62]

A few years later, Burckhardt once again had cause to comment on the political affairs of Prussia. By early 1847, Prussia was entering a period of political and social unrest that would culminate, a year later, in revolution. In order to find a solution to the growing crisis in Prussia, Friedrich Wilhelm called the provincial estates together to form a United *Landtag*. Like many of his contemporaries, Burckhardt hoped that the *Landtag* would lead to positive reform. But when the king refused to acknowledge anything more than the advisory function of the assembly, the violence and opposition only increased. By now Burckhardt no longer believed that a constitution would solve Prussia's social, economic, and political ills, especially in a country with no democratic traditions, an incapable parliament, and a strong bureaucracy. While he felt that the king had acted unwisely in dissolving the *Landtag* in June 1847 – an act that only further intensified the constitutional crisis, and was a missed opportunity for reform – he guardedly praised Friedrich Wilhelm's throne speech. It was "tragically touching," he commented; "an historian in 100 years time (if the world is still standing on its legs by then) will find that the speech was not unworthy."[63] Thus, when faced with the choice between the destructive force of radical democracy and the despotism of the Prussian regime, he "took the side of the king and his throne speech, feeling in this situation suddenly very Swiss."[64]

. . .

Burckhardt's relationship with his German friends serves as a barometer of his political views. Particularly so was his friendship with Gottfried Kinkel, with its glimpse of the various shades and contours of

62 Ibid.

63 Ibid., 3:67. Ranke was much more effusive in his praise of the same speech, claiming that never "since David had a king spoken so beautifully," quoted in Kaegi, 3:141.

64 Kaegi, 3:143.

Burckhardt's political principles and commitments. It is clear that their friendship was based on shared literary, artistic, and academic interests, rather than political views. Between 1841 and 1843, the time of his sojourn in Germany, Burckhardt did not seem to be overly concerned about Kinkel's political activities. In any case, despite the growing tension between the Rhinelanders and the Prussian authorities, Kinkel's opposition had not yet crystallized into a revolutionary political program. Indeed, after Burckhardt's return to Basel, they corresponded regularly, discussing their scholarly and literary endeavours at great length. However, Burckhardt's tone changed perceptibly as Kinkel became more active in opposition politics. He tried to warn Kinkel about the violence of radical liberalism in Switzerland and the dangers of his politically inspired poetry that was causing heads to turn in Berlin. Despite Kinkel's growing radicalism and political indiscretions, and even though it became increasingly difficult, Burckhardt continued to support him. He recognized, though, that fundamental personality differences threatened their friendship: "The Lord made you *so* and me *differently* and if we behave rationally, then people can enjoy being with both of us, without wanting to compare me to you. 'In my father's house are many rooms'." [65]

During the mid-1840s, the friendship became increasingly untenable for Burckhardt. The more radical Kinkel became, the more Burckhardt distanced himself from him. As a Rhinelander, Kinkel was bitterly opposed to Prussian rule; although a Protestant, he was sympathetic to the grievances of the Rhineland's Catholic population. Given his temperament, it was almost inevitable that, during the crisis years of the late 1840s, his liberal, democratic political views would be galvanized into opposition activities. By 1846, Kinkel was predicting a revolution; two years later he had found a home within the ranks of the revolutionary liberal opposition. In 1848, along with Karl Schurz, he founded the Bonn Democratic Club, which enjoyed considerable success, numbering six hundred members by the autumn. As a leader of the democratic movement in Bonn, Kinkel's influence was considerable; he soon played a leading role in local politics and entered the national spotlight. [66]

In the early months of 1848, Kinkel tried to chart a moderate course, believing that political freedom and German national unity could be achieved through a constitutional monarchy. After the frustrations and

65 *Briefe*, 3:66.
66 Sperber, *Rhineland Radicals*, 275.

setbacks of the democratic movement in the early summer of 1848, especially in the wake of the conservative victories in the elections to the Frankfurt National Assembly – "the five fingers of despotism, clergy, nobility, moneybags, soldiers, officials, have triumphed and will dominate the parliaments,"[67] Kinkel claimed with despair – he adopted a new political strategy. When he assumed the post of editor of the *Bonner Zeitung* in August 1848, he published a pamphelt, "Artisans: Save Yourself!", which publicly proclaimed for the first time his commitment to the republican cause.[68]

As its title suggests, this pamphlet was not primarily concerned with republican forms of government, but was specifically directed at artisans, whose economic situation was being dangerously eroded by industrialization. In a call for political action, Kinkel argued that the artisans' task in the revolution was to pave "the way for the republican form of government."[69] In the atmosphere of general protest against the Prussian authorities in the Rhineland and at a time when subtle ideological differences were often blurred, his pamphlet was initially welcomed. Upon reflection, however, many radicals on the left found it lacking. Their criticism focused on Kinkel's passionate defence of the guild system, which had been abolished in the Rhineland by the French during the Napoleonic era. As well, many observers considered his ideas to be anachronistic. His proposal was not a concrete solution to the economic and social crisis faced by the independent craftsman, who, because of lack of favourable access to market, an increased burden of debt, and overcrowding in the trades, was quickly being proletarianized. Rather it was a program that restricted the growth of trades. Occupational freedom, the cornerstone of liberal economic demands elsewhere, was, according to Kinkel, nothing less than an "exploitative action of a reactionary government," and as such could not exist in a democratic *Volksstaat*.[70] This and his lack of understanding of the social and economic changes taking place in Germany opened him up to ridicule and scathing criticism from local working-class organizations; it also alienated him from the radical left which, among other things, called for the abolition of the guilds.

67 Quoted in Ibid., 183.
68 De Jonge, *Gottfried Kinkel as Political and Social Thinker*, 14–17.
69 Ibid., 18.
70 Sperber, *Rhineland Radicals*, 275.

In many respects Kinkel was a "romantic" revolutionary, with little practical knowledge and experience of the problems of economic modernization, capitalism, or revolution. Certainly this was Burckhardt's later opinion. When it came to political and economic matters, Burckhardt wrote to Hermann Schauenburg in 1849 after receiving news of Kinkel's fate, "he understood nothing except how to make a sensation ... '[M]an shapes his own destiny'."[71] But Kinkel, undaunted by criticism of his program from the revolutionary rank and file, continued to joust at windmills. In the spring of 1849, as the revolutionary movement flared again following the Prussian king's refusal to accept the German crown from the Frankfurt Assembly, Kinkel decided to take up arms. On the evening of 10 May 1849, during fighting between Prussian troops and revolutionaries, Kinkel participated in the storming of the arsenal in Siegburg, near Bonn; he then planned an uprising in the Palatinate. Seven weeks later, on 29 June, Kinkel was seriously wounded in a skirmish with Prussian troops near the Badenese town of Durlach. Arrested, tried, and sentenced to death, he was only spared through Bettina von Arnim's personal intervention with the Prussian king. Shortly afterwards, with the help of Karl Schurz, Kinkel escaped from Spandau prison and fled to England. By this time he had become something of an international sensation – a martyr to the revolutionary cause in Germany.

Kinkel's popularity was a source of considerable aggravation to the radical left, which regarded him as a sham. In an 1852 pamphlet entitled "The Great Men in Exile," Marx and Engels tried to destroy the myth that had developed around Kinkel and his activities. They wrote vindictively: "Who better fitted for the task of enacting this great passion farce than our captive passion flower, Kinkel at the spinning wheel, able to emit endless floods of pathetic sentimental tears, who was in addition, preacher, professor of fine arts, deputy, political colporteur, musketeer, newly discovered poet and old impressario all rolled into one? Kinkel was the man of the moment and as such he was immediately accepted by the German philistines."[72]

After returning to Switzerland, Burckhardt followed Kinkel's radicalization with growing alarm. By the time of his imprisonment, however, they had not corresponded for over two years. Whereas Kinkel had

---

71 *Briefe*, 3:112.

72 Quoted in Ashton, *Little Germany*, 152. See also Warnke, "Jacob Burckhardt und Karl Marx," 141ff.

adopted a violent, more extreme political agenda, Burckhardt had followed the opposite course. Repeatedly, he tried to warn Kinkel of the dangers posed by his extreme radicalism. One year after their last meeting in August 1847, Burckhardt commented that Kinkel would "fall between two stools in the most shameful way," because he lacked entirely the "noble discretion" and "inner balance" that even Republicans required.[73] Over the course of the last two years, he added, he had expected that Kinkel's political activities would eventually lead to his ruin, because the combination of professional difficulties and an increasingly radical perspective had made him irrational and angry. Burckhardt sadly recalled, that when they had met for the last time in Berlin in 1847 it was no longer possible to speak with him: "He wanted revenge and was going to smash his head against the wall sooner or later; if it had not been against this wall, then it would have been against another."[74] Moreover, Burckhardt continued, Kinkel's experience of radical politics in Switzerland during the early 1840s and the bloody revolution of 1848 had convinced him that democracy was a potentially destructive force; in his opinion both "democrats and proletarians, despite their most furious efforts, will have to give way to an increasingly violent form of despotism, since our lovable century is made for everything except genuine democracy."[75]

73 *Briefe*, 3:105.
74 Ibid., 3:112.
75 Ibid.

3

Swiss Liberalism and Political Journalism

BEFORE RETURNING TO BASEL in early October 1843, Burckhardt embarked upon an extended journey to France. In May 1843, en route from Berlin, he attended the wedding of Kinkel and Johanna Matthieux in Bonn, before travelling on to Brussels and his final destination, Paris, which he reached June 8.[1] Once in the French capital, he began a daily routine of research and copying in the Bibliothèque Royale and other libraries, spending a great deal of time visiting churches, museums, national monuments, and theatres. In addition, he wrote a number of articles for the *Kölnische Zeitung*, the most important of which was a piece entitled "French Literature and Money,"[2] which criticized the Parisian literary scene and its degeneration into a mere money-making enterprise driven by greed, power, and ambition. Emphasizing the negative role of both public opinion and the unrestricted freedom of the press on literary creativity, Burckhardt argued that France's *literati* had, in their unbridled desire for momentary fame and fortune, unrepentently bowed to the whims of the "Paris public," sacrificing true artistic creativity and genius in the process, and thereby renouncing all further bonds with the nation.

1 Burckhardt departed Berlin under a small cloud. At the beginning of January he published in Kugler's journal, *Kunstblatt*, the first of a series of articles reviewing a major Berlin exhibit of modern German art. As will be discussed later, his criticism evoked hostility from certain circles of the German art world. The controversy continued even as Burckhardt travelled to France, only coming to an end with the timely intervention of Kugler in the debate. See "Bericht über die Kunstausstellung zu Berlin im Herbste 1842," *Kunstblatt*, 3 January 1843 to 21 March 1843. See Kaegi, 2:226–43, and Schlink, *Jacob Burckhardt und die Kunsterwartung*.

2 "Die französische Literatur und das Geld," in *Unbekannte Aufsätze*, Oswald, ed.

This article not only provides an interesting assessment of literary and political life in pre-1848 Paris; it also represents the first tentative articulation of the important themes which were to dominate Burckhardt's mature political thought: his fear of centralization and militarism; the rise of new Caesars and their manipulation of public opinion and the "masses;" and his enthusiasm for the *Kleinstaat*. Intended in part as a lesson for his German audience, he played upon the fear of revolution and social unrest in France, which in Germany in the early 1840s had been only a half-serious premonition. He sensed that the French masses had great anxieties about the future, that they had forgotten the lessons of the French Revolution and no longer trusted the "republican form of the July dynasty or the constitution."[3] This was a paradoxical situation for Burckhardt, especially when contrasted with events in Germany. He argued that in France, despite a constitution and a parlimentary form of government – both of which he agreed Germany required – "lamentable political decay and social confusion" were the uncontested masters. Paris, he said, had become a large barracks. He predicted an eventual sort of alliance between the king and the masses, and a descent into misrule.[4] The full implications of this paradox became much clearer to Burckhardt a few years later, during the political crisis in Switzerland of the mid-1840s, when he was to conclude that, without a mature public life, popular sovereignty and the trappings of constitutionalism were no panacea for deeper political and social ills.[5]

According to Burckhardt, the cause of the social and political unrest in Europe and, more specifically, the disaffection in Paris during the summer of 1843 was the inexorable drive towards the centralization of political authority. With Germany as his point of reference, he emphasized the role played by the *Kleinstaat* in the development of the *Kulturnation* and individual liberty, echoing a theme first broached in his work on Conrad von Hochstaden. Only in the *Kleinstaat*, he argued, could individual liberty be fully expressed and creative energies allowed to mature. In Germany, in contrast, where no dominant cultural centre existed and political centralization was not yet fully realized, "our great poets lived in small cities on the Rhine, in Swabia, in Thuringia, in numerous middling jobs and positions and have received nothing from their work except the honour of their nation and

3 *Briefe*, 2:17 and 37.
4 Ibid., 2:35; "Die französische Literatur und das Geld," 67.
5 See for example, *Briefe*, 2:154.

immortality."[6] In France, however, where Paris exercised artistic as well as political hegemony, art lived or died according to the whims of the great Parisian public. This, said Burckhardt, had important implications for political life. The possibility existed that in small, decentralized states a politically mature public life and a high degree of individual liberty might emerge for the educated citizenry. The small state, Burckhardt summarized many years later, "exists so that there may be a spot on earth where the largest possible number of its inhabitants are citizens in the fullest sense of the word."[7] Citizenship and the respectability and responsibility this entailed, when combined with a sense of a common past and future destiny, united people more than constitutions, written laws, and strong central government. His impression of Paris was that everyone was living day to day, that everything was in motion and transition. "It will not be long before there is a new explosion," he concluded.[8]

. . .

On his return to Basel in October 1843, against the backdrop of the excitement of Paris and his fond memories of Berlin and the Rhineland, Burckhardt predicted a much more tedious existence for himself. "The good times are over for me," he complained. "A life of reserve and politeness awaits me in Basel," which he characterized as money proud and far too pietist. As for its inhabitants, "I can trust nobody completely and there is nobody with whom to cultivate an open intellectual relationship."[9] In May 1843, Burckhardt had been promoted to *doctor philosophiae* at the university of Basel on the basis of his two essays for Ranke's seminars: "Carl Martell," which as his official dissertation he

6 "Die französische Literatur und das Geld," 61 and 65.

7 WB, 259.

8 *Briefe*, 2:17.

9 Ibid., 2:24 and 34. Burckhardt's criticism of pious, purse-proud Baslers echoed a staple of the liberal opposition movement in Basel and Switzerland generally. According to the *Schweizerische Nationalzeitung*, 9 January 1844, in Basel "money is the surrogate for talent, ability, knowledge, dignity, and virtue ... But money isn't the only thing; for no matter how rich Basel is, it still has a pious reputation ... Basel is a city of wonders; the rich enter heaven easier than camels through the eye of a needle. Piety is worth a lot; almost as much as wealth. Almost ..." Quoted in Kaegi, 2:396.

translated into Latin; and "Conrad von Hochstaden." Now he looked forward to working hard and establishing himself, as he began to prepare his first lectures for a course in the history of art at the university, where he had received an appointment as lecturer.

Burckhardt's expectations were only partly fulfilled after he returned to his native city. Over the course of the next two years, his life was certainly not boring. Although he had more than enough work to occupy him – a few weeks after his return he began writing articles on art and art history for the ninth edition of the Brockhaus *Konversationslexikon*[10] – the peace and quiet he desired eluded him. Instead, the political situation in Switzerland was even more volatile than that in France or Germany. His return to Basel had coincided with a period of serious political strife, bordering on anarchy, within the Swiss Confederation; strife that – between the liberal, progressive, and Protestant cantons and the conservative, traditionalist, and largely Catholic cantons – would eventually lead to civil war in 1847. Moreover, during this tense and violent prelude to civil war, Burckhardt agreed to become editor of the city's main newspaper, the conservative *Basler Zeitung*. Consequently, not only did he become directly involved in political life for the first and only time; he also became embroiled in political conflict and, for a while, was a favourite target in the opposition press.

Burckhardt's job as editor began on 1 July 1844 and lasted nineteen long, unpleasant months. This was not his first experience as a journalist. As we have seen, he had also written articles for the *Kölnische Zeitung*, and continued to write regularly for this paper throughout his time as editor in Basel, providing Rhinelanders with a running commentary on the chaotic Swiss domestic political scene. From the start, Burckhardt never seriously considered journalism as a career; he continued to view this job as a stop-gap measure until a suitable university position opened up and as a means to earn some money for travelling abroad. Even Andreas Heusler, who had hired him, recognized that his talent lay elsewhere, writing that Burckhardt "was made for better things than a newspaper writer."[11] In fact, although Burckhardt was an avid reader of newspapers, he regarded journalism with a certain disdain, seeing it as an instrument of propaganda and manipulation, and a potentially

10 Rehm, "Jacob Burckhardts Mitarbeit am Konversationslexikon." See also Kaegi, 2:524–50. Burckhardt worked on the articles for about three years. He also wrote approximately 70 new articles, revising and expanding more than 300.

11 Quoted in introduction to *Jacob Burckhardt als politischer Publizist*, Dürr, ed., 8.

dangerous force in modern society. While he generally supported freedom of the press, he lamented the poor quality of most newspapers as
well as their sensationalism, feeling that the press, when uncontrolled,
served as an agitator of public opinion and radicalism. These views only
intensified with age. Remember that from Paris, he had even praised
the necessity and effectiveness of the censor in Germany.[12]

Burckhardt initially approached his new job with a certain degree of
optimism. It provided him with a platform for his views and the opportunity to put his convictions to the test. He also hoped that he would be
able to exert some influence on public opinion. The goal of his political
journalism, he explained, was a two-pronged attack against the forces of
absolutism and the "screaming radicalism" of the Swiss.[13] In the highly
volatile world of Swiss politics, Burckhardt believed his would be the
voice of reason and moderation; naively perhaps, he thought his articles
would teach the educated public to avoid the errors of the more radical
elements of Swiss liberalism and reactionary conservatism.

This optimism was short-lived, however, as he quickly became disillusioned with his new employment. One reason was that he felt his position contributed to his already strong sense of alienation from Basel
society. He often complained to his friends about his loneliness, claiming that he was living a "dog's life," that he could not have been more
isolated if he were living amongst savages. He tried hard to maintain
close contact with his German friends and yearned for their letters and
visits.[14] In addition, his work for the newspaper was much more time
consuming than he had anticipated. At first, his main responsibilities included writing the lead article on domestic affairs, and compiling and
writing the important section on international news, in addition to the
more mundane tasks associated with the general production of the
newspaper. With this busy schedule leaving him little time for the things
he enjoyed doing, he bemoaned the unfortunate fact that "all literary,
academic and other interests must remain silent for the next little
while," that the "political devilry" in Switzerland was keeping him too
busy. "It's unbelieveable how destructive this political excitement is to
the musas basilienses," he complained.[15]

12 See his essay, "Die französische Literatur und das Geld." In general, though Burckhardt did support freedom of the press. See *Briefe*, 2:43. It also appears that, unbeknownst
to the Prussian authorities, Burckhardt took part in a demonstration for freedom of the
press in Berlin in 1841. Kaegi, 2:247, note 2.

13 *Briefe*, 2:86.

14 Ibid., 2:123 and 125.

15 Ibid., 2:117 and 161.

For the first time, Burckhardt also became a public figure, subject to attack by political opponents. His debut articles as a journalist were extremely controversial and thrust him immediately into the political limelight. Although not completely unexpected, the attacks were somewhat disheartening. As he wrote to Kinkel a few months before he assumed his editorial responsibilities, he anticipated attracting, "like all previous editors of the *Basler Zeitung,* a continuous stream of personal attacks of the most common sort."[16] These acrimonious debates reflected not only the hostility that had existed between the liberal and the conservative camps since the early 1830s, but also Basel's extremely politicized press. The *Basler Zeitung,* regardless of Burckhardt's own moderate position, was the organ of both the Basel elite and the government. This newspaper, originally founded to counter radical agitation in the countryside during the Basler *Wirren* and to combat the "revolutionary violence" thought to be the "main source of all the evil being suffered by the confederation," presented itself as the guardian of the traditional values of "justice and equal rights" – the cornerstones of all "true civilizations."[17] Under Heusler's energetic direction, it had become the most important conservative newspaper in Switzerland. During the 1840s, its main political competition was the liberal *Schweizerische Nationalzeitung,* published by the Basel lawyer, Dr Karl Brenner, who considered it the purpose of both his newspaper and the liberal movement to engage in "a free and open battle against the system of our government." By this time, Brenner's newspaper had become one of the leading voices of liberal criticism of the patriciate.[18]

In total, Basel supported four newspapers during the 1840s. It was a hotbed of political journalism, an important sign of the changing political culture, the emergence of a public sphere, and the struggle by those excluded from political power to shape and influence the terms of political discourse in the city. Political life in Basel was experiencing a shift away from the extremely restrictive administrative and constitutional spheres – even the press, traditionally a passive vehicle for the transmission and dissemination of events and news from the Grand Council, had prided itself on reflecting the dignified, if not somewhat pious, tone set by the government – and into the broader public arena. Political debates were becoming accessible to the masses for the first time. The changing nature of the press and its new role in the "process of social

16 Ibid., 2:86.
17 *Basler Zeitung,* 2 January 1844.
18 See Sarasin, "Sittlichkeit," 74.

education" was recognized by Heusler, who commented that "social life no longer only expresses itself in the constitution and in official authorities; there are other levers powerfully moving today's world; the chief among them are the press and the associations."[19]

The change in the nature of political discourse and in the role of the press in Basel no doubt contributed to Burckhardt's growing fear of the masses, especially over the course of the next few months as the nation's passions were ignited by the so-called Jesuit Question. This crisis soon dispelled Burckhardt's concern about personal attacks in the press; he quickly developed a "skin like a crocodile," and even found some humour in being dragged through the mud by the radical press.[20] Even more than the controversial appointment of the radical theologian David Friedrich Strauss to a professorship at the university of Zürich in 1839, the Jesuit Question pitted Catholic against Protestant, conservative against liberal, canton against canton, and canton against the federal government. It inspired the poetic voice of Gottfried Keller and the protesting voice of the radicals and militant partisans, who, when government failed to solve the sensitive issue according to their desires, resorted to violence against the Catholic population and open rebellion against cantonal and federal authorities in what had become an unfortunate pattern in Swiss political life in the first half of the century. However, whereas the Strauss affair toppled the liberal government in Zürich, the Jesuit Question was to lead to civil war in 1847.

. . .

During the first half of the nineteenth century, political life in Switzerland was characterized by extreme passion and violence; civil strife and partisan conflict were endemic and almost synonymous with being Swiss. In many respects, the Basel *Wirren* of 1830–33, perhaps the most extreme manifestation of the tension that existed in the country during the 1830s, served as a prelude to future, and much more serious, national conflict. It was an ominous sign of things to come. The liberals, whose origins were in the many educational, patriotic, and charitable associations that had played such an important role in public life during

19 *Basler Zeitung*, 9 November 1846.
20 *Briefe*, 2:105.

the late eighteenth and early nineteenth centuries, had won impressive victories in the cantons following the July Revolution of 1830. By the 1840s, Swiss liberalism was far less fragmented and localized. Through its active press, its emphasis on popular sovereignty and civil rights, and its program of economic reform, liberalism had succeeded in winning substantial mass support and had become an increasingly cohesive, national political movement. One of its main strengths was its commitment to nationalism and the process of nation building. From the perspective of the liberals, the creation of a viable national state was the ultimate goal of human evolution and progress. This required a far-reaching reform of the political structure in order to ensure the creation of a strong central government and to eliminate the more odious elements of Swiss particularism, which had, in the liberals' opinion, kept the country as a "bundle of states" and prevented the emergence of a modern, centralized nation-state. This agenda was at odds with Switzerland's historical federalism. Liberal success in many cantons notwithstanding, the lack of a "national centre" – reflected in the rotation of the seat of the federal government between the directorial cantons of Bern, Zürich, and Lucerne – the persistance of strong regional loyalties, and the very novelty of nationalism and the concept of the nation, meant that nationalism was suspect to many conservatives and traditionalists. A significant number of conservative cantons still fought to preserve their political sovereignty and independence within the loose federation. By the early 1840s, that included the city of Basel and the cantons of Valais, Fribourg, Schwyz, Lucerne, Neuchâtel, Uri, and Unterwalden.

By and large, Switzerland's ideological divide mirrored confessional division. Questions of faith, as much as political ideology, dominated the highly nuanced world of Swiss politics; religious conflict, in evidence since the Reformation, always simmered dangerously below the surface. The combination of political ideology and confession was an explosive mixture in the 1840s, pitting the "enlightened," "progressive," and predominantly urban, liberal Protestants against the "backward," "irrational," predominantly rural, conservative Catholics. (Basel, as had often been the case, did not fit neatly into this formula, being both conservative and Protestant.) Tension was especially acute in those cantons with a mixed religious population. There an uneasy system of confessional parity existed which, regardless of demography, guaranteed Catholics and Protestants equal representation in cantonal government. As throughout Europe, the Roman Catholic Church came under attack by liberals and radicals who saw the Church as a rival for power and loyalty. The liberals, whose goal was a secular state, sought to subordinate the Church, and in a number of regenerated cantons the fate of church orders, institutions, and property were openly discussed.

The first round of this conflict began on 5 January 1841, when a referendum in the predominantly liberal canton of Aargau approved a plan to revise the constitution and abolish the system of representation based on confessional parity. The new electoral system for the Aargau Grand Council was now based on direct vote count, which gave the Protestants and liberals a majority. This was a serious setback to Aargau's Catholic population, whose members were naturally outraged at their sudden loss of political influence. Interpreting the new liberal constitution as a direct assault on their faith, many Catholics refused to accept the revisions and began to agitate for a separate canton. The government, perhaps fearing a repetition of the earlier violence in Basel, promply arrested a number of secessionist leaders. This sparked a series of riots throughout the Catholic districts, which were soon crushed by government troops.

In an act designed to punish the Catholic population, liberal and radical Protestants in the Aargau government used the riots, which Burckhardt believed had been deliberately provoked by the radicals,[21] as a pretext to attack the Catholic clergy and the monasteries, which they blamed for the unrest in the canton. On 13 January 1841, a majority in the Aargau Grand Council voted to dissolve the four monasteries and four convents in the canton. The decision came into effect one week later; with only forty-eight hours notice, and in the dead of winter, the monks and nuns were expelled from the canton, and the property of the monasteries confiscated.[22] This unconstitutional step was soundly condemned by all non-liberal cantons, the conservative press, the Catholic Church, and the international community. The Austrians were especially angered because the Benedictine abbey at Muri, one of the oldest in Switzerland, had been founded by the Hapsburgs.

The matter was brought before a special session of the federal diet. It soon became clear, however, that the crisis could not be solved within the parameters of the Federal Treaty, the inadequacies of which, in this

21 Ibid., 2:152. See also Biaudet, "Der modernen Schweiz entgegen," 940ff.

22 Biaudet, "Der modernen Schweiz entgegen," 941. The monasteries were Muri, Wettingen, Baden, and Bremgarten; the convents were Fahr, Hermetschwil, Gnadental, and Baden. The Aargau Grand Council was motivated by more than the fact that the monasteries were a source of opposition to liberalism. It was also tempted by the vast wealth of the monasteries, which it hoped would cover the increased expenses of government. See Schefold, *Volkssouveränität und repräsentatvie Demokratie*, 43–4.

instance, were glaringly obvious. Although the dissolution of the monasteries was a clear violation of the treaty, which expressly guaranteed their continued existence, the treaty also upheld cantonal sovereignty in internal domestic affairs. Despite this, in April, following a vote in the federal diet, the government of Aargau was declared in violation of the constitution and was ordered to reinstate the monasteries. When the Aargau government prevaricated, another vote in the federal diet took place, with the same result. This time the canton reinstated three of the convents, but over the next two years refused to capitulate to all of the demands of the federal government, despite internal protests and international pressure from Rome and Vienna. Finally, in 1843, the government of Aargau reluctantly agreed to reinstate the last convent. Later that summer, the federal diet declared itself satisfied with the result and dropped the monastery question from its agenda.

The final decision by the federal government did not satisfy Swiss Catholics, whose resolve had been strengthened by the events in Aargau. In the predominantly rural Catholic cantons of central Switzerland, where liberalism had been slow to gain a foothold among the peasantry, there was now a resurgence of political Catholicism and ultramontanism. Reaction was especially widespread in Lucerne. Lucerne had been one of the first cantons to be "regenerated" in the aftermath of the July Revolution of 1830, and had been a leading member of the liberal *Siebnerkonkordat*. In the spring of 1841, the liberals suffered a major setback when conservative forces under the leadership of the wealthy Catholic landowner, Joseph Leu, successfully campaigned for the revision of the cantonal constitution. The conservative victory in Lucerne represented not just a defeat for the liberal movement; as one of the three directorial cantons, Lucerne was able to exert considerable influence over the agenda of the federal government and assumed an important leadership role among Swiss Catholics and conservatives. More significantly, Leu gave a powerful voice to political Catholicism. A conservative, Leu was able to mobilize the rural masses by incorporating democratic ideas, such as the abolition of privileges and "one man one vote,"[23] into his political program. Inspired by Leu's success, Catholic Switzerland approached the Aargau monastery crisis increasingly

23 Although Leu was called the champion of "clerical democracy" and the "Catholic Democrat," Burckhardt called him a "fanatical peasant" in the *Kölnische Zeitung*. See *Jacob Burckhardt als politischer Publizist*, Dürr, ed, 60. Widely respected by many of his opponents for his integrity and devotion, Leu was murdered in 1845 at the height of the crisis. See Biaudet, "Der modernen Schweiz entgegen," 938; Remak, *A Very Civil War*, 25. See Burckhardt's assessment of the murder in *Jacob Burckhardt als politischer Publizist*, Dürr, ed., 138–9.

confident that they occupied the moral and legal high ground and more than ever determined to defend its rights and independence. When the federal diet failed to resolve the crisis to their satisfaction, and with their faith under siege, the Catholic cantons decided to take matters into their own hands. Despite possible risks to the federation, they began negotiations to form a special defensive union to preserve the constitution and to prevent any further liberal aggression.[24]

In the midst of this highly charged political environment Leu and his ally, the former radical, but now archconservative politician Konstantin Siegwart-Müller, pursued an openly ultramontane policy destined to antagonize not just the radicals, but the moderate liberals and their Protestant conservative allies as well. Once in power, the conservative regime in Lucerne pushed forward with a highly contentious plan to invite the Jesuits into the canton to organize and run the education system. Although the government was aware of the difficulties this would cause – the issue divided families and even the Catholic Church expressed reservations – it was determined to conduct its affairs as it saw fit. The recalling of the Jesuits had been controversial even before the Aargau expulsion order. Siegwart-Müller had once publicly condemned the Jesuits, declaring that they were like "crab lice": "Once you have them you cannot get rid of them." But the closing of the monasteries had changed the equation, and Siegwart-Müller's opinion. It was not just Swiss Catholicism that was under attack, but the sovereignty of the cantons and the constitution. For the government of Lucerne, the Jesuit question was much more than a simple question of faith; it had become a symbol of existential, political importance. Everyone knew that the independence and sovereignty of the cantons and the integrity of the federal system were at stake. Despite his dislike of the Jesuits, Siegwart-Müller proclaimed that the people of Lucerne would "take orders neither from rebels nor from Protestants on what teachers it may invite, or to whom it will entrust its young clerics, or what form its Catholicism should take."[25]

The attempt to reinforce cantonal sovereignty, to reassert Catholicism politically, and to thwart the gains of liberal and radical Protestantism within the Confederation, backfired miserably. Despite the fact that Lucerne's government was clearly acting within its legal rights, it was

24 Three of the cantons – Uri, Schwyz, Unterwalden – were the original members of the union (the "Urkantone") that formed the Eidgenossenschaft in 1291. The others were Lucerne, Fribourg, Valais, Zug.

25 Quoted in Remak, *A Very Civil War*, 26.

flirting with political dangers it could not easily control. For liberals, conservatives, Protestants, and, in fact, many Catholics, permitting the Jesuits to return to the canton, never mind allowing them to control education, was a grave political error. The liberals regarded the Jesuits as anathema to modern, enlightened thought. They represented "the empire of darkness and superstition" and "a dark power that had crept in from abroad." They embodied everything the liberals were trying to destroy in the Switzerland of the old regime. According to many Protestants and liberals, they aimed to "bring back the age of barbarism, of the Inquisition and the auto-da-fé," and threatened to destroy the liberal dream of a secularized, modern state; to weaken the stability and integrity of the country from within; and to turn back the achievements of the Swiss Reformation.[26] In many Protestant regions, the Jesuits, an obvious target for paranoia and conspiracy theories, aroused in the popular consciousness widespread and dreadful traditional fears, superstitions, and hatred. In pamphlets and songs that flooded the countryside Jesuits were described as "Damned corrupters of men's minds / Falsehood's satanic teachers / Reason's sinister enemies / From the guild of hocus-pocus." In 1843, Gottfried Keller, Switzerland's most important literary figure of the nineteenth century, became involved in the seemingly endless discussion with an abusive poem entitled "The Jesuit Parade."[27]

The timing of the liberals' opposition to the Jesuits and their desire to interfere in the affairs of Lucerne struck many, including Burckhardt, as crassly opportunistic. For a long time, Burckhardt recalled, the Jesuits had been in Fribourg and Valais. Although they had also moved into the mountain canton of Schwyz, they had conducted themselves well. They had not become involved in politics and their presence had been accepted without acrimony.[28] But in the early 1840s the radical liberals were suffering setbacks – in Zürich following the Strauss affair and the so-called *Züriputsch*, which overthrew the liberal regime in 1839; in Lucerne; and after May 1844, in the canton of Valais. In order to counter these defeats and the "boundless anger" they had caused, the radicals fell back on the one issue that was bound to spark popular outrage. Consequently, anti-clericalism and anti-Jesuit sentiment became a symbolic focal point in liberal political discourse and an important element of

26 Quoted in Sarasin, "Sittlichkeit," 80.
27 Remak, *A Very Civil War*, 28. Remak provides an excellent translation of this poem.
28 *Briefe*, 2:153.

their strategy to regain political momentum and power. Liberals' outrage found expression in the shrill crescendo of slander and abuse in their newspapers, which according to Heusler, by no means a neutral observer, was reaching a feverish pitch. In his commentaries in the *Basler Zeitung*, Heusler took special aim at the liberal press in Bern, Aargau, and Zürich, which he felt was inciting violence and intensifying the crisis through thoughtless, inflammatory criticism of Catholicism. This, he felt, raised serious questions about freedom of the press and responsible journalism. He reprinted the texts of two federal government decrees from 1816 and 1819, which made it an offence to slander either confession, and appealed to all governments to stop the abuse of the Catholics in the press, calling it the "sacred duty" of the state.[29]

The liberals and the radicals had no intention of moderating their attacks. Moreover, they did not content themselves with witty verse, slander, and public outrage. Throughout the Protestant, liberal regions, anti-Jesuit associations were formed; they organized petitions and protests, in an attempt to force the federal government to expel the Jesuits once and for all. When this failed, they mobilized groups of partisans, whose objective was to overthrow the ultramontanist regime in Lucerne. In December 1844 and in March 1845, partisans invaded Lucerne. In both cases, however, they were outnumbered and defeated by troops loyal to the canton. The rise of the *Freischärler* was ominous and portended the collapse of political authority. As Burckhardt pointed out, a power vacuum had emerged in Switzerland. The governments of the cantons – even the liberal ones – were unable and often unwilling to control the partisans. Likewise, the federal government was powerless. Faced with the anarchy of partisan warfare, the federal diet proved incompetent and useless. While men were dying, the federal government "played at diplomacy" (*gediplomätelt*). Only the parties seemed to possess any authority and they were thoroughly embittered and hostile.[30] In any case, Lucerne received no assistance from the federal authorities and, in December 1845, it formalized an alliance with the seven other Catholic-conservative cantons, the so-called "Special Federation," or *Sonderbund*, which was prepared to use arms to defend its rights and interests. Burckhardt, who as a journalist was obliged to follow events closely, feared that the mounting conflict between Catholics and Protestants had brought the country to the brink of destruction. He believed that a civil war, if not an outright religious

---

29 BZ, 13 August 1844 and 13 December 1844.
30 See *Burckhardt als politischer Publizist*, Dürr, ed., 95 and 98.

war, was imminent. As well, he predicted the possible intervention of foreign powers, which in fact was only avoided in 1847 by the rapid defeat of the Catholic cantons in the *Sonderbund* War and the timely manoeuvring by the English prime minister, Lord Palmerston.

. . .

Burckhardt's career as a journalist began in the midst of this volatile religious and constitutional crisis. He entered the political fray with a number of articles on the national sharpshooting festival, held in the summer of 1844 in Basel. This competition, which drew sharpshooters from throughout the country, was Switzerland's largest and most important national celebration. Although ostensibly non-political, the festivals in reality had been dominated by liberal and radical democratic clubs for many years and served as a platform for political agitation. In the wake of the *Kantonstrennung* and the hostility that event had generated towards liberalism and the federation, the canton of Basel-City had not participated since 1831. The occasion of the Basel festival was consequently seen by some as an act of reconciliation between the canton and the federation. While the Basel authorities hoped that the festival would remain non-partisan – "The festival should once and for all stop being what it has been for a decade: a focus of radical activities and a parade ground for overambitious people"[31] – liberals and radicals ensured that the pressing constitutional and confessional conflicts remained high on the agenda. Much to the disappointment of Basel's governing elite, which had only reluctantly agreed to host the national festival in the first place, their worst expectations were fulfilled. At gatherings in taverns and inns, at rallies and marches in the streets, and at speech after speech, liberal and radical politicians and their supporters called for the complete revision of the Federal Treaty, condemned cantonal nationalism and particularism, and vented their spleen on the Jesuits in Lucerne. At one such speech, the crowd was urged to "unite in a holy war to drive out these vermin."[32]

Burckhardt had harsh words for the opposition's political grandstanding and violent rhetoric. He deplored its radicalism and condemned it

31 Dürr, "Das eidgenössische Schützenfest," October 1937, 341.
32 Ibid., 345.

for using the festival as a stage for their political fights.[33] His editorial also implied a criticism of Swiss nationalism. Like so many conservative Baslers, Burckhardt had by no means come to terms with the *Kantonstrennung* of 1833, nor with the role played by the liberals and the federal government in that disaster. As he had revealed a few years earlier in a letter from Germany, he was by no means sympathetic to Swiss nationalism; nor, as Emil Dürr has remarked, did he join "the patriotic pathos of the Basel and Swiss liberals and radicals." Instead, he concluded his final commentary on the event of 26 July by pointing out that, instead of fostering reconciliation between Basel and the Swiss confederation, the radicals had sown discord by abusing the hospitality of their hosts.[34]

Burckhardt's criticism of liberal and radical nationalism did not go unnoticed by the opposition press. Shortly after his first editorial appeared, he wrote to Kinkel that the *Schweizerische Nationalzeitung* had led with an article entitled "The Editor of the *Basler Zeitung*: Traitor to the Fatherland."[35] Nonetheless, he did not relent in his criticism of the radical, democratic left, and his articles on the *Schützenfest* set the tone for his more important commentaries on the deteriorating political and confessional situation in Switzerland. His discussion of the Jesuit crisis, coming so soon after his condemnation of Swiss liberalism and radicalism and during this high point of Swiss nationalist sentiment, provoked an immediate response from the liberal press and embroiled him in further controversy.

Burckhardt claimed that his Jesuit article had been well-received in local conservative circles, but, in fact, it was poorly conceived and ill-timed; moreover, it revealed a definite lack of political and journalistic experience. The initial difficulty with this piece stemmed from the fact that Burckhardt appeared to argue both sides of the issue, and consequently satisfied no one. Burckhardt, whose attitude towards organized religion had undergone profound changes over the previous few years, was no friend of the Jesuits and opposed the ultramontane policies of the government of Lucerne. In words not much different from those spoken a few weeks earlier during the shooting festival by radical politicians in Basel, he accused the Jesuits of being "a curse on all lands and

---

33 *Burckhardt als politischer Publizist*, Dürr, ed., 46ff and 54ff. For his attitude towards festivals, see *Briefe*, 2:99 and 101.

34 *Burckhardt als politischer Publizist*, Dürr, ed., 10 and 56.

35 *Briefe*, 2:115.

individuals into whose hands they fall ... We know a little bit about their scientific triviality, the deplorable superficiality of their education methods, their false presentation of our history, and their agitation."[36] But then Burckhardt seemed to do a *volte-face*: it was wrong, he continued, to persecute the Jesuits without any legal basis and in open violation of the constitution. Any such action, he feared, would only make martyrs of the Jesuits. He concluded that although the Jesuits were indeed a plague on the land, they could not be persecuted since they had a legal right to settlement in any canton that so permitted. However, the main thrust of his argument – that the rule of law had to be maintained – was weakened by his initial statement. His call for more education, patience, determination, and loyalty, not to mention his criticism of the emotionalism and empty slogans of the liberals, appeared weak and contradictory, and fell on deaf ears.[37]

The liberal press pounced on Burckhardt. They maintained that if the Jesuits were a plague, then it behooved everyone, whether liberal or conservative, and regardless of legal niceties, to expel them before the disease spread and infected the entire country. This was no time for forbearance or legal niceties; direct action was the only "true education." As Karl Brenner, editor of the *Schweizerische Nationalzeitung*, remarked in a response that took particular aim at Burckhardt, "Either – Or!" He concluded by reminding his newspaper's readers that Burckhardt's articles, beginning with the shooting festival, had aroused "righteous indignation" throughout the entire land. He then warned the young editor not to pretend to be a "great statesman," suggesting instead that Burckhardt express himself more gently in the future, because he was now forever branded in the eyes of Swiss liberals.[38]

The liberals' response to the Jesuit article was of no great concern to Burckhardt. However, the fact that the commentary inadvertently caused considerable embarrassment to the newpaper's publisher, Andreas Heusler, worried the young editor a great deal. Heusler, in addition to acting as publisher of the *Basler Zeitung*, served as a professor of law at the university and was one of the canton's leading politicians. As Basel's representative to the federal diet, he was actually in Lucerne trying to mediate the crisis when Burckhardt's article appeared. The article, in fact, threatened to ruin his delicate diplomacy, because it

---

36 *Burckhardt als politischer Publizist*, Dürr, ed., 50.
37 Ibid.
38 Quoted in Kaegi, 2:412.

angered many Catholics in central Switzerland. It also made Heusler look hypocritical: just three days previously, he had condemned the liberal press for slandering Catholicism. In a letter to Burckhardt, he apparently suggested that the young editor was trying to change the newspaper's editorial policy on this sensitive issue.

Burckhardt, who vehemently denied that he had changed the newspaper's editorial position, tried to pursuade Heusler that he shared his conservatism, asserting that although their views might be nuanced he agreed wholeheartedly with the direction of the *Basler Zeitung*. In his response to Heusler's accusation, he emphasized with pride his contributions to the fight against liberalism and radical democracy. There was no doubt in his mind, he claimed, that the main enemy of Switzerland and Basel was the growth of extreme radicalism. "I consider it the happiest coincidence of my life," he protested to Heusler, "that I know and have learned to understand quite plainly the radicalism of all the more important nations, that I have perceived and been able to study first hand and at times against my will the political mechanism of the Carbonaro and the Paris radicals, the Berlin 'Freien', and the Basel loudmouths." Furthermore, he could not understand how he had changed the paper's direction: "The paper will never assume a different direction from the one that has been determined for years by your leading articles, and this is the direction to which I also adhere."[39] Nevertheless, shortly after Burckhardt's editorial on the Jesuits, and despite his protestations, Heusler took over responsibility for the lead articles.

Burckhardt continued to work for the *Basler Zeitung* and to write newspaper reports about the political crisis in Switzerland, but these articles now appeared in the Rhenish newspaper, the *Kölnische Zeitung*. Although their general tone is somewhat different – not least because he was reporting to a readership unfamiliar with the context and nature of events in Switzerland – his views were consistently conservative and remained close to the official position of Heusler and the government of Basel. In these articles he openly identified himself as belonging to the forces of Swiss conservatism, those individuals who "wanted no agitation at all, but instead would like to maintain peaceful progress under the constitutions of 1831 and 1832. With these agree all of those proprietors, industrialists etc. who demand peace at all cost, as well as the more moderate elements of the Catholic party."[40] Although he was criti-

---

39 *Briefe*, 2:110 and 106. See also Kaegi, 2:411ff. Heusler's letter to Burckhardt no longer exists.
40 *Burckhardt als politischer Publizist*, Dürr, ed., 57.

cal of the ineffectiveness of the federal government and understood that the Federal Treaty was far from perfect, he believed, like many other conservatives, that the liberals and radicals had begun to transcend the bounds of political reason.[41] Their politicization of the confessional issue had so exacerbated the crisis that a measured response was hardly possible any longer.

Burckhardt's greatest concern was that the principles of Swiss constitutionalism were being undermined. The radicals' assault on the Jesuits was simply a pretext for their continued attack on the Swiss constituiton. For Burckhardt and his conservative allies, the Jesuit question had become a fight for the historical, constitutional rights and democratic traditions of the cantons against the forces of centralization, a fight that had become hopelessly complicated and sidetracked by the confessional antagonism. Although the radical forces were content to attack the Jesuits, they also understood the conflict in terms of the "unity of the fatherland," and the need to strengthen and modernize Switzerland, versus the "aristocratic federalism" of the conservatives, which had weakened central authority and perpetuated national division. That the government of Basel was trying to mediate the crisis within the legal confines of the existing political arrangement antagonized the liberals, and some conservatives in Basel, who accused the local government officials of supporting the Catholic interests.[42] For many liberals, the distinction between the "the power of the Roman priests" and the local "aristocrats" had become increasingly blurred.

The conservatives clearly saw the liberals and the more extreme radicals as a dangerous revolutionary force. They had declared open war on the constitution, paying no heed to the legal rights of the cantons and the Catholics, and were determined to achieve their political objectives by whatever means suited them, whether legal or illegal – indeed, they were prepared to destroy the rule of law if need be. For conservatives such as Burckhardt, rule of law was paramount, despite the fact that the constitutional structure was imperfect and reform was necessary. He believed that by whipping up popular fears and creating national hysteria, the liberals were using the Jesuit question to mask their revolutionary agenda, which was the destruction of both the federal constitution and the legitimate authority of those conservative cantons, whether Catholic or Protestant, that refused to adopt liberal constitutions. While the

41 Ibid., 72.
42 The government was taken to task for its "awkward position in Swiss affairs." See the *Intelligenzblatt*, 25 April 1845; 10 April 1845; 11 April 1845.

liberals argued that they could disregard existing laws because the *Volk* was endangered by the presence of the Society of Jesus, their real objective was political revolution. As Burckhardt commented in an article for the *Kölnische Zeitung*, even if the government of Lucerne withdrew its invitation to the Jesuits, the radicals would simply find another excuse for continuing their political agitation.[43] While the Jesuits may have been a curse, he said, they were at least tolerable because they were law-abiding. The liberals and radicals, however, were no longer satisfied with legal avenues to reform and, through their violence, represented a more serious threat to the continued stability and security of Switzerland. By exposing what he considered to be the underlying motives of the liberals and pointing out the illegality and violence of their political action, Burckhardt made public the double standards of the movement. As he privately confided to Willibald Beyschlag, Swiss liberalism, with its empty phrases of freedom, equality, and popular sovereignty, had become "a thoroughly laughable phenomenon."[44]

The formal political and constitutional questions that concerned the modern state, perhaps given short shrift by Burckhardt in his later historical writings, were of great importance to the young editor in the context of Swiss domestic affairs. Although his experience elsewhere had taught him that consitutions were no panacea to society's ills – he knew that constitutions only worked if the public was willing to uphold them – he recognized that the survivial of most small states depended upon the rule of law, both domestically and internationally. He quickly became a staunch constitutionalist and federalist, arguing that "a federal republic must go to pieces if the federal states do not abide by their reciprocal rights."[45] He compared the situation in his homeland to that of Germany. If Prussia or Saxony had suddenly decided to invade Bavaria in order to get rid of the Jesuits, this would have represented the grossest of violations, leading to war and disaster. This was unimaginable, but, translated into the "lilliputian relations" of Switzerland, this was precisely what he saw happening. The constitution clearly stated that the federal government could only interfere in the affairs of individual cantons if requested by that canton. In effect, a canton could hand over its education system to the Turks, he proclaimed, if that afforded it pleasure: "Here the cantons are sovereign."[46]

43 *Burckhardt als politischer Publizist*, Dürr, ed., 70.
44 *Briefe*, 2:154.
45 Ibid., 2:153.
46 Ibid., 2:154.

While liberals might have regarded this as the principal weakness of the Swiss constitution and a just reason for restricting the cantons' authority, politically engaged Baslers intent on maintaining their political power and independence considered the rights of the cantons to be sacrosanct. Given the natural limitations of the *Kleinstaat*'s power, constitutions and the rule of law (and the will to abide by them) were the only guarantees to their continued existence, as the smaller German states had learned to their disappointment. Consequently, the primary concern of the city's emissaries to the federal diet was to uphold the treaty and keep the liberals from sacrificing cantonal rights in the name of a strong, centralized state. Only ten years earlier, Baslers had fought against a hostile central regime in order to prevent the diminution of their powers, and had lost. The Basel elite knew what the increased authority of a central, unitary state apparatus meant to its power and autonomy. They consequently watched with increased alarm during the winter of 1844–45 as the liberals, in a new level of violence, twice attempted to overthrow the constitutionally elected government of Lucerne.

As Switzerland lurched towards full civil war, Burckhardt commented on the fear and instability apparently destroying his country. The "concepts of federal law" had become "totally blurred," he said, respected by the liberals only when convenient. "Everything would have been happily solved and avoided, if only they had adhered to the basic word of the constitution." But this was not the case. Instead, the liberals – the "apostles of freedom" – wrapped themselves in the "mantle of liberty," believing they were the "bearers of the fate and hopes of Switzerland." They followed a "higher law" to which only they, apparently, were privy.[47] In the name of popular sovereignty and liberty, the liberals with their "leveling ideas of 1830" had aroused the revolutionary zeal of the masses, posing a far greater danger to individual liberties than the Jesuits ever could. "The word freedom sounds so beautiful and round," he commented to Kinkel, "but only he who has seen with his own eyes the slavery imposed by the screaming masses, called the *Volk*, and has patiently and observantly endured civil unrest, should talk about it ... I know too much history to expect anything else from this despotism of the masses than a future tyranny, which will mean the end of history." Although careful to emphasize the role of a politically mature people – an educated citizenry that could and should participate in political life – Burckhardt was sure that this did not exist in either Germany or Switzerland. Rather, these countries were now faced with the daunting

47 Ibid., 2:154–5.

prospect of volatile, explosive masses who, being uninformed, were consequently ripe for manipulation and destruction. While characterizing the citizens as still "political children," he admonished Kinkel to give thanks to God "that there are Prussian garrisons in Cologne, Koblenz and other places, so that the first crowd of communized boors can't fall on you in the middle of the night and carry you off bag and baggage." Fortunately, following the abortive partisan incursion into Lucerne in the spring of 1845, Burckhardt could write with a certain degree of pleasure that "the mobile anarchy, whose leaders thought they could go from canton to canton and mess everything up, has in the meantime run into a wall at Lucerne."[48]

In his correspondence as well as his newspaper reports, Burckhardt openly celebrated the defeats of the radicals. Following the successful defence of Lucerne against radical partisans in the second *Freischarenzug* in the spring of 1845, he described for his *Kölnische Zeitung* readers "Lucerne's sparkling victory" and the radicals' "humiliating defeat."[49] Indeed, the defeat was decisive. Ill-provisioned, poorly trained, and incompetently led, the ragtag forces under the charismatic captain of the Swiss General Staff, Ulrich Ochsenbein, lost over one hundred against a vastly outnumbered force from Lucerne; almost eight hundred prisoners were taken.

It would be a mistake to assume that because Burckhardt celebrated the defeat of the radicals he disapproved, in general, of democratic principles. As Kaegi has correctly pointed out, Burckhardt did not attack democracy per se, but rather the Swiss demagogues who, with their slogans and "sweet but meaningless phrases about freedom and civilization," deceived and manipulated the people.[50] As far as Burckhardt was concerned, the liberals had neither respected Swiss democratic traditions, nor behaved according to the spirit of democracy. Indeed, the chief accomplishment of Swiss liberalism had been to mobilize the discontented elements of society into a highly aggressive army, with complete disrespect for the existing constitution, private property, and life. To an extent, though, Burckhardt felt that the masses were not to blame. He believed that they had been seduced by the rhetoric of the radicals, about which the moderates could do little.[51] For the young

48 Ibid., 2:156–7.
49 *Burckhardt als politischer Publizist,* Dürr, ed., 105.
50 See Kaegi, 2:448–9.
51 *Burckhardt als politischer Publizist,* Dürr, ed., 105.

journalist, the future certainly looked dim. His fear went beyond that of continued radical agitation and confessional war. He spoke of two spectres haunting the nation. First was the lack of political moderation and the escalating violence in Switzerland; these, he felt, created a situation in which the neighbouring powers, France, Prussia and Austria, might be obliged to intervene for their own security, a threat that became likely two years later. Second, and perhaps more dangerous than foreign intervention, was his fear of religious and class warfare, for, as Burckhardt claimed, communism had already gained a foothold.[52]

. . .

When Burckhardt quit working for the *Basler Zeitung* at the end of 1845, he swore that he had put active political life aside altogether. Almost a year earlier, he had written that "the entire Helvetian political scene" had become "an albatross around my neck."[53] Over the course of his career as a journalist, he had developed a remarkable contempt for the political dealings that confronted him daily. With his last corrections for the newspaper completed, "the hour of his liberation rang out ... Since then, the world looks much different to me."[54] He longed to escape from "this dreadful racket, this inopportune public opinion, this crazy party politics,"[55] to Italy, where he hoped to resuscitate his creative energies and avoid political confrontation. To Hermann Schauenburg, he wrote that while his friends were "getting deeper and deeper into this wretched age," he had rejected it entirely. Thus he was escaping

to the beautiful, lazy south, where history is dead, and where I, who am so tired of modernity, will be refreshed by the thrill of antiquity as by some wonderful, peaceful tomb. Yes, I want to escape from everything: from the radicals, the communists, the industrialists, the intellectuals, the pretentious, the reasoners, the abstract, the absolutists, the philosophers, the sophists, the state fanatics, the idealists, the 'ists' and 'isms' of every kind. On the other side, I'll only meet Jesuits and among the 'isms' only absolutism, and foreigners usually know how to avoid

52 Ibid., 107.
53 *Briefe*, 2:153.
54 Ibid., 2:188–9.
55 Ibid., 2:197–8 and 2:189.

both. On the other side of the mountains, I must forge a new relationship with life and poetry if I am to become anything in the future.[56]

Towards the end of March 1846, Burckhardt made true his escape to the south. His destination was the eternal city of Rome, which would later occupy such an important place in his thoughts and work. Unfortunately, his stay was cut short by an invitation from Franz Kugler, in Berlin, to work in the Prussian capital revising his *Handbuch der Geschichte der Malerei* (Handbook of the History of Painting). Although happy to be once more among Kugler and his Berlin acquaintances – he was especially relieved that he was not in Basel, which he found so boring and philistine that it made a winter in Berlin an appealing prospect – Burckhardt loathed having to leave Rome: "Oh how hard it has been for me to leave Rome this time. I know now that I'll never be really happy outside of Rome."[57] Almost one year later, in late 1847, Burckhardt returned to Rome, where he stayed for six months. As Max Burckhardt has written, this was to be Burckhardt's major visit to Rome; although not a study or working visit, it was nonetheless productive in terms of his own artistic creativity.[58] It was also during this visit that he wrote a short, but important, article for the art journal, *Kunstblatt*, "Andeutungen zu einer Geschichte der christlichen Skulptur"(Suggestions about the History of Christian Sculpture).

During 1847 and 1848, Burckhardt, unable to avoid the political and social turmoil that held Europe in its embrace, found himself in the midst of much more serious political upheavals in Prussia and, later, in Rome. In effect, his second trip to Rome in late 1847 coincided with an uprising in the north against Austrian rule. Although in principle he supported the *risorgimento* in its struggle, he was once more critical of the emptiness of the liberal slogans of liberty and progress. Despite his intention to leave politics forever, between November 1847 and April 1848 he continued to write articles on events in Italy for the *Basler Zeitung*. Deeply disturbed by the scenes of chaos and anarchy, he felt overwhelmed by the sheer force of the masses and its potential for destruction. If anything, the experience of the Revolution of 1848 in Italy reinforced his fears of liberalism and mass democracy.

56 Ibid., 2:208.
57 Ibid., 3:36.
58 M. Burckhardt, "Rom als Erlebnis und geschichtliches Thema," 7–17.

By the time he returned to Switzerland in the spring of 1848, the political situation in his homeland had been irrevocably altered. The policies of Burckhardt and Heusler – their attempts to uphold the
constitution and mediate the crisis over the Jesuits – had won few con-
verts and had failed miserably. Even the Basel authorities were no
longer convinced of their efficacy.[59] Burckhardt found himself in Italy
during the war of the *Sonderbund* (October-November 1847), which saw
the Catholic league army dispatched, in record time and with minimal
casualties, by the federal army commanded by General Guillaume
Henri Dufour. Much to everyone's great relief, the European powers
did not have time to intervene. Nonetheless, it would be a mistake to
deny the seriousness with which the major European powers followed
events in Switzerland during the autumn of 1847. While conservative
politicians and rulers feared the consequences of a liberal victory, liberals across the continent rejoiced at the demise of the *Sonderbund* and the
subsequent proclamation of a liberal constitution. The Swiss success inspired them to actions of their own. As one recent commentator has
written, the Swiss civil war "acted as the catalyst for the series of revolutions that shook the continent in 1848."[60]

The civil war fundamentally changed the Swiss political landscape in
two main ways. First, rather than destroy the Swiss union, which could
have happened had the *Sonderbund* emerged victorious, the liberal victory consolidated the federal state and the union of cantons. Second,
the liberal constitution, based on the principles of popular sovereignty,
laid the foundation for the democratic system of today. In addition,
government and administration were modernized. Basic civil rights, for
instance, freedom of speech and religion and equality before the law,
were entrenched. Moreover, various reforms were introduced to enhance trade and industry, such as the establishment of a single currency, uniform weights and measures, and a federal postal service.
Equally significant, the constitution removed a major source of political

---

59 Kaegi, 2:454–5.
60 King Friedrich Wilhelm IV of Prussia wrote in a letter to Queen Victoria that "saving
Switzerland from the hands of the Radicals" was "simply a vital question." Remak continues,
"For if the side of the 'Godless and lawless' ... were to triumph in that 'most abominable
Civil War, then in Germany likewise torrents of blood will flow ... Thousands of emigrated
malefactors wait only for a sign ... to pour forth beyond the German border', where that
'godless band will march through Germany', intent on the 'murder of Kings, Priests and
Aristocrats'." See Joachim Remak, *A Very Civil War*, 155–156 and 175. See also Erwin
Bucher, *Die Geschichte des Sonderbundkrieges*, Zürich, 1966.

violence and conflict by outlawing secessionist movements and ending the cantons' traditional right to sign treaties with each other. As a last note, the Jesuits were banned altogether.

Despite strengthening the powers of the central state, the federal constitution of 1848 conceded enough to the cantons to make it palatable to conservative administrations. Thus a major source of contention, the guild system, remained intact in Basel and, elsewhere, a matter of cantonal jurisdiction. Although the constitution was accepted in Basel, it posed little threat to the continued hegemony of the patriciate, which successfully resisted any infringement on its authority until 1875.[61]

61 See for instance, M. Burckhardt, "Politische, soziale und kirchliche Spannungen in Basel," 49.

4

"Eminus Conservator"[1] – Burckhardt and Modernity

CONSERVATISM AS A SELF-CONSCIOUS political movement and ideology emerged during the late years of the eighteenth century in response to the "advance of modern forces" that threatened the "institutions, conditions, and principles of the *ancien régime.*" Its raison d'être, according to Klaus Epstein in his classic study of German Conservatism, was "conscious opposition to the deliberate efforts of the Party of Movement to transform society in a secular, egalitarian, and self-governing direction." In the case of Germany, and, we might add, Switzerland, the essence of conservatism as a specific historical phenomenon was resistance to the challenge of radicalism and the forces of modernity that threatened the traditional social and political order.[2]

A number of political theorists have identified the "belief in the [intellectual] imperfection of human nature as the theoretical foundation of conservatism in both its religious and secular forms."[3] This understanding of human nature stands in stark contrast to that generally espoused by philosophers of the Enlightenment and to the discourse of laissez-faire or classical liberalism as it developed over the course of the nineteenth century. These credos postulated that individuals are inherently rational, and that through the application of reason – and the self-interest that motivates the rational individual – society and human beings can achieve a better, more perfect world.

---

1 The quotation is from Burckhardt's poem, "Versenkt mich ins Tyrrhenische Meer," *Briefe,* 3:57.

2 Epstein, *The Genesis of German Conservatism,* 5–7.

3 Sigurdson, "Jacob Burckhardt's Liberal-Conservatism," 490.

The notion of the imperfectibility of mankind was deeply rooted in Burckhardt's consciousness. It found expression in his scepticism and pessimism, in his scholarly work, and, equally as important, in his fundamentally conservative political *Weltanschauung*. This basic assumption about human nature was deeply rooted in Basel's orthodox Protestant theological heritage. According to Thomas Howard, Burckhardt's thought was characterized by "a deep-seated historical and cultural pessimism inherited from the idea of original sin."[4] The Basel Confession of 1534 states: "For the power of sin and imperfection is so strong in us that reason cannot follow what it knows nor can the mind kindle a divine spark and fan it."[5] The Basel Confession, which consolidated the Reformation in the city-republic and remained the basis of Basel orthodoxy well into the nineteenth century, occupied a prominent place in Burckhardt's early religious upbringing. In the catechism written by his father for use in the religious instruction of Basel's children, which the young Burckhardt would have known by heart, emphasis was placed upon original sin. "That I by nature am inclined to sin, as the Scripture says," the children of Basel would incant; "every thought and action of the human heart is evil from childhood on."[6]

Burckhardt Sr.'s catechism, with its emphasis on imperfectibility, reflected the world view of many of Basel's leading citizens and was also an important manifestation of the continued attempt by the city's orthodox religious elite to protect the legacy of the Reformation in Basel from the external threats posed by the "modern scientific consciousness" of the "*philosophes, Neologen,* and *Aufklärer*." Its target was twofold: the principles of modern historical criticism, which threatened to undermine the "humanist synthesis between learning and faith" that characterized Basel's orthodox theology; and the enlightened, liberal notion of the perfectibility of mankind (and its corollary, the belief in historical and moral progress) as it manifested itself in the decades following the French Revolution of 1789.[7] It consequently had significant conservative political and social implications: it rejected radical change to the status quo and reinforced the existing structures of society and the power of the governing class.

4 Howard, "Historicist Thought in the Shadow of Theology," 323.
5 Quoted in Ibid., 276.
6 Quoted in Ibid., 298.
7 Ibid., 263–4 and 268. As Howard writes: "That changing society ipso facto meant improvement was in many respects unthinkable to these men, deeply steeped as they were in a religious *Denkweise* unsympathetic to the progressive ideologies of the Enlightenment," 275–6.

Despite Burckhardt's decision to abandon his theological studies and his subsequent apostasy, the concept of original sin (or the imperfectibility of mankind) continued to exert a strong residual influence on his personal beliefs, on his approach to history, and on his understanding of the historical process. He rejected the core ideas of the Enlightenment (which for Burckhardt were summed up in the works of Rousseau) that held that "human nature [is] assumed to be good once the barriers are taken down." Calling Rousseau a "plebeian," Burckhardt thought his *Confessions* were characterized by an "unnerving dreaminess, and virtuous feelings rather than virtue." Because Rousseau made "no use of the real, concrete life and sorrows of the French common man," he remained a "theorist, a utopian."[8]

The task Burckhardt assigned to himself as an historian, in contrast, was based on the study of the harsh reality of the human condition. "Our point of departure," he claimed, was "the one possible and remaining centre – man, suffering, striving, doing, as he is, was, and forever will be."[9] The study of history from this perspective revealed to Burckhardt, the "patrician," that the past contained no dreams, the present and future no utopias. Rather, there was good and evil, fortune and misfortune: "the life of mankind is a unit whose fluctuations in time and place constitute an up and down, a weal or woe." As a result, he spurned Rousseau's vision of an "ideal past," referring in his lectures to the "optical illusion with regard to so-called golden ages in which great spiritual capacities come together in a society, as though 'happiness' had a definite address or domicile at some *time* or in some *place*." He seemed to take special delight in pointing out to his students "how much general and inevitable *human* misery was present."[10]

Just as he rejected past golden ages – or for that matter dark ages – Burckhardt also spurned the Enlightenment belief that reason would liberate mankind and lead to happiness or perfection. The notion of progress was a myth, as was the possibility of utopia.[11] Here Burckhardt made an important distinction between progress as an historical value

8 JHH, 243.
9 WB, 226.
10 JHH, 24–6.
11 "Conservatives believe that the modern goal of establishing an earthly utopia – that is, a society characterized by universal happiness – is intrinsically unrealizable. It is unrealizable because the main handicap to establishing the millenium is not some easily overcome external social obstacle, such as monarchy, aristocracy, or clericalism, but rather the internal obstacle which exists in each individual as ineradicable original sin," Epstein, *The Genesis of German Conservatism*, 14.

or judgment (in the sense of improvement leading to perfection or happiness) and change, development, and growth over time (in the sense of technological and economic developments, or changes in ideas and values). Change occurred in both the material and spiritual worlds, he said, but this did not necessarily translate into historical or moral/ intellectual progress, or into individual or universal happiness. The meliorist vision of society offered by liberal philosophy was nothing less than self-deception and delusion. According to Burckhardt, it was a sign of spiritual or intellectual bankruptcy, of the triumph of a crude, destructive materialism. Because "we always have the criterion of material well-being before our eyes," he argued, we risk destroying existing systems, beliefs, and cultures, rather than creating new ones; furthermore, by rejecting the legacy of the past as inadquate and inherently flawed, we inevitably betray a condescending attitude towards the past and our cultural heritage. As he stated in his lectures: "We resist illusions – first of all, the illusion that humanity had been eager and longing, in the highest degree, to get out of the Middle Ages as a dark, unhappy situation. In a large view, the Middle Ages may have been a time of salutory delay. If it had exploited the earth's surface as we are doing, we would perhaps not be around at all. (Would that be a loss?) Let us assume that the period concerned was there, at least primarily, for its own sake rather than for ours."[12] Indeed, the commonly held assumption in the nineteenth century that people were living in an age of moral progress was, Burckhardt contended, "supremely ridiculous"; neither the human spirit nor brain "has demonstrably developed in historical times: [human] faculties in any case were complete long before."[13] As a result, Burckhardt maintained, what many people mistakenly considered to be moral progress was, in reality, nothing other than the abdication and "domestication of the individual" in the material world, brought about by the versatility and wealth of culture, and the enormous increase in the power of the state. Burckhardt even doubted the possibility of intellectual or scientific progress; indeed, he said, quite the opposite was probable. In one articulation of a favourite theme, he complained that "the progress of *Kultur* might have increasingly narrowed the consciousness of the individual. In the sciences, the discovery of isolated facts is already obscuring the general view."[14]

12 JHH, 65.
13 WB, 133 and 282.
14 Ibid., 282.

Equally erroneous as the belief in the possibility of moral progress, declared Burckhardt, was the popular argument that "our age is the consummation of all ages, or very nearly so, and that the past is to be regarded as fulfilled in us."[15] Burckhardt considered that the belief in historical progress was best typified in the philosophy of Hegel. He consequently took Hegel to task for assuming to be "privy to the purposes of eternal wisdom" when he argued that it is a given in philosophy "that the world is rationally ordered, and that history reveals the rational, inevitable march of the world spirit" towards freedom. This was nothing less than "the cautiously introduced doctrine of perfectibility, that is, our old friend, progress."[16]

Burckhardt's belief in the imperfectibility of mankind and his rejection of the notion of progress and the possibility of utopia places him within the general framework of European conservative thought and antimodernist discourse. As a political discourse, conservatism contained many different shades and offered highly nuanced analyses of, and solutions to, contemporary problems. Despite common goals and origins, conservatism represented more than just the defence of the political and social status quo when confronted by the challenge of radicals. Epstein's typology of conservatism – status quo conservatism, reactionary conservatism, and reform conservatism – is particularly useful in elucidating the specific dialects of conservative political discourse. Generally speaking, the primary characteristic of status quo conservatism is the belief that the existing order is satisfactory and ought to be defended. Reactionary conservatives, in contrast, believe that the existing order is fundamentally flawed and ought not be conserved; instead, they are embittered by the present and look back to the restoration of an earlier age. Finally, reform conservatives differ fundamentally from status quo and reactionary conservatives by accepting the inevitability of historical change and development, although they may not entirely approve of it. According to Epstein, the reform conservative enters into "voluntary cooperation with history," because "changes *will* occur either with the active cooperation of men like himself, who will spare whatever can still be preserved from the past, or by Radicals, who will frequently go much farther than necessary in destroying the *ancien régime* and will place no value whatsoever upon maintaining the maximum possible historical continuity."[17]

15 Ibid., 226.
16 Ibid., 152–3.
17 Epstein, *The Genesis of German Conservatism,* 7–11.

If we accept Epstein's typology, then Burckhardt best fits the description of a reform conservative. He definitely could not be categorized as a reactionary conservative, as was his colleague Johann Jacob Bachofen, for he understood that it was neither desirable nor possible to turn back the clock. As Burckhardt once claimed as a young man, restorations were no longer possible, and the "princes would do well if they recognized how their former position differs from their present one."[18] Moreover, although he often stated that his goal was to preserve the culture of "old Europe," he did not believe in "ideal pasts." Likewise, Burckhardt certainly was not a simple defender of the status quo. Often critical of the social and economic elite in Basel, as well as the government party, which itself was divided, he recognized the need for political changes both in Basel and the Swiss Confederation. He believed, however, that these changes were best achieved through gradual reform within the constitutional framework, thereby maintaining continuity with existing institutions and ideas, rather than through violence and revolution.

Although not wedded to the monarchical principle, conservatism in Basel, based as it was on the tradition of civic-republicanism, shared many features with early nineteenth-century German conservatism. Indeed, James Sheehan has commented that "the distinctive feature of early nineteenth-century German conservatism was its 'Janus-like' opposition to both bureaucratic absolutism and radical democracy, which conservatives regarded as parallel threats to religious orthodoxy, local autonomy, and traditional social institutions. Bureaucrats and democrats, they believed, advocated an abstract, universal notion of freedom behind which despotism inevitably loomed; both sought a legal and social equality through which society's organic cohesion and essential diversity would be destroyed."[19] These words capture the essence of Burckhardt's conservative world view, which he articulated when he described the purpose of his journalism as being to combat the "contemptible sympathies that reign here with all forms of absolutism (e.g., the Russian form)" and "the screaming radicalism of the Swiss."[20] While Burckhardt was not too keen to defend religious orthodoxy – indeed, he rebelled against it as a youth and was very critical of ultramontanism during the crisis years of the 1840s, a reflection of his general support

18 *Briefe*, 1:201.
19 Sheehan, *German History*, 592–3.
20 *Briefe*, 2:86.

of the separation of church and state – his desire to preserve local autonomy and traditional social (and cultural) institutions from the threat posed by reactionary, authoritarian rulers on the one hand, and by mass democracy on the other, was a defining feature of his political discourse.

Where Burckhardt's thought began to diverge significantly from that of German and Prussian conservatives was in his understanding of the state and power and their quest for national unity. Whereas in the 1840s and 1850s, conservative theorists like Friedrich Julius Stahl actively promoted the "progress from corporate particularism to national unity, from a patriarchal to a statist or constitutional system,"[21] the defining feature of Basel's conservative (and constitutional) tradition of civic-republicanism was its particularism. In this, we find an echo of the ideas of the prominent Swiss conservative theorist Karl Ludwig von Haller, who claimed that "smaller states are the true, simple order of nature, and one way or another she will always return to them eventually."[22] Haller, a member of the Bernese patriciate, was the author of the six-volume *Die Restauration der Staatswissenschaft* (1816–1822), which was intended to combat the "Ideas of 1789" and to create a sound theoretical basis for the restoration of the absolutist system of rule that had existed during the *ancien régime*. One of the most important conservative treatises of the early nineteenth century, it lent its name to the period. While most Baslers might not have agreed with his reactionary conservatism, Haller's particularism struck a positive chord among most conservative Swiss. Although Burckhardt may not have been directly familiar with Haller's writings – it seems highly likely, though, that he was – we know his father was, for some of Burckhardt Sr.'s writings drew on Haller's *Staatswissenschaft.*[23] Nevertheless, throughout Burckhardt Jr.'s work, we find a strong echo of Haller's particularism; a generally positive assessment of the value of the small state; and a negative disposition towards the evolution of modern, centralized power. In contrast to Swiss liberals, who sought to establish a centralized, unitarian state, Burckhardt was a federalist; along with other conservatives, he fought for the maintenance of a decentralized, particularist confederation of states or cantons in which the sovereignty and independence of the cantons would be preserved.

The struggle for the preservation of local autonomy against the pressures for centralization of political authority was not only a recurring

21 Sheehan, *German History*, 594–5.
22 Ibid., 591–2.
23 See Kaegi, 1:159.

theme in Burckhardt's correspondence and historical work, it also provided the justification for his jousts with Swiss liberalism and radicalism.
As well his particularism concurs, in general, with his understanding of
political power and his delineation of the role of the state and the individual in society. It lies, too, at the root of his conception of *Bildung* and
culture in general, and is manifest in his criticism of party politics, liberalism, nationalism, and militarism. In short, more than any other political concept, particularism best encapsulates Burckhardt's opposition to
contemporary political developments and his attitude towards the process of modernization in the nineteenth century.

. . .

Generally speaking, political philosophies are an attempt to articulate
ways in which society should be organized. As such, most political philosophy attempts to delineate the role of the state in society. A uniquely
German conception of the state has been identified as one of the "peculiarities" of German history. According to Georg G. Iggers, in German
political philosophy and in much of nineteenth-century German historiography, the state was "neither the nation in Michelet's sense nor [was]
it embodied in the history of parliamentary institutions in the British
meaning"; instead, it was modelled on the "enlightened *Obrigkeitsstaat*"
[authoritarian state]. Iggers concludes: "In place of the utilitarian concept of the state, as an instrument of the interests and welfare of its population, German historiography [and political philosophy] emphatically
places the idealistic concept of the state as an 'individual', an end in itself, governed by its own principles of life."[24] The state, then, was not
just the embodiment of power, but also of morality; only through a
strong, powerful state could liberty, prosperity, and cultural development be ensured. In his 1836 essay, "A Dialogue on Politics," Leopold
von Ranke added another important dimension to the discussion about
the nature of the state: it was now a "spiritual substance" which contained "a trace of the divine."[25]

---

24 Iggers, *The German Conception of History*, 8.

25 Ranke, *The Theory and Practice of History*, 129. The essence, perhaps, but not the substance, which Burckhardt captured when, as a student, he repeated to his sister that Ranke
had claimed that "Nations [*Völker*] are the thoughts of God!" *Briefe*, 1:161.

This organic conception of the state was not just limited to conservatives such as Ranke. Even German "moderate liberals" such as Johann Gustav Droysen or Friedrich Christoph Dahlmann rejected the mechanistic, utilitarian conception of the state that was central to classical liberal doctrine; they maintained instead that the state was not only "a natural product of historical forces," but also "a positive good, an ethical value without which culture and morality were impossible."[26] As both conservative and liberal historians and theorists wrestled with the problem of determining the essential locus of sovereignty in a modern society where the traditional source of power was moving away from the monarch to the *Volk* or nation, the organic conception of the state became a convenient refuge for those liberals caught between the desire to empower the *Volk* and to affirm or reaffirm the power and sovereignty of the state.[27]

Despite two years in Ranke's seminars, Burckhardt was not convinced by Ranke's theories of the state. Burckhardt condemned the growth of strong, centralized states and their coercive power. He considered the state to be neither a moral entity, the formation of which was the divinely conceived purpose of historical development and which was necessary for the realization of true individual and intellectual freedom, nor the repository of ethical values. In contrast to Ranke, for example, who subordinated individual liberties and rights to the needs of the state, Burckhardt saw the state, through its monopoly of power, as severely limiting free cultural expression and the freedom of the individual. He began his discussion of the coercive power of the state in *Reflections on History* by countering Rousseau's concept of the social contract. Like Haller, Burckhardt objected to the social contract theory because it postulated the fundamental natural equality of all individuals. He argued that history revealed that no state had ever been established by a general contract entered into freely and equally by all sides, and that none would ever be established this way.[28] Rather, the origins of states, primitive or modern, were to be found in coercion and the exercise of power. Force, he maintained, was always the primary consideration, necessatating an unequal

26 Iggers, *The German Conception of History*, 94.

27 It is generally assumed that the "organic" view of the state was the reserve of conservative thinkers. See for example, Sigurdson, "Jacob Burckhardt's Liberal-Conservatism," 491. However, as Iggers and Sheehan demonstrate, this was not the case, although Sheehan argues that a "deep ambivalence ... characterized most liberals' attitudes towards the state," Sheehan, *German Liberalism in the Nineteenth Century*, 39–40.

28 WB, 256.

relationship. "We are never at a loss as to its origin, because it arises itself through the inequality of human gifts. Often the state may have been nothing more than its systematization."[29]

"Now power," Burckhardt wrote, "is of itself evil, whoever wields it. It is not a persistent force, but is a lust and ipso facto insatiable; therefore it is unhappy in itself and must make others unhappy."[30] This, he claimed, was true not only for traditional, absolutist systems of government where power was wielded with violence and force against external and internal forces, but also for the modern, bureaucratic state where the means of exercising power were more subtle and refined. For Burckhardt, the state was the embodiment of power. His famous description of the "state as a work of art" in the *Civilization of the Renaissance in Italy* highlights the extent to which political power in the Italian states was rationalized, and the instruments of authority and coercion concentrated and systematized in the hands of a few despots. Burckhardt's conception of the state and its role in society, which cannot be separated from his understanding of the nature of power, reveals the extent to which his views of the state diverged from those that dominated both the conservative and liberal intellectual traditions in Germany. His analysis of the development of the Renaissance state, for example, revealed a mixture of good and evil that he claimed he found difficult to judge.[31] Still, he did judge, and found the state lacking in morality and legitimacy. In the two forms of polities he examined, republics and despotisms, he found for the first time "the modern political spirit of Europe, surrendered freely to its own instincts, often displaying the worst features of an unbridled egotism, outraging every right, and killing every germ of a healthier culture."[32] For Burckhardt, political power was not justified because it furthered the "ethical aims of the state," as many German intellectuals argued.[33] Indeed, he maintained unequivocally that the state was not a moral or ethical entity; as he put it, "The realm of morality lies quite outside that of the state."[34]

Although to some extent, Burckhardt regarded society as an organic, complex whole, he disagreed with Ranke, and most German intellectuals, who maintained that the state was a "natural and organic entity." On

29 Ibid., 257.
30 Ibid., 302.
31 CRI, 28.
32 Ibid., 20
33 See Iggers, *The German Conception of History*, 96.
34 WB, 262.

the contrary, he considered the state to be "an artificial, external, humanly-fabricated institution," the purpose of which was the exercise of power. As one recent commentator has noted, Burckhardt made a fundamental distinction between society and state: "Society is the repository of the cultural ideals of a people, while the state is an artificial instrument of coercion intended only as a guarantor of a people's security." From this conclusion, one of the central features of Burckhardt's approach to cultural history becomes clear: his rejection of nineteenth-century historiography's focus on the process of state formation.[35]

Still, Burckhardt could not ignore the historical importance of the state, and argued that the state should nonetheless strive to serve as the "'standard of the just and good' which must be set up somewhere, but ... is no more than that."[36] Burckhardt realized, however, that this ideal was rarely instituted. Here, his conception of the nature and role of the state most closely resembles that of the classical liberal theorists. In essence, he recognized that the state was an historical necessity but, because it was based on power and power was by its very nature evil, he advocated a strictly limited function for the state. Thus, the best way to ensure the liberties of the individual was, he felt, the non-interventionist state as implied in laissez-faire liberalism – the "nightwatchman's state," which through the exercise and maintenance of the rule of law regulated competing interests within society and provided basic security for the individual.[37]

Unfortunately, the exercise of power could not be easily reconciled with the freedom of the individual, a dilemma recognized by other nineteenth-century political theorists and philosophers. One of the most important historical trends Burckhardt (along with Mill and de Tocqueville) identified in his own century was the steady enhancement and growth of the state through the "lawless centralization" of political authority. Centralization, he declared, was a product of modernity. Burckhardt saw this process accelerating in the eighteenth century and reaching its apogee with the crisis of the French Revolution. According to him, political centralization represented nothing less than a "new

35 Sigurdson, "Burckhardt's Liberal-Conservatism," 491 and 500ff.

36 WB, 262.

37 Sigurdson correctly describes Burckhardt's support of the limited state as "grudging." It was not a "good in itself; it is the best of a bad situation," Sigurdson, "Jacob Burckhardt's Liberal-Conservatism," 500–1. But as Kahan also points out, the state in and of itself was not by nature a "mere nightwatchman, or the result of humanity's demand for justice." It was a "manifestation of power," Kahan, *Aristocratic Liberalism*, 60.

concept of the extent of the state's power." The growth of the state's monopoly of power during the Revolution arose, he argued, during a time of "danger to the fatherland" and was enhanced by the reduction of the independence of the church.[38] Through its manifold incursions into spheres of life that had previously been off limits, centralized states and administrative power represented the most dangerous threat to the liberty of the individual, while seriously reducing the authority and autonomy of local governments and administrations. The end result of centralization, avowed Burckhardt, was despotism and cultural and spiritual mediocrity.[39] Thus he portrayed the concept of equality, on which centralization was based, as a double-edged sword: "It turns into the abdication of the individual, because the more universal any possession is, the fewer individual defenders it finds. Once people have become accustomed to the state as the sole guardian of rights and public welfare, even the *will* to decentralization no longer helps."[40]

It is no coincidence that Burckhardt's most critical writings about the modern state and the process of centralization were advanced during the key development phases of the modern, federal Swiss state and during the Prussian-German state building of the late 1860s. In the latter years of the 1850s, he had explored the origins of the modern state in his study of Renaissance Italy. Over the course of the next decade, when the impact of centralization was being more strongly felt on the continent, he explored the problem in his *Reflections on History*, and in his lectures on the French Revolution. The Prussian-Austrian War of 1866 marked an important turning point. Not only did Burckhardt fear the end of many small states due to the increasing influence of nationalism and militarism – Prussian annexations confirmed this fear – but he also worried that this was the beginning of further, more dangerous conquests on the part of the Prussians, which, he believed, would eventually lead to a general European conflagration. Although the Franco-Prussian War did not turn into the expected large-scale continental war, Burckhardt believed it exemplified a now-ingrained temperament in the public spirit, an attitude both of permanent dissatisfaction with the way things were and of insatiable lust for power and expansion. He warned that the ensuing alarming sense of the provisory, unstable nature of political and social life could cast a dark shadow over traditional

38 JHH, 218–19. See also Kahan, *Aristocratic Liberalism*, 6off.
39 *Briefe*, 5:96.
40 JHH., 219.

relationships. "More serious than this is the complete despair about everything small ... Whoever does not belong to an Empire with 30 million people cries: Help us Lord, we're sinking! The philistine, like the devil, wants to eat from the biggest bowl, otherwise it no longer tastes as good." He waited with curiosity, he continued, for the time when hate for Prussia would bubble to the surface again in Southern Germany.[41] Such was the overwhelming desire for power, that it was little wonder that the general public viewed power as historically inevitable and indispensable. Only through the actual exercise of power, or belonging to a great political power, could the modern individual find satisfaction. Any form of decentralization of political authority in the age of nationalism, state building, and power politics was therefore abhorrent to modern ears.[42] Burckhardt's fears for the continued existence of the small state were especially acute during this time of European unrest and were restricted not just to the future of the smaller German states, but to Switzerland as well. Like many Swiss, he feared that Switzerland would enter into an alliance with France, thereby destroying Swiss neutrality and possibly provoking Prussia's wrath.

Despite Burckhardt's "flight to Italy" and his general rejection of Germany and the Middle Ages, his fears about Germany's future were concrete. Notwithstanding Bismarck's military victories, or indeed because of them, he had serious doubts about the future of a strong, united Germany; he worried, too, about the continuity of his much valued German cultural heritage in a state governed by the destructive forces of extreme nationalism and militarism. As Burckhardt argued in his *Reflections on History*, apropos the relationship between state, religion, and culture, the state posed a direct threat to cultural production because culture unsettled the authority of the state and religion, the influence of culture on the two constant powers [state and religion] being one of perpetual modification and disintegration. "It is their critic, the clock which betrays the hour when their form and substance no longer coincide."[43] According to Burckhardt, the state, when confronted by this challenge, inevitably sought to control cultural production, the only possible result being the general standardization of culture and conformity, or the domestication of the individual. Bismarck's state building confirmed Burckhardt's hypothesis and reaffirmed his doubts and fears.

41 *Briefe*, 4:226–7.
42 See wb, 302.
43 Ibid., 174.

"A people cannot be culturally and politically important at the same time," he maintained. "Germany has now made politics its guiding principle, and now it must bear that burden. O how the eyes of those wise men who are now celebrating Prussiandom, how they will open wide when they are forced to see that the desolation of Germany's spirit is dated from 1870."[44] More importantly, he believed that Germany's rulers had begun a process that they not only could not control, but which, in the end, would prove the source of their own destruction. Germany, he averred, would suffer the same fate it had inflicted upon its unsuspecting neighbours. As he reportedly claimed: "The Hohenzollern are digging their own grave. The huge movement that they have stirred up will pass over their body. I won't experience it, but you will. Altogether they are undermining the monarchy, because if the Prince no longer respects the monarchy, then who is supposed to? If in 1866 the Hohenzollern were able to push aside princes, with whom one had so often dined, then who can still respect monarchy?"[45]

· · ·

Not surprisingly, Burckhardt believed that the political entity best suited to the individual and the *Kulturvolk* was not a politically powerful nation-state, but the smallest of all possible political units; that, alone, could provide for the maximum of individual liberty and security of person. This was the essence of Swiss particularism and the centuries-old Basel tradition of civic republicanism. It was also the cornerstone of the conservative political discourse of Basel's governing class and of the city's policy with regard to the Swiss government during the first half of the nineteenth century. Burckhardt's particularism – and that of Basel's other conservatives – stood in sharp contrast both to the declared aims of Swiss liberalism and radicalism, which fought for increased centralization of political power and the creation of a unitarian state structure; and to German liberalism, which also sought the establishment of a strong, national state to counter the centrifugal forces of particularism.

Because Burckhardt considered that the vast increase in the power of the state over the subject in modern industrial society destroyed the

44 Quoted in Wegelin, "Jacob Burckhardt und der Begriff der Nation," 180–1.
45 Quoted in Kaegi, 5:555.

creative spirit of the individual and led to the domestication and abdication of that individual,[46] he admired and, indeed, at times idealized the
small state. However, he feared that a small state would lose its identity
and traditions if subsumed within a greater political entity; he feared,
too, that it and its citizens would lose their freedom. In other words,
there was a cost to pay for being small. Small states were often unstable
and susceptible to the aggressions of larger ones. Nevertheless, for
Burckhardt, the benefits outweighed these costs, because the small state
"exists so that there may be a spot on earth where the largest possible
number of its inhabitants are citizens in the fullest sense of the word."
This, he noted, was because the small state "has nothing but real, actual
freedom, which ideally will fully compensate for the powerful advantages of the big state, even its power."[47] In effect, Burckhardt never attributed to the system of small states in Germany (*Kleinstaaterei*) the
derogatory meaning given small states by Swiss liberals and German nationalists. He always believed that the golden age of German culture, the
age of Schiller and Goethe, had only been possible because of
Germany's numerous small nation-states that had enabled Germans to
hold European, as well as German, sympathies. The same was true of
Switzerland, he believed, where regional loyalties enabled the cultured
individual to look beyond the confines of the Confederation.

According to Burckhardt, the ideal of the small state was most closely
realized in the Greek *polis*, with its unequaled harmony between the individual, liberty, and the state. In contrast to the modern state, "which
desires that no one escape its material hold," the relationship between
the Greek city-state and the individual was based on a reciprocal sense
of duty and involvement; there the individual, recognized as a full, spiritual participant in society, was not isolated and antagonized by alien material forces.[48] Burckhardt spoke of the "unfettered" individual as
someone unified, not alienated, by government and power: "The complete individual in antiquity, is, above all, part of the state to a degree of
which we now, in the present mode of connection between the individual and the state, have no idea. Whenever one breaks with the *polis* or
when it is lost, it is a tragedy every time."[49]

46 WB, 282.
47 Ibid., 259.
48 Ibid., 297.
49 JHH, 6.

In contrast to his own "power-drunken century," the age of the city-state embodied, for Burckhardt, a harmony between politics and culture that enabled the greatest freedom for spiritual creation. It is no coincidence that Burckhardt compared the Renaissance Italian city-republic of Florence with the Greek *polis*. Florence and Athens were "great centres of intellectual exchange," he noted, where culture blossomed and mediocrity could not establish itself in the diverse, balanced, and fertile soil. Granted, there developed "a strong local prejudice." But, he maintained, this was based on the knowledge "that there was nothing one could not do, and that here was the best society and the greatest stimulation. They produce from their own citizens a disproportionate number of important individuals."[50] We could perhaps add another city to that list, namely Basel. Basel, which inspired in Burckhardt the same local prejudice and respect for culture, was home to its fair share of important intellectual figures. Indeed, it is Burckhardt's strong ties to Basel and his sense of *Heimat* that unifies the *Kulturvolk* and the *Kleinstaat*, the two poles of his loyalty. And it is a connection that could only be made by true citizens. Never was there any real doubt as to where Burckhardt's principal loyalty lay. Like the Athenian or the *uomo universale* of Renaissance Florence, it lay with his *Heimat*, the city-republic of Basel.

. . .

Despite his criticism of Basel's pietism and pettiness, Burckhardt remained throughout his life one of its most loyal citizens. His attitude towards Switzerland, though, is much more ambivalent. While it may have been his *Vaterland*, it never did have the same emotional pull as that of his *patria*. Indeed, if we can speak of a hierarchy of loyalties, it was certainly subordinate. This is clearly reflected in his politics. Although he never participated actively in political life, within the context of Swiss politics he remained essentially a conservative federalist. The debate between the defenders of the traditional "republican, federal system" and the liberal advocates of a centralized, unitary state did not end with 1848 and the creation of the modern, liberal state. Indeed, it reintensified during the discussions around the revision of the federal constitution in the early 1870s. Like many conservative federalists in Basel,

50 WB, 318–19.

Burckhardt's attitude towards federal politics was somewhat distanced and ambivalent, a reflection of loyalties divided between his *patria* and his *Vaterland.* He stoically accepted the new constitution of 1874, which further diminished the authority of the cantons and enhanced the power of the central government; but he criticized the liberals who dominated the government and continued to oppose further centralization. As late as 1891, he wrote that he was off to the polls in order to cast his vote "against this increase in the authority of the *Bund.*"[51]

The federal constitution of 1874 necessitated consititutional changes at the cantonal level. In 1875, with the overwhelming support (81 percent) of those able to vote, a new constitution was adopted in Basel. With its introduction of popular sovereignty – in which all Swiss residents of the canton, not just the Basler "*Altbürger,*" could vote – the constitution of 1875 brought an official end to the rule of the patriciate and the dual city/cantonal administration, ushering in an era of liberal/radical (*freisinnige*) government. For some, this "silent revolution" was a disaster: no longer was Basel a proud, independent republic; it had been ignominiously reduced to the status of a municipality.[52] Many of the old conservative elites nonetheless easily accommodated themselves to the new constitutional arrangement. However much they opposed it in principle, they continued to play a dominant role in the political life of the city until well into the twentieth century.[53]

Burckhardt's response was less accommodating, and his political views became much more pessimistic in tone. Events in Germany, as well as in Switzerland and Basel, no doubt contributed to this, his dislike of Bismarck's demagoguery being no less than his fear of democracy. His greatest concern with regard to political developments in Basel was not that a six-hundred-year tradition of civic republicanism had come to an end. Rather, he worried about the rise of mass democracy, which, he believed, would lead to socialism and the despotism of the masses. It seemed that his fear of the masses, first expressed during the religious and political crisis of the 1840s, had borne fruit. In contrast to the more "optimistic" 1860s, when Burckhardt made an attempt to accept the "healthy sense of the people,"[54] he was now confronted by the "ultra-democratic transformation" in Basel politics, and forced to drink from the "chalice of

51 *Briefe*, 9:325–6. See also Kaegi, 7:182ff.
52 Kaegi, 7:124. See also Kaegi, 5:503, "Basel Republic becomes Swiss Canton."
53 See Schaffner, "Geschichte des politischen Systems," 49–50, and Kaegi, 7:137.
54 *Briefe*, 4:127.

radicalism." He found that he "was no longer capable, in his advanced years, of finding these developments pleasant."[55] Burckhardt, whose sympathies during these years were with the conservative *Eidgenössischer Verein* and its principal organ, the *Allgemeine Schweizer Zeitung,* never doubted that socialism and radicalism were on the rise.[56] To his way of thinking, the triumph of democracy in 1874 in Basel was just the first step towards the despotism of the masses, and, possibly, the destruction of cultural life through the levelling effect of mass opinion and mass culture.

Even though the "democratic wind" blowing through Basel was in reality but a gentle breeze, rather than the hurricane he had envisioned, Burckhardt was determined to "remain at his post." "No matter how things go in Basel," he wrote to his German friend, Friedrich von Preen, "I'll be here."[57] In spite of the changes that had occurred in Basel – the rapid growth in population, the rise in construction, the intensified industrialization, the expansion of the working class, and the democratization of Basel's political structures – not to mention his opposition to many of the canton's officials and policies, Burckhardt remained loyal to his *patria.*

Burckhardt's loyalty to Basel is somewhat paradoxical. At times he appears to have been more loyal to the ideal of the humanist city-republic of free citizens, than to the actual city. Despite his criticism of the ruling class's philistinism, he continued to believe that the humanist ideal, consisting of civic duty and virtue, still existed and was worth nurturing. The notion of civic virtue or *Heimatsinn* has often been underestimated in the formulation of an individual's national sentiment and political identity. This was especially so in Burckhardt's case. Celia Applegate, in her work on the Palatinate, has demonstrated the central importance of regional loyalties in German political culture and in the development of identity. *Heimatsinn* was expressed in a wide variety of "regionally directed activities," such as writing local histories, organizing festivals, or even picking up litter – all of which were portrayed as a "civic-minded contribution to the health of the community."[58] In fact, regional identity or *Kantönligeist* has been a major factor in the formation of political culture and identity in Switzerland. Geographic, historical, cultural, religious, and linguistic

---

55 Ibid., 5:237 and 6:73.

56 Ibid., 6:73. On the *Eidgenössischer Verein,* the *Allgemeine Schweizer Zeitung,* and Basel politics during the last quarter of the nineteenth century see, Roth, *Die Politik der Liberal-Konservativen in Basel.* On Burckhardt's sympathies with this circle, see *Briefe,* 6:342, "Anmerkungen zum Brieftext."

57 *Briefe,* 5:237 and 225, and ibid., 6:68.

58 Applegate, *A Nation of Provincials,* 3.

differences inordinately determined, and still determine today, individual identity. That *Heimatsinn* could hinder the establishment of a strong national identity or consciousness was known only too well by Swiss liberals, who, try as they might, were unable to dismantle the political, ideological, and cultural barriers to cantonal particularism.

The expression of *Heimatsinn* through civic virtue has long been considered a particular characteristic of the Swiss. Gordon Craig identifies civic virtue, with its deep historical roots, as "a necessary condition of national existence in a world dominated by great powers." Whether as a response to the Great Powers, to the cultural and linguistic composition of Switzerland, to the unique political constellation of the federation, or to geographic obstacles only overcome in the nineteenth century, Craig is correct in emphasizing civic virtue as a cornerstone of Swiss political culture. Of course, Craig is at pains to point out how this was an especially liberal phenomenon: Swiss liberals "were more explicit in their invocation of the principle than had been true in the past and, when they were in power, used the schools and popular festivals to exalt it as a patriotic obligation of the individual."[59]

However, public manifestations of civic virtue were by no means restricted to the political agenda of the liberals. In Switzerland in general, and Basel in particular, demonstrations of civic virtue served a conservative political agenda; whether uniting regional traditions and loyalties as an alternative to the demands for a strong central, national state, or providing a legitimating discourse for the political and social status quo. One such evocation of civil virtue has been the subject of recent historical inquiry. The "Basel Unification Festival" of 1892, considered by its organizers as a unifying exercise during "a time of social tension and alienation in an increasingly anonymous large city,"[60] was enormously successful, attracting thousands of spectators and, with few exceptions, holding the residents of the city spellbound for its duration. One exception was Jacob Burckhardt. Perhaps he still recalled the unpleasantness of the Swiss sharpshooting festival held in Basel almost half a century earlier. Regardless, he did not approve of this type of display and expressed his scorn to von Preen: "At present our existence here is totally dominated by one of the most senseless and gigantic festivals ... the glorification of the year 1392, when Gross-Basel and Klein-Basel became one city ... For my part, I am naturally excused because of age, and

59 Craig, *The Triumph of Liberalism*, 237.

60 See Sarasin, *Stadt der Bürger*, 308ff; and ibid, "Domination, Gender Difference and National Myths," 144.

don't have to participate, and will be completely satisfied only if the whole pathetic fraud passes without incident."[61]

For Burckhardt, such festivals were food for the masses: bread and circuses. Such prominent displays of patriotism and nationalism were the embodiment of a type of mass culture, the *Kulturfäulnis*, that he despised. They examplified what David Gross has referred to, albeit in a different context, as the "sort of culture – perhaps kitsch is a better word – [that] was manufactured for the majority ... designed merely to entertain or titillate, not to elevate. It was a pseudo-culture without soul and led to what Burckhardt called 'universal falsification'."[62] As a consequence, Burckhardt believed that such parades tended to diminish civic pride, rather than enhance it. They were no substitute, he felt, for true *Bildung* and *Kultur*.

Burckhardt's own strong sense of civic virtue found expression in another forum, in his deeply felt obligation to the cultural education and development of his fellow Basel citizens. He, along with others such as Bachofen and Overbeck, considered it their duty to preserve Basel's "cosmopolitan tradition of *Bildung* under modern conditions that were hostile both to it and to the survival of the patriciate that had nurtured and sustained it."[63] In this case, *Bildung* represented a conservative vision of civic virtue, one explicitly directed at cultivating the elite of Basel society rather than educating the masses. This was the driving force behind Burckhardt's dedication to his university, his teaching, and his students. As one commentator has observed, this form of "civic humanism" that "extols the intellectual, aesthetic, and moral cultivation of the individual as a necessary requirement for worthwhile community life in a free society" was, according to Burckhardt, the "only proper role for an intellectual in mass society."[64]

. . .

61 *Briefe*, 10:36. Ironically, Burckhardt's views coincided with those of the local Social Democrats, who also called the pageant a "pathetic fraud." See Sarasin, "Domination, Gender Difference and National Myths," 144. He also expressed his disdain at the *Eidgenössische Sängerfest* that was held in Basel in 1875. See *Briefe*, 6:72, and Kaegi, 7:140–1. Gross-Basel refers to the main city on the south side of the Rhine, Klein-Basel to the smaller section on the north or German side of the Rhine.

62 Gross, "Jacob Burckhardt and the Critique of Mass Society," 398–9.

63 Schorske, "Science as Vocation in Burckhardt's Basel," 206.

64 Sigurdson, "Jacob Burckhardt: The Cultural Historian as Political Thinker," 420.

The ideal of *Bildung* came to the forefront of educational theories during the last decade of the eighteenth century and the first decade of the nineteenth century. The central concept underpinning the new discourse of neohumanism, it found its most poetic and complex expression in Friedrich Schiller's *Über die ästhetische Erziehung des Menschen* (1795). Equally as important were the various writings of Wilhelm von Humboldt.[65] In simple terms, the concept of *Bildung* (and neohumanism in general) arose in reaction to the rationalism of the Enlightenment and the egalitarianism of the "Ideas of 1789." The notion of *Bildung*, or "genuine cultivation" according to Anthony J. La Vopa, was conceived specifically in contrast to "mere instruction or training, and indeed against mere education (*Erziehung*) in the rationalist sense. The key words of Enlightenment orthodoxy – merit, service, duty, usefulness – were ignored, or dismissed contemptuously, or given entirely new connotations."[66] The attempt to redefine the terms of education, humanity, and ultimately individuality, which was explicit in the concept of *Bildung*, served a particular sociological and ideological function: the attempt by the growing class of educated middle-class Germans (the *Bildungsbürgertum*) to redefine and enhance their status within Germany's aristocratic, hierarchical society. *Bildung* became "a neoaristocratic surrogate for pedigree and courtly breeding; as a distinctly bourgeois assertion of educational achievement and personal merit in the face of aristocratic pretensions; as a hybrid, at once aristocratic and bourgeois, legitimating a mixed elite."[67] While it had pretenses towards equality of opportunity – for example, it was possible for the poor, through individual effort, to acquire the requisites of *Bildung* – its requirements and goals automatically set it against the uncultivated masses and above the mere technical expert. In the German states, the ideal of *Bildung* would ostensibly provide both an avenue into the ranks of the bourgeoisie and an avenue, for the bourgeois, into the public service and positions of authority; at the same time it kept separate those socially below them.

The successful penetration of the concept of *Bildung* into the consciousness of the rising middle classes was due in large part to its "chameleon-like capacity to refract the social norms of several groups at

---

65 Of particular importance are two essays by Humboldt: "Theorie der Bildung des Menschen" (1793), and "Über das Studium des Altertums und des griechischen insbesondere" (1793), in which he develops a holistic conception of the study of antiquity.

66 La Vopa, *Grace, Talent, and Merit*, 264.

67 Ibid., 266.

once."[68] In Germany, where the middle classes were defined as much against the aristocracy as against the lower orders, *Bildung* was easily adapted to the liberal cause. *Bildung* was associated with liberation, with spiritual and political reform.[69] In other regions and in different historical circumstances, *Bildung* refracted a different set of social norms and served a conservative political agenda. Perhaps the most important example, here, is Basel. For members of Basel's upper middle class, which ruled in its own right and did not have to define itself against an aristocracy – indeed, this class was regarded (and regarded itself) as a de facto "aristocracy" or "patriciate" – *Bildung* could and did provide a legitimizing ideology, by providing opportunities for the youth of the elite to enter the ranks of government and administration on the one hand, and by conferring legitimacy on the corporate political and social structures of the city-republic, on the other. If in Basel the patriciate was not technically an aristocracy, because birth was not a prerequisite for privilege and entry into the upper echelons of society, then *Bildung* certainly became that surrogate.

As Lionel Gossman has recently shown, the debate over the merits of *Bildung* was played out in Basel in the early decades of the nineteenth century in discussions about educational reform. On the one hand, liberals supported a French model of "enlightened," modern education that stressed practical, technical studies. On the other, the conservative elite, including many of the most important merchant families, supported the concept of *Bildung*, with its emphasis on "humanist" studies (i.e., languages, classics, history).[70] Although the authorities in Basel tried to balance the "realist" and "humanist" camps – Basel, after all, had not become an important commercial and trade centre by being unpragmatic – the concept of *Bildung* remained paramount to the formation of Basel's ruling elite. And it continued to define the function of the university which, as the symbol of elite *Bildung* and neohumanism, was continually attacked by liberals.[71]

Burckhardt's strong sense of civic responsibility and identification with Basel is inextricably linked to the concept of *Bildung*, and in this sense it was inherently conservative. Even with its obvious political and ideological implications that reached back to a past ideal, *Bildung* never

68 Ibid.
69 See Sheehan, *German Liberalism in the Nineteenth Century*, 14–18.
70 Gossman, "The 'Two Cultures' in Nineteenth-Century Basel," 99.
71 Basel's *Pädagogium*, where Burckhardt also taught, blended the "realist" and "humanist" curriculum. The latter served as preparation for university.

lost sight of the present. Gossman best sums up the connection between *Bildung* and the ideal of civic-republicanism that formed the basis of Basel conservatism when he writes that "the core of the neohumanist idea of education is a vision of the state, inspired by the Greek *polis*, as a liberal community of free, independent, and well-rounded citizens. Through its emphasis on the freedom and integrity of the individual with respect to the state, that vision is opposed both to the feudal-absolutist *ancien régime*, even in its 'enlightened' guise, and to the absolute centralized power claimed by the revolutionary regimes." Indeed, Gossman maintains that "the elevation of the Greek signified the affirmation of culture and 'spirit' in face of power (and even of politics) or 'matter'."[72] For Burckhardt there was little doubt that the neohumanist tradition of *Bildung* was the better path to take. It provided a model suited to the needs of both the *Kleinstaat* and the *Bürger*, the education of whom was Burckhardt's highest duty.

Bildung was much more than a legitimizing ideology as far as Burckhardt was concerned. It was also well-suited to his psychological temperament, his critique of modernity, and his understanding of the intellectual's role in modern society. Hardtwig has outlined how Burckhardt's *Amtsethos* (sense or ethic of duty) merged with his conception of *Bildung* and asceticism in opposition to the phenomenon of power, in both the historical world and its subsequent representation in historiography, as well as the very practical world in which he lived.[73] In an age of crisis and revolution, individuals cannot escape the impending sense of powerlessness and alienation through recourse to materialism, egotism, or violence; rather they must seek the solution within themselves and within the spiritual continuum of the past that unites all humankind. *Bildung* consequently provided Burckhardt with the necessary bridge between his day-to-day existence and his ascetic and aesthetic impulses. The very centrality of the goal of holistic self-realization to *Bildung* reveals the extent to which it was conceived as an essentially ascetic phenomenon. The pursuit of inner knowledge and self-exists cultivation as a spiritual calling, as a means of personal salvation in a time of crisis. *Bildung* consequently represents ascetic self-mastery and self-possession, the requirement of true culture and education. Devotion to this ideal empowers and liberates the subject. An exercise in the power of mind

---

72 Gossman, "The 'Two Cultures' in Nineteenth-Century Basel," 100–2.

73 See Hardtwig, "Wissenschaft als Macht oder Askese," his *Geschichtskultur und Wissenschaft*, 161–88.

over body, it represents a self-imposed dedication to the spirit and the control of corporeal temptation. In an age in which both the mind and the body were being increasingly managed by a society that was refining its controls over the subject, *Bildung* emerged as the only source of true individual freedom.

In his study of history, Burckhardt proceeds from an examination of good and evil in history to the problem of survival in modernity. In a final repudiation of the Enlightenment, he argues that *Bildung*, not happiness, must be the goal of life: "We have imperceptibly passed from the question of happiness and unhappiness to that of the survival of the human spirit, which at the end appears as the life of one person. This life, as it becomes self-conscious *in* and *through* history, must capture the gaze of the thinking man, and the general explanation and pursuit of this must lay claim to his efforts so that the concepts of happiness and unhappiness will more and more lose their meaning." In a footnote, he added that the "goal of those capable – nolentium, volentium – is not happiness but knowledge: 'Maturity is Everything'."[74]

These sentiments, also mirrored in his correspondence, reflect Burckhardt's darker mood of the 1870s. Writing in the aftermath of Prussia's war with France, he worried not about the continuation of French culture, which would survive defeat, but for German culture, which he believed had been sacrificed on the altar of militarism and faced defeat in victory. Believing contemporary German society was modeling itself on the military, that its forms, symbols and concepts were penetrating and reshaping German society and culture in its image, he argued that the only solution, if Germany was to avoid the specter of totalitarianism, lay in a return to the spiritual. To his friend Arnold von Salis, he counselled that "the new, the great and the liberating must emerge from the German spirit and in contrast to power, wealth and business; it will have to have its martyrs."[75] Like Nietzsche, with whom he shared his fears, he was afraid of the growing nationalism and militarism and was critical of the cultural philistinism which seemed to him, but not to Nietzsche, to be embodied in the work of Wagner. After Prussia's disturbing victory over France in 1871, Burckhardt wrote to von Preen that the national spirit and soul of the people could only be revived by "ascetic people."[76] He therefore viewed asceticism as a condition of survival and rejuvenation, not just for himself but also for humankind.

---

74 WB, 245.
75 *Briefe*, 5:159 and 160–1.
76 Ibid., 5:183.

Part 2   Burckhardt and History

5

History: Science versus Poetry

IN APRIL 1841, after an exhausting, somewhat lonely, but still worth-while trip from Berlin, Burckhardt arrived in the Rhineland city of Cologne: "Sancta Colonia." The goal of Burckhardt's spring journey was the summer semester at the university in Bonn. The objective of this particular trip to Cologne was the cathedral: "St. Martin's appeared first, then out of the trees arose the Cathedral. The city took shape, ev-erything so glorious! I quickly settled the business of my arrival and raced like mad to the Cathedral."[1] Like many Germans, young and old, Romantic or conservative, Burckhardt's enthusiasm for Cologne cathe-dral knew no bounds. It was, he thought, like no other church in the world, "the inexplicable revelation of an incomparable, heavenly ge-nius."[2] Over the next few years, the cathedral would play a significant role in Burckhardt's life. Besides showering it with praise in his *Kunstwerke der belgischen Städte* (1842), he used it as a central theme of his major work on Conrad von Hochstaden (the founder of the cathe-dral) written for Ranke's seminar. It became a concrete symbol of his enthusiasm for Germany, the Middle Ages, and Germany's cultural heritage.

Burckhardt's arrival in Cologne came just a few months after the Prus-sian King, Friedrich Wilhelm IV, made official the decision to complete the cathedral. For many decades, the Cologne cathedral, unfinished since the Middle Ages, had been a rallying point for German liberals and romantic nationalists. Writing in the *Rheinischer Merkur* in 1814, the journalist Josef Görres, who had made his name as an opponent of the

---

1 *Briefe*, 1:174.
2 Ibid., 1:175.

French occupation of the Rhineland during the 1790s, emotionally re-called the spirit of the past in order to proclaim his exuberance for the future: "In its fragmented incompleteness and bleakness," the Cologne cathedral had long been a symbol of a Germany in a state of confusion. Now, however, it would become "a symbol of the new Empire that we want to build."[3] With Friedrich Wilhelm's official sponsorship, the cathedral now became the focus of a strand of increasingly prominent, conservative German nationalism. At the festival of 1842, which celebrated the start of construction and served as a conservative, nationalist counterfestival to the earlier liberal festival at Hambach, "the Cologne cathedral ... was to be seen as a symbol of an unfinished German national unity, whose construction would be carried out by the existing authoritarian states, rather than involving their reform or destruction, as left-wing nationalists wished."[4]

Besides reflecting the need for national symbols and serving as a potent source of nationalist pride – even Franz Kugler called the Cologne cathedral "the most sublime monument of the German spirit"[5] – the German public's passionate enthusiasm for it represented something much more enduring: a new and intense interest in history and the historical. The cultural critic, Stephen Bann, has described the early nineteenth century as the "forcing period of historical mindedness."[6] During this time of great transition, as individuals began to come to terms with the violence and rapidity of historical change that followed in the wake of the French Revolution and the Napoleonic Wars, and as the bourgeoisie became increasingly aware of its new-found importance and power within civil society, history assumed a crucial element in the identity of the literate public sphere and of the nation itself. In short, historical consciousness, perhaps more than anything else, defined the cultural literacy of the age.

With its enthusiasm for the Middle Ages, this new historical awareness was a defining element of particular intellectual movements, such as romanticism. However, the awareness, rather than being restricted to the elite or to intellectual circles, penetrated all levels of society, especially

3 Quoted in Jenderko-Sichelschmidt, "Die profane Historienmalerei," 98.

4 Quoted in Jonathan Sperber, *Rhineland Radicals*, 114. The presence at the festival of the King, Archduke Johann of Austria, and of Metternich "underscored its political intent." On 4 September 1842 the king laid the first stone in a national ceremony.

5 Quoted in Kaegi, 2:112. Kugler and Burckhardt visited Cologne together in the summer of 1841, possibly August. See Gilbert, "Jacob Burckhardt's Student Years," 260.

6 Bann, *The Clothing of Clio*, 2.

the middle classes. Public excitement about the plans for the Cologne cathedral represented just one powerful, highly visible manifestation of the passionate concern for public historical monuments.[7] Historical themes also became a dominant feature in the literary world, with the proliferation of historical novels, and in the art world, with the revival of the genre of historical paintings, which were shown at exhibitions criss-crossing Germany and were seen by thousands of people in galleries and via the new reproductive techniques. Similarly, the public's desire to re-capture, record, and relive the past found expression in the mania for collecting; in the proliferation of local historical and antiquarian societ-ies (*Geschichtsvereine*) (over forty by 1844); and in the establishment of local and regional museums dedicated to the collection and preserva-tion of artifacts and the compilation of local histories. Although these societies often only served local interests, thereby strengthening and preserving the particularism that characterized Germany during the *Vormärz*, they nonetheless played a crucial role in cultivating the public's historical consciousness and identity. Membership in these societies was drawn not from the ranks of professional historians, although some were certainly members, but primarily from the educated middle class, the *Bildungsbürgertum*, which included teachers, civil servants, lawyers, merchants, physicians, and librarians, among others.[8] More than at any time previously, and perhaps since, at almost every level of society, peo-ple were expressing a new consciousness of the past and of how history shaped their lives and world.[9]

Nowhere was this awareness of history more evident than in academic and intellectual circles, where historical knowledge was considered the only basis for understanding human, social, and cultural development. The study and interpretation of law, art, economics, and theology – in short all aspects of social, political, and cultural development – became historicized. Many scholars recognized this as a particular characteristic

7 The elevation of the Gothic to the status of a national, "German" style – even if most art historians agreed that Gothic architecture was of French origin – was another manifes-tation of this. See Kaegi, 2:112.

8 Hartmann, "Die deutsche Kulturgeschichtsschreibung," 68–72.

9 Telman states that the historical profession "created the need for historical knowl-edge and argued that such knowledge contributed to the self-understanding and thus to the well-being of the community," in Telman, "Clio Ascendant," 461. While the latter point is certainly valid, it could also be argued that the development of the historical profession was partially a response to an existing need, given the extent of informal, public interest in history going back well into the eighteenth century. One must also avoid equating histori-cal knowledge solely with that offered by professional historians.

of their age, Burckhardt included. Indeed, Burckhardt justified his lectures on the study of history by emphasizing how "history and the historical observation of the world and time has generally begun to penetrate our entire education and culture."[10]

. . .

The emergence or discovery of this "historicity" has been the subject of much discussion and debate. This, of course, is not to suggest that previous generations were somehow lacking in historical sensibility, a sensibility that, once lost at some indiscriminate point in the past, subsequently required rediscovery. Hayden White correctly reminds us that the transition from Enlightenment historiography to historicism did not "so much signal the rebirth of a *genuine* historical sensibility as mark an important transition from one *form* of historical thought to another."[11] The issue, however, remains clouded, in large part because "historicism," the term employed to define the emergence of this "historical mindedness" or "historicity," has multiple meanings. For the purposes of this general overview, historicism refers both to a theory of historical knowledge and to a specifically German practice or tradition of historiography. Otto Gerhard Oexle refers to these two phenomena respectively as Historicism I and Historicism II.[12] To avoid confusion, I shall use the term historicism to refer to the theory of historical knowledge. Thus, when I discuss the German tradition of historiography, I shall refer either to the German historical school or to German historicism.

Traditionally, German intellectual historians and philosophers have argued that a radical transformation occurred during the last decades of the eighteenth century and the first decades of the nineteenth century. The nature of this radical transformation was captured by Karl Mannheim in 1924 when he argued that historicism represented a development from the "static philosophy of Reason" of the Enlightenment, to a "dynamic historical philosophy of life" that was to become the defining feature of modern thought. Historicism, in other words, was nothing less

10 WB, 83.

11 White, *Tropics of Discourse*, 138.

12 Oexle, "Historismus," 119–55 and "Die Geschichtswissenschaft im Zeichen des Historismus," 17–55. For references to the vast literature on historicism and the best recent surveys see Iggers, "Historicism," 129–52, and the article by Telman, Review Essay, 249–65. Iggers, *The German Conception of History*, remains indispensable.

than a revolution in thought, representing the rejection of the philosophy of natural law, "the idea of the persisting identity, the eternal sameness, and the *a priori* character of the formal categories of Reason" – all of which characterized Enlightenment thought.[13] This argument was further developed by Friedrich Meinecke in his work, *Die Entstehung des Historismus* (1936). Briefly, Meinecke attempted to place this new "historical mindedness," or historicism, within a clearly defined conceptual and contextual framework and to distinguish this new intellectual spirit, the "age of historicism," from what preceded it. Essentially, Meinecke argued that a new theory of historical knowledge gained currency during the late eighteenth and early nineteenth centuries, as individuals began to apply new standards to judging human nature and historical time. In general terms, like Mannheim, he agreed that "modern historical thought" or "historicism" resulted from the rejection of the "two-thousand-year domination of the theory of natural law, and the conception of the universe in terms of 'timeless, absolutely valid truths which correspond to the rational order dominant throughout the universe'." Following the work of Giambattista Vico (1668–1744) and, most importantly, Johann Gottfried Herder (1744–1803),[14] Meinecke maintained that man made history – that there was not one single, coherent history, but many histories – and that all human values, culture, and thought were conditioned by history and were unique or individual. In other words, no reality or meaning existed outside of history; "every age must be viewed in terms of its own immediate values"; and "there is no progress or decline in history, but only value-filled diversity." With the triumph of historicism, then, "the recognition that all human ideas and values are historically conditioned and subject to change, had become the dominant, inescapable attitude of the Western world."[15] It was, in Mannheim's words, a *Weltanschauung*, or what we might today call a discourse or a "grand narrative," that provided unity, meaning, and totality, and constituted a coherent and self-referential way of both seeing and conceptualizing the world. No "fad" or "fashion," no mere "intellectual current," it had indeed become "the very basis on which we construct our observations of the socio-cultural reality." In short, historicism had become the very condition of modern existence.[16]

13 Mannheim, *Essays on the Sociology of Knowledge*, 91 and 93.

14 Vico's *New Science* appeared in 1725; Herder's more influential *Auch eine Philosophie der Geschichte* appeared in 1774.

15 Iggers, *The German Conception of History*, 5 and 30; Iggers, "Historicism," 133. Thus Ernst Troeltsch would write that historicism was the "fundamental historicization of all our thought about mankind, his culture and his values," *Gesammelte Schriften*, 3:102.

16 Mannheim, "Historicism," in *Essays on the Sociology of knowledge*, 85.

The work of Mannheim, Meinecke, and Ernst Troeltsch was of fundamental significance in defining this new theory of historical knowledge.
Meinecke and Troeltsch, in particular, emphasized that historicism was
a uniquely German phenomenon. It was, they said, "Germany's greatest
contribution to Western thought since the Reformation and 'the highest stage in the understanding of things human attained by man'." It
represented the key to distinguishing German thought from that of
Western Europeans, who remained committed to the "natural law patterns" that characterized Enlightenment thought.[17] Central to this interpretation was the assumption that modern, historicist thought
constituted a radical break or structural change in historical thought
from that of the Enlightenment, which according to Meinecke remained "pre-modern," "pre-scientific," and unhistorical (even anti-
historical).[18] Of course, such bold and broad claims have not gone un-
challenged over the decades. In the first place, as contemporary scholarship has revealed, Meinecke's assumption that Enlightenment thought
was somehow unhistorical can no longer be sustained. Not only did a
great many historians practising in the academies and universities of
eighteenth-century Germany and throughout Europe produce a prodigious amount of scholarship in books and in dozens of historical journals, but they also made significant contributions to the development of
historical theory, taking important strides towards the institutionalization and professionalization of the discipline.[19]

Secondly, many scholars over the years have asked what exactly distinguished this modern theory of historical knowledge from that of the
Enlightenment. Was there a shift in paradigm? If so, what and where are
its discontinuities? If not, what are its lines of continuity? According to

17 Iggers, *The German Conception of History*, 5. In the 1920s, Troeltsch argued that historicism was in a state of crisis. The study of history "progressively showed the relativity and
hence invalidity of the values and beliefs of Western Culture," Iggers, "Historicism," 133.

18 Or, indeed, it represented a paradigm shift. See the vast literature produced by the
"Bielefeld School," which essentially maintains Meinecke's categorization of Enlighten-
ment history as "pre-scientific." Rüsen, *Konfigurationen des Historismus*; Jaeger and Rüsen,
Geschichte des Historismus; Blanke and Rüsen, eds. *Von der Aufklärung zum Historismus*; Blanke,
Historiographiegeschichte als Historik; Muhlack, *Geschichtswissenschaft im Humanismus und in der
Aufklärung*, 1991.

19 On the importance of theoretical developments in the Enlightenment, see Blanke
and Fleischer, eds. *Theoretiker der deutschen Aufklärungshistorie*; and Blanke, *Historiographiegeschichte als Historik*. See also Iggers, "The University of Göttingen, 1760–1800," 11–37; Reill,
The German Enlightenment and the Rise of Historicism; and Bödeker, Iggers, et al., eds.
Aufklärung und Geschichte.

Peter H. Reill, those features specifically labelled "historicist" – "the concept of development and the idea of individuality" – were certainly present, if not dominant, in the work of the Aufklärers.[20] Perhaps even more distressing from the perspective of those who are determined to see modern historiography firmly rooted in early nineteenth-century German soil is Donald R. Kelley's classic study of French Renaissance humanism. Kelley employs essentially the same definition of historicism – "Historicism refers to that cast of mind which, consciously or not, turns not to nature but to the world of man's making; which seeks out not the typical but the unique; which emphasizes the variety rather than the uniformity of human nature; which is interested less in similarities than in differences; and which is impressed not with permanence but with change."[21] However, Kelley maintains that historicism, and hence modern historical thought, "was not simply a byproduct of the *Freiheitskriege* [the Wars of Liberation] ... There were indeed, as Lord Acton noted, brave men before Agamemnon." Rather, the origins of historicist thought can be found in the humanists of the Renaissance. These "were the first men to make a conscious and concerted effort to revive a dead past with some appreciation of temporal perspective and willingness to examine antiquity on its own terms."[22]

If there were indeed brave men before Agamemnon, we must ask what distinguished Ranke's historiography from that of Gatterer, Gibbon, or for that matter Guizot, since it seems that, in most of the literature, German historicism (Historicism II) – or what Iggers has referred to as the "German academic tradition of writing history" in the nineteenth and part of the twentieth century[23] – essentially applies this new theory of historical knowledge to historiographic practice. If the theoretical principles and concepts that supposedly define nineteenth-century German historicism can, in fact, be traced back to the Enlightenment or even the Renaissance, the term historicism becomes less important in defining the German tradition of historical writing. Suddenly, in fact, the arguments of Rüsen, Blanke, and Muhlack – that German historicism represents the "paradigm" of modern historical discourse; that prior to it there was no "scientific history;" and that it "constitutes the highest

20 Reill, *The German Enlightenment and the Rise of Historicism*, 214.

21 Kelley, *Foundations of Modern Historical Scholarship*, 4–5.

22 Ibid., 5 and 7. Iggers now emphasizes the similarities rather than the differences between enlightenment and modern historical thought. See most recently Iggers, "Comments on F.R. Ankersmit's Paper," 162.

23 Iggers, "Historicism," 142. Iggers has also refered to historicism as a form of historiographic practice as "historism," or "classical historicism."

form of historical understanding"²⁴ – appear quite parochial. Indeed, the supposed accomplishments of the German historicists – the modernization of historical discourse and the complementary processes of objectification and de-rhetoricization (i.e., scientificization) – important as they may seem to have been, were neither contingent upon a radical transformation in the understanding of the historical process and the emergence of a new theory of historical knowledge, nor especially unique to Germany.

What made the historiography of the German historical school unique, and what distinguished the historical writing of Ranke from that of his predecessors and contemporaries in France or England, was not that the German historicists had achieved the possibility of "true knowledge" or *wahre Erkenntnis* (as opposed to "probable knowledge" or *wahrscheinliche Erkenntnis*) through the establishment of "scientific" history.²⁵ Rather, I would suggest that what was new was the very belief that *wahre Erkenntnis* was indeed possible, that German historicists believed they had discovered the means by which this could be achieved, and that their approach to understanding the past could achieve relative hegemony within the historical profession. In short, the writing of history was now characterized by the adoption of new discursive strategies, such as chronological, explanatory narratives, and was motivated by the desire to achieve scientific objectivity and the "ideal of life-like representation," or historical realism, in their work. In other words, the distinguishing feature of nineteenth-century historiography was not that historicists had discovered a "science" of history; rather it was the general emergence, not just in Germany but throughout Europe, of a new language of historical representation based upon the privileging and legitimizing rhetoric of science. Historians could now proclaim that it was possible to arrive at absolute Truth and certainty through historical knowledge.²⁶

. . .

24 Ibid., 145.

25 Muhlack, *Geschichtswissenschaft im Humanismus und in der Aufklärung*, 421.

26 Bann, *Clothing of Clio*, 14ff. Ankersmit argues that Enlightenment historiography was characterized by "ontological realism" and historicist discourse by its rejection. Iggers argues precisely the opposite. Clearly, historicists who attempt to de-rhetoricize historiographical representation – and the close relationship between history and rhetoric during the Enlightenment – support the position of Iggers and Bann. See the debate between Ankersmit and Iggers in HT.

The emergence of this new language of history based on the rhetoric of science must be understood within the context of the new sense of historical mindedness that pervaded the ideology of the emerging bourgeois public, as well as the radically altered social and political situation of historians in early nineteenth-century Germany. Spurred by Wilhelm von Humboldt's reforms to the education system in the early years of the nineteenth century, the professionalization of the historical discipline – whereby the study of history became an independent, autonomous discipline within the academic world – transformed historians. Once generalists, literary figures devoted to pedagogical goals, historians became prominent, privileged figures of intellectual authority, the purveyors of scientific knowledge within society, whose objectives were "research, discovery, and specialization."[27]

In Germany, the practice of history, although institutionalized during the eighteenth century, was never professionalized. While numerous historians worked in the famous academies of Berlin or Munich, and some achieved prominent positions in the universities of Protestant Germany, most notably Göttingen and Halle, the study of history was considered, at best, an ancillary discipline for philology, theology, or jurisprudence and, consequently, had a relatively low status within the academic community. Chairs of history certainly existed, but they were often filled by non-historians; lacking the prestige of specialization and authority, in effect "the lowest position on the institutional ladder," they were often abandoned over time.[28] Furthermore, as Telman, Turner, and Jarausch have persuasively demonstrated, eighteenth-century historians had not developed the prerequisites for professionalization – expertise, credentialing, and autonomy – and, as a consequence, there was neither a "professional ethos" nor a "disciplinary community."[29] As Jarausch has concluded, in the eighteenth century, "history was not a discipline with firm boundaries but rather an emerging disciplinary complex in several faculties ... During the *Aufklärung* the discipline therefore found itself in a 'peculiar state of suspension' emerging out of a service role, but not yet firmly established in its own scholarly right."[30]

27 Turner, "University Reformers and Professional Scholars in Germany," 2:531.
28 Telman, Review Essay, 261. See also Turner, "University Reformers and Professional Scholars in Germany;" Jarausch, "The Institutionalization of History in 18th-Century Germany," 25–48; Iggers, "The University of Göttingen 1760–1800," 11–37.
29 Telman, Review Essay, 260.
30 Jarausch, "The Institutionalization of History in 18th-Century Germany," 36–7.

During the first half of the nineteenth century, the study of history was professionalized in Germany. Chairs of history were filled with individuals dedicated to the discipline; standards of training and credentialing were established; and history, once subordinated to other fields of study, was studied in its own right. The professionalization of historical studies at the university reflected what history had become for society at large: the dominant form of social and cultural knowledge. However, the process whereby history became an autonomous discipline within the university was gradual and complex. Related to this process was the growing recognition that history required more than set standards of teaching and credentialing; if history were to be raised above the status of an ancillary field of study, it needed its own method, theory, and form of practice to distinguish it from other disciplines and, simultaneously, grant it autonomy. Consequently, the development of a new form of historical discourse based on the rhetoric of science – the process of "scientificization" – became an important criterion for the discipline's professionalization. Once reconceptualized as a form of science, history could fulfill and legitimize the demands of the educated public; lend credence to the historians, their work, and the academic institution; and enable the historians to become authorized interpreters and guardians of the past and regulators of public opinion in the present.[31]

This process was implicit in the historians' attempts during the first half of the nineteenth century to establish the epistemological break between history and literature, seen as essential to the emancipation of history from the realm of general literature and philosophy. This effort was by no means new. Although many eighteenth-century historians recognized the rhetorical origins of historical writing, a number were still motivated by the same desire to establish the scientific status of history. But, as Telman points out, the nature of what actually constituted "scientific" in the eighteenth century was not the same as in the nineteenth century, "for the standards a discipline must meet to qualify as a science are subject to constant revision."[32] These changing standards for assessing the criteria of what constitutes science reflected the changing social values and levels of cultural literacy; certainly, few nineteenth-century histori-

---

31 As Iggers has correctly pointed out, it is a mistake to confuse professionalization with scientificization, as Rüsen, Blanke et al. tend to do. See Iggers, "Der Programm einer Strukturgeschichte des historischen Denkens," 331–5.

32 Telman, Review Essay, 257.

ans would have regarded the historical work of their eighteenth-century predecessors as scientific.

The gradual reconceptualization of history as a science rather than a form of literature reflected not only the higher expectations awarded the source criticism and theory of the academic community as it became professionalized, but also the broader transformation within the nineteenth-century academic and elite cultural discourse. However, the end product was not a uniform, universal conception of science; there was no unity of scientific method for the study of society and culture. John Hooper, in his study of the French historian Jules Michelet, has outlined the process by which history came to be seen as a science; he follows the fortunes of Michelet's reputation within the context of the professional academics' relatively active campaign to re-evaluate and re-categorize the historical discipline.[33] As he explains it, from the 1820s to the 1840s, it was acceptable to admire the literary qualities of Miche-let's work, because, to a large degree, history was still flexibly defined as a literary genre. For example, reviewers such as John Stuart Mill, a great admirer of Michelet, could still praise his ability to combine poetic greatness with scientific veracity. However, in an age of rapid scientific and technological change usually equated with progress and material advancement, public expectations, as well as those of the academic community, dictated that history adopt a much more systematic approach. Empiricism, along with the rejection of hypothesis, an extraordinary faith in facts, and a belief in the neutrality of science, became the hall-marks of a culture that placed enormous value on authenticity, accuracy, and objectivity and that also believed that the scientific method could unveil and explain the mysteries of the natural and human world.

By mid-century in England and France, historical positivism became the gage by which to measure the scientific qualities of historical schol-arship.[34] This meant, however, that just as Thomas Babington Macaulay's reputation waned and Henry Thomas Buckle's rose as model English historians, so too Mill and other commentators began emphasizing the positivistic aspects of historical writing in their reviews, proclaiming in the 1840s the need for a "more systematic philosophical approach to the 'reality' of History."[35] The more scholars and the pub-lic expected history to emulate scientific research methods in the search

33 Hooper, "Changing Perceptions of Jules Michelet as Historian," 283–98.
34 The best recent study of historical positivism is Fuchs, *Henry Thomas Buckle.*
35 Hooper, "Changing Perceptions of Jules Michelet as Historian," 288.

for accurate reproductions of "reality," the more Michelet's reputation declined. By the 1850s, the majority of reviews would criticize the "unscientific" characteristics of his work and even question Michelet's status as an historian. Thus, Gustave Planche, writing in 1850 in the *Revue des Deux Mondes,* claimed that "M. Michelet does not appear to understand clearly the duties of the historian." Likewise, Hyppolite Taine criticized Michelet's "poetic imagination" and "lyrical epic," arguing that these were incompatible with the more desirable "qualities of science" in historical writing.[36]

The attempt to achieve an objective, scientifically verifiable history was clearly part of a European-wide trend. One can see similar developments in Germany during the first half of the nineteenth century, where professionalization occurred much earlier than in France or England. A quick glance at the evolution of the meaning of the German word for science, *Wissenschaft,* reveals this transformation. Initially, *Wissenschaft* referred to an individual's personal knowledge of a given subject. One said that someone had *Wissenschaft* of something particular. Towards the end of the eighteenth century, however, the meaning of this concept shifted away from personal ability towards general erudition. Accordingly, *die Wissenschaft,* using the definite article, came to imply "scholarship" or learning in general, while *eine Wissenschaft,* using the indefinite article, encompassed an entire body of knowledge, in effect a scholarly "discipline."[37] In the early nineteenth century, through the process of professionalization, history became an autonomous discipline, a separate academic *Wissenschaft,* in the German university system. But despite the obvious differences between "discipline" and "science," the term *Wissenschaft* gradually began to assume meanings that implied a "scientific" character. The modifier *wissenschaftlich,* for example, suggested the certitude of knowledge and the possibility of achieving a "superindividual, universally valid truth" from the employment of methodological principles.[38] Implicit in the claim that historical knowledge was a *Wissenschaft* or discipline, therefore, was the belief that an objective truth could be discovered in the past and verified through the use of the appropriate methodology.

The desire for an objectively verifiable historical truth was the goal of German historicists and positivists alike, and both adopted the rhetoric

36 Quoted in ibid., 292 and 293
37 See Ringer, *The Decline of the German Mandarins.*
38 Hardtwig, *Geschichtskultur und Wissenschaft,* 61–2.

of science for their cause. But it was in the conception of science that historical scholarship in Germany differed from that of France or England. German historians rejected the nomothetic, positivist conception of science practised by Comte and Buckle, arguing that the methods of the natural sciences could not be applied to the study of humankind and society. In contrast, it was the development of historical hermeneutics and the application of the principles of source criticism, adopted from classical philology, that gave German investigations scientific legitimacy within the broader context of the university and society.

Hermeneutics may perhaps best be defined "as the theory of interpretation or science of the principles (or rules) of proper textual exegesis."[39] Although the principles of general hermeneutics had been known and practised for many centuries, philosophers and historians during the second half of the eighteenth century began to distinguish between general and historical hermeneutics, pinpointing the latter as the extrapolation of "a more narrowly textual meaning into a broader contextual meaning and ultimately an even broader historical meaning."[40] In other words, historical hermeneutics emphasized the relationship of the part to the whole. It signalled, in effect, the revival of the traditional Aristotelian categories in literary and historical studies, which held that the essential difference between history and literature was that "the historian speaks of what has happened, the poet of the kind of thing that can happen. Hence also poetry is a more philosophical and serious business than history; for poetry speaks more of universals, history of particulars."[41] Only through the study of the particulars or individualities of history, which were conceived of as expressions of the human spirit, could one arrive at an understanding of the whole.[42]

Central to this science of the particular – and to how one arrived at an understanding of the whole – as it developed in the first half of the nineteenth century in Germany was the concept of *Verstehen*, or empathetic

39 Ermarth, "Hermeneutics and History," 195.
40 Ibid., 194.
41 Quoted in Gossman, *Between History and Literature*, 231.
42 Iggers, *New Directions*, 20, writes: "History was made up of 'individualities', each possessing their internal structure and a meaning and purpose unique to them alone. Not only persons possessed the qualities of individuality but in an even more profound sense so did the great collective bodies which had grown in the course of history – states, nations, cultures, mankind. These individualities were not merely fleeting appearances but each 'represented an idea rooted in actuality'."

understanding. Implicit in the theory of historical hermeneutics was the belief that through *Verstehen* "the interpreter can arrive at an immediate grasp of the objects that he is interpreting. In textual hermeneutics, this was taken to mean that the interpreter can come to grasp the mind of the author; in historiography, it meant a recovery of the past 'as it actually was'."[43] Through the combined use of source criticism, textual exegesis, and *Verstehen*, scholars believed that the meaning of historical phenomena could be explained and interpreted. Furthermore, it was then possible to achieve an immediacy in the understanding of the past. In other words, the theory of historical hermeneutics seemed to provide scholars of the German historical school with a means to an end – that end being objective, historical truth.

The development and widespread acceptance of the theory of historical hermeneutics by the German historical profession in the early nineteenth century radically altered the practice of history. But the theory also had numerous practical advantages for the professionalization and modernization of the discipline. For historians, it provided sound methodological principles that gave their research legitimacy. Anchored in the certitude of scientific veracity, it now served to distinguish historical scholarship from literature as well as the methods of the professional historian from that of the amateur. An argument could now be made that historical studies, following the generally accepted "scientific" criteria of the day, were objective and promised a scientifically verifiable accuracy in their historical reproduction. This was crucial to both the authority and the autonomy that historians sought for the discipline. As the only legitimate science of history and source of truth in the past, historical hermeneutics had enabled historians and theoreticians to ward off the double threat posed to the autonomy of the discipline by philosophy of history and historical positivism. Thus legitimized methodologically and theoretically, the study of history would be accepted as an autonomous discipline, the professional status of historians would be greatly enhanced and ensured, and the discipline would achieve institutional integrity.

The application of hermeneutics to the study of history was most clearly articulated and advanced by Johann Gustav Droysen, perhaps the greatest historical theorist of the nineteenth century. Droysen was convinced that the "science of history is the result of empirical perception, experience and investigation," and that historical truth, which he be-

---

43 Megill, *Prophets of Extremity*, 22. Quoting Gadamer, Megill calls Romantic hermeneutics "the reproduction of an original production." See also Iggers, *New Directions*, 18–26.

lieved was resident in moral forces, could be recovered unmediated by the scholar's use of the correct methodological principles – "*understanding by means of research*" ("*forschendes Verstehen*"). Droysen consequently had little doubt about the scientific nature of historical studies. "Historical things have their truth in the moral forces," he argued, just "as natural things have theirs in the natural 'laws', mechanical, physical, chemical, etc." Indeed, the main difference between the natural sciences and the study of the past was, to him, the "scientific" method employed, not the final goal. Droysen maintained that three scientific methods were available to scholars: the speculative, the physical, and the historical.[44] Despite the fact that the positivists attempted to apply the inductive methods of the natural sciences to the study of society and that the historicists employed the methods of hermeneutics, the goals and the rhetoric of historical hermeneutics and historical positivism remained the same: scientific authenticity, accuracy, and objectivity.

For Ranke, Droysen, and their followers, this meant reliance on the critical evaluation of original documents, the "criticism of correctness or validity," in order to "determine what relation the material still before us bears to the acts of will whereof it testifies."[45] This could then be incorporated unproblematically into a historical narrative by the objective narrator. But while the Germans continued to distinguish between the *Naturwissenschaften* and the *Geisteswissenschaften*, the unifying thread was the common search for a theory of objectivity, the belief that meaning was natural, and that it could be retrieved unmediated by the scholar through the use of sound methodology. By creating a scientific system and delineating the boundaries between history and literature, scholars would be able to distinguish between truth and falsehood, fact and fiction.

· · ·

Despite the contentious question about the inherent differences between historical and fictional narrative, it is nonetheless possible to delineate specific transformations in the narrative structure of historical texts during the first half of the nineteenth century. From there, one can see how changes in the rhetoric or "poetics" of historical represen-

44 Droysen, "Outline of the Principles of History," 104–8.
45 Ibid., 113.

tation reflected the emergence of objective/scientific historical discourse. Of particular importance is the changing function of the narrator within the historical and literary text. Lionel Gossman, for instance, basing his work on the ideas of Roland Barthes, argues that narrative can be divided into two general categories. The first, *histoire*, is characterized by a covert narrator who tries to eliminate any obvious indications of authorial presence through a pure narration of events. The second, *discours*, is characterized by an overt narrator who is very much aware of his or her active participation in the act of narration and who provides the unifying centre of the text.[46]

Eighteenth-century historiography, like fiction, privileged rhetoric as an essential element of historical discourse. Historians were "keenly aware of the role of perspective and of the literary and aesthetic aspects of historical writing,"[47] Iggers has written; as well, he notes, in the work of eighteenth-century historians, obvious signs of the presence of the author, such as text commentary, were not eliminated, but served a vital function within the structure of the narrative. In particular, the presence of the narrator served to create a distance between the narrative and the author, who, by engaging the reader as an ironic spectator of the historical scene, facilitated the creation of a dialogue between the reader and the past. A fundamental distinction was made in the work of Voltaire, for example, or Hume or Gibbon, between text commentary and the actual narration of events; the separation of the subject and object was emphasized in a manner that ultimately reinforced the freedom of the subject. Accordingly, Gossman believes:

History, in the eighteenth century, raised questions and created conditions in which the individual subject, the critical reason, could exercise and assert its freedom. It did not present itself as an objectively true and therefore compelling discovery of reality itself. On the contrary, its truth and validity were always problematic, provoking the reader's reflection and thus renewing his freedom. In an important sense, therefore, historical narrative and fictional narrative were constructed in fundamentally similar ways in the eighteenth century.[48]

In the early nineteenth century, however, *histoire* became the dominant form of historical discourse in the academic world. Based on a

46 Gossman, *Between History and Literature*, 243ff.

47 Iggers, "Comments on F. R. Ankersmit's Paper," 162. Ankersmit essentially maintains the opposite and argues that Enlightenment historiography was characterized by "ontological realism" or the ontology of the "true statement."

48 Gossman, *Between History and Literature*, 244.

deep-rooted mistrust of language, professional scholars considered proper historical observation to be extralinguistic. In effect, historical discourse was characterized, in the words of one recent student of poetics, "by a fundamental confusion between, in Saussurean terminology, the signified and the referent. Indeed, this discourse claims to bypass the signified and to make the signifier into a direct, unmediated representation of the world."[49] In effect, this "attempt to grasp reality (the referent of language) beyond the screen of language,"[50] in the name of objective historical science, meant that all inherently subjective elements of poetry, style, and rhetoric were banished from the historical narrative.

As Rüsen has pointed out, the process of "de-rhetoricizing" (*Entrhetorisierung*) historical discourse was a conscious goal of historians concerned with establishing an objective, scientific writing of history; moreover, it was one of the most important signposts in this process.[51] But it was not just rhetoric, or the poetics of language, that was eliminated by the evolution of *histoire*. In the name of objectivity and science, the direct presence of the author in any given historical text was no longer desired. The persona of the narrator in nineteenth-century historical and fictional texts consequently assumed a covert function, a privileged position above or outside the text. According to Barthes, "on the level of enunciation ... historical discourse is basically without a speaker: promoting an 'objective subject' (*personne objective*), it seeks to cancel the 'emotional subject' (*personne passionnelle*)."[52] The author strived to become what in essence was a neutral "reporter recounting what happened."[53] Epistemologically, this presumed the existence of the "coherence of a transparent primary or natural authenticity" between the text and the reader, an assumption that facilitated the creation of a form of direct representation without any possibility or need for authorial mediation.[54] By ignoring the ambiguity and the very rhetorical nature of language and by presuming its transparency, rational discourse, in effect, tried to kill off the author, the goal being to repress all elements of subjectivity and to create an objectively fixed reality. The author's task became simply one of presenting, in as unpoetic, unambiguous language as possible, the events of the past as accurately as possi-

49 Carrard, *Poetics of the New History*, 27.
50 Pomata, "Versions of Narrative," 13.
51 Rüsen, *Konfigurationen des Historismus*, 64–5.
52 Carrard, *Poetics of the New History*, 26.
53 Gossman, *Between History and Literature*, 244.
54 Mah, "Suppressing the Text," 13.

ble. At no time ought the author's guiding hand be felt within the course of the narration, because this would be construed as an obvious sign of authorial presence. This is precisely what Ranke had in mind when he wrote that his goal in writing history was "to extinguish my own self, as it were, to let things speak and the mighty forces appear which have arisen in the course of centuries."[55]

In other words, the primary aim of *histoire* was the attempt to recreate historical authenticity, or an historically authentic milieu, through the objective reading of primary sources. Historical realism, to borrow a term from art history, became the order of the day. And it reflected an important shift away from a mediated form of historical representation, the goal of which was mimesis or imitation, to a "life-like" form of representation, the goal of which was authenticity. This new form of historical discourse had a number of advantages for the historian. First, it created a "reality effect," which had the benefit of being "science-like" in its attention to detail and accuracy and its adherence to form, and which, in turn, created the illusion of authenticity. Secondly, by establishing history as the "very paradigm of realistic discourse," realism also conformed to the new code of cultural literacy, based on the language of science, which had become dominant during the century. Finally, it provided an authenticating experience of the past that sustained present-day values, as well as a system of information that could be used to form and mould the cultured individual or citizen. Thus other forms of discourse were ruled out as "utopian, idealist, mythical, illusory, reductionist, or otherwise distorted."[56]

But was the development of historical realism a response to a sense of loss in a world of rapid and often violent change, as Foucault and Bann have argued? Or, in what essentially amounts to the same thing, was it a response to a profound "crisis of orientation," as Rüsen suggests? Whatever the answer, it did offer the comfort of certitude and stability based on chronological, progressive narrative.[57] Moreover, in its lack of ambi-

55 Quoted in Krieger, *Ranke: The Meaning of History*, 5.

56 White, *Content of the Form*, 101.

57 Foucault writes that "all this is a surface expression of the bare fact that man found himself emptied of history, but that he was already beginning to recover in the depths of his own being, and among all the things that were still capable of reflecting his image ... a historicity which was linked to him essentially," *The Order of Things*, 369. Bann writes that "the restoration of the life-like is itself postulated as a response to a sense of loss. In other words, the Utopia of life-like reproduction depends upon, and reacts to, the fact of death. It is a strenuous attempt to recover, by means which must exceed those of convention, a state which is (and must be) recognised as lost," *The Clothing of Clio*, 15; Rüsen, *Konfigurationen des Historismus*, 21.

guity, this form of historical representation also had a certain utilitarian value, in that the meaning of the text was presumably clear to the audience and therefore required minimal interpretation skills. As Gossman writes in his summation of the ideas of Roland Barthes, the cultural pattern of realism, whether in history, literature, photography or art in general, "points to an alienating fetishism of the 'real', by which men seek to escape from their freedom and their role as makers of meaning. The 'real' appears to him as an idol."[58]

The irony, of course, is that rhetoric was not eliminated; instead, it assumed a different guise, namely the language of science and facticity. The fetishness of the rhetoric of realism is perhaps best exemplified by Ranke's famous dictum that he wanted "to show what actually happened" (*wie es eigentlich gewesen*). This statement encapsulated the historiographical ideal of generations of historians and signified, among other things, Ranke's attempt to recreate an historically authentic milieu. In his theoretical writings, Ranke attempted to develop a theory of historical knowledge that would demonstrate the possibility of reproducing an objectively fixed reality in the past. He outlined these goals in "On the Character of Historical Science," in which he echoes Aristotle, who maintained in the *Poetics* that the business of history is the study of the particular. For Ranke, it is in the realm of the particular that "reality" is to be found. In contrast to philosophy or poetry, "history has to rely on reality" and therefore must move away from the ideal to the real.[59] But Ranke could not theorize rhetoric out of existence, inasmuch as language mediates between the particular and the general. Initially, Ranke seemed to have straddled both sides of the fence in the debate over whether or not history was, in fact, science or literature. What distinguishes history from other sciences, he declared, is that history is both art and science. It is scientific in the collection and discovery of sources; it is art in what the historian then does with this array of material, the re-creation of the past (authentically, as verified in the documents).[60] For Ranke, the artistic element of history lay in the act of writing. However, the historian, he felt, did not require any special talent or skills. "Art rests on itself: its existence proves its validity."[61] It is natural, it comes with the territory, it is unavoidable, he seems to be saying, almost apologetically. Rüsen claims that there is no reason for the

58 Gossman, *Between History and Literature*, 250.
59 Ranke, *The Theory and Practice of History*, 33–4.
60 Ibid., 33.
61 Ibid., 34.

mutual exclusivity of rhetoric and rational science. This is indeed true. Despite the claims of nineteenth-century historians, rhetoric could not be eliminated, as even Ranke realized. But by claiming that art rested on itself, Ranke minimized the rhetorical nature of historical discourse into insignificance. As Rüsen writes, "For Ranke, rhetoric is negated by scientific research, and there is only a residue of rhetoric remaining in a fundamentally changed form: the aesthetics of historiography." Ranke's overwhelming emphasis on the scientific nature of the research imperative consequently subsumed the "residual" rhetorical moment. It was smothered out of existence, as is the "aesthetics of historiography." The same can be said of Droysen, who emphasized that his *Historik* was not intended as "a discipline for the artistic composition of history."[62] Rüsen has also suggested that art (and perhaps language) did not constitute a subversive moment in Ranke's conception of history.[63] But Ranke's attempt to minimize the role of language suggests that it did threaten to undermine his concept of history and historical objectivity, and that the relationship between language and meaning was by no means as transparent as he presumed.[64]

. . .

Historians have often compared Burckhardt with Ranke. Despite obvious differences – Friedrich Meinecke and Felix Gilbert, for example,

---

62 Droysen, "Outline of the Principles of History," 104 and 109.

63 Rüsen, "Rhetoric and Aesthetics of History," 195. See also Rüsen, *Konfigurationen des Historismus*, 124.

64 Bann captures this process wonderfully: "If Truth is, as Nietzsche liked to imagine, a woman, then style is the sharp instrument which pierces the veils that conceal her. Or, as Kipling put it in his clever short story 'A Matter of Fact', the only resource of the writer in possession of the remarkable story is to 'tell it as a lie': 'for Truth is a naked lady, and if by accident she is drawn up from the bottom of the sea, it behoves a gentleman either to give her a print petticoat or to turn his face to the wall and vow that he did not see'. Against the orthodoxy of this position, Ranke raises up, in the days of his chivalrous youth, a redoubtable standard. For Truth, that abstract and over-extended lady, is substituted the homelier figure of Clio. And Clio, or History personified, will be revealed in untrammelled nakedness: is not the primary sense of *bloss* (*er will bloss zeigen*) precisely that of nakedness? *Eigentlich*, whether we translate it 'actually' or 'essentially', becomes no more than a means of assuring us that all the veils are off: there is not even a print petticoat for the sake of her modesty, and *a fortiori*, no need of the probing style (*stylus*) to make intrusive jabs into her secret places," *The Clothing of Clio*, 12.

thought that Burckhardt was the greatest practitioner of cultural history, Ranke the greatest political historian – historians, in general, still tend to relegate Burckhardt, however peripherally, to the German historical school. According to Rüsen and Jaeger, Burckhardt is "one of the most famous representatives of historicism," even if they consider him an outsider within this tradition.[65] Yet, Burckhardt himself viewed his position differently. Early in his career, while he was still a student, he staked out very different ground from Ranke and the scientific, conceptualized history practised by German historicists. Not only did he begin to practise cultural history, as opposed to political history, but he also rejected the theoretical and ideological assumptions of Ranke and the German historical school.

Burckhardt's theoretical position can perhaps best be seen in his famous statements about the nature of history. In sharp contrast to Ranke, Burckhardt regarded history unreservedly and unconditionally – and unrepentantly – as a form of literature; as an art, not a science. When his friend Willibald Beyschlag asked him in 1842 about the nature of history and what it meant to him, he answered that history "to me is for the greater part always poetry; it is for me a series of the most beautiful and artistic compositions."[66] Burckhardt took a personal stance in the ongoing discussion about whether or not history was science or literature and made an important statement about the nature of historical discourse. At one level, his response signified a rejection of the most important principle of historicism and historical hermeneutics; namely, the overriding concern for the particular. While Ranke did not deny the interconnectedness of history, he contended that any understanding of the whole depended primarily upon the study of the particular.[67] By viewing history as poetry, however, Burckhardt was agreeing with Aristotle, that poetry is a more profound medium than history, and with Schopenhauer that art achieves more for the understanding of the human spirit than history. Poetry, and consequently Burckhardt's conception of the historical enterprise, was concerned with the universal, whereas history, as it had come to be conceived in his own age, was primarily concerned

65 Jaeger and Rüsen, *Geschichte des Historismus*, 42 and 122. This of course depends on how one defines historicism. Rüsen and Jaeger define it so broadly as to include virtually all forms of historical discourse; i.e., Historicism I.

66 *Briefe*, 1:204. If Burckhardt did not always consider this to be the case, he nonetheless continued to see poetry as the "perhaps never reached, but always strived for, example of historical scholarship," Flaig, *Angeschaute Geschichte*, 34.

67 Ranke, *The Theory and Practice of History*, 57–59.

with the particulars of the world. Poetry, therefore, as a more sublime form of expression, provided greater insight into human nature. By elevating history to the status of poetry, Burckhardt envisioned a much higher task for historical studies than merely explaining the meaning of the past. The goal of history and historical observation became identical to that of poetry, both of which sought to capture the ideal or the "image of the eternal,"[68] and both of which dealt with form as well as content.

While Burckhardt disagreed with Ranke about whether or not history was an art or a science, both shared a mutual distrust for speculative philosophy of history. Their stand against philosophy of history reflected a number of concerns, including the desire to counter Hegel's continued influence at the university in Berlin. They hoped to bring the study of history out from under his lengthy shadow and to establish it as an autonomous discipline. Ranke's hostility to philosophy of history, at least during the 1830s and 1840s when he was increasingly preoccupied with it, was certainly motivated by his rejection of Hegelianism. As Telman writes, Ranke "believed that human beings were the active agents of history, and he thus objected to what he saw in the Idealist philosophy of history as the reduction of human history to the playing out of superhuman ideas." Ranke believed that Hegel's teleology effectively undermined the principle of individuality, which formed the basis of Rankean historiography, because philosophers "saw the infinite only in the totality," whereas the historian "viewed in each individual being the infinity of creation." As a consequence, more than any mode of historical analysis based on principles derived from the natural sciences, Hegel's philosophy of history threatened to undermine the methodological soundness of historicism and, with it, the autonomy of history as an academic discipline.[69]

On the other hand, Ranke considered philosophy inappropriate to the study of history because it was akin to poetry. In his outline of the characteristics of history, he sought to demonstrate how history was distinguished from philosophy through its methodology, its reliance on the real, and its subjection to empirical analysis. Accordingly, Ranke claimed that philosophy was very similar to poetry, both of which "move within the realm of the ideal," and, consequently, was not subject to empiricism. Although he contended that history "demands a union of the intellectual forces active in both philosophy and poetry under the con-

68 WB, 382 and 285.
69 Telman, "Clio Ascendant," 429 and 430.

dition that the last two be directed away from their concern with the ideal to the real," he noted that poetry and philosophy share common characteristics, making them basically incompatible with the study of the past.[70]

Burckhardt shared Ranke's criticism of Hegel's teleology, the "idea of the cunning of reason." However, Burckhardt's critique of the philosophy of history went further than that of Ranke's, to include the entire realm of conceptual thought. In some ways a hallmark of his mature historical thought, Burckhardt's reluctance to engage in speculative theories and concepts was quickly picked up by his detractors during his lifetime and became a dominant theme in their criticism of his work. Wilhelm Dilthey, for example, commented in 1862 in a then anonymous review of *The Civilization of the Renaissance in Italy*, that the work was conceptually weak.[71] But Burckhardt was prepared to accept this criticism; in fact, he acknowledged it to be true. He wrote that, as a student, he had "never thought philosophically" and had never had a thought "that was not connected to something external."[72] Just as he would later disavow any attempt to formulate a theory of speculative aesthetics in his art history, so he would begin his lecture cycle on the study of history, *Reflections on History*, with a disclaimer against all philosophies of history. There would be a "renunciation of everything systematic." He would make "no claim to 'universal historical' ideas," and would similarly refuse to examine the ideas behind a work of art, concentrating instead "only on perceptions." The simple goal of his lectures, he said, was to present "transverse sections of history in as many directions as possible." Once again, he reiterated, his lectures would contain "above all else, no philosophy of history."[73]

The reason Burckhardt gave for this was that philosophy was concerned with origins and looked for hidden meaning within the historical process. "Your system," he wrote to his philosopher friend, Karl Fresenius, "penetrates the depths of the secrets of the world, and for you history is a source of knowledge, a science, because you see, or believe to

70 Ranke, *The Theory and Practice of History*, 33–4.

71 Dilthey, *Gesammelte Schriften*, 11:73. It was only with the publication of Dilthey's collected works that his authorship of this review became known. It appeared originally in the *Berliner Allgemeine Zeitung*, 10 September 1862. Burckhardt knew the review but not who wrote it, and was instrumental in bringing Dilthey to Basel in the late 1860s. See Kaegi, 3:715–22 and 7:196–206.

72 *Briefe*, 1:204.

73 WB, 225.

see, the primum agens where for me there is only mystery and poetry."[74]
He consequently distinguished between the speculative concepts of the
philosophers and his own historical project. He reported in two extensive letters from June 1842 – having decided to pursue cultural history
instead of political history and during a time of intense study of the philosophy of history – on the progress of his historical studies and the
course of his thinking. In particular, he had intensified his "certainly casual but daily thinking about the philosophy of history of the last two
years."[75] Now, he was planning to study Hegel, among other philosophers, to see if he understood his work and whether or not it suited his
beliefs.[76] But, clearly, he had his doubts. Although Burckhardt had the
highest respect for philosophy, he warned that, "the speculations of another person, even if I could acquire them, could never console me or
even help me." Considering himself something of an oddity for going
against the trend, he asked only that he be left alone at this "lower level,"
in order that he might "experience and feel history instead of understanding it from the perspective of first principles ... The never ending
riches that flow through me from this lower form of immediate sensation already makes me overly happy, and will surely enable me to accomplish something, even if it is in unscientific form, that will perhaps even
be of use to philosophers."[77]

Neither human experience, this "lower form of immediate sensation," nor perception could be simply shackled by a priori theories or
concepts said Bruckhardt; they had to be given free reign. This, then,
explains his defensive, at times deliberately confrontational, demeanor
and tone towards philosophy of history and theory in general. His famous scheme of the three powers (state, religion, and culture), outlined
in *Reflections on History*, should not be taken as the first step towards a
general historical plan or theory of historical development. Admittedly
arbitrary and consciously antithetical to chronological philosophies of
history, it was conceived expressly as a tool with which to facilitate his
students' historical observation and contemplation, not as· a theory of
historical knowledge.[78] More of a typological, rather than teleological,
schemata for ordering history, it provided his students with the basis for
formulating analogies and articulating the similarities and continuities

74 *Briefe*, 1:208.
75 Ibid., 1:154.
76 Ibid., 1:207.
77 Ibid.
78 WB, 254.

within the historical flux. Never was it designed to make a theoretical connection between history and philosophy, as was Johann Gustav Droysen's more famous *Historik* (1857). On the contrary, Burckhardt recognized that "every method is open to question, and none is universally valid"; ultimately, he said, method is shaped by the individual.[79] He went even further than this, however, making the explicit connection between the historians' pretensions to scientific status and the uncertainty of theory, writing that "history is actually the most unscientific of all disciplines, only that it transmits so much that is worth knowing. Clear conceptual definitions belong to logic, but not to history, where everything is in flux, continual transition and combination."[80]

While Burckhardt argued against philosophies and systems of thought in general, his comments were specifically directed against Hegal's philosophy of history, the most important and influential philosophy of his day. Some debate surrounds the extent of Burckhardt's reception and assimilation of Hegel's ideas. Many see similarities, especially in the understanding of *Geist*, or spirit. Ernst Gombrich, for example, writes that Burckhardt's cultural history "has been built, knowingly and unknowingly on Hegelian foundations which have crumbled."[81] As well, Rüsen has argued that Burckhardt's three powers act in his work much as the Hegelian thesis, antithesis, and synthesis.[82] Whether or not this is the case, Burckhardt nonetheless postulated his own approach to history in specific contrast to Hegel, whose systematization of history was paradigmatic of the teleological approach that dominated contemporary philosophy of history. Like Ranke, he questioned the legitimacy of Hegel's speculations because they followed history, providing "longitudinal" sections chronologically, in order "to penetrate a general program for the development of the world, mostly in a highly optimistic sense."[83] He argued that the subordination of one event or action to another im-

79 Ibid., 227.
80 Ibid., 293.
81 Gombrich, *In Search of Cultural History*, 6.
82 Rüsen, *Konfigurationen des Historismus*, 310. There seems to be some confusion, because later Rüsen argues that they are symptomatic of Weberian ideal types, the use of which enabled Burckhardt to see history as both continuity and change, and able, therefore, to take into account both an historicist vision of change and a teleological vision of human continuity. Ibid., 315. In contrast to Rüsen, Flaig argues that the Weberian ideal type, as an heuristic device designed to serve the progress of knowledge, is inappropriate to Burckhardt, as he did not see history in terms of progressive knowledge. Flaig, *Angeschaute Geschichte*, 36.
83 WB, 226.

posed structures and models of development that, rather than emerging directly from the historical flux, were applied with the benefit of hindsight. As such, contended Burckhardt, philosophy of history, in its search for origins, was condemned to speak more to the future than of the past.[84] Like art, said Burckhardt, the past existed for itself, in itself, and not for our own existence in the present.

Burckhardt argued that the belief in progress and absolute values was consequently the ultimate expression not only of the modern individual's condescension to the past but also of egotism of the modern age. The assumption that "our time was the consummation of all time, or very nearly so, that the past may be regarded as fulfilled in us, while it, with us, existed for its own sake, for us, and for the future,"[85] was, for Burckhardt, a gross overestimation of human wisdom. Burckhardt felt that it represented the arrogant complacency of the modern bourgeoisie, even as the notion of progress and its corollary, the moral superiority of the present, provided the historical and philosophical justification for the process of modernization. Moreover, argued Burckhardt, while there may have been definite material, scientific, and technological advances, these had the negative effect of alienating the individual still further from the objective world. According to Burckhardt, this worldly progress was made at the cost of culture, as human creativity became increasingly linked to market values. As he put it: "Literature and culture are appreciated, to be sure. But literature has unfortunately become an industry as well in most cases. Alongside it, the literature of the eighteenth century appears all to be written with the heart's blood. Today very few things are still produced out of inner necessity. The *raison d'être* of the vast majority of creations is the honorarium or the hope for a position."[86] Despite all the evidence of material progress, Burckhardt maintained that human nature had remained more or less unchanged throughout the ages. No moral and ethical advances or transformations accompanied this progress. In effect, the promises of unremitting confidence in mankind's rationality were deceptive; the scientific and technological innovations having given rise only to greater, more complex social and ethical problems, while diminishing mankind's capacity for spiritual enrichment and enlightenment. But Hegel, by arguing that history represented the continuous development towards the perfectibility

84 Ibid., 227.
85 Ibid., 226.
86 JHH, 222–3.

of humankind in the present, implied that this process was guided by universal principles that could be discovered through the application of conceptual, rational thought.[87] As a consequence, Hegel's work came to symbolize for Burckhardt a misguided faith in the ultimate rationality of human nature and in the historical progress that was embodied in philosophy of history.

Burckhardt's misgivings about philosophy of history thus went much beyond the belief that philosophy subordinated past events and facts to preconceived structures, an opposition he shared with Ranke.[88] Burckhardt placed in doubt the very possibility of rational discourse. As a result, Burckhardt objected to any attempt to conceptualize the past: by subordinating human action to ideas or theory, he said, the realm of human experience and intuition was straightjacketed. Such subordination created an unbridgeable gap between immediate perceptions and instincts, smothering human perception and the whole of sensate life. In a manner similar to Nietzsche, Burckhardt ultimately decided that the theoretical mind, in its isolation and rationalization of subjectivity, was by its very nature hostile to art and a threat to myth; it could not possibly represent a creative force, because creativity emanates from "the instincts, the passions, the unconscious – from the dark, hidden recesses of the human spirit."[89] Culture and art, Burckhardt emphasized, cannot be restricted by artificial theoretical constructs; it must be allowed to occur spontaneously. It was "the world of the variable, free, not necessarily universal; of that which lays no claim to compulsive authority."[90] Conceptual thought, however, laid claim precisely to this universal, compulsive authority, rendering artistic creation impotent in its wake, destroying the latter's spontaneity, and robbing it of its innocence.

In his lectures on Greek cultural history Burckhardt advanced this thesis of the destructive impact of conceptualized thought – "thought was the enemy of the beautiful and lavish visualizations" – on the devel-

87 See especially WB, 152.
88 In his discussion of the principles of history, Ranke took the philosophers to task for the way they started from a truth, "which has been found elsewhere and in a way particular to him as a philosopher, constructs all of history for himself: how it must have taken place according to his concept of mankind. Not satisfied to test whether his idea is right or wrong, without deceiving himself, in terms of the course of events which have really occurred, he undertakes to subordinate the very events to his idea. Indeed, he recognizes the truth of history only insofar as it subordinates itself to his idea. This is a mere construct of history," in *The Theory and Practice of History*, 35–6.
89 Megill, *Prophets of Extremity*, 55.
90 WB, 254.

opment of art saying that rational philosophy threatened to reveal the mysteries of art and myth.[91] The general implication was that Greek visual art achieved such glorious heights because the artists were hostile to philosophy. This, however, was not the case with Greek poetry, he contended, which subsequently lost its "naïveté" with the rise of philosophy. Writing about Greek culture of the fourth century B.C. in his lecture on art in antiquity, Burckhardt maintained that great poetry ceased to be produced after Euripides and Sophocles, and that, "on the whole, poetry died because of democracy and political and philosophical reflection."[92]

Burckhardt's thoughts on the decline of ancient Greek poetry paralleled his interpretation of art in his own day. Both, he felt, had lost their naïveté. Convinced of the destructive materialism and cynicism of a modern world obsessed by power and greed; convinced of the domestication of the individual and the pernicious nature of the celebration of the new "objective" consciousness – embodied, he believed, in modern, rational scientific thought, political democracy, and Hegel's speculative philosophy, and which killed human subjectivity – Burckhardt could only conclude, uncomfortably, that authentic experience was no longer possible in the modern world. His solution was to return, in his writings and his observation and contemplation of the past, to that world of aesthetics destroyed by the modern, rational, and scientific consciousness.

91 GA, 10:48ff and WB, 319.
92 Quoted in Kaegi, 6:342.

6

Burckhardt and the Development
of Cultural History

IN THE MONTHS IMMEDIATELY FOLLOWING his semester of study at the University of Bonn during the summer of 1841, Burckhardt made a decision that determined the course of his career as an historian. Instead of following in the footsteps of his mentor, Leopold von Ranke, he chose to pursue the study of cultural history. This decision effectively removed him from the historiographical mainstream as represented by the German historical school. Although there is nothing to suggest that it caused tension between Burckhardt and Ranke – on the contrary, Ranke was always supportive of his student – the decision nonetheless reveals the extent to which Burckhardt's views on history, while still a student, diverged from what would eventually become the dominant paradigm of historical scholarship in the German academic world. In effect, it signalled a rejection of the "scientific" pretensions of the German historical school and of the narrative model of traditional fact and event-oriented political history established by Ranke and his followers.[1]

Shortly before his death, Burckhardt reportedly said to the young historian Kurt Breysig that "he had never been interested in political history; he had no talent for it."[2] Political history, which in the German historical school focused almost entirely on the historical understanding and development of the state, dominated the German historical profession and in many respects was the "official" history. It reflected the prevalent belief in German intellectual circles that the state was a higher

1 On Burckhardt's rejection of event-oriented history, see Hardtwig, *Geschichtsschreibung zwischen Alteuropa und moderner Welt*, 189–90; Siebert, *Jacob Burckhardt*, 78ff.

2 Quoted in Röthlin, "Burckhardts Stellung in der Kulturgeschichtsschreibung des 19. Jahrhunderts," 397. Burckhardt discussed the latest developments in cultural history with Breysig. See *Briefe*, 10:303–4.

order, an organic entity governed by its own principles, from which all social and cultural life emanated and to which it was subordinated.[3] Although the great political historians of the nineteenth century, such as Heinrich von Treitschke or Heinrich von Sybel, for example, did not necessarily ignore social or cultural life, they proceeded from the assumption that politics and the state determined the nature of social and cultural development. Society, according to Treitschke, could only exist within and through the state, and not as an autonomous entity. As a consequence, the only real history could be the history of princes, politicians, generals, and diplomats; not surprisingly, Treitschke defined history as *Staatswissenschaft.*[4]

. . .

Cultural history has been somewhat neglected in the study of nineteenth-century German historiography, even though it constituted an integral element of historical scholarship and had roots going back to the Enlightenment. As one recent commentator has noted, "From its beginnings, cultural history has been written chiefly by and for those who are excluded from power."[5] During the eighteenth century, it was the historiographic domain of those Enlightenment philosophers and university professors who represented the aspirations of the emerging bourgeoisie, challenged the fundamental legitimacy of the absolutist state, and sought

3 Iggers, *The German Conception of History*, stresses the unique conception of the state and has demonstrated how it was a defining feature of German historicism. It was considered an "end in itself," and was closely connected to the concept of the *Machtstaat.*

4 Hartmann, "Die deutsche Kulturgeschichtsschreibung," 138–41. The relationship between historians, politics, and the state is discussed in Simon, *Staat und Geschichtswissenschaft.* Simon writes that historians were "the political scientists of the day ... Gervinus, Waitz, Dahlmann, Duncker, Droysen taught 'politics' in order to show how the state was the product of historical forces and to demonstrate that politics was applied historical scholarship," 3. Not only was the state was seen as an "ethical force," it was "the subject of historical development and consequently the worthiest object of historical research," 76–7.

5 Gossman, "Cultural History and Crisis," 404. Recent studies of German cultural history include: Hans Schleier, "Deutsche Kulturhistoriker des 19. Jahrhunderts: über Gegenstand und Anfgaben der Kulturgeschichte," *Geschichte und Gesellschaft* 23 (1997): 70–98. Hans Schleier, "Kulturgeschichte im 19. Jahrhundert: Oppositionswissenschaft, Modernisierungsgeschichte, Geistesgeschichte, spezialisierte Sammlungsbewegung, in *Geschichtsdiskurs*, vol. 3, edited by W. Küttler, J. Rüsen, E. Schalin. Frankfurt am Main: Fischer Verlag 1997, 424–46.

to shape the "public sphere."[6] Its founder, or at least "prototypical representative," was Voltaire (1694–1778). His famous historical works, *Le siècle de Louis XIV* (1751) and *Essai sur les moeurs et l'esprit des nations* (1756), represented an important shift away from the vast collection and compilation of facts and data that characterized the work of the traditional polyhistorians; these historians also placed social and cultural development, not accounts of the lives of important individuals or of military and political events, at the centre of the historical narrative. "Do not let the reader expect here … minute details of wars, of attacks on towns taken and retaken by force of arms," Voltaire wrote in his introduction to his study of the age of Louis XIV. Rather, he declared, "In this history we shall confine ourselves to that which deserves the attention of all time, which paints the spirit and the customs of men, which may serve for instruction and to counsel the love of virtue, of the arts and of the fatherland."[7] In its broadest sense, therefore, cultural history was not simply the history of what we would call "high culture" or the arts, but the history of society and civilizations. It sought to integrate all aspects of social life, including material culture, customs and values, institutions, as well as economic and cultural developments into a unified, cohesive narrative.[8]

Despite the almost mandatory criticism of Voltaire by the historians of the German *Aufklärung*, his work essentially set their agenda during the second half of the eighteenth century. Like Voltaire, the great eighteenth-century cultural historians such as Johann Gottfried Herder, Isaak Iselin, and Johann Christoph Adelung viewed the historical process from a "philosophical-anthropological" perspective that placed mankind

6 This important dimension of German cultural history is discussed at length in Hartmann, "Die deutsche Kulturgeschichtsschreibung." On the history of cultural history in general, see also the brief discussions in Siebert, *Jacob Burckhardt*, 25–36; and Gilbert, *History: Politics or Culture?* 81–92.

7 Voltaire, *The Age of Louis XIV*, in *Candide and Other Writings*, New York: Everyman Books 1956, 225. Likewise he begins his account: "It is not merely the life of Louis XIV that we propose to write; we have a wider aim in view. We shall endeavor to depict for posterity, not the actions of a single man, but the spirit of men in the most enlightened age the world has ever seen," 221.

8 What Hartmann refers to as cultural history in the eighteenth century – namely, the integration of the study of social, economic, political and cultural conditions – is called *Zivilisationsgeschichte* by Muhlack, who prefers to use the term *Kulturgeschichte* to refer to "the area of culture in the narrower sense." Muhlack also makes a distinction between *Zivilisationsgeschichte* and *Universalgeschichte*, whereas Hartmann claims that they were more or less identical, adding to the confusion of terms. Muhlack, *Geschichtswissenschaft im Humanismus und in der Aufklärung*, 254–5.

in the centre of a rational, progressive development towards perfectibility and enlightenment. Following the lead of Herder and Iselin, the concept of culture was specifically defined as, in this case by Adelung, the "transition from more sensuous and animal-like conditions ... The entire sensuous, that is the entire animal-like condition, the true position of nature, is the absence of all culture." From such a definition of culture, the objective of cultural history became to trace humankind's progressive development from this primitive state towards the higher state of human affairs that existed in the latter eighteenth century.[9] As a result, cultural history in the broadest sense became the history of humanity (the *Geschichte der Menschheit*), encompassing all peoples who were considered "civilized"; that is to say, those peoples who were conscious of their past and who had left records to this effect.

During the first decades of the nineteenth century, the practice of cultural history remained heavily indebted to the earlier histories of *Menschheit*. It focused on describing the progressive stages of general human development and was still committed to what we would describe today as an anthropological approach to history. Echoing his Enlightenment predecessors, the cultural historian Wilhelm Wachsmuth, for instance, wrote in his *Entwurf einer Theorie der Geschichte* (1820) that the "the principal idea is to describe how human rationality has progressively developed from raw, physical conditions." This was to be achieved first of all through the "presentation of the primitive conditions of humanity prior to the formation of the state, at which point one advances to real history and then pursues these threads with philosophical observations and developments up until recent times."[10]

Although Wachsmuth's work remained anchored in eighteenth-century conceptualizations, cultural historians continuously strived to establish the autonomy of their discipline during the *Vormärz*. Part of this process was the deliberate articulation of cultural history as an "oppositional form of scholarship" (*Oppositionswissenschaft*). Throughout the nineteenth century, cultural historians claimed to be presenting an

9 Quoted in Hartmann, "Die deutsche Kulturgeschichtsschreibung," 29. See also, Hans Schleier, "Kulturgeschichte der Völker als Evolution und Vervollkommnung des Menschen. Deutsche Kultur historiker Ende des 18. Jahrhunderts," in *Europa in der frühen Neuzeit: Festschrift für Günter Mühlpfordt*, vol. 4, edited by Erich Donnert. Weimar: Böhlan Verlag 1997, 619–42.

10 Cited in Dilly and Ryding, "Kulturgeschichtsschreibung," 18. See also, Hans Schleier, "Wilhelm Wachsmuths 'Entwurf einer Theorie der Geschichte' aus dem Jahre 1820." *Jahrbuch für Geschichte* 37 (1988): 103–35.

alternative form of historical discourse to standard political history. This opposition was essentially twofold. First, cultural history was directed explicitly against traditional political history, which focused on the state, war, diplomacy, and the actions and writings of leading political figures. Thus, in contrast to this "court historiography," or *Hofhistoriographie*, cultural historians were concerned with all aspects of human activity, firmly subordinating the role of high politics and the state in historical development. Instead of concentrating on such "external events," they focused on the "internal conditions" of society: intellectual and religious life, social institutions, manifestations of popular and elite culture, and long-term economic developments. This did not mean that they ignored political life altogether. On the contrary, they were concerned with what might be called the primacy of domestic politics, which included constitutional and legal history, the relationship between the population and the state, and the general material and spiritual development of people and society. In other words, they often focused on social, cultural, and economic transformation – in short, the process of modernization.

The second defining feature of this opposition derived from the first. By focusing their energies on "internal conditions," what we might consider the results or consequences of events, rather than on the "external events" themselves, cultural historians rejected the principles of the event-oriented historiography of the German historical school. Instead of an analytical or explanatory narrative structure, they employed a descriptive narrative form. In addition, from the perspective of the cultural historians, Ranke's famous dictum – that the task of the historian was to show "what actually happened'" – became clouded in prejudice, precisely because explanation and interpretation depended upon the subjectivity of the historian. Thus, in 1843, Georg Friedrich Kolb announced that it was an "absurd imposition" to expect historians "to sink in the mud of the prejudices of all ages." Historians, he believed, too easily confused their own judgments and opinions with those of the past; as a result, he declared, they were unable to distinguish properly between the connection of events and their presentation (*Darstellung*).[11]

By the late 1840s, cultural history had undergone a significant reorientation. With relatively few exceptions, cultural historians had abandoned the attempt to write the history of *Menschheit*, focusing their attention on Germany instead. While this narrowed their perspective

11 Ibid., 16–17.

substantially, it enabled them to broaden the scope of their enquiries by addressing specific issues related directly to Germany's past. From geography to economics, these studies had one common denominator: the *Volk*. Rather than humanity in general, the *Volk* became the new organizing principle of cultural history. This conceptual framework was perhaps most extensively developed in the histories of the journalist and historian Wilhelm Heinrich Riehl (1823–97). Riehl, who based his work on an organic conception of the *Volk*, was influential in the development of the discipline of *Volkskunde* or ethnography. A further trend can be seen in the work of certain historians who wished to go beyond tracing the internal development of the *Volk*. For example, Friedrich von Hellwald, in *Kulturgeschichte in ihrer natürlichen Entwicklung bis zur Gegenwart* (1875), sought to incorporate Social Darwinism into his cultural histories, and "the evolution of culture became tied to the notion of the fight for existence."[12] Others, such as Gustav Klemm, attempted to transform cultural history into something akin to racial history and to prove, through the presentation of seemingly incoherent facts and artifacts about material, spiritual, and social life, that the world was divided into "passive" and "active" races; he claimed that only the "active" races, to which Germany belonged, developed culturally. According to Heinrich Ritter von Srbik, Klemm was no less than the father "of the nordic doctrine of Blood and Spirit."[13]

Despite the reconceptualization of cultural history in the late 1840s and 1850s and its increasing popularity – in 1856 the first journal dedicated to cultural history, *Die Zeitschrift für deutsche Kulturgeschichte*, was founded – it remained extremely problematic. The greatest difficulty faced by cultural historians was the field's lack of conceptual and methodological rigour. In most cases, cultural history was defined not according to a well-conceived set of theoretical or historical principles, but in contrast to the political and event-oriented history of the German historical school. As a result, the very definition of what constituted the subject matter of cultural histories – that is to say, a working definition of culture – remained extremely varied and often vague. For Wachsmuth, for example, culture referred primarily to "creative and ennobling rational activity." Quite in contrast to Wachsmuth was the definition put forward by Gustav Klemm, who, in 1843, restricted his field of study to "how people of earlier ages ate, drank, lived and

---

12 Gilbert, *History: Politics or Culture?*, 83.
13 Srbik, *Geist und Geschichte*, 2:352.

dressed."[14] Without more precise conceptualization, the term cultural history was destined to embrace a myriad of historiographical practices, ranging from historical anthropology, to art and literary history, to the history of ideas and the history of everyday life, to ethnology and a type of "racial science."

Similarly, those practising cultural historians who strove to produce comprehensive histories of society, while maintaining that society was an organic whole, could not realize their goal of a *Sozialwissenschaft* or *Gesellschaftswissenschaft* because they focused on describing historical conditions, rather than explaining social and cultural development. As well as losing the universal perspective of eighteenth-century cultural histories, most tended to concentrate on particular elements of social development at the expense of the general. Bereft of theoretical reflection, their work became, in the words of Roger Chickering, the history of "the minutiae of manners and morals, of *Lebkuchen* and *Totenbretter*, with little sense of historical context."[15]

This seriously harmed the reputation of the discipline, and it subsequently faced many obstacles in its search for autonomy and legitimacy, especially within the professional academic community. Although cultural history was extremely popular with the educated middle class, in large part because of its relevance to the present, it was poorly represented in the universities. Increasingly, it became the preserve of local, amateur historians who were active in the *Vereine*, and of the occasional specialist, who focused on the minutiae of everyday life or the compilation of regional histories.[16] The dilettantish reputation of cultural history was further reinforced by the fact that, for the most part, it was directed not towards an academic audience, but rather towards the general reading public. Although the *Zeitschrift für deutsche Kulturgeschichte* sought to place cultural history on a firm theoretical and methodological footing – so it could compete with mainstream historiography and shake off its reputation as popular, not scholarly, history – the journal never entirely succeeded and ceased publication in 1859.

Despite their important contribution to the understanding and preservation of local history and the history of the *Volk*, the work of German cultural historians was generally scorned by professional historians because it ignored political life. Many believed that its focus on the history

14 Dilly and Ryding, "Kulturgeschichtsschreibung," 18.
15 Chickering, *Karl Lamprecht*, 155.
16 Hartmann, "Die deutsche Kulturgeschichtsschreibung," 64–72.

of everyday life and on local history, instead of on the state, and its lack of conceptual precision meant that cultural history could not become a "scientific," scholarly field of study. Mainstream historians' reviews of Gustav Klemm's ten-volume cultural history, to cite just one example, were consistently negative. Friedrich Jodl, for one, condemned the work as "spiritless collecting." Nowhere did Klemm attempt to relate this myriad of facts to general principles, "to draw conclusions, to find causal connections and patterns in occurrences ... and to transform the unconnected details into living knowledge."[17] This attitude was summed up in the 1850s by Johann Gustav Droysen, by no means an impartial observer, who echoed the opinion of many academics when he claimed that the current state of cultural history was "of highly doubtful scholarly and scientific value and had a much too dilettantish standing."[18]

Despite their overwhelming position of dominance within the German university – or perhaps because of it – the *Politologen* responded defensively and sometimes with extreme hostility to those scholars outside the mainstream who dared to challenge the hegemonic rule of state-oriented political historical discourse. Cultural historians were favourite targets. The infamous Lamprecht controversy, the most explosive clash between political and cultural historians, has been the subject of many enquiries in the history of German historiography.[19] However, this battle over historiographical turf, from which the political historians emerged as the unquestioned champions, was in fact only the climax of many decades of rancourous squabbling and jousting between cultural and political historians.[20]

Throughout the decades preceding the Lamprecht controversy, cultural and political historians engaged in an on-again, off-again war of

17 Jodl, *Die Culturgeschichtsschreibung*, 22. This reminded Carl Neumann, an early Burckhardt scholar, of the Germanische Nationalmuseum in Nuremberg, which he claimed consisted "of many rooms of old ovens, pots, shields, toys, books and pictures." He compared it to a "washing list," lacking all systematization. Quoted in Siebert, *Jacob Burckhardt*, 33, note 16. Two of the men actively involved in the founding of the Germanisches Museum in 1852, Johannes Falke and Johann Müller, became editors of the most important journal devoted to cultural history, *Zeitschrift für deutsche Kulturgeschichte*, in 1856. See Gilbert, *History: Politics or Culture?*, 84.

18 Droysen, *Texte zur Geschichtstheorie*, 27.

19 On Lamprecht and the Lamprecht-Controversy, see Chickering, *Karl Lamprecht*, and Schorn-Schütte, *Karl Lamprecht*.

20 See for example, Heinrich von Treitschke's 1858 "Kampfschrift," in which he criticized some of the most noted cultural historians of the day, including Wilhelm Heinrich Riehl (1823–97), Treitschke, *Die Gesellschaftswissenschaft: Ein kritischer Versuch*.

words. The debate within the German historical profession flared once more, in 1888, with the publication of the lecture, *Das eigentliche Arbeitsgebiet der Geschichte*, by Dietrich Schäfer, a former student of Treitschke. Schäfer, who thought that cultural histories were "sprouting from the ground like mushrooms," based his attack on two essential points. First, he argued that the state had to be the central locus of history and historical writing because its development was the primary motivation of human behaviour and because it, alone, provided the necessary unity of human activity, society, and culture. Second, he contended that the entire cultural historical enterprise was plagued by methodological and conceptual weaknesses. Not only was its subject matter diverse and ill-defined; it also possessed no clear means of integrating this material into a comprehensive, unified framework. Schäfer concluded by intimating that the best status cultural history could hope to attain was as an auxiliary to political history. As it stood, however, the enterprise remained at an "unscientific," popular level.[21]

Schäfer's comments provoked the young Karlsruhe historian, Eberhard Gothein, to respond. In his work, *Die Aufgaben der Culturgeschichte* (1889), Gothein attempted to establish cultural history as a specialized field of study, as a legitimate and respected scholarly enterprise that would not just compete successfully with political history, but would also challenge its authority and official status within the academic community.[22] Gothein viewed the development of cultural history as "a necessary consequence of the course of development of the modern spirit." Whereas traditional political history by its very nature concentrated on one particular aspect of human history, cultural history made possible the integration and synthesis of all aspects of social life or "cultural systems" – religion, the state, art, economics – into a "higher unity."[23] However, although fine in theory, this was much more difficult to put into practice. Indeed, such was the ambiguity of Gothein's conceptualization

21 Schäfer, *Das eigentliche Arbeitsgebiet der Geschichte*, 29. See also Chickering, *Karl Lamprecht*, 151–6.
22 Gothein, *Die Aufgaben der Culturgeschichte*, 50. Both Schäfer and Gothein evoked Burckhardt's name in defence of their cause, but Burckhardt adroitly avoided any public participation in the discussion. He even returned a copy of Gothein's book to the author claiming "regretfully," but caustically, that he was unable to form a "systematisches Bild," of *Die Aufgaben der Culturgeschichte*, *Briefe*, 9:196. This must have been a disappointment to Gothein, who had modelled his work on Burckhardt's and had even visited him in Basel. See Peter Alter, "Eberhard Gothein," in Wehler, ed. *Deutsche Historiker*, 8:43–4.
23 Gothein, *Die Aufgaben der Culturgeschichte*, 6.

of cultural history and his dependence on the historicist principle of individuality, that he concluded that cultural history, in its purest form, was not the history of civilization, but rather the history of ideas.[24]

Gothein's intervention on behalf of cultural history did not make the field of study more acceptable to the German historical profession, and it was to remain in the historiographic shadows for most of the nineteenth century. The incredible hostility of the German professional historical community, led by Friedrich Meinecke, towards Lamprecht's attempt at a synthesis of economic, social, and cultural history further hindered the development of cultural history in Germany, ultimately to the detriment of German historiography in general. Consequently, throughout the nineteenth century, the field of cultural history languished in a grey area between parochial, popular history and acceptable, professional scholarship. On the one hand, cultural historians had difficulty overcoming the barriers of official academic history and the institutional structure of the profession, thus ensuring methodological, theoretical, as well as ideological conformity.[25] On the other hand, however, as Schäfer correctly claimed, the study of cultural history was also handicapped, and ultimately marginalized, during the nineteenth century by its own conceptual and methodological imprecision and vagueness. In short, cultural historians were unable to agree on a precise definition of what constituted culture or cultural history. In the end, the inability of cultural historians to develop a sound theoretical framework and the methodological principles that would provide it with unity and coherence left the emerging discipline fragmented and open to accusations of dilettantism, amateurism, and unprofessionalism.

Finally, cultural history existed as an *Oppositionswissenschaft* not only on theoretical and methodological, but also political grounds. Although cultural historians rejected the Rankean historical paradigm, they did share at least one feature with the German Historical School: as the work of Wilhelm Heinrich Riehl and many others demonstrates, cultural history was as overtly politicized as the work of such mainstream political historians as Sybel or Treitschke. Even in its Enlightenment form, cultural history was motivated by didacticism and intense patriotism. Many early nineteenth-century works of cultural history were ex-

24 Ibid., 50.
25 On the institutional structure of the German historical profession see Iggers, *New Directions in European Historiography*, 80–5. Significantly, Gothein never occupied a chair of history. In Bonn and Heidelberg he held the chairs for national economy.

plicitly conceived as *Vaterlandsgeschichte*. As already noted, what distinguished cultural history from political history was that the latter represented the history of the political elite – kings, princes, ministers, generals, and diplomats – whereas the former was considered the history of the "nation" or *Volk*, understood to be primarily the middle classes. As Hartmann has persuasively demonstrated, cultural history since the eighteenth century had been written by middle-class historians for a middle-class audience. Cultural history, in other words, was the history of the rise to prominence of the *Bürgertum*; in contrast to political history, this represented the "specific interests of the bourgeoisie" and, through its patriotism and didactic intent, sought to reproduce a "bourgeois vision and ideal of history."[26]

These factors did not make cultural history acceptable to the establishment or to the professional historical community. Throughout the nineteenth century, cultural history unrepentantly bucked the dominant political attitudes of the establishment, continuing to associate itself with opposition to the political status quo. In the period prior to 1848, for instance, cultural historians' attempts to raise the political consciousness of the *Volk* and to represent it as the core of the political nation, stood in sharp contrast to the reactionary conservative agenda of the Prussian state. After the failure of German liberals to establish a *Volksstaat* in 1848, those cultural historians who opposed the *kleindeutsch* movement for German national unification and were "anxious to show that the autonomy of the German states had roots in the way people lived in these various regions," were stigmatized by the establishment as agents of political particularism.[27] Finally, the fortunes of cultural history suffered later in the century as well, after the growth of the political left in Germany and Bismarck's campaign against Social Democracy. Even though a liberal historian such as Riehl consistently condemned the "leveling" tendencies of the socialists in his journalistic writings, cultural history's emphasis on the habits and customs of the *Volk*, rather than on the "primacy of politics," earned it the label of "subversive"; to some it appeared to appeal to dangerous democratic tendencies in society, as Dietrich Schäfer made clear in his 1889 polemic against cultural history.[28]

. . .

26 See Hartmann, "Die deutsche Kulturgeschichtsschreibung," 64–95.
27 Gilbert, *History: Politics or Culture?*, 85.
28 Schäfer, *Das eigentliche Arbeitsgebiet der Geschichte*, 6.

178   *Burckhardt and History*

Despite its insecure status within the German scholarly community and
its lack of clear conceptualization, cultural history was by no means an
alien field to the young Burckhardt. Indeed, he was drawn to it very early
in life. He first encountered the full and varied potential of cultural history as a student at high school, where he studied the works of the great
contemporary French historians: Guizot, Thierry, and Barante. He was
also very familiar with Voltaire's writings and considered him to be the
founder of cultural history.[29] Perhaps more significant for the course of
Burckhardt's future development as a cultural historian, however, was his
close friendship with the Freiburg historian, Heinrich Schreiber, thought
by many to be one of the best local historians of his day.[30]

Burckhardt and Schreiber first became acquainted in 1835, when
Schreiber, who was then working on a study of the sixteenth-century poet
and scholar Heinrich Glareanus, asked the seventeen-year-old to conduct
archival research in Basel. Their friendship lasted until Schreiber's death
in 1872. Burckhardt attributed much of his success as an historian to
Schreiber's influence; he certainly provided the young Basler with the
inner strength to follow his convictions and to abandon his theological
career in favour of history. Shortly before he departed for Berlin, Burckhardt expressed his appreciation: "Should I ever achieve anything of
significance in the field of history ... the honour will be due to you ...
Without your stimulation – even though you might not be aware of it –
and without your encouragement when you found out about my decision
[to abandon theology and study history], and finally, without your shin-
ing example, it would probably not have occurred to me to seek my vocation in historical research ... I hope to be able to repay ... you later."[31]
Burckhardt ultimately kept his promise, dedicating his first major work
of cultural history, *The Age of Constantine the Great*, to "Herrn Professor
Dr. Heinrich Schreiber in Freiburg with respectful gratitude."

29 Kaegi, 1:353 and 6, 1:107; See also Röthlin, "Jacob Burckhardts Stellung in der Kulturgeschichtsschreibung," 397.

30 In many respects, Schreiber's work embodied the very best of contemporary German
cultural history. Throughout his lifetime he wrote on an enormous range of topics, including literature, art, archaeology, theology, and history. His most famous works were his studies of the social and cultural life of Freiburg, beginning in 1820 with his *Geschichte und
Beschreibung des Münsters zu Freiburg im Breisgau*, and his multivolume *Geschichte der Stadt
Freiburg im Breisgau* (1857–58), which sought to integrate material and intellectual culture
into the historical narrative. On Schreiber see, Rieke, *Heinrich Schreiber*.

31 *Briefe*, 1:122. Rieke, *Heinrich Schreiber*, 78ff; Kaegi, 1:251ff.

In fact, what may have been new for Burckhardt at this time was not cultural history, but rather the Rankean approach to political history, which he encountered first hand as a student in Berlin. Whether or not Burckhardt's dislike of Ranke as a person contributed to his decision to avoid traditional political history is difficult to say. He certainly mocked Ranke's aristocratic pretensions and "civil service" attitude and, over time, grew suspicious of his strong allegience to the Prussian state and its authoritarian regime. Seen from this perspective and within the context of his German experiences, Burckhardt may have viewed cultural history's subordination of political history, its reputation for dilettantism, and its broader public appeal as an antidote to the reactionary conservatism of Ranke and Prussia and as a confirmation of his allegience to his middle-class origins and to the German *Volk*.

No prominent cultural historians were then in residence at the university in Berlin. However, Burckhardt did come into close contact with many professors who incorporated various aspects of cultural history into their work. The most notable were the art historian Franz Kugler, who sought to integrate art history and cultural history, and the great classicist August Boeckh, whose course on Greek antiquity Burckhardt attended during the winter semester of 1839–40. The work of both scholars differed substantially from the typical cultural histories of the time. For them, cultural history was neither local history, nor the history of material civilization. They rejected the mundane recording of the facts of daily life in favour of a more comprehensive, coherent, and universal examination of those aspects of human creativity and spiritual life that gave definition to the historical era under consideration. For Kugler, who viewed art from the broader perspective of cultural history, it was crucial that art historians demonstrate how a work of art evolved from the intellectual and social context in which it was conceived and created. He saw art as providing crucial evidence about the cultural developments of a given period. Much as Kugler sought to capture the spirit of a period through its art, Boeckh viewed cultural history as history that focused on "the conditions existing when actions took place." He likewise avoided what would today be called the "history of everyday life," trying instead to establish the dominant ideas – whether political, philosophical, or cultural – that formed the essence of any given period of history.[32]

---

32 Gilbert, "Jacob Burckhardt's Student Years," 265; See also Siebert, *Jacob Burckhardt*, 45 and Kaegi, 2:48–53.

Despite the important influence of these two scholars, Burckhardt did not make a decision to pursue cultural history until either during, or shortly after, the 1841 summer semester he spent studying in Bonn. The few months he spent in the Rhineland were of great significance.[33] Although Burckhardt did not think very highly of the university,[34] the level of scholarship was sound and he was exposed to much more cultural history than was the case in Berlin. Indeed, if his course schedule is any indication, he chose to avoid lectures on political history, concentrating instead on cultural history and related subjects.

The university in Bonn, like that in Berlin, was a product of Wilhelm von Humboldt's effort to reform and modernize the Prussian education system. Founded in 1818 as a Protestant institution in a predominantly Catholic region, it was seen by the authorities as a valuable instrument in the Prussianization of that part of the Rhineland recently annexed to the Kingdom of Prussia. Despite being plagued by political and religious tensions during the *Vormärz* – the controversy surrounding Gottfried Kinkel's decision to marry a divorced Catholic is a case in point – the university was by no means a mirror image of the university in Berlin. More liberal and certainly less influenced by the thought and work of Hegel, it had a number of prominent cultural historians on its faculty, including Karl Dietrich Hüllmann and Johann Wilhelm Löbell. Although we cannot be sure that Burckhardt ever attended Hüllmann's lectures on medieval cultural history, he was certainly familiar with Hüllmann's massive study of medieval towns, *Städtewesen des Mittelalters* (1826–7) (which he cited in his work on Conrad von Hochstaden), and was in close contact with the professor. Likewise, Burckhardt does not seem to have had any contact with Löbell, although he knew his book on Gregory of Tours published in 1839.[35] We do know, however, that Burckhardt studied medieval philosophy with Christian August Brandis. We know, too, that he attended lectures on English history given by the geographer Georg Benjamin Mendelssohn, brother of the musician Felix Mendelssohn and grandson of the philosopher Moses Mendelssohn, a course Burckhardt seemed to find particularly stimulating, even though

33 Besides Kaegi, 2:95–179, see also Gilbert, "Jacob Burckhardt's Student Years," and Schieder, "Jacob Burckhardt und die Rheinlande," 163–82

34 *Briefe*, 1:176.

35 See Gilbert, *History: Politics or Culture?*, 46–8, and ibid., "Jacob Burckhardt's Student Years," 266–7. Hüllmann gave Burckhardt permission to use the university library. *Briefe*, 1:176. He refers to this work by Löbell in *Briefe*, 1:231, a work that was thematically close to Burckhardt's study of Carl Martell.

it discussed economic history at great length. Finally, we know that Burckhardt attended a course on ancient Greek art history by the philologist Friedrich Gottlieb Welcker, which created a lasting impression.[36] The only course that might have had a strict political content was one Burckhardt attended on Rhenish history by the young *Dozent* and student of Ranke, Heinrich von Sybel. There is, however, little indication that Burckhardt enjoyed Sybel's lectures; Werner Kaegi even doubts that he "remained loyal until the end of the semester."[37]

The most important evidence of the direction Burckhardt's historical thought was taking at this early point is his study of Conrad von Hochstaden, the early thirteenth-century archbishop of Cologne and founder of the Cologne cathedral. Inspired by the summer he spent in the Rhineland and his widespread enthusiasm for the cathedral, Burckhardt wrote an essay after his return to Berlin for Ranke's seminar.[38] This essay, like his earlier study of Carl Martell, certainly reflects an intellectual debt to Ranke. This is perhaps most evident in its chronological discussion of political developments and its narrative structure. However, Burckhardt was clearly trying to chart an independent course by integrating analyses of the cultural and intellectual conditions of early thirteenth-century Cologne into the narrative; as such, the essay represents an important transitional work.

As stated in a letter to Kinkel, Burckhardt, like other cultural historians, tried to write for a general audience. For example, it was the public, not Ranke, that he kept in mind while writing his essay on Conrad. Indeed, although Ranke was in fact very pleased with Burckhardt's work and even suggested he publish it,[39] the work ultimately reflected more of the influence of Burckhardt's friend and teacher, the art historian Franz Kugler, and perhaps even of Karl Friedrich Hüllmann, than of Ranke. During the summer of 1841, Burckhardt had spent eight days in Cologne with Kugler, who, a few months later, published an article on the cathedral, the

36 Kaegi, 2:139ff. Brandis and Welcker were the university's "twin pillars of anti-Hegelianism." The influence of Brandis's course on medieval philosophy can be seen in Burckhardt's *Conrad von Hochstaden*, especially his section on the Cologne scholar Albertus Magnus. Burckhardt also attended a course by Ernst Moritz Arndt, which he did not find impressive.

37 Kaegi, 2:143. Sybel, only one year older than Burckhardt, began studying in Berlin in 1834 and attended Ranke's seminars with two other well-known Ranke students, Georg Waitz and Wilhelm von Giesebrecht. In 1842, Friedrich Christoph Dahlmann began teaching in Bonn.

38 *Briefe*, 1:194.

39 *Briefe*, 1:194–5.

first of many to appear over the next few years.[40] Moreover, at the same time, Burckhardt was also writing his guidebook to Belgian art, *Die Kunstwerke der belgischen Städte*, which was published in 1842. Perhaps the latter inspired him to incorporate his new understanding of cultural and art history into his studies and to explore the complex relationship between monumental art and history in *Conrad von Hochstaden*.

It was no coincidence that after his trip to the Rhineland and the completion of his study of Conrad von Hochstaden, Burckhardt announced to Kinkel his decision to devote his energy to the study of cultural history: "As far as my historical research is concerned, the background is for me the main thing, and it forms the basis of cultural history, to which I primarily want to devote my energies."[41] Despite his determination to pursue cultural history, Burckhardt was initially very hesitant about accepting the advice of Ranke and his friends in Bonn to publish the manuscript. However, by the late autumn of 1842, he overcame his reluctance after seeing the recently published work on Hochstaden by the Zürich Germanist Ernst Ettmüller, which he felt was "careless and tendentious."[42] Burckhardt's new found confidence in his work did not last long. Another study soon appeared on the same theme, this one by Heinrich von Sybel, his former teacher in Bonn and a scholar whose credentials were far more prestigious than those of Ettmüller.[43]

A number of scholars have argued that Burckhardt's *Conrad von Hochstaden* is a "typical work of the Ranke school," given its critical scholarship "based on an examination of all the available primary sources." As Gilbert concludes, "This is a work of Ranke's school in that the single event, despite the care which is given to its correct presentation, is presented in the perspective of the basic trends of the period."[44] However, despite the fact that Burckhardt paid close attention to chronology,

40 Kugler, "Der Dom zu Köln und seine Architektur."

41 *Briefe*, 1:197.

42 *Briefe*, 1:218. Ettmüller, *Pfaffentrug und Bürgerzwist oder die Kölner Erzbischöfe Konrad von Hochstaden und Engelbert von Falkenburg*, Zürich, 1842. On Burckhardt's decision to publish, see Dürr, Introduction, GA, 1:xxxvii-ix.

43 Sybel, "Erzbishof Conrad von Hochstaden und die Bürgerschaft von Köln." The appearance of Sybel's work seems to have made Burckhardt nervous; perhaps that was why he claimed, in a letter to Schreiber, that Kinkel had published his manuscript behind his back, which was certainly not the case. See *Briefe*, 1:232. However, Sybel praised Burckhardt's work, although he "corrected" some details. See GA, 1:xxxix.

44 Gilbert, "Jacob Burckhardt's Student Years," 258. Similarly, Kaegi, 2:158, argues that because "the whole is presented as a narrative in chronological order," this is a sign of the influence of the Rankean School.

made critical use of source material, and was careful about presentation – methods, incidently, that were not invented by Ranke – his essay was not typical of the Rankean school. It was at worst an atypical, at best an early (if not entirely successful) attempt by the young scholar to write cultural history. This becomes especially clear when one compares Burckhardt's *Conrad* with Sybel's early contribution to the history of Cologne in the thirteenth century.

These two works by students of Ranke on the same theme, appearing as they did within a short time of each other, provide a remarkable glance at the ideas of two of Europe's most prominent historians during the formative period of their careers. The sharp contrast between the two studies reveals the extent to which Burckhardt had distanced himself from the traditional political history and embraced cultural history, and the extent to which Sybel had remained a loyal pupil of Ranke (for without question, his was a "typical work of the Ranke school"). Indeed, Heinrich von Sybel (1817–95), the founder of the prestigious journal, *Historische Zeitschrift*, along with Droysen, Georg Waitz, Georg Gervinus, and Friedrich Christoph Dahlmann, was to become a leading member of the so-called "Prussian School" of historical thought. Often considered as representative of the "high point of historical optimism," the historians of the Prussian school were highly politicized scholars who, generally speaking, began their careers as liberals during the Revolution of 1848 but, once disillusioned with the failure of the Frankfurt Parliament to unify Germany, abandoned liberalism in favour of unification from above under the auspices of the Prussian army. In the wake of Bismarck's wars of conquest and national unification, they became staunch adherents of the German *Machtstaat* and later *Weltmachtpolitik*.[45]

By all accounts, Sybel's article on Conrad von Hochstaden is consistent with his mature work. Despite later ideological and theoretical differences with Ranke, Sybel clearly shared his teacher's view of the state as an ethical entity and the driving force of historical development to which all else in society was to be subordinated. As early as 1843, Sybel was already harnessing his conception of political history to the historical mission of Germany as articulated by the Prussian School: namely, German national unification. He began and ended his essay on Conrad von Hochstaden and the city of Cologne during the thirteenth century with a lament about Germany's lack of national unity, and the impossibility of

---

45 See Iggers, *The German Conception of History*, 90–123.

"bourgeois public spirit" continuing to exist in a state in which "the natural or historical solidarity is broken into pieces." That this was the case in the thirteenth century was partly the fault of Conrad, who, with other territorial princes, had presided over the fragmentation of the German nation into a multitude of small provinces and thus effectively prevented the emergence of a strong territorial state.[46]

Burckhardt's presentation of the history of Cologne and the founding of its cathedral could not have been more unlike that of Sybel. While Sybel's work was a classic example of German political history, Burckhardt's sought to integrate cultural history within the general framework of his narration of the events of Conrad's life. Burckhardt was not entirely successful, confined as he was by the work's restrictive chronological structure. Nonetheless, he attempted to create the desired effect by separating and highlighting the strictly cultural historical sections from the main structure of the narrative. As a result, the three main cultural historical excursuses – on the cultural life of Cologne during the time of the building of the cathedral, the figure of the great medieval scholar Albertus Magnus, and the city's constitution – became in many respects the central focus and outstanding features of the study.

The strong influence of Kugler is clearly evident in Burckhardt's *Conrad von Hochstaden*, especially the manner in which he desired "to show precisely the inner connection between the rich artistic developments and the cultural conditions of each epoch."[47] For Burckhardt, as for Kugler, this was an important key to writing cultural history. As Burckhardt fully admitted, however, he was unable to proceed with such a task and, in the end, was content merely to refer to the "rapid increase in well-being and culture in this time," not exploring more fully the implications of this relationship. However, he did examine the specific cultural conditions. In his discussion of Rhenish life, he provided a thorough sketch of various aspects of medieval urban social life, including economic, artistic, and spiritual developments; he also incorporated discussions of political culture, including most importantly a section on the city's unique constitutional situation.

Unlike most contemporary cultural history, Burckhardt's work did not ignore high politics – he devoted considerable space to descriptions of the political conflicts between the archbishop and the city of Cologne and the various emperors and princes. Likewise, he did not attempt to

46 Sybel, "Erzbischof Conrad von Hochstaden," 122–3.
47 GA, 1:221.

write the history of the *Volk*. Moreover, the specific sections on cultural history in *Conrad von Hochstaden* cannot simply be reduced to the purposeless rendering of "detailed descriptions of social life" or the "recording [of] the daily life of society and all its groups," as Gilbert suggests.[48] More compelling, though, was Burckhardt's attempt to integrate these discussions into the general framework of his examination of "the climax of epic poety," which began with the reign of Friedrich II "and concluded with the Cathedral at Cologne ... the triumph of the entire pagan and Christian, eastern and western architecture."[49] In this regard, there are certain similarities between this work and his masterpiece, *The Civlization of the Renaissance in Italy*. In particular, Burckhardt was primarily concerned with what he described in his earlier letter to Kinkel as the "background", or the study of the social, political, and cultural conditions or prerequisites necessary for the creation of noteworthy cultural achievements. (Although the Cologne cathedral occupies a central place in his study of Conrad von Hochstaden, the work is not about the cathedral per se. Similarly, we cannot understand the significance of the Italian Renaissance without an appreciation of the art, even though it is not discussed at length.) There are other similarities, most notably that both works describe periods of endemic political strife. But ultimately, although the perpetual violence of the age has a tremendous impact on cultural development, it neither shapes the period nor is it, in the long run, the characteristic feature of the age. On the contrary, the bloodshed and violence that accompany the various political confrontations form the historical background; what emerges as the defining feature of the age is the enormous creative energy, which in the case of Cologne was embodied in Albertus Magnus and the tremendous spiritual and intellectual force behind the creation of the cathedral. "Cologne was the garden where the most beautiful blossoms of that great age opened up," Burckhardt claimed. It bore witness to the "grandeur and glory of those intellects whom we must honour as the bearers of the culture of that period."[50]

Burckhardt found the "bearer of culture" and the representative figure of the age not in Conrad, but in the figure of the scholar Albertus Magnus, the dominican monk who designed the cathedral and brokered the peace between the inhabitants of the city and the ambitious,

48 Gilbert, *History: Politics or Culture?*, 47–8.
49 GA, 1:204–5.
50 Ibid., 1:205.

arrogant archbishop. An individual of rare intellectual genius of world historical significance, Albertus had connections throughout Europe and was none other than the teacher of Thomas Aquinus, the "Wagner to this Faust."[51] More than any other individual, he represented the very universality of medieval culture, symbolizing for Burckhardt the cultural and spiritual unity of the age. He was, in effect, the very antithesis of Conrad and became, in the words of Schieder, "a representative of real historical greatness in the sense of *Weltgeschichtlichen Betrachtungen*, behind which Conrad von Hochstaden and with him the world of the state and politics disappear."[52]

While Burckhardt attempted to integrate cultural history into his account, it would be incorrect to describe *Conrad von Hochstaden* as a cultural history in the sense of Burckhardt's later works. In many respects, Burckhardt did not succeed entirely in the task he set for himself; he recognized his limitations, while at the same time expressing his desired objectives. But his attempt to elevate the "bearers of culture" over the "bearers of naked power" was a significant step in the direction of an independent cultural history. Moreover, the emphasis on the spiritual and cultural unity of thirteenth-century Germany stood in sharp contrast to Sybel's main thesis; namely, the overwhelming disunity and fragmentation of political life and the disintegration of empire. Perhaps at no other point do we so clearly see the distinction between Sybel's political orientation and Burckhardt's emphasis on cultural development than in Burckhardt's final excursus on Cologne's consitutional situtation.

Burckhardt's trip to the Rhineland coincided with the highpoint of his romantic enthusiasm for Germany and, as we have seen, his subsequent patriotic outbursts to his sister Louise in Basel. In the Rhineland, and more importantly in his studies of medieval Germany, Burckhardt believed he had found "the real Germany." However, his opinion of what constituted this reality differed from that of Sybel. Where Sybel saw the striving for political unity, Burckhardt emphasized the spiritual and cultural unity of the German lands; where Sybel saw the collapse of the drive towards a unified nation-state, Burckhardt saw the realization of a system of independent, small states, unified not by naked power, but by culture. This was "the real Germany" that Burckhardt admired in the Rhineland. "The German Middle Ages, in its endlessly rich forms of political and bourgeois life, often reminds us of a forest of strong young

51 Ibid., 1:230.
52 Schieder, "Burckhardt und die Rheinlande," 180–1.

trees," he wrote. "From the same soil numerous independent beings, the roots of which are mysteriously entangled, are growing upwards, so that their branches and tops touch and become intertwined above the earth."[53] This vision of Germany – a Germany with countless independent existences – corresponded, as Kaegi has argued, with a vision of Germany to which Switzerland "as a free member was able to belong and to which it had once belonged until the imperial, unitarian reform of the Empire tried to transform it into a great state and brought an end to the old circumstances: until the conflict with Maximilian," that is, during the Swiss War of 1499 and the crisis of the late fifteenth century.[54] However, Burckhardt continues, "finally the few more powerful trees climb above everything into the heights and draw with them the remaining air and light. In Germanic Europe the state has also finally become master over all those independent entities. It patronizes everything and draws everything into its ambit."[55]

In a work written for Ranke's seminar, and during a time of heightened enthusiasm for Germany, Burckhardt suggested a uniquely Swiss and Basel interpretation of German medieval history, an analysis that reflected his political ideal of the *Kleinstaat*. According to Burckhardt, it was no coincidence that the "golden age" of medieval German culture occurred during a time when this ideal most closely reflected political and social reality. Furthermore, his particularist ideal was expressed in distinct opposition to the liberal, nationalist tendencies of the day. In effect, because the internal structure of this political entity was based on the guilds, Burckhardt was expressing a corporatist vision of society that clashed with modern political objectives: "they were freely joined unions of free urban residents who formed a community based on law [*Rechtsgenossenschaft*], with the common duty of the protection of public security and the preservation of law and rights."[56] This was the very system of government and type of political association with the Swiss cantons that Basel had belonged to since the early sixteenth century, the roots of which were to be found in medieval Germany; now, however, it was under attack from liberals and radicals throughout Switzerland. It was a system threatened by the power and growth of the modern, centralized state. It is also no coincidence that when the ideal of the

53 GA, 1:238.
54 Kaegi, 2:164.
55 GA, 1:238.
56 Ibid.

"intellectual unity" of the German lands was replaced by power-hungry
visions of German "political unity" during the revolutionary excitement
of the late 1840s – when "in Germanic Europe the state has finally become master over all independent entities" – Burckhardt abandoned
political history for cultural history, medieval history for ancient history
and the history of the Renaissance, and Germany for Italy.

. . .

Burckhardt's first major work of cultural history was *The Age of Constantine
the Great*, which appeared in late 1852. Burckhardt was aware that "with
this book he was offering something that nobody had offered before."[57]
The book, which most likely originated in Kinkel's early plans for a history of paganism, was the product of ten years of study and reflection
about ancient and medieval history and the task of cultural history. It offered not just a new interpretation of the age of Constantine, the decline
of the Roman Empire, and the rise of medieval Europe; of greater significance, it presented, in the words of Irmgard Siebert, a "new methodological conception" of history.[58] In effect, with *The Age of Constantine the Great*,
Burckhardt began to redefine the practice of cultural history.

The general thrust of *Constantine* can be briefly outlined as a discussion of a period of profound crisis and flux, the period of the transition
from paganism to Christianity, from Roman antiquity to the Christian
Middle Ages. One of Burckhardt's principal motivations was the desire
to debunk myths surrounding the triumph of Christianity; the division
of the Christian world into a western half, with its centre in Rome, and
an eastern half, with its centre in Constantinople; and the decline of paganism, especially the dominant opinion that the triumph of Christianity was somehow inevitable or preordained. His particular historiographical vendetta was directed against early Christian historians,
such as Lactantius and Eusebius, as well as contemporary theologians.
He was particularly critical of Eusebius, whom he described as "the first
thoroughly dishonest historian of antiquity. His tactic, which enjoyed a
brilliant success in his own day and throughout the Middle Ages, con-

57 Siebert, *Jacob Burckhardt*, 73.
58 Ibid.

sisted in making the first great protector of the Church [Constantine] at all costs an ideal of humanity according to his lights, and above all an ideal for future rulers."[59] Instead, Burckhardt portrayed Constantine as a cynical manipulator of the Church for his own political ends; as a genius driven by "ambition and lust for power"; and as a man of little faith, who was "essentially unreligious," despite the image he put forward of himself.[60] In contrast, Burckhardt attempted to rehabilitate the reputation of Diocletian, despite his persecutions of the Christians who had suffered great harm at the hands of the Christian authors.

Such an interpretation of Constantine and the late Roman Empire was not necessarily new. It followed the critical evaluations of the early Christian historians by Montesquieu, Voltaire, and Gibbon.[61] What was new in Burckhardt's intepretation was its derivation from his secular view of Christianity, which deprived Christianity of its role as an historical agent in the collapse of the pagan Empire. Instead of being a great spiritual force motivating men and women, Christianity became, in Burckhardt's rendition, just another historical power. Indeed, at one point he describes the triumph of Christianity as a "historical spectacle of the greatest magnitude."[62] As such, he minimized the influence of Christianity both on its own triumph and on paganism's general decline. He argued that its role in the decline of the Empire had traditionally been too highly rated by other scholars, including Gibbon. In contrast, as Burckhardt explains at the beginning of his work, the success of Christianity was the result of "an internal development in paganism itself."[63]

Burckhardt's objective was to study these internal developments and conditions within pagan society, which eventually resulted in its collapse when confronted by the rise of Christianity. He did not want to trace the origins of this collapse, however. Hence the concept of "decline" is not entirely appropriate, inasmuch as it implies an examination of cause and effect, a teleological process. Instead, Burckhardt attempted to represent what might be called a "state of being" characterized by two particular conditions – "*Veraltung*," or antiquation, obsolescence, or senescence; and "*Erstarrung*," or paralysis – as the defining features of late Roman society. During this time of internal political and economic

59 *Constantine,* 283.
60 Ibid., 292.
61 See Kaegi, 3:379–82.
62 *Constantine,* 257.
63 Ibid., 12.

chaos, he said, the Empire existed in a state of permanent crisis, the effect of which was that political, religious, and cultural institutions became obsolete or paralyzed. Pagan society had lost its spiritual bearings; in the process, its "essential content" became "directly analogous to Christianity" and, consequently, ceased to provide answers to the questions that preoccupied men and women during this time of crisis. Christianity, in contrast, was able to provide "answers which were incomparably simpler, and which were articulated in an impressive and convincing whole, to all the questions for which that period of ferment was so deeply concerned to find solutions."[64]

The "twilight of paganism" revealed the extent of the "crisis in the life of the ancient world." Burckhardt argued that Christianity did not cause the "senescence and corruption of conditions in the Empire," and that the Church was in no position to bring it new strength: it could not "bestow a second youth upon the senescent Roman Empire."[65] Quite the opposite was true. The Church profited from the decay of pagan culture. In his descriptions of this condition, Burckhardt discussed the impact of internal and external processes, structural and contextual factors, and material and intellectual developments. He argued that internal political and religious developments and the corruption of classical art revealed the exhausted state of pagan culture. In painting, architecture, and poetry, the classical ideal had been abandoned and replaced. Art and literature in the fourth century, Burckhardt tells us, had betrayed its decay by its "laboured and tortured form, by [the] heaping up of *sententiae*, by the misuse of metaphor for the simple and commonplace, by modern turgidity and artificial archaic aridity." What this signified to Burckhardt was nothing less than the end of "beauty and freedom." Burckhardt ended his discussion with the probing question:

Does a formal decline in poetry and representational art always imply a people's national decline also? Are those arts not blossoms which must fall before fruit can mature? Cannot the true take the place of the beautiful, the useful of the agreeable? ... But anyone who has encountered classical antiquity, if only in its twilight, feels that with beauty and freedom there departed also the genuine antique life, the better part of the national genius, and that the rhetorizing ortho-

64 Ibid., 214.
65 Ibid., 215–16.

doxy which was left to the Greek world can only be regarded as a lifeless precipitate of a once wonderful totality of being.[66]

In short, the triumph of Christianity revealed "a sad picture of essential devolution," in which the "inward man" was left famished and demoralized;[67] it signified the end of classical individualism and the beginning of the Middle Ages.

Burckhardt's interpretation of the age of Constantine and the collapse of the Roman Empire was not well received by the academic community in general. This was something he had anticipated, and it may explain why he did not refer to the book as a cultural history in the first preface. Despite his determination to be a dilettante and to go his own way, he still valued the approval of his colleagues.[68] Significantly, he did not believe that the content of his work would cause criticism, but rather its form. *Constantine*, he feared, "would be reproached for its lack of a consistent principle of representation."[69] Indeed, instead of modeling his work on German scholarship, he had consciously emulated the French. As he reported to a colleague shortly after the work's publication: "I have attempted a form of representation based on the French rather than the German example, and now I don't know how this will be welcomed."[70] The great early nineteenth-century French historians such as Barante, Guizot, and Michelet, he believed, had successfully managed to blend sound scholarship with graceful style. As a student he became convinced that this distinguished their work from German academic scholarship, and he made a promise to emulate the French style of writing history. "I have made a vow to myself," he announced, "to try to write a readable style my whole life long, and to aim for what is interesting, rather than dry, factual completeness." He thought that most German historians, with the exception of Ranke, were only read by scholars; that the Germans had cut themselves off from the broader reading public. "For a long time," he noted, "the French have been much wiser in this

66 Ibid., 242–3.
67 Ibid., 312–13.
68 "But if the new conclusions which he [the author] believes he has reached in the area here treated meet with the approval of specialists, he will value such approval highly," Ibid., 11.
69 *Briefe*, 3:170
70 Ibid. On the influence of French cultural history on Burckhardt, see Röthlin, "Burckhardts Stellung in der Kulturgeschichtsschreibung des 19. Jahrhunderts."

regard."[71] In the end, one of the hallmarks of Burckhardt's dilettantism was his determination to write not for professional historians, but rather for "thoughtful readers of all classes."[72]

But this, as it turned out, was only a minor concern of the reviewers. Critics in the German academic press repeated professional historians' standard complaints about cultural history. Although his old teachers were lavish in their praise, most reviews in the various scholarly journals expressed concern about the lack of methodological and theoretical precision. According to the reviewer in the journal *Grenzboten*, the book's "lack of scientific completeness was only very partially compensated by its artistic composition"; meanwhile, another reviewer complained that it had no "logical, methodological order" and, missing the point completely, that it was a "biography or history without a beginning or end." Of the many reviews, however, only one was truly hostile. Not surprisingly, the *Zeitschrift für lutherische Theologie* condemned the work as perfidious and infamous because of its disrespectful treatment of the early Christian historians, Constantine the Great, and Christianity in general.[73]

That his work did not live up to the expectations of the German professional historical community was no surprise to Burckhardt. Like most contemporary cultural histories, *Constantine* was conceived in opposition to the principles of German historicism and traditional event-oriented political history.[74] Although Burckhardt still had some doubts about the course he was embarking upon, he had made a conscious decision to distinguish his work from mainstream German historiography. But he was also taking a stand against the contemporary trends in the

71 *Briefe*, 1:197.

72 *Constantine*, 11. This had been an objective of Burckhardt's for a very long time. In 1848 he wrote from Italy that he intended to write a "library of cultural histories," a series of short, readable volumes aimed at the "popularization of scholarship," *Briefe*, 3:94. This was a trend within cultural history as Hartmann has demonstrated. See also wb, 83, in which Burckhardt describes his introduction to the study of history as being "not only for the historian ex professio," but for the "educated individual."

73 Ranke, for instance, thought *Constantine* "gave evidence of the spirit of research and the gift of representation in an unusual degree," quoted in Brennan, "Burckhardt and Ranke on the Age of Constantine the Great," 54. Likewise, Kugler's review in the *Deutsches Kunstblatt* was extremely positive. For an examination of the reviews, see Kaegi, 3:418–21.

74 Some argue that Burckhardt's "philological-critical approach to the primary sources" is an indication that he belongs to the German historicist tradition (e.g., Brennan, "Burckhardt and Ranke on the Age of Constantine the Great," 55). But, as I have asserted above, this was not unique to Ranke and the historicists, but was common to all historiography.

practice of cultural history in Germany. In his preface, he claimed that it was not his intention to write "a history of the life and reign of Constantine," which would have been the task of narrative political history; nor "an encyclopedia of all worthwhile information pertaining to his period," a critical reference to standard German cultural histories. Rather, he would take the unusual step and describe "the significant and essential characteristics of the contemporary world" and to outline and shape "a perspicuous sketch of the whole."[75]

What did Burckhardt mean by "the significant and essential characteristics" of the age? How was this cultural history? More specific clues about his conception of cultural history at this time can be found in the introduction to his first lectures on the study of history from 1851, written while he was still working on *Constantine*. In the first place, in explicit contrast to traditional historiography written from one "point of view," such as "the history of states, with regents, conquests and losses of land, war, etc.," Burckhardt regarded cultural history as opening up new dimensions to the study of the past. It viewed the past from many perspectives and significantly broadened the scope of historical enquiry. "Besides the history of states etc., there is now an infinitely broad cultural history." This did not mean that he ignored politics or the state; indeed, he always regarded them as integral elements of cultural history. However, it did mean that the historian had to cast his net wider in the search for source material. Written evidence, such as political, military, and diplomatic documents, privileged by most political historians, was now complemented by another type of record, the non-written text or document: "Everything that remains becomes a talking witness of the particular epoch, a monument." Thus, according to Burckhardt, cultural history became a type of historical archaeology in which all sorts of evidence were now integrated into the historical picture and treated like a text. "Research," he maintained, "stands to gain an enormous breadth ... The main task for us is to point out the historical content of *all* monuments."[76]

Perhaps the most obvious example of this in *Constantine*, as in *Conrad von Hochstaden*, was his attempt to substantiate his descriptions of the decay of the antique world by incorporating evidence from art and

---

75 *Constantine*, 11 and 13. This was more succinctly articulated in the preface to the second edition of 1880, where he said that his task had been to provide "not so much a complete historical account as an integrated description, from the viewpoint of cultural history."

76 WB, 84.

literature. The attempt to integrate the study of art into general cultural history, certainly one of the characteristic features of Burckhardt's study of the age of Constantine, reflects the continued influence of Franz Kugler. At this time, Burckhardt was preoccupied with the difficult relationship between art and history, hoping to achieve some kind of effective combination of the two disciplines. In his letter of application for the position of professor of art history at the newly founded Federal Polytechnical University in Zürich, he refered to Constantine as "an example of the combining of art history with cultural history in general, which I believe is my highest objective."[77] In the end, however, it proved impossible for Burckhardt to achieve this goal completely in *Constantine*; he was forced to limit his discussion of art to those artistic tendencies that revealed specific cultural historical tendencies of the age. This would have implications for his art studies and his later cultural history; for the time being, however, it meant that art history remained an auxiliary discipline subordinated to cultural history. Eventually, Burckhardt gave up trying to integrate the two disciplines altogether and in his masterpiece, *The Civilization of the Renaissance in Italy*, declared that he would deal with Renaissance art in a separate volume.

Given the breadth of cultural historical enquiry and the scope of its available source material, it no longer sufficed to collect facts "according to definite external relationships."[78] Burckhardt did not regard cultural history as a science of the particular, the objective of which was to recount singular events in a linear, temporally ordered, explanatory narrative. Rather, his intention was to study the past from a "universal perspective," where the facts and events revealed the "characteristics of the age": where they told what things were like, not what happened, in the past. As such, cultural history sought generalizations about society derived from the integration of all forms of evidence into the historical narrative (including traditional written records). His studies sought to integrate or synthesize aspects of both material and ideal culture in a way that would reveal the dominant metaphors of the age, or the features and traces of the collective mentality that provided definition to the whole of the epoch or civilization under consideration.[79] In the age of Constantine the

77 *Briefe*, 3:197.

78 Ibid.

79 Karl Lamprecht admired Burckhardt's work because "every cultural epoch is delineated by a center of psychic life." Although Burckhardt may have objected to the use of the term "psychic," this effectively captures the essence of his approach to cultural history. Quoted in Chickering, *Karl Lamprecht*, 53.

Great, this can be summarized in the metaphors of senescence and paralysis; in the *Civilization of the Renaissance in Italy*, it is individualism.[80]

. . .

A number of historians have pointed out that *Constantine* represents what may be perhaps best described as a personal odyssey. For example, Peter Gay, in his essay on Burckhardt, the "poet of truth," argues that the book was "Burckhardt's final reckoning with Christianity, a personal debate with a personal adversary. It stands against piety, edification, and hypocrisy. It is the last reverberation of a private struggle that Burckhardt had fought out years before in his correspondence and in family discussions, but which he still lacked the sovereignty to treat with the serenity of true distance."[81] In the decade following the completion of his studies, Burckhardt had overcome the religious crisis of his youth and had achieved the independence he desired. He had emancipated himself completely from the "loathsome orthodoxy" of his forefathers and had succeeded in developing a truly secular interpretation of the past. Put another way, he attempted, in the words of Franz Overbeck "to execute [his] task as a historian entirely without recourse to Christianity."[82]

Other scholars have argued that *Constantine* represents, as well, an indirect attempt to come to terms with the crisis of modernity. As Hayden White has written: "The *Constantine*, a study of cultural decline, consciously evoked a comparison of the fall of the Roman Empire with the coming end of European civilization."[83] There are many similarities be-

80 This is significant because it suggests that Burckhardt included in his conception of culture much more than what we would call "high culture," or the arts, what he himself described as "the entire sum of intellectual developments which occur spontaneously and without compulsive authority," w B, 276. Burckhardt defined culture more broadly to include all forms and structures of human existence – social and economic activity, customs and traditions, systems of belief, scholarly and artistic achievements, as well as general political culture. Ibid., 254.

81 Gay, *Style in History*, 166; See also Kaegi, 3:399; Howard, "Historicist Thought in the Shadow of Theology," 346ff. Howard reminds us that the terms *Übergangsperiode* or *Übergangszeit*, "which Burckhardt used to describe his inner state after his religious crisis, are the same terms used to describe the period under discussion in his *Constantine*." Ibid., 347–8.

82 Quoted in Howard, "Historicist Thought in the Shadow of Theology," 352.

83 White, *Metahistory*, 236; More recently Brennan, "Burckhardt and Ranke on the Age of Constantine the Great," 59, has also argued that the work "mirrors many of his own nineteenth-century concerns and represents his working out of a number of personal dilemmas."

tween Burckhardt's portrait of the decaying Roman Empire and his understanding of nineteenth-century Europe. His description of the decline of myth and idealism and the rise of realism in late antiquity, for instance, was a theme that surfaced in his early studies of the Renaissance and in his criticism of modern art. Similarly, we can find reflected in *Constantine* his hostility towards military regimes and dictators, in addition to his fears about the growing power of the state and the masses, all of which were an articulation of his ongoing attempt to understand the forces at work in his own century. His interpretation of the old regime of Europe as obsolete and paralyzed parallels his description of late pagan antiquity. In many respects, the French Revolution assumes the same historical magnitude as the triumph of Christianity, and has a similarly degenerate impact on art, life, and the individual.

Although they approach Burckhardt from different perspectives, both Gay and White imply that *Constantine* was based on a projection of the historian's present, that Burckhardt's historical impressions were informed and formed by his overwhelming concern for the present and for the fate of modern culture. In many respects, the defining feature of Burckhardt's approach to history and hence his understanding of cultural history was precisely this confrontation between the forces of modernity and history. This conflicting relationship was played out in *Constantine,* as well as in the *Civilization of the Renaissance* and his other works. I would like to suggest, therefore, that the study of the age of Constantine represents a personal reckoning in one final sense: namely, that the work signalled Burckhardt's coming to terms, in his own mind, not just with the task of cultural history in general, but also with the legacy and implications of the tradition of German historicism.

The existing tension in Burckhardt's historical work between modernity and history originated in his profound belief that the contemporary world was in a state of crisis. It was resolved, at least in part, through his writings and his understanding of history. This necessitated, in the first place, the rejection of the principles of scientific, objective history, which with its progressivist, explanatory orientation perpetuated the myth of purposeful historical development, obscured the nature of the crisis of modernity, and presumed to be privy to "eternal wisdom" and capable of recovering truth and meaning in the past. Second, any resolution of the confrontation between modernity and history could only be achieved through a reorientation of the relationship between historians and the past, the authors and the text. Any attempt to "extinguish" themselves, as Ranke desired, from the process of historical reconstruction would simply remove the authors from active involvement in the historical process. As "neutral reporters" relating events from the past, the historians would abdicate their responsibilities for the present and, ultimately, for the future as well.

The performative function of the historians is thus of crucial importance to understanding Burckhardt's work. History was not science, it was poetry; historians were not neutral, objective observers who simply exposed or discovered the past, but poets with a voice that (re)created the past and had a very real stake in that recreation. Moreover, the author's role was not denied or denounced, but welcomed and embraced. In this regard, I believe that Burckhardt's approach to history was in its essence "holistic." By this I mean not simply that he sought unity, coherence, and synthesis in his reconstuctions of past epochs and civilizations, or that he wanted to write "total" history. Rather, I take the term to imply a form of wholeness or completeness that exists between the author and the past, the historian and the text. In this specific sense of the term, holism implies a dialogic, as opposed to monologic, conception of historical knowledge where the past only becomes "whole" when it is connected to the present via the mediation and performance of the author. Cultural history enabled Burckhardt not only to relate the past to the present in an organic relationship, but to trace those elements of continuity in the past that constituted the spiritual continuum of Western culture. It created an authentic milieu, not of the past, but of the present, because it provided Burckhardt with a means by which he could confront the cultural imperatives of his own day.

In general, holistic thought was an attempt to overcome the fragmentation and atomization of modern life. Through the rejection of modernity, it became an *Oppositionswissenschaft*. Its reputation today rests largely on the fact that in the early twentieth century it became the handmaiden of reactionary thinkers, with abominable consequences.[84] But in its more innocent days following the death of Goethe, it took modern scientific and historical (positivist-empirical) thought to task, arguing that its emphasis on the particular – on facts and on scientific, mechanical precision – threatened further to alienate the individual and atomize society. Burckhardt's project should be seen as originating in contrast to the mechanistic metaphors that dominated nineteenth-century social and cultural discourse, where everything and everyone was reduced to the level of machinelike rationality, where the individual

84 Harrington, *Reenchanted Science.*

was reduced to a cog in that machine and domesticated and alienated from society and culture. Burckhardt, through the language of his cultural history, tried to bring together material and ideal culture in an attempt to reunify the subjective and objective individual into a meaningful whole. Cultural history consequently became the ultimate aesthetic expression – a defiant, rebellious statement against the atomization and alienation of the individual in modern society.

7

Burckhardt and Anschauung

THE PROBLEM OF CRISIS occupied a central role in both the life and historical work of Burckhardt. Without a doubt it shaped his historical perspective and even his unique form of cultural history. As an historian he was most concerned with periods of radical historical upheaval and crisis, such as the dissolution of the Roman Empire and the transition from paganism to Christianity, the transition from the Middle Ages to the modern world, or the era of the French Revolution. At the same time, his lived experience of modernity – first in the political, then in the cultural realms – convinced him that the present represented a major break in the continuity of Western culture and that he was living in a time of crisis. His approach to history, he claimed in *Reflections on History*, would consequently be to a "certain extent pathological" in nature.[1] In other words, he considered his task as an historian to be the study of the symptoms of the diseases or crises that afflicted the world and the individual.

Many factors contributed to his perception that he was living in a time of crisis: the seemingly unstoppable growth of industrial capitalism and the ever-increasing power of economic interests; democracy, popular sovereignty, and the rise of the centralized state; the rise of mass society and mass culture; and the increasing dominance of public opinion. Burckhardt's diagnosis of the impact of modernity on the individual, in this respect similar to that of Marx, was that modernity destroyed the creative spirit and led to the progressive alienation of the individual. This alienation of the individual and destruction of the creative spirit cut loose the individual from his or her bearings in the past, thereby

1 WB, 226.

suggesting that modernity destroyed the possibility of authentic experience. This led to a paradox. If authentic experience and the coherence of a past reality were no longer possible in the modern world, then what remained for the historian but myths and fictions that must, in turn, assume the place of reality? The sense of living in a time of crisis, and the belief that the dominant cultural forces or modes of explanation could no longer account for "reality," but that they, in fact, distorted the reality of the human condition and fed myth, gave rise to the need for an alternative form of discourse. A new frame of reference was required; a new language, in effect, became necessary. The old, traditional formulations were no longer adequate.

Much has been made of Burckhardt's gloomy, pessimistic pronouncements about modernity and the future of Western civilization. However, his dedication to the study of history and to *Bildung* – his determination to keep alive the culture of "Old Europe" in the face of modernity's onslaught – suggest that he was not pessimistic to the point of despair and that he did see the possibility of future cultural renewal. "Certainly a new existence, built on old and new foundations, will arise out of the storm," he remarked in a passage much quoted by historians; "our destiny is to help rebuild after the crisis is past."[2] History played an important role in this process, because it provided an essential link between past and present, an anchor for the modern individual. If the study of history for Burckhardt was ultimately pathological, it is crucial to remember that he also believed that the study of the past contained a potential remedy to the sickness of modern society: the therapeutic value of contemplation.

Burckhardt was also aware that as a form of therapy, the study of history could achieve the opposite effect: it could lull one into a false sense of security and complacency. Thus he objected to simplistic notions of historical progress and the naive "optimistic will" of the Enlightenment. He maintained that history written from these presuppositions only served to reinforce this ideological and intellectual status quo. Consequently, he relished his status as dilettante and outsider and rebelled against the dominant mode of historical discourse in the nineteenth century; that mode, he avowed, in its accommodation to the ideological premises of modernity, only served to mystify further the crisis of modernity. Instead of adhering to the traditional form of historical narrative

---

2 *Briefe*, 2:211. Likewise, he continued to believe in the possibility of cultural renaissance: "One characteristic of higher cultures: their capacity for renaissances," WB, 283.

practised by his contemporaries of the German historical school, he sought to undermine modernity and to solve the derelict, meaningless experience of his own day and the problematic of crisis through the creation of a new historical language of aesthetics based on *Anschauung,* or the spiritual contemplation and observation of history.

Burckhardt's reliance on *Anschauung* not only signifies a rejection of the principles of German historicism; it also reveals that he proceeded from a fundamentally aesthetic position. It is an aesthetic position for two reasons. First, Burckhardt was especially concerned with those historical and psychological forces behind the spirit of creativity; he desired to capture the domain of perception, sensation, and experience, and to show how it shaped the world. Second, he was interested not just in content, but also in form. *Anschauung* implies the active participation of the author or reader in the historical reconstruction and the inherent subjectivity of the historical undertaking. Viewing history first and foremost as a form of art or poetry, Burckhardt rejected the prevailing attitude that the reality and truth of history could be grasped in its immediacy if studied scientifically and according to theoretical concepts. Like Schopenhauer, whose work Burckhardt greatly admired in later life, he regarded history as a form of representation, rather than explanation or interpretation, and suggested that historical meaning did not exist for the past, but only in the present, and that this meaning is made and remade.[3]

This notion is fundamental to understanding the confrontation between history and modernity that characterized Burckhardt's work. It is also fundamental to understanding his position in the intellectual history of nineteenth-century Europe. If his goals were to preserve the "spiritual continuum," to demystify the crisis of modernity, to rehabilitate the past, and to secure future cultural renewal, then he and his audience had to be active participants in the reconstruction of historical meaning. In short, *Anschauung* anticipated a radical new function for the author. Whereas traditional nineteenth-century German historiography, represented perhaps best by Ranke, was essentially monologic – that is to say, following Dominick La Capra, it assumed "a unified authorial voice providing an ideally exhaustive and definitive (total) account

3 Much has been written about the influence of Schopenhauer's thought on Burckhardt. See for instance White, *Metahistory,* 237–43, who argues that Schopenhauer provided philosophical justification for Burckhardt's pessimism. In contrast, Howard, "Historicist Thought in the Shadow of Theology," 371, argues that Burckhardt's ideas were formed before he became familiar with Schopenhauer's work.

of a fully mastered object of knowledge"[4] – *Anschauung*, in contrast, posited a dialogical relationship between the author, the past, and the text, and in so doing resuscitated the voice of the historian as an active maker of the past and the present.

. . .

During the summer of 1842, a year after his important semester at the university in Bonn and a number of months after his decision to pursue cultural history, Burckhardt began an intensive study of the philosophy of history. Over the course of the summer, as he became engaged in a running dialogue with his friends about the relative merits of philosophy, his ideas about *Anschauung* and the study of the past crystallized in his mind for the first time. He became convinced that *Anschauung*, which focused on the essential elements of history and human nature, had become his "surrogate" for philosophy. "I stand on the edge of the world and stretch out my arms towards the origin of all things," he proclaimed somewhat melodramatically; "this is why history is sheer poetry for me that can only be mastered through *Anschauung*."[5] Certainly he felt he had discovered the driving force behind his insatiable thirst for the past. *Anschauung* had become as necessary to him as oxygen. "If I can't start from *Anschauung*," he claimed in a letter to his friend Willibald Beyschlag, "then I can't achieve anything. Naturally I include in this intellectual *Anschauung*; that is to say, the historical, which emerges from the impression of source material." But he had also found the justification for his understanding and approach to history. He formulated his ideas in specific contrast to philosophy of history and conceptual thought in general, and to the claims of scientific history. "What I create historically is not the result of criticism or speculation," he maintained, "but rather of the imagination which fills the gaps of *Anschauung*. History for me is still for the greater part poetry, a series of the most beautiful artistic compositions ... [B]ut where there is no inner picture to be set down on paper, it must remain insolvent."[6] He consciously compared the process of writing history to that of painting and the historian

4 LaCapra, *History and Criticism*, 36.
5 *Briefe*, 1:206 and 208.
6 Ibid., 1:204–5.

to the artist, claiming a few days later in a letter to a different friend that he should "think of me as a learning, striving artist because I too live on images and *Anschauung.*"[7]

But what exactly is *Anschauung* and how did Burckhardt translate this process into historical practice? As with many other German terms, such as *Bildung, Wissenschaft,* or indeed *Kultur,* the multiple connotations of the term are difficult to capture in English translation. In effect, *Anschauung* means both contemplation and the act of visual perception. In Burckhardt's usage of the term, both of these literal connotations are discernible. However, his understanding of *Anschauung* was informed by other meanings as well. Without question, the language of *Anschauung* for Burckhardt was primarily aesthetic, a language of visualization and perception. It was the language of art and as such it implied the opposite of rationalized, conceptual thought. It was neither objective in the empirical sense, nor passive, as Peter Gay has written.[8] Rather, it was based on human instinct and proceeded from the active stimulation of the sensate world of immediate experience. It is not surprising that Burckhardt compared the historian who proceeds from the principle of *Anschauung* with the artist who transcribes or projects the world of physical perception through his or her subjective experience onto the canvas; similarly, Burckhardt consistently employed visual metaphors to explain his train of thought. His vocabulary, consisting of such words as "images," "pictures," "artistic compositions," and "impressions," reveals the extent to which he sought to create written history based on the subjective experience of the process of physical, visual sensation or perception.

At the same time, however, these images and impressions could only emerge through the process of active contemplation of the source material of the past, either in the form of written documents or physical monuments. The active process of *Anschauung* contains not only the visual metaphoric connotations of physical perception; it also implies an almost spiritual contemplation that creates a uniquely personal bond between the subject and the objective world under consideration. It suggests that through active dialogue or communication with the past as represented by the historical sources – in other words through the subjective experience of the past – the essential lines of continuity can be grasped from the flux of the historical process, and that a spiritual, almost mystical awareness of the past is attainable. This points to a defin-

7 Ibid., 1:208.
8 Gay, *Style in History,* 176–7.

ing feature of *Anschauung*, to which we will eventually return. As an inherently subjective and active means of understanding the past, it is a consciously mediated form of historical representation. It is possible only through the recognition of the active, creative role of the observer as the translator of the immediate visions or images onto the canvas.

In an echo of the traditional Enlightenment philosophy of aesthetics, the young Burckhardt relegated aesthetic thought to a status secondary to rational, theoretical thought, when he asked to be left alone at this "lower" level of *Anschauung* in order to "feel" history.[9] However, in his mature work he evidently ceased to regard it as a lower level of understanding. Clearly, *Anschauung* and the need to "feel" history indicate that in no way did he believe that aesthetic thought was subordinate or inferior to conceptualized thinking. On the contrary, throughout his writings he challenged the very legitimacy of the "a priori point of view" of the philosophers of history and its application to historical thought. For Burckhardt, *Anschauung*, and art in general, did not simply form a bridge between reason and the senses; he was not trying to rationalize the aesthetic, but to aestheticize the rational. Reason, he maintained, emerges from the instinct for cohesion and an ordered, explicable universe in the same way that art emanates from the drive for creativity, the *Kunsttrieb* or *Schönheitstrieb*. But both are a response to, and both fulfill, primary aesthetic needs.

While both art and *Anschauung* reflected the human need for form and coherence, neither, declared Burckhardt, stood in the service of truth. As a consequence, he refused to give Schiller the last word on the function of art in the education of mankind. Art in and of itself, argued Burckhardt, was not a solution to the crisis of modernity or the alienation of the modern individual, although it may have been a response to these forces, because the beautiful is not "a transition point or education for the Truth. This does not suffice because to a high degree art exists for its own sake."[10] Again, his choice of vocabulary reveals the extent to which he viewed the process of artistic and historical creativity as emanating from the aesthetic realm. Neither philosophical speculation nor scientific theories, he emphasized, could discover the revelations of the spirit of an age. This could only be achieved through feeling, experience, and imagination.

9 *Briefe*, 1:207.
10 WB, 278.

At first glance, this highly subjective understanding of *Anschauung* appears to be merely a different way of describing the classical hermeneutic conception of *Verstehen*. Indeed, contemplation of the historical seems to be the first, necessary step in the empathetic understanding of the past (*Verstehen*), so central to historicism. *Verstehen*, as understood by German historicists, was not just an essential component of the theory of historical hermeneutics; it was a means of achieving value-free, objective, and hence scientific history and a vehicle for the discovery of meaning in the past. The irony is that Ranke and Droysen sought to achieve objective, scientific history by employing the vocabulary of aestheticism and tried to rationalize and objectify what was essentially an aesthetic phenomenon by cloaking their language in the rhetoric of science. Whether *Verstehen* is taken to mean intuition, divination, or emphathetic or sympathetic understanding, it clearly could not be achieved through the critical faculty of reason. The credibility of the claim for objective, scientific historical scholarship, which Droysen made in his *Historik*, was thus undermined by the very vocabulary he employed. "The science of history is the result of empirical *perception, experience* and investigation," Droysen maintained. "All empirical knowledge depends upon the '*specific energy*' of the *nerves of sense*, through the *excitation* of which the mind receives not 'images' but *signs* of things without, which *signs this excitation* has brought before it."[11]

While *Verstehen* may have freed the historian from the limitations of *a priori* philosophical thought, it was nonetheless an integral component of the theory of historical hermeneutics, itself a way of conceptualizing the past, and a means of achieving objective, rational history. Burckhardt, in contrast, proceeded from precisely the opposite assumption. *Anschauung*, he said, neither represented a theory of history, nor assumed such a "high office" as to relate the past "wie es eigentlich gewesen" [to show what actually happened]. History, he argued, was poetry rather than science. These basic assumptions behind the historical enterprise resulted in important differences – not just in historical content, but also in the form of narrative discourse employed by the historian.

A number of scholars have argued that the academic culture of the Western world has been dominated by the need to explain natural phenomena and historical events. The primary objective of most scientific scholarship and historical studies has been to establish causation, to

11 Droysen, "Outline of the Principles of History," 106 and 104. The emphasis is mine.

answer the question of why and how something happened in a chrono-logically ordered sequence.[12] Explanation has therefore been the most prevalent form of historical narrative, displacing that of description in the nineteenth century. Perhaps more than any other rhetorical device or methodological innovation, the explanatory narrative form con-formed to the dominant notion of what constituted the primary task of science and historical studies in the nineteenth century. The classifica-tion and organization of knowledge in a causal relationship enabled the scientist not just to explain natural phenomena, but also to endow them with meaning. Likewise, the task of the historian became identified with the search for meaning in the past by establishing causation of events in a chronologically ordered narrative.

Nineteenth-century hermeneutic theory, despite resting primarily on the intuitive element of empathetic understanding, was conceived as a means of explaining, not simply describing, the historical process as re-vealed in the documents of the past. For historians, numerous benefits accrued to this development. First, explanation, the uncovering of causes, was of immediate interest to those scholars trying to establish meaning in history and historical agents. By establishing a causal nexus, not only was the past interpretable and understandable, but it could also be understood in terms of the present. Second, explanation assumes that "the past is a meaningful whole" that can be comprehended by the historian. Because explanation assumes the immediacy of knowledge, it makes the task of the historian relatively easier; it takes for granted, in the words of one scholar, "that essentially the past is a sea of historical phenomena that have to be described and explained" and prescribed a meaning.[13]

The philosopher of history F.R. Ankersmit has proposed an alterna-tive narrative vocabulary to that of description and explanation for histo-rians. He suggests a third possibility – the vocabulary of representation – and compares the historian using this narrative strategy "to the painter representing a landscape, a person, and so on." At first glance, this may appear similar to the language and purpose of description. But there are significant differences. As I interpret Ankersmit, representation does not carry the conceptual baggage and rhetorical burden of scientific his-tory and of description, which, like explanation, implies the possibility

12 For instance Ankersmit, "Historical Representation;" and Megill, "Recounting the Past."

13 Ankersmit, "Historical Representation," 206.

of objective, value-free narration and places an overwhelming emphasis on the meaning of the past. On the contrary, argues Ankersmit, representation implies "a plea for a *rapprochement* between philosophy of history and aesthetics." Furthermore, unlike explanation or description, representation is explicitly concerned with form as well as content; it acknowledges the necessary performative role of the author. As Ankersmit explains, "The vocabulary of representation has the capacity to account not only for the details of the past but also for the way these details have been integrated within the totality of the historical narrative."[14]

Ankersmit's formulation of historical representation is useful not just as an agenda for future historiographical practice; it can also be applied to the study of the history of historiography. It is my contention that Burckhardt sought precisely this type of *rapprochement* and that the language of *Anschauung* can best be compared with the vocubulary of representation. Moreover, Burckhardt's understanding of *Anschauung*, which is structured according to the metaphor of visual perception, suggests that his primary narrative objective was neither description nor explanation, but rather representation. At one level, for example, Burckhardt's work on the Italian Renaissance does away with explanation. It did not seek, for instance, answers as to why the transition from the Middle Ages to the Renaissance occurred. In a sense this transition is accepted as a given, and his aim was rather to present the contrasting conditions of the two ages in order to provide an historical *Bild*, or picture, of the Renaissance. At a different level, it is a lesson on how to visualize the past, a reflection on the re-creation of historical form and representation. He presented cross-sections of the past, woven together, not chronologically but thematically, into a vivid tapestry designed to give us glimpses and impressions of his creation. At every moment, however, we are conscious of the author's design. The object of historical study provides its essential form; it is treated like a text that functions in the present as well as the past. But the text exists in a dependent relationship. Like the narrative form of representation, Burckhardt's work places the onus on the author or viewer, not just on the text. The emphasis in representation is therefore on the process of seeing and visualizing, on the active, re-creative function of the observer, and on the distance between any given reality in the past and the observer of that reality.

14 Ibid., 209.

Unlike the historian who seeks to explain the past, the historian who prefigures his or her narrative according to the principles of representation is, like an artist, conscious of the distance between the reality of what is out there and the text or canvas that is the production of the creative mind. In assuming the immediacy of the past, explanation pays little heed to the vagaries of language, to the fact of an unbridgeable gulf separating the language of the author and the reality he or she is trying to explain. Assuming the universality of historical meaning and the objectivity of a scientific historiography, explanation takes for granted that the past can be perceived in an unmediated, immediate form by the historian. As Iggers has written, *Verstehen* "is possible only if we cast ourselves into the individual character of our historical subject matter,"[15] if, in other words, we can do away with our own subjectivity.

However, by accepting as a given the immediacy of historical knowledge, historians have fallen into what Gadamer, Megill, and others have described as the trap of "hermeneutic naïveté," by which is meant "the viewing of the historical account as if it were a 'view from nowhere', instead of – as it decidedly is – a view from some particular interpretive perspective."[16] *Verstehen*, as a form of narrative based on explanation, consequently implied that the author, through the use of proper historical method, could achieve an objective immediacy with the text. The difficulty that arises from this belief in "immaculate perception"[17] is that it gives short shrift to the very problem of historical perspective and the role of the author as interpreter of the past. In contrast, historians who prefigure a narrative structure according to the principles of representation are very much concerned with these issues; not only are they aware, but they will be "interested in the gap between language and reality or between appearance (representation) and reality."[18] It is precisely in this gap that the "poetry" of history, at least for Burckhardt, existed. The indifference or failure to recognize this essential distance has been recognized as a common feature of historicist thought by a number of scholars. Iggers writes, for instance, that "the Rankean school did not

15 Iggers, *The German Conception of History*, 10. He continues, writing that "this process is not accomplished by abstract reasoning, but by direct confrontation with the subject we wish to understand and by contemplation (*Anschauung*) of its individuality, free of the limitations of conceptual thought. All historical understanding, Humboldt, Ranke, and Dilthey agree, requires an element of intuition (*Ahnung*)."

16 Megill, "Recounting the Past," 636.

17 Ibid., 632.

18 Ankersmit, "Historical Representation," 219.

confront the problem of selection and perspectivity of which the Göttin-gen historians had at least been aware,"[19] a sign perhaps not of the progressive modernization of the historical profession in the nineteenth century, but of its progressive naïveté.

Despite his basic hostility towards the principles of the Enlightenment, Burckhardt at least shared this perspective with eighteenth-century historians. Not only was the problem of perspectivity central to his approach to history, but, as one recent commentator has noted, the paradigm of perspective provided him with a dominant structuring metaphor.[20] By adopting a point of view, by writing history from his "Archimedean point outside events," he was highlighting not only the conscious distance between the representation and the reality, but also the role of the historian as participant, around which "anchor of perception" the narrative revolves and evolves. He addressed this issue openly and unproblematically at the very beginning of his work on the Renaissance. Aware that the historian viewed the past from the perspective of his own time, abilities, and interpretation, he wrote that his book was "an essay (*Versuch*) in the strictest sense of the word." Indeed, he continued, "the possible ways and directions are many; and the same studies which have served for this work might easily, in other hands, not only receive a wholly different treatment and application, but also lead to essentially different conclusions."[21] This, of course, raises the question of the role of language and the historian's style in the writing of history, reminding us once again of the historicists' aim of "de-rhetoricizing" history. Indeed, if Ranke wanted to extinguish himself from the text, Burckhardt sought precisely the opposite. One of the underlying assumptions of *Anschauung* was the need to resurrect the author as an active participant in the making of history.

. . .

For Burckhardt, history was poetry and the historian a poet. And like a poet, the historian carefully selected and shaped from the multitude of

19 Iggers, *New Directions in European Historiography*, 21. See also Bann, *The Clothing of Clio*, 25–31.
20 See Holly, "Burckhardt and the Ideology of the Past."
21 CRI, 19.

sources and experiences those elements required for the final composition. Hence Burckhardt's concern for perspective went beyond that of the author to the very root of the historian's task: the selection of facts. However, this task, as he knew too well, was far from unproblematic, shaping as it did the nature of historical discourse. Facts and facticity were not just the bread and butter of positivists, they were essential components of all historical explanation. But they meant more to historical discourse than just adherence to sources or the establishment of events and truth in the past. They ensured the sophistication of methodology and the integrity of narrative structure; they guaranteed historical veracity, objectivity, and scientific detachment; they lent authority to the historian and legitimacy to the discipline. If the historian who did not adhere to this carefully crafted agenda was considered by mainstream academics to be a heretic, then Burckhardt was a heretic.

The "cult of the fact" became a hallmark of nineteenth-century cultural literacy. It had its roots in the crude notion that scientific explanation and a realistic form of presentation were possible if one strictly collected facts and adhered to empirical evidence. Scientific authority and exactitude were sought in all ways of life – the objective not only of historical studies, but also of literature and art. The realist novel or painting consciously employed techniques, rhetorical or artistic, specifically designed to create the illusion of scientific precision and objectivity. For instance, all signs of authorial presence were eliminated in the novel, while the artists, in their desire to reproduce as accurate and detailed a portrait as possible, were reduced to the status of neutral, impartial observers of empirical data. Their goal, like that of photographers, was less to interpret or describe than to present a lifelike portrayal of historical reality; to let the facts, accurately portrayed, speak for themselves, that is to say, to explain the past.

The novels of Flaubert, Zola, and Dickens, or the massive popularity of the genre of realist painting, reveal the extent to which the nineteenth-century artistic world had absorbed the scientism of its age and adopted the rhetoric of science to its cause. Whether it was Flaubert modeling himself on the scientist, or Zola believing that art had to serve science, the cultural language of the time, with few exceptions, expressed an ebullient faith in the value of empiricism, technology, and scientific progress to overcome the ills of society and point the way to a better future. This prevalent spirit of utilitarianism and scientism is effectively captured by Charles Dickens, in his classic portrait of nineteenth-century English industrial life in *Hard Times* (1854), when he introduces

"Thomas Gradgrind, sir. A man of realities. A man of facts and calculations." What Gradgrind wanted, sir, was "Facts." "Teach these boys and girls nothing but Facts. Facts alone are wanted in life. Plant nothing else, and root out everything else ... Stick to Facts, sir! ... In this life, we want nothing but Facts, sir; nothing but Facts!"[22]

While the "cult of the fact" may have reached its height in the historical world towards the end of the nineteenth century with the extremely popular historical handbook by Charles Victor Langlois and Charles Seignobos, its roots extended back to the notions of a progressive, objective *Wissenschaft*. The extent to which this overwhelming preoccupation with facts penetrated historical consciousness can be seen not just in the work of the so-called *Faktenpositivisten*, but also in the work of German cultural historians who, in pursuit of the minutiae of everyday life, revealed "an enormous sensualization and almost manic longing for empirical experience."[23] This characterized those historians Burckhardt critically referred to in his correspondence as the "*viri eruditissimi*," those most erudite of men who believed that the historical enterprise consisted almost entirely of the discovery of new facts, an understanding of science that depended on the Rankean view that the author could be extinguished and that the facts could speak for themselves. In other words, the task of the author was merely to gather the information that, by its own inner logic, would contain an inherent coherence. It patently ignored the rhetorical and literary strategies employed by historians in the construction of the historical text and the reconstruction of the past; or at least it reduced the role of the historian to the most minimum of requirements, to that of facilitator of historical truth, so as to create the effect of unmediated representation and knowledge.

While this may have been a natural outcome of the rapid scientific and technological changes of the industrial age in which he lived, it signalled for Burckhardt the triumph of a Biedermeier mentality driven by materialism and rationalism. By eliminating authorial presence and by serving immediate material interests, history became a means of justifying the present. It was necessary, wrote Burckhardt in his introduction to his lectures on the French Revolution, for the historian to pass judgments on events and to question the facts in order to avoid misrepre-

22 Dickens, *Hard Times* (Harmondsworth: Penguin Books, 1969), 47.

23 Dilly and Ryding, "Kulturgeschichtsschreibung vor und nach der bürgerlichen Revolution von 1848," 20. The extent to which this also dominated American historical scholarship towards the end of the nineteenth century is discussed in Novick, *That Noble Dream*, 21–46.

senting the function of knowledge as the "idolization of success." That is, the historian must try, to prevent the emergence of the belief that historical knowledge exists to justify certain developments, which leads to the approval of the *fait accompli*,[24] precisely the course adopted by the Prussian School.

This notion profoundly contradicted Burckhardt's conception of traditional, humanist *Bildung* – in which scholarship represented a calling, and knowledge and culture served the individual's spiritual needs and his or her understanding of history, as well as the task of the historian. For Burckhardt, history was above all else a source of culture or *Bildung*. His approach contrasted starkly with the dominent trend of nineteenth-century historical studies, in which history was viewed as a science and historians were assigned the task of research or *Forschung*. The central importance of the research imperative to nineteenth-century historical science was perhaps best articulated in Droysen's statement that "the essence of historical method consists in understanding through research." Whether or not Droysen considered the aim of research to be empirical knowledge or interpretation,[25] research did attempt to establish the theoretical and methodological foundation of "scientific" history.

Burckhardt directly opposed the type of scholarship that, in the name of progressive, scientific knowledge, was based on the gathering of facts. *Forschung* destroyed not only the poetry of history, he attested, but threatened to reduce a noble pursuit to the status of an enterprise, a business transaction. Such an enterprise was competitive, responding only to the demands of the academic marketplace, and was harnessed by bureaucratic organizations. In short, history as a science (*Wissenschaft*) governed by the research imperative (*Forschung*) commodified knowledge and the past. Burckhardt was not the only intellectual who voiced opposition to the destruction of history as a form of *Bildung*. His Basel colleague, the philologist Johann Jacob Bachofen, also shared this view, as did Burckhardt's colleague and former student, Wilhelm Vischer-Heussler.[26] In the 1850s and 1860s, Bachofen was engaged in a type of intellectual feud with the German historian of ancient Rome, Theodor Mommsen. According to Lionel Gossman, whose work on the Basel intellectual elite of the nineteenth century stresses the cultural divergence

24 Burckhardt, *Geschichte des Revolutionszeitalters*, 13.

25 Iggers, "Historicism," 140.

26 On Vischer-Heussler, see Gossman, "The Boundaries of the City," 36–7. On Burckhardt and history as *Bildung*, see also Mali, "Jacob Burckhardt: Myth, History and Mythistory," 100ff.

between Basel and Berlin, Bachofen regarded Mommsen as the "transla-
tor/traitor par excellence," who killed "the living word, the marvelous
poetry of ancient symbol and myth, and transform[ed] them into the
dead concept, the modern prose of economics and class conflict. The
work he does is scientific, we might say, rather than poetic. In
Bachofen's eyes, however, what the jackbooted Mommsen 'translates'
and delivers over to his readers is not the lover's knowledge of the
'Goddess herself' – the object of Bachofen's quest – but the anatomist's
knowledge of a cadaver."[27]

Likewise, Burckhardt was involved in a lifelong (profoundly ascetic)
quest for the "Goddess herself." Facts, he insisted, could not simply be
collected and presented as if they contained the essence of history and
represented objective historical reality. This was precisely the problem
of modern thought in general and German historiography in particular. "People are always talking about the art of writing history," Burckhardt complained, "and many believe that they have done enough
when they have replaced Schlosser's labyrinthine constructions with an
obdurate narrative comparison of the facts." But this was not the point.
"No, good people," he announced, "now it is a matter of sifting
through the facts, of selecting that which can interest *mankind*."[28] The
process of selection and representation was the principal task of the historian. For Burckhardt, the facts did not point to what had happened
in the past, but to the possibility of *Anschauung* and further interpretation. The problem faced by the historian becomes what one can do
with the facts. Interpretation, he maintained, is involved every step of
the way, from the initial selection of the fact, to the choice of where it is
to appear in the narrative structure. Facts, by some inherent quality in
themselves, do not dictate where they shall appear in the text or what
meaning they shall possess. Understanding this, Burckhardt was consequently aware of the need not for more facts, but for more interpretation. Any textbook or monograph could provide enough facts. For
those who really wanted to learn – "i.e., become spiritually rich" – a few
well-selected sources were sufficient. The point, he felt, was not to lose
all sense of proportion, but to keep the facts in perspective and be willing to learn for learning's sake.[29]

27 Gossman, "Basle, Bachofen and the Critique of Modernity," 179.
28 *Briefe*, 1:197.
29 WB, 249 and 251.

The obsession with facts led to specialization within the discipline, a trend that Burckhardt severely condemned. This, he believed, posed a number of dangers both to the historian and the study of history. Specialization, he was convinced, was a serious threat to the historians' mental health, causing general weariness in those who preoccupied themselves too long with themes of limited interest. He even attributed Henry Thomas Buckle's "paralysis of the brain" to his intensive study of seventeenth and eighteenth-century Scottish sermons.[30] Not only was it misplaced energy, he warned; it was also a misinterpretation of the historian's task. In effect, it was a reflection of contemporary historians' obsession with the collection of facts, as well as their underlying assumption that the more facts they accumulated, the more scientific and authoritative history would become. "It is indisputable," noted Burckhardt, "that there are namely a dozen people who believe that scientific progress consists of the archival accumulation of single facts." He suggested that this unnatural and unhealthy focus on the particular was made at the cost of perspective and generalization. Fortunately, he declared, there are a few contemporary historians whose work "presents life and has ideas" that "pass over the heads of these gentlemen to their occasional great astonishment."[31] He advised his younger historian friend Bernhard Kugler, the eldest son of Franz Kugler, to choose themes of world historical significance that would interest the greatest number of people – which he had had the good fortune to do in the past – and to leave behind "the detritus of mere facts – not out of your studies – but certainly out of your presentation. One really only needs to use those external facts that are the recognizable and characteristic expression of an idea, a general thought, a vivid feature of the respective time ... The strength of our nerves and light for our eyes are too good to waste on exploring external facts from the past ... Long before the rubbish collectors have gotten up from their carts, in order to shout something unpleasant to us, we are already over the mountains."[32]

According to Burckhardt, historians whose primary intention was *Anschauung* privileged form over content. They would simply be unsuccessful, he avowed, if they placed too much emphasis on the collection of

30 WB, 123.

31 *Briefe*, 5:133.

32 Ibid., 5:76–7. See also WB, 248–9. In words that could be Burckhardt's, Ankersmit writes: "The wild, greedy, and uncontrolled digging into the past, inspired by the desire to discover a past reality and reconstruct it scientifically, is no longer the historian's unquestioned task," in "Historiography and Postmodernism," 152.

facts. To his way of thinking, the contemplative, observing, and discerning historian was actively involved in the historical process and carefully selected only those relevant sources and facts required for the overall presentation. Such an historian painted the canvas with broad brush strokes, capturing in these lines of the image the perceived characteristics of the past (but not the past itself), and did not get lost in detail. Facts might provide information, but rarely were they illuminating. On the contrary, too many facts and details risked cluttering the limited representational, historical landscape; irrelevant, they distracted the observer from what was important, much like a realist painting that, in the name of historical accuracy, showed every last painful particular, to the ultimate disadvantage of the whole. Like Bachofen, Burckhardt believed that the past was too important to be left in the hands of scientists and researchers who destroyed myth with facts.

Only those facts, he would write in his introduction to his lectures on Greek cultural history, "that are in a position to reveal a real connection with our spirit and to awaken a real interest, whether it is through affinity or through contrast with us," belonged in cultural history.[33] As a result, Burckhardt did not shy away from using as legitimate sources material that would have been considered unscientific and dangerous. His use of anecdotes is perhaps the most obvious example. In many respects, they created the ideal "inner connection with our spirit." Anecdotes, at once "nowhere yet everywhere true," serve as more than a mere source of stylistic flare in Burckhardt's work.[34] They were the original historical "slips of the tongue," or "*Fehlleistungen,* of the past, the rare moments when the past 'let itself go', where we discover what is really of importance for us."[35] For Burckhardt, they served independently of facts – indeed, they flaunted facticity – in order to provide an overall view both of the past and of historiography. They awakened in the reader a sense not just of the ideas or mentalities of the historical subject, but also of the reader's

33 GA, 8:4.

34 CRI, 31. The English translation refers in this instance to Burckhardt's anecdote as a "story," although the original is "Anekdote." Thus Burckhardt distinguishes between the sources and the facts of history. As Felix Gilbert writes: "The cultural historian does not want to learn from his sources the 'facts' of the past; he studies the sources because they express the spirit of former times. It does not matter, therefore, whether they are factually correct, whether they lie or indulge in exaggerations or inventions. Even misleading statements may tell us something about the mind of a former age," Gilbert, *History: Politics or Culture?*, 89.

35 Ankersmit, "Historiography and Postmodernism," 148.

own active, participatory role in creating the past. Anecdotes, according to Burckhardt, facilitated the creation of a dialogue between the reader, the author, and the past because they required of the reader a creative leap of imagination, from fiction to reality.

· · ·

While the task of the historian may have been to an extent pathological in nature, Burckhardt by no means envisioned himself as an eager pathologist or anatomist engaged in the rigorous post-mortum of the cadaver of history. This he left to the scientific specialists, those myopic *viri eruditissimi.* His objective was rather to expose the disease, not explain its course. This represented an important reconsideration of the task of history. In traditional historiography, in which the primary goal is explanation, meaning in the past is derived through the establishment of causation. To say what caused what is not just to explain historical phenomena as a coherent sequence within a chronologically (temporally) bound narrative, but to accredit meaning to events that, in and of themselves, they do not necessarily possess outside of this sequence.

In a manner unique in nineteenth-century historiography, Burckhardt's major cultural historical achievements signify the deconstruction of the phenomenon of cause and effect, the cornerstone of modern science and historiography. In *Constantine*, for instance, he eschewed the temptation to write a chronological, explanatory narrative, emphasizing instead that "the author's design" was "to describe" the period between the accession of Diocletian and the death of Constantine, to present an "integrated description, from the viewpoint of cultural history."[36] Indeed, none of his mature work is diachronically organized. Instead, each chapter, for instance, in the *Civilization of the Renaissance*, is spatially and topographically organized according to themes that can be read independently of the whole. In a manner similar to Nietzsche,[37] Burckhardt's understanding of *Anschauung* reversed the traditional hierarchy of diachronic cause and effect. Causation assumed secondary status within his project, as did the search for origins; indeed, by its very nature, *Anschauung* posits that the primary concern of the historian is the effect itself,

36 This he stressed in both prefaces from 1852 and 1880. *Constantine*, 11, 13, 15.
37 See for example, Ankersmit, "Historiography and Postmodernism," 141-2.

not the causal chain leading to the effect. The effect, or perception, and the conditions of the past are what one encounters first, and what makes historical phenomena present, or accessible, to the historian in the first place; that, according to Burckhardt, had to be the starting point of any historical enquiry, even if the goal is explanation.[38]

The elimination of the causal nexus in Burckhardt's historiography does create a certain ambivalence in the relationship between the reader and the text. In effect, it tends to dissolve any internal reference point for the reader or observer that might otherwise have been established through the explanatory links of cause and effect. But this is not just intentional; it is also a necessary part of the performative function of the author. Moreover, it is necessary if the audience is to be successfully engaged in the historians' dialogue with the past. The audience is not presented with a *fait accompli*, or an objective, exact rendition of history that requires no obvious critique or interpretation. On the contrary, the ultimate meaning of the canvas/text derives from the active involvement of the viewer/reader who is obliged to enter into a dialogue not just with the text, but with its author.

In this respect, Burckhardt's historical work is analogous with impressionist painting.[39] This is by no means an idle comparison. In realist art and historiography, the problem of perspective is reduced to the establishment of a "single-point" perspective, created in large part by internal reference points derived through the chronological recounting of events within the narrative structure. As has already been pointed out,

38 See for example, WB, 166 and 225.

39 Hayden White has made this comparison. He writes: "Burckhardt, for all his Schopenhauerian pessimism (or perhaps because of it), was willing to experiment with the most advanced artistic techniques of *his* time. His *Civilization of the Renaissance* can be regarded as an exercise in impressionistic historiography, constituting, in its own way, as radical a departure from the conventional historiography of the nineteenth century as that of the impressionist painters, or that of Baudelaire in poetry ... Like his contemporaries in art, Burckhardt cuts into the historical record at different points and suggests different perspectives on it, omitting, ignoring, or distorting as his artistic purpose requires. His intention was not to tell the *whole* truth about the Italian Renaissance but *one* truth about it, in precisely the same way that Cézanne abandoned any attempt to tell the whole truth about a landscape. He had abandoned the dream of telling the truth about the past by means of telling a story because he had long since abandoned the belief that history had any inherent meaning or significance. The only 'truth' that Burckhardt recognized was that which he had learned from Schopenhauer – namely, that every attempt to give form to the world, every human affirmation, was tragically doomed in the end, but that individual affirmation attained to a worth of its own insofar as it succeeded in imposing upon the chaos of the world a momentary form," *Tropics of Discourse*, 44.

the universality of explanation implies that history is a meaningful whole, and that this meaning can be adduced by the historian. In impressionist art and Burckhardt's "impressionist" historiography, the content or object of study tends to recede in importance. Instead, the observer places the emphasis on the tone or the representation of the object as perceived by the artist/historian through the distortions of instant vision. The goal is not to create mimesis or exactitude, in the precise manner of the draftsman or photographer, but to reflect immediate (historical) impressions – momentary aspects of life, warts and all – as though the subject were unaware of the intrusive observer. In other words, it is as if one were to view the world for the first time without the benefit of prior knowledge.

Burckhardt's reliance on *Anschauung* and his desire to study the "background" suggests an ambivalence not only about detail and fact, but also about establishing meaning in history. Clearly, background can only be achieved through the artist's subtle manipulation of perspective, which consists of foreground, middle ground, and background. Perspective has been described as the "expression of a desire to order the world in a certain way: to make incoherencies coherent, to objectify subjective points of view, to turn the shimmering world of visual experience into a richly fixated construct."[40] But perspective is more than a rationalization or a "science" of the process of visualization. As a representational device, perspective is also concerned with the contours and discrepancies of this process. It is very much a "symbolic form" as well, the coherence of which is dependent upon the artistic form imposed by the artist. It is not in and of itself "reality," but only a representation of reality. The only meaning is the viewer's interpretation.

Although Burckhardt was interested in establishing continuities in history, he was not concerned with general laws of historical development or explanation. "Representation," Ankersmit has remarked, "is indifferent to meaning." By this, he maintains that meaning only arises subsequent to representation; that meaning exists not in the representation itself but evolves instead "from our recognition of how other people (historians, artists, novelists) represent the world," or from their interpretation of the representation. As in an impressionist work of art, then, meaning is derived from the various contours created through this manipulation of perspective from the only reference point possible, that of the viewer. In terms of historiography, it was thus not enough to

40 Holly, "Burckhardt and the Ideology of the Past," 63.

analyze what an historical text meant; the goal was to examine how the text subsequently worked within the broader historical context and the historiographic narrative. Ultimately, the urgent desire to seek coherence and meaning in the historical text through the process of explanation obscures not only vital differences and passions, but also the way text functions.

Burckhardt's employment of the vocabulary of representation and *Anschauung* indicates that his mode of historical thought operates within the parameters of aesthetic discourse. Rather than basing his approach to history on conceptualized theories or scientific methodologies that stressed the importance of explanation, meaning, and facticity, his unique form of cultural history is derived from his viewing of the past as a text to be interpreted or decoded through the realm of sensate experience. In Burckhardt's cultural histories, aestheticism meets with the asceticism that shaped his personal experience (his quest for the "Goddess herself"), thereby forming the primary structuring element or ordering principle of his thought and life. But how does this translate into Burckhardt's historical practice? If he viewed the historical process aesthetically, how was this reflected in his work?

Perhaps the single "truth" that Burckhardt wished to expose was that history was not a rational process, and that human beings were not rational creatures. Accordingly, reason represented an instinctive, yet absurdly impetuous desire of humankind, which, in its striving for coherence and order, attempted to break away from the very aesthetic realm of instinct to which it belonged, in order to create a disjuncture between experience and intellect, subject and object, content and form. Reason was a divisive myth designed to reveal the world as it is and was and to celebrate and justify the present, the ultimate result of which was spiritual alienation and the creation of a self-perpetuating antagonism between subject and object. In this sense, reason was an all-inclusive and hegemonic discourse, designed to create order in the social and cultural realms through control of the individual's aesthetic sensibilities of mind and body.

However, in Burckhardt's histories there is another force at work, a force that he also referred to as the *Geist.* This was not a rational spirit that drove humankind. Rather it was the embodiment of the irrational side of humankind, the sensual, passionate side of human nature that does not follow rational laws but instead obeys the instincts. This purely aesthetic side governed human behavior and was not subordinated to rationality; rather it embraced what is both good and evil in humankind: lusts, greeds and appetites, as well as the longing for beauty, love, and peace. Instead of following a rational, progressive course, historical life represented the continual conflict between these elements. It surged violently here and there in "a thousand forms." It was "complex and under all manner of disguises, free and unfree, speaking at times through the masses, at times through individuals, now in an optimistic, now in a pessimistic mood. It built and destroyed states, religions and civilizations, and was at times in itself a vague mystery, at times accompanied by reflection, but more often by dark feelings transmitted by the imagination, rather than led by reflection."[41] These "dark feelings" of the human spirit, which create and destroy earthly life and forms, always building anew what will only later be destroyed, represented the spiritual continuum that Burckhardt sought to capture in his texts. But this world of the human spirit could not be approached through concepts and rational thought. According to Burckhardt, "We must inevitably, as people of a definite time, pay our passive tribute to this whole being (historical life), but at the same time we must approach it through the spirit of observation."[42]

. . .

Like Burckhardt's earlier study of the age of Constantine the Great, the *Civilization of the Renaissance in Italy* is an intensely personal work. The Renaissance was a theme that was "sympathetically and mysteriously connected to [his] inner being," a product of "inner necessity."[43] The book was undoubtedly Burckhardt's most famous and influential; like *Constantine*, as one recent scholar has shown, it reflects his serious religious doubts, the consequences of his crisis of faith and apostasy, and his secular understanding of history.[44] But more than simply serving to confront his own doubts about Christianity, Burckhardt's *Renaissance* was perhaps his most important reckoning with modernity and history, an attempt to come to terms with the ideas that dominated the contem-

41 WB, 229.
42 Ibid.
43 *Briefe*, 5:74 and 4:76.
44 Howard, "Historicist Thought in the Shadow of Theology," 36off.

porary world. In short, it is a confrontation with modernity and a repudiation of the promise of the Enlightenment. In addition, however, Burckhardt was making a statement about human nature when he sought to demonstrate that the optimism regarding the eternal goodness of mankind – Rousseau's great "optimistic will" which so irritated Burckhardt – was misguided, misplaced, and based upon a faulty understanding of human beings. His is a critique of the new religion of rationality, enthroned by Hegel's progressive *Geist* and the doctrine of perfectibility, that led not to liberation of the subject, nor to moral or intellectual progress, but rather to greater transgressions and to cynicism, which in turn ultimately destroyed the subjective instincts, myth, and beauty. Finally, *The Civilization of the Renaissance* represents Burckhardt's attempt to capture and recount in his historiography the "dark feelings" or the naive, instinctive state of human nature. In this seminal work he demonstrates how this state, translated into the creative experience, provides not only the content of *quattrocento* history, but also its form. The story of the rise of the individual and the modern state is one of intense, passionate conflict. Here, horrifying tales of death and destruction exist side by side with the most glorious spiritual and intellectual achievements. It is a journey to the heights of human creativity and the depths of human depravity, the story of the forces of good and evil that exist side by side within the human spirit.

The antagonism between the forces of good and evil, the story of human suffering, Burckhardt was at pains to stress, was by no means unique to the Renaissance, but is a characteristic of human history in general. With the recognition of this simple truth, Burckhardt turned both Hegel and Ranke aside and followed a path already prepared by Schopenhauer, the philosopher with whom Burckhardt is most often compared. Burckhardt was one of the few serious scholars to confront the issue of evil in history. Hegel, for instance, did not consider the problem of evil in history to be significant; it was merely the unavoidable cost of the progress of world history, which required sacrifice and victims. In Hegel's dialectic, fate and tragedy, as explanations for the recurrence of evil in history, are replaced by reason, logic, and necessity in the name of human progress. Likewise, according to Ranke, human misery is unfortunate but necessary; in the end, he too believed that it was eventually compensated for by the course of history and human progress. But for Burckhardt, as for Schopenhauer, history was indeed a tragedy, the story of evil and suffering; it was "the long, difficult, and confused dream of humanity" in which the history of the individual became the history of humankind.[45]

The problem of good and evil in history assumed great importance in Burckhardt's study of the Italian Renaissance. For one thing, Burckhardt showed that the period represented the development of social and political structures that were to govern contemporary society. It was significant, too, because it demonstrated that while this conflict could indeed be a creative force – giving rise not only to the modern individual or the "state as a work of art," but also to the creative genius of the humanists and the artistic heritage of the Renaissance – that very duality also contained the seeds of the period's own destruction. Hence Burckhardt's picture of the Renaissance is a tragedy in the most literal sense. The human instinct, he maintained, is as capable of producing the sublime as it is the wicked. In effect, the forces responsible for the rise of humanism in the fourteenth century are the same as those contributing to its decline and to the sixteenth century's subsequent descent into political and social chaos.

The work also provides an important parallel to *Constantine*, in which Burckhardt described the decline of pagan individualism. For Burckhardt, the collapse of pagan individualism facilitated the consolidation of Christianity in the fourth century. In Renaissance Italy, the process was reversed; it was the decline of medieval Christianity, accompanied by a renewed interest in classical antiquity, that made possible the rise of the modern individual. To Burckhardt's eyes, the distinguishing feature of both the pagan and the modern individual, liberated from the veil or myth of Christianity, was that the rational drive and the cultivation of the self exist side by side, often in violence, ambivalence, and contradiction. The new individual of the Renaissance, modern man, expressed his individuality in extremes of good and evil, in brutality and creative genius. "Through his gifts and his passions," Burckhardt wrote, "he has become the most characteristic representative of all the heights and all the depths of his time. By the side of profound corruption appeared human personalities of the noblest harmony, and an artistic splendor which shed upon the life of man a luster which neither antiquity nor medievalism either could or would bestow upon it."[46] But Burckhardt's work was not the celebration of the artistic achievements of the age. It is the story, as Wolfgang Hardtwig correctly states, of the unleashing of an

45 See also the insightful work by Flaig, *Angeschaute Geschichte*, 14ff.
46 CRI, 289.

outrageous amorality, of the "liberation of the evil in human nature. There emerges the picture of a public life transfixed by force and crime, by cruelty and despotism, by lack of justice and instability."[47]

It is no coincidence that Burckhardt ended the first chapter, "The State as a Work of Art," with an account of the Borgias. His story so far had been about the structural transformation of Italian society. In this context, he uses the phrase "state as a work of art" to describe, in contrast to the Middle Ages, the objective, rational treatment of politics and governance. This new, objective approach to statesmanship – the attempt to control the external world through the force and tyranny of reason – was perhaps, for Burckhardt, the most significant outward sign of the new relationship between the object and the subject, between the individual and society. The emergence of a newly found secular power, however, also bears the decisive imprint of the subjective individual, because the "state as a work of art" is shaped and executed according to the designs and wishes of its rulers, without moral compunction or the restraint of tradition, according to his own rules and wishes. Burckhardt's story, therefore, is, according to Hardtwig, one of blood-chilling violence and degradation, of blatant disregard for laws and rights, and of total lack of restraint, and it culminates in the Borgia's conquering of both secular and religious authority. The signature of the age, as Hardtwig claims, emerges from this tale of evil, from its megalomania, its voluptuousness, and its greed.[48]

As Burckhardt's work demonstrates, this Dionysian side existed not just in the form of the *condottieri* or the infamous Sforza, the dukes of Milan. The humanists, too, were characterized by the same psychological drives that motivated the actions of the soldiers of fortune, albeit in milder and less violent forms. Scholars and poets alike, in an attempt to express their individuality, were also driven by an unbridled egotism; by the same insatiable lust for power, fame, glory, and immortality. "Amid all these preparations outwardly to win and secure fame, the curtain is now and then drawn aside, [Burckhardt's "instant vision" of the unaware subject] and we see with frightful evidence a boundless ambition and thirst after greatness, independent of means and consequences." The desire to produce something that would guarantee a place in the "great pantheon of world-wide celebrity" was motivated, avowed Burckhardt, not by an "extreme case of ordinary vanity, but [by] something

47 Hardtwig, "*Geschichtskultur und Wissenschaft,* 195.
48 Ibid., 197.

demonic, involving a surrender of will, the use of any means, however
atrocious, and even an indifference to success itself."[49] In this age of
"overstrained and despairing passions," one corrective to fame could be
found in the Renaissance passion for ridicule and wit, designed for the
most bloodthirsty of character assassinations. Base motives and actions
thus exist side by side with artistic splendour in Burckhardt's representation of the Renaissance; good and evil cohabitate, in a type of osmotic
relationship, and are distinct media, although they absorb and transfer
their qualities from one to the other. Sometimes one will dominate,
sometimes another, but always both are present, threatening ambiv-
alently and randomly to create and to destroy. This is not to deny the genius of Renaissance cultural creativity. Instead, it is a recognition that
cultural expression, the domain of true spiritual freedom and consciousness, comes at a cost. Peter Gay summarizes: "Renaissance man's
central problem is pervasive and unvaried: each of his virtues produces
its vice, each vice produces its antidote which is itself imperfect, so that
the struggle of the individual is perpetual, and the result of his conduct
ambiguous. The freedom of Renaissance man is a strange semislavery; it
is half blessing, half curse."[50]

Burckhardt did not minimize or neglect to recount the forces of evil
that occupy such a central position in his interpretation of the Renaissance. In fact, Burckhardt at times appeared to relish his vivid descriptions of this Dionysian side of Renaissance life. This is part of his
broader attempt to shatter the myths of modernity and the development of the modern individual, which presumed that human beings are
by nature good and that history and humanity are driven by rational,
progressive forces. His history of the Renaissance individual in fact reveals precisely the opposite: that human beings are not by nature good,
and that they contain within themselves a tremendous capacity for evil,
which is "a part of the great economy of world history." In a Darwinian
moment, he explicitly equates the struggle for survival and dominance
in the natural world with that of the historical world.[51] This does not
mean that he praised the victors or the successes of history; by no means
was the stronger the better. His point was that these successes were the
result of tremendous human suffering; not that they were "good," as

49 CRI, 109–10.
50 Gay, "Burckhardt's *Renaissance*," 204.
51 WB, 239–40.

much as that they were a result of humankind's natural instincts, which also consisted of potential for "evil."

In his essay on fortune and misfortune in history, Burckhardt examined in greater depth the implications of the duality of good and evil in history. Once again, this duality serves to reinforce his fundamental aestheticist position with regard to not only historiography but also life in general and his critique of modernity. At the core of his study of happiness and unhappiness in history is the rejection of the Enlightenment credo of human rationality and progress, which in many respects represented a denial of the Dionysian side of human nature. Although Burckhardt recognized the historical existence of good and evil, he did not judge history accordingly. Judgments according to this principle were the result of an "optical illusion," he maintained, and a characteristic of the modern age; they were "thinkable only as a result of the new business of history," the purpose of which was, in Foucault's language, "the production of truth." Such judgments, declared Burckhardt, are only possible in a public age in which a "kind of literary consensus, which has been accumulated from the wishes and reasonings of the Enlightenment and from the true or fanciful conclusions of a number of widely read historians," could become established. According to Burckhardt, these crude attitudes became part and parcel of the public consciousness and were turned into trendy journalistic arguments, exercising an unprecedented hegemony over public discourse and consciousness. But this public use of reason did not enlighten or liberate, he argued. On the contrary, it further enslaved mankind through its hegemonic power to exclude and disenfranchise and, consequently, became the deadly enemy "of true historical insight."[52]

In particular, Burckhardt's criticism was an indictment of those who would pass moral judgment on the past from the perspective of modernity. Modernity, according to Michel Foucault, places a high value on the present: "Modernity is the attitude that makes it possible to grasp the 'heroic' aspect of the present moment. Modernity is not a phenomenon of sensitivity to the fleeting present; it is the will to 'heroize' the present."[53] Since the Enlightenment – or specifically the acceptance of Rousseau's optimistic will, which not only assured us that humankind was by nature good, but also instilled the belief in moral progress and in the theory of perfection – the present had been glorified as the "heroic

52 Ibid., 232–3.
53 Foucault, "What is Enlightenment?" in *The Foucault Reader*, 38.

age," the result of which was "the arrogant belief in the moral superiority of the present."[54] Burckhardt's history of the human *Geist*, however, sought to demonstrate not just that the roots of modernity were to be found in a state of profound amorality, but also that morality could not be found in institutions such as the state or religion, which depended upon, and embraced, power. Moral virtue, he believed, was best nurtured in the private realm, where the individual was free to develop the self ascetically and aesthetically. "It's an evil world," Burckhardt liked to proclaim.[55] Not surprisingly, perhaps, the individuals Burckhardt admired most in the Italian Renaissance were those secular ascetics who professed scepticism towards the claims of both the Church and modern society, and who retreated from the world in order to devote themselves to lives of scholarship and learning.

. . .

It is in the nature of the modern historical enterprise that historians desire to have the last word; that they must seek and find cohesion, coherence, and closure in the study of the past. Unfortunately, Burckhardt's conscious decision to chart his own historiographical course has made it exceedingly difficult for commentators to arrive at some sort of concensus about how to categorize his work within the context of nineteenth-century historical discourse. That unlike Ranke, for example, Burckhardt did not train a generation of historians who could develop his ideas into a school of historical thought only complicates the matter. Still, on a number of specific issues there is basic agreement. Most people, for instance, would agree that Burckhardt's approach to history was synchronic, rather than diachronic, and that he did not seek to explain the development of historical processes or look for origins. As scholars have long recognized, this approach is most clearly articulated in Burckhardt's famous statement from *Reflections on History*, in which he declares that his aim is to present the "constant, typical, and recurrent" and to examine transverse sections of the past, rather than to provide a chronologically organized explanation of events.[56] To that end, he believed that

54 JHH, 230 and 243. See also WB, 283.
55 Kaegi, "Die Idee der Vergänglichkeit," 209.
56 WB, 227.

writers of cultural history "need to be released from mere narration which may be given by handbooks," and to attempt "to group phenomena more according to their inner relations in which they form conditions, lasting states of affairs ... What we really aim at is an understanding of all the more significant and effective forces in general, and thus of the more or less constant conditions created by them." Although he recognized that cultural history would then "long have a subjective and dilettante appearance," he was not overly concerned. What counted was that in the pursuit of the study of cultural history "each individual will proceed according to his personal insight."[57]

What this ultimately signifies within the broader tradition of European historiography, however, is not at all clear. Hence, there are as many interpretations about his approach to history as there are scholars who study and write about him. Siebert has tentatively – and tantalizingly – suggested that Burckhardt's emphasis on the "broad lines, the general tendencies," the "exploration of conditions, general dispositions and structures," and, ultimately, his rejection of the "narration of particular events" and "event and person-oriented history" anticipated various aspects of modern structural history. In particular, she suggests the possibility of an important connection between Burckhardt's work and that of the French *Annales*'s school.[58] Like Siebert, I would hesitate to go so far as to say that Burckhardt prefigured the work of the *Annales*. However, the comparison may not be that far-fetched. As in the work of Fernand Braudel, for instance, Burckhardt sought the unity and coherence of a period not in the "*l'histoire événementielle*, that is, [in] the history of events: [the] surface disturbances, [the] crests of foam that the tides of history carry on their strong backs," but rather in the "deeper realities of history, of the running waters on which our frail barks are tossed like cockleshells."[59]

If there is any value in comparing the work of Jacob Burckhardt with that of the *Annales* historians, I would suggest that it lies in that school's practice of the history of mentalities rather than in its history of social and economic structures and systems. Indeed, more so than the history

57 JHH, 29.

58 Siebert, *Jacob Burckhardt*, 78. Hardtwig identifies Burckhardt's form of cultural history with *Geistesgeschichte* and *Gesellschaftsgeschichte* without suggesting any similarity with that of the *Annales* school. Hardtwig, *Geschichtsschreibung zwischen Alteuropa und moderner Welt*, 165ff.

59 Fernand Braudel, *The Mediterranean and the Mediterranean World in the Age of Philip II*, vol. I (New York: Harper & Row, 1972), 21.

of ideas, or Hardtwig's *Gesellschaftsgeschichte*,[60] the history of mentalities approach seems to come closest to reflecting the intent of Burckhardt's conception of cultural history. Witness its concern with attitudes and ideologies; its universal-historical emphasis; its use of descriptive rather than explanatory narrative; and its topological and spatial, rather than temporal, organizing principles.

There are fundamental differences, however, between Burckhardt's cultural history and the history of mentalities as practised by the *Annales* school, especially regarding the latter's conceptualization of history. Whereas the primary objective of the *Annales*'s historians has been the "search for a science of history,"[61] Burckhardt explicitly rejected the notion that history was a science and could be written objectively. Whereas the *Annales*'s historians claim to reject positivist methodology and theory, a strong positivist residue remains in their work at the discursive level of textualization and enunciation. Burckhardt, in contrast, because he started with the belief that history is an art, not a science, does not share the logocentrism of the *Annales*'s historians.[62] He was much more conscious of history's origins in rhetoric, and of the performative function of the historian in the reconstruction of the past.

Other historians have pointed out that this emphasis on the constant, typical, and recurrent indicates that Burckhardt's understanding of history was typological; that is to say, he sought to present those typical aspects of the past or historical types from the flux of events and time that give history its coherence and form. Rüsen has argued that Burckhardt's typology closely resembles Weberian ideal types – both have "the character of a utopia" – which enables him to go beyond chronologically ordered narrative.[63] Egon Flaig, in contrast, argues that while Burckhardt's "typical presentation" may resemble Weber's idealtype "because of its amazingly similar means of construction," it served a different function altogether. Flaig denies that Burckhardt's typology was an heuristic devise designed to serve the progress of knowledge as a means of accounting for teleological change in history.[64] Burckhardt's typology, he maintains, is essentially indifferent to causal explanation, chronological narrative, factual empiricism, and historical meaning or

60 Hardtwig, *Geschichtsschreibung zwischen Alteuropa und moderner Welt*, 173.
61 See Iggers' *New Directions in European Historiography*, 43–79.
62 On this positivist residue, see Carrard, *Poetics of the New History*.
63 Rüsen, *Konfigurationen des Historismus*, 315.
64 Flaig, *Angeschaute Geschichte*, 36.

truth. Rather, it is a means of configuring the past, a representation. Indeed, Burckhardt's typological approach does serve a vital function in the process of historical representation. In many respects it is a lesson in *Anschauung*, a means by which Burckhardt was able to aestheticize history and cultural history. Defined according to their "inner relations" and derived from the "personal insight" of the historian, his admittedly subjective "*Potenzenlehre*" (the three powers of state, culture, and religion) were ultimately "mere constructions"; "yes, simply reflections of ourselves ... that are transmitted through the imagination."[65] His was a subjective "metalanguage," which stood in contradistinction to the historical positivists' search for meaning, truth, and certainty in knowledge. It enabled Burckhardt to interupt the stream of history at isolated and, at times, arbitrary moments in order to examine those voices, metaphors, allusions, and texts that constituted the myths of past ages; it enabled him to touch the poetic core of human frailty, meaninglessness, and eternal posturing.

One of Burckhardt's most important statements defining his approach to cultural history was made in the introduction to his lectures on Greek cultural history, begun in 1872 and later posthumously published as *Griechische Kulturgeschichte*. Aware that he was assuming a position outside the mainstream of contemporary cultural and political history, he sought to broaden the scope of enquiry. He wanted, thereby, to enable cultural historians to go beyond the mere collection of facts about ways of life and to provide a more integrated, coherent account that would capture the dominant ideas, trends, and spirit of the age. He indicated that he was not interested in "the treatment of that which only belongs to the usual external life"; instead envisioning a higher task for the cultural historian, one that was concerned primarily with the instinctive forces of human nature, those same forces he felt were being destroyed by the encroachment of the state and the rise of liberalism and free-market capitalism in his own day. Rooted in the idea that history was a creative process, that it was poetry, Burckhardt's unique form of cultural history concerned itself with "the inner qualities of past humanity and proclaims how it was, what it wanted, how it thought and saw, and what it was capable of." In other words, his goal was to seize "the inner core of mankind." Citing Schiller, he summarized the goal of his cultural history of Greece: "The man whose inmost heart I have once

65 WB, 227 and 229.

probed / Is known to me in all his will and deeds."[66] His starting point, as he had earlier stated in his lectures on the study of history, was to examine the past from the "only remaining and possible centre for us, from the suffering, striving and acting man, as he is, was and will be."[67]

This last statement has received considerable attention by scholars, most of whom agree that it is a sign of Burckhardt's anthropological approach to history. In this context, anthropological refers to the notion that Burckhardt was convinced of the constancy and uniformity of the motivational forces of human nature throughout the ages, and that this negated the possibility of teleological change.[68] This approach serves an extremely vital function in Burckhardt's historiography: not only does it reinforce his conception of the basic continuity of the historical process; it ultimately allows him to come to terms with his own age of crisis as a momentary break in this continuity, and as one that will inevitably be restored according to the logic of human nature. In addition, the anthropological aspects of his thought take into account his dualistic understanding of human nature, with its underpinnings of instinct and intellect and its propensity for good and evil, for the beautiful and the monstrous, and for truth and illusion. While I am not questioning the overall significance of Burckhardt's anthropological position – to a certain extent all historiography is anthropological – the main issue goes beyond the question of the unity of human behaviour. Although the anthropological standpoint may be an underlying assumption of his work, it is not its driving force. It is possible to argue, from a slightly different perspective, that the anthropological presuppositions can be seen as means to an end, that end being an aesthetic history. Burckhardt's desire to study "suffering, striving, acting man" reveals his deep-rooted concern with precisely that "naive," instinctive state of inner conflict within mankind that gives rise to art, creativity, and culture and which, in his own age, had been lost. This goal reaches back to the creative instincts of mankind, the *Kunsttrieb*; back to the very inner core of aes-

66 GA, 8:3 and 6. The quote is from *Wallensteins Tod*, Act II, scene 3. "Hab ich des Menschen Kern erst untersucht, / so weiß ich auch sein Wollen und sein Handeln." Translation from the excellent new edition of Burckhardt's cultural history of Greece, *The Greeks and Greek Civilization*, 5.

67 WB, 226.

68 Rüsen, "Jacob Burckhardt: Political Standpoint and Historical Insight on the Border of Post-Modernism," 241. See also Rüsen, *Konfigurationen des Historismus*, 311, and Hardtwig, *Geschichtsschreibung zwischen Alteuropa und moderner Welt: Jacob Burckhardt in seiner Zeit*, 51 ff.

thetics; to the original realm of human perception and sensation unfettered by the "higher" truths of pure thought; and to the original realm
of human desire and subjectivity untamed by rational praxis. In other
words, by raising sensate life to the primary locus of experience, by viewing history as an art, and by rejecting the notion of history as a rational
science, Burckhardt was not trying just to dephilosophize or deconcep-
tualize history. More importantly, he wanted to aestheticize it in order to
capture the whole of human society and history as an aesthetic product
in which art and free spiritual creativity have world-making significance.

8

Burckhardt and Contemporary Art

IN THE BRIEF AUTOBIOGRAPHICAL SKETCH written towards the end of his life, which in the Basel custom was read at his funeral, Burckhardt recalled that "besides history, the observation of art had always had a powerful attraction ... and among the rich intellectual stimulation of all kinds which Berlin provided ... the museums there were from the beginning a source of learning and of longed-for enjoyment."[1] Clearly, the study of art occupied a central position in Burckhardt's professional life. When viewed as a whole, his extensive work in the field of art history not only reflects the same diversity and wide-ranging knowledge that characterized his historical work, but forms a comprehensive, unified history of the entire scope of Western art from classical antiquity to the modern age. His first publications, on art and historical themes, reflected his strong passion for architecture. When he was just nineteen years old, he published his reflections of the cathedrals of Geneva, Lausanne, Basel, and Zürich in the *Zeitschrift über das gesamte Bauwesen* in order to earn money for a planned journey to Italy.[2] As a student in Berlin, he continued to study art history with Franz Kugler and, after an excursion through Belgium in 1841, he published a short book, *Die Kunstwerke der belgischen Städte*, a popular guide and his first "Cicerone," designed to introduce the casual traveller to the most important aspects of the golden age of Flemish art. In 1855, after completing *The Age of Constantine the Great*, Burckhardt published his enormously popular guide to Italian art, *Der Cicerone*, the work that cemented his interna-

---

1 GA, 1:viii.

2 Burckhardt, *Bemerkungen über schweizerische Kathedralen.* The articles were originally published over the course of 1837–39. In his "Bilder aus Italien," a record of his second trip to Italy in 1838, he also provided brief sketches of the history and architecture of Milan, Pisa, Florence, and Genoa. See Burckhardt, *Reisebilder aus dem Süden*, 56–149.

tional reputation as an art historian.[3] In addition to this book and numerous essays and lectures, one other important monograph was published during his lifetime, *Die Geschichte der Renaissance in Italien* (1878); initially, it was published as *Die Geschichte der neueren Baukunst*, the architecture volume in Kugler's series *Geschichte der Baukunst* (1867). Finally, his famous study of Peter Paul Rubens, *Erinnerungen aus Rubens*, published posthumously in 1898, serves as the culmination of his lifelong interest in the Flemish artist who had caught his attention on his first trip through Belgium.

Burckhardt's accomplishments in the history of art are even more impressive. For twelve years, he held the chairs of history and art history concurrently; he was also active in the field for most of his life. His first teaching position was as a lecturer (*Privat Dozent*) of art history at the university in Basel during the 1843–44 academic year. In 1855, he was appointed professor of art history and archeology at the newly established federal polytechnical institute at Zürich, where he taught for three years before returning to Basel in 1858 as full professor of history. Between 1858 and 1874, Burckhardt taught only history, but was involved in local artistic life as a member of the commission for Basel's public gallery, the Öffentliche Kunstsammlung. In 1874, he accepted the chair of art history at the university as well and, even after retiring from the chair of history in 1886, continued to teach art history in an official capacity until 1893, when he retired completely from all university responsibilities.

Burckhardt's interest in art was not just professional. There was an intense personal dimension to his relationship with art that transcended both the academic world and the realm of immediate visual pleasure and stimulation. This can be seen at a number of levels. On the one hand, it found expression in the cultivation of his own substantial creative energies and talents. For example, like many young men of his time, he tried his hand at poetry. His early letters reveal numerous literary plans, as well as frustration at his perceived inability to achieve success in what he believed to be one of the highest forms of artistic expression. This was perhaps more a sign of his insecurity and self-deprecation, than of a lack of real ability. Although by the age of twenty he had resigned himself to not achieving fame as a poet – heading instead for the more mundane notoriety of an historian – his literary

3 *Der Cicerone* caused somewhat of a sensation. It was the subject of an 80-page review by Gustav Waagen, director of the Royal Art Gallery in Berlin, in the journal *Deutsches Kunstblatt*, 21 June 1855 to 9 August 1855.

endeavours nonetheless brought him a certain degree of celebrity in Basel. Indeed, Burckhardt was considered one of the most important Basel-dialect poets. His book of poetry, *E Hämpfeli Lieder,* published anonymously in 1853, was well received because of its unpretentious use of dialect as a literary form.[4] Burckhardt's gift of *Anschauung* also found expression in hundreds of sketches, drawn primarily during his numerous excursions to Germany and Italy. These drawings fall into two general categories: those designed to assist his art studies as a mnemonic device for recalling particular architectonic styles and forms; and those more detailed sketches of landscapes and monuments that served as a personal document of his travels and life. In any case, he was not a natural drawer. It did not come easily to him, and he always viewed himself as a dilettante. As photography advanced and became more accessible, he stopped drawing and began, instead, to collect photographs of most of the more important artworks.[5]

On the other hand, the contemplation and observation of art had an intensely metaphysical dimension for Burckhardt. Art assumed the mysterious qualities of a religion; the enjoyment of art became a spiritual, mystic experience, at once a source of inspiration and a "healing power" in his life. The value of art, according to Burckhardt, lay in its worth as a representational form and in its ability to transform humankind and the world. Art was a tranquil oasis of pleasure and freedom in which the subject could be liberated, if only temporarily, from the oppression and disharmony of the objective world; it was a sublime moment in which an ideal, utopian spirit penetrated the recesses of the mind and imagination. A true work of art, declared Burckhardt, expressed at once what the world was and what the world should be. "In the midst of our hurried age," wrote Burckhardt, art provides us with "a domain of general contemplation, of which past centuries knew little or nothing; it is a second dream existence in which quite exceptional spiritual senses come to life and consciousness."[6] Yet the sheer power of the artist's imagination and the monumental will behind artistic creation,

4 For the circumstances surrounding these poems and his other dialect poetry, see Kaegi, 3:240ff. See also Burckhardt *Ferien: Eine Herbstgabe,* and Burckhardt, *Gedichte,* 1926. See also Hoffmann, *Jacob Burckhardt als Dichter,* and Gass, *Die Dichtung im Leben und Werk Jacob Burckhardts.*

5 *Briefe,* 6:241. See also M. Burckhardt, "Jacob Burckhardt als Zeichner," Boerlin-Brodbeck, "Jacob Burckhardts römische Skizzenbücher," and Boerlin-Brodbeck, ed., *Die Skizzenbücher Jacob Burckhardts.*

6 "Über die Kunstgeschichte als Gegenstand eines akademischen Lehrstuhls," (1874), in GA, 13:25.

however apparent to the student of art, could not, avowed Burckhardt, alone explain art's force or its unique ability to stimulate the sensibilities of the observer. Although art was an "historical phenomenon of the first degree," it was one that he felt was a "high, active power in life."[7] Like poetry, art was often the best that remained of an age; the highest and most noble expression of individuality and, indeed, of humanity. As a source of the past, he felt it represented a summation of history and humankind's most glorious achievements; in a world of violence, disharmony, and radical change, the artistic and intellectual heritage of the past constituted the foundation of humankind's "spiritual continuum." Thus, for Burckhardt, beauty had to be "elevated over time and its changes," and its contemplation should not be seen as a right or duty, but as a higher need. In effect, it represented "our freedom in the midst of our awareness of enormous, universal dependence and of the stream of necessities."[8]

Because for Burckhardt art was a wonder, he considered it almost inaccessible to our mortal pretensions and immune to historians' systematizing schemes. The true meaning of art, as of life, was not readily apparent to the scholar, he felt, but remained cloaked in mystery. In his inaugural address as professor of art history in 1874, which afterwards served as a general introduction to his cycle of art history lectures, Burckhardt maintained that "art, with the exception of poetry, is that spirit which does not talk, but builds, creates and portrays; it is the unspoken as such, that which consequently lives in forms and tones because it is not able to live in words. Therefore, one can never speak of the true mystery of the particular work of art, and with continued research the deepest reason behind art generally only becomes even more mysterious, and all discussions of the same more or less futile."[9] Since it is almost inaccessible to our mortal pretensions, he argued, all that we can truly experience of art are those "mysterious vibrations which are communicated to the soul. What these vibrations release is no longer individual or temporal but immortal and of symbolic significance."[10]

For Burckhardt, because art seemed to defy and transcend the rhetoric of the scholar, its sublime and eternal character posed special difficulties for those engaged in its study. Despite being a "language of all

---

7 Ibid., 26.

8 WB, 229 and 230.

9 "Über die Kunstgeschichte als Gegenstand eines akademischen Lehrstuhls," 26. Meier discusses this lecture in "Zu Jacob Burckhardt und Friedrich Nietzsche," 101.

10 WB, 278–9.

nations," it was mute at this very conjuncture. Burckhardt seemed to be questioning the very possibility of language when he asked his readers to rely on contemplation and observation, the very essence of his own historical being. Language, itself mortal and this-worldly, was vague and imprecise, he said, at once incapable of coherence and accurate representation and unable to achieve parity with the spiritual and everlasting.

Burckhardt felt it was an unfortunate sign of the vanity, lack of spirit, and general "historylessness"[11] of the modern age that, rather than recognizing these vibrations and fragments – the only traces left to our "restoring ability" – as part of a more mysterious, enchanting force, the modern individual viewed art, like language, as transparent to meaning. In the optimistic age of scientific positivism, rapid technological change, and laissez-faire capitalism, he argued, art was treated as though its meaning was hidden just below the surface, waiting to be delivered to the expectant, curious viewer through the rigours of scholarly analysis. This then was the task early nineteenth-century art historians set for themselves; this was what the interested art public demanded. However, Burckhardt consciously avoided speaking of the "idea" or meaning a work of art supposedly transmitted. He did not believe that one could penetrate the "idea of the artwork"; this, he maintained, was a "laughable pretension."[12] While it might be possible for natural scientists to reveal the secrets of nature, the mysteries of art remained for the most part impenetrable to the impertinent probings of the scholar.[13] Likewise, Burckhardt argued that the increasingly pervasive desire to discover the "idea" behind a work of art was potentially harmful in its implications; this was the intellectual property of the "most dreadful of philistines," into whose hands he feared the discipline of art history had fallen.[14]

However, the modern educated public of Burckhardt's time, not just the art historians, demanded meaningful art; art had to have a more immediate and direct relevance for them and for society as a whole. Throughout the century, as the audience for art grew and its production became tied to the demands and values of the marketplace, art was expected to fulfill the aesthetic preferences of the public and to serve its

11 Ibid., 229.

12 In his rejection of the argument that art was anchored in ideas, Burckhardt adhered to what one recent commentator has described as a "post-Kantian" aesthetic. See Siebert, "Zum Problem der Kulturgeschichtsschreibung bei Jacob Burckhardt," 258.

13 "Über die Kunstgeschichte als Gegenstand eines akademischen Lehrstuhls," 26.

14 *Briefe*, 3:68.

ideological and moral needs. In other words, modern art increasingly had to prove its actuality and to justify its very existence in social and economic terms, a process that eroded creativity and destroyed artistic independence.

An important reminder of the new authority and influence of the bourgeoisie in the art world was the increasingly widespread notion of "*Kunstleben,*" or "artistic life." This particular understanding of art and its relation to society had important implications for artistic development, and was perhaps best embodied in the proliferation of art associations in Restoration Germany. These particular organizations, like other social, academic, or political clubs in Germany, were of tremendous importance in the development of a mature, politically conscious public sphere. The art associations served a variety of functions. They actively promoted local artistic talent, creating a new market and a valuable source of patronage. As well, they offered the middle classes a veneer of culture and prestige, conferring on them social status and a means whereby they could help articulate and shape not just artistic, but also political discourse.

But as the art historian Nikolaus Meier has explained, *Kunstleben* implied much more than the sum of art associations, public art exhibitions, museums, or art academies. It was more than the "art scene" or "cultural politics"; rather, it represented a redefinition of the concept of art. *Kunstleben* was an ideal – a type of utopian, organic, synergetic entity based upon the understanding that art was public property, produced for a market and, theoretically, accessible to all, not a luxury or simply a representational form produced for the pleasure of a traditional, elite clientele such as the court, church, and aristocracy. Furthermore, within the context of this ideal, it was understood that art provided life with a special meaning, spirituality – a certain fulfilment – and that there was a special bond between the artist, the general public, and the art historian, whose inspired task it was to transform this ideal into practice.[15] As a consequence, art was expected to play a role as both vehicle and servant of public interest. Throughout Germany and the rest of Europe, theorists and intellectuals debated the public function of art; they explored the possibility of harnessing art and its production to the national cause and of creating an environment that would assist in the mobilization of

15 See Meier, "Kunstgeschichte und Kulturgeschichte oder Kunstgeschichte nach Aufgaben."

artistic creativity, the formation of patriotism, and the cultivation of "bourgeois virtues," all in the service of the nation and state.[16]

The promotion of the national *Kunstleben* was actively pursued by some of the leading politicians and intellectuals of the day. Men such as Freiherr vom Stein, Wilhelm von Humboldt, Fichte, and even Goethe were enlisted by the state in the aftermath of Germany's liberation from French domination to help shape a national *Kunstleben*. Indeed, perhaps more than at any other time in Germany's past, the state became an active participant in artistic life. As one recent commentator has claimed, the state, acting alongside the market, "provided the institutional matrix for nineteenth-century culture. As patron, educator, and regulator, governments influenced what got built and produced, taught and studied, published and performed."[17] And with few exceptions, this development was regarded as a positive virtue. However, it was ultimately a double-edged sword. Although state munificence opened up new possibilities for artists, they often paid a high price in terms of artistic freedom and integrity: if the state was expected to support the arts, the arts were expected to support the state.

The proliferation of public art projects throughout Germany is testimony to the seriousness with which officials and politicians viewed art as a tool for the political education of the *Volk*.[18] Calls for a more relevant, patriotic art were not just made by bureaucrats, but also by art historians and critics, who saw art as an important expression of national pride and patriotism. Indeed, art historians played an especially significant role as the semi-official choreographers (in conjunction with the artists and bureaucrats) of the national *Kunstleben*, where art theory and practice were supposed to coincide. Besides being involved in various public projects, art historians had to demonstrate the connection between various cultural phenomena and art – for instance, how the spirit of the people manifested itself in all forms of life, whether the state, religion, or art. Seen from this perspective, it was but a small step to becoming advocates

16 Meier, "Kunstgeschichte und Kulturgeschichte," 415–16. The completion of the Cologne cathedral, which was considered an example of the potential of a national *Kunstleben*, was a high priority. See also Großmann, "Verloste Kunst: Deutsche Kunstvereine im 19. Jahrhundert," and Büttner, "Bildung des Volkes durch Geschichte." For similar developments in Great Britain, see Hurtado, "The Promotion of the Visual Arts in Britain."

17 Sheehan, *German History*, 524.

18 See Büttner, "Bildung des Volkes durch Geschichte." See also Burckhardt's comments in his lecture "Über erzählende Malerei," in *Jacob Burckhardt, Vorträge, 1844–1887*, 251.

for the creation of a "patriotic program for the arts" that would promote national spirit and the values of the bourgeoisie, based on the belief that art was a reflection of certain moral, intellectual, and spiritual characteristics of a people. The influential art historian Karl Schnaase was not alone in arguing that art was an expression of the *Volksgeist* and should therefore be actively promoted. Many of the projects Franz Kugler planned as an official in the Prussian ministry of education and culture, such as the organization of a national curriculum for fine-arts education, or the preservation of monuments and heritage buildings of national significance, reflected this underlying belief in the nature of artistic expression and the need for a national program for the arts.

Kugler's desire for a national artistic life in which the state, art, and scholarship were actively allied was therefore consistent with the dominant tendencies and interests of the day, not only in Germany, but elsewhere in Europe. The example of Great Britain, where in 1835 a House of Commons Select Committee on the Arts and Manufacturers was created in order to study the benefits of promoting fine-arts education amongst the middle and working classes, illustrates the contours of the relationship between art and politics and the debate over the public function of art. Members of this committee were motivated by a complex set of factors, and their arguments reveal the extent to which the relationship between art and the public had become a subject of political and patriotic interest. As Shannon H. Hurtado effectively demonstrates, it had also become a significant matter of national economic and social interest.

Education in the visual arts, it was assumed by the House of Commons committee, could serve as a viable and highly public instrument not only in the "humanization" and pacification of the subordinate classes of English society, but also in the continued struggle of the ruling elite to preserve its political and social hegemony. Art's practical appeal as a means of socialization and education was clearly recognized by Sir Robert Peel, who spoke for the political leadership in Great Britain when he articulated the hope that "angry and unsocial feelings might be much softened by the effects which the fine arts have ever produced upon the minds of men." Not only would exposure to the exalted world of art, culture, and ideas enrich the working classes spiritually and intellectually, it would also deaden revolutionary fervour and produce complacency and compliance. In theory, it would also enrich the masses and the nation, economically. At its core, promotion of the arts and instruction of the working classes in the practical principles of design and drawing would create a "middle class of artists" capable of producing superior products, thereby enhancing and "maintaining Britain's supremacy in the manufacturing sector," and developing a new market for the mass consumption of domestic goods.[19]

Nationalism and patriotism also played a substantial role in the minds of the select committee members, who envisioned armies of proud British workers producing manufactured articles with a distinct, superior British style. In order to fulfill its agenda, the committee even solicited the advice of the director of the Royal Gallery in Berlin, the noted art historian Gustav Waagen, who suggested that Britain should encourage more education in the fine arts; initiate a policy of purchasing art for the nation; and engage local artists to decorate and design public buildings, a common practice on the continent. Moreover, drawing on the German example, he suggested emulating, in Britain, the establishment of art associations to popularize art, a practice successful in Germany. All in all, Waagen concluded, and the committee concurred, the process of the "democratization of art," a byword for bringing art to the masses, would be a welcome benefit to the nation and "practical exposure to the arts would have a salutary moral and economic effect upon the British manufacturing population."[20]

In contrast to many of his colleagues, Burckhardt expressed reservations about the value of state involvement and manipulation of the arts. The root of this skepticism can be found in his deep mistrust of the state and its insatiable desire and need for power. Although he recognized that the culture of the Greek *polis* was to a large degree determined by the state, Burckhardt believed this to be a product of unique historical circumstances, inapplicable to modern bureaucratic, centralized state structures. In general, his attitude was that the interests of the state and culture were largely incompatible. He maintained that, in demanding power, the state inevitably had a negative impact on the freedom of individual creativity. When contemplating his own century, he saw that culture, in looking to the state for resources and approbation, had become locked in a power struggle. To Burckhardt, it was clear which side would win and which side would suffer.[21] Although fully cognizant of the fact that historically, cultural development was often determined by religion

19 Hurtado, "The Promotion of the Visual Arts in Britain," 60 and 62.
20 Ibid., 63.
21 WB, 300.

and the state, he believed culture could only be truly autonomous if it evolved without the restrictions imposed by these two powers. In the nineteenth century, however, the politicization and commodification of art meant that its value was determined according to its functionality. Unlike his contemporaries, Burckhardt was therefore highly suspicious of any form of state interference in the world of artistic creativity. While he recognized the need for public support of exhibitions, museums, and institutes of higher education, he did not trust politicians who wanted to direct artistic development; nor did he share Kugler's hopes for a national program for the arts. As Meier aptly remarks, "He did not think highly of the *Kulturstaat*."[22]

This did not mean that Burckhardt was not an active supporter of a national *Kunstleben*. For many years he served as a member of the Commission for the Public Art Gallery in Basel, whose job it was to purchase works of art, promote artists, and stimulate public interest in their work.[23] However, as Burckhardt's choice of pictures for the public art gallery reveals, his primary objective was not the political education of his fellow citizens. Rather, it continued to be their general *Bildung*. He was motivated by the desire to expose the public to the "the entire panorama of art"; to break down prejudices against secular artistic genres, such as landscapes; and to cultivate taste and appreciation. Burckhardt drew the line, then, at the growing demand that art have a more immediate, practical, and increasingly political relevance to society. However much he may have welcomed the redefinition of political authority in the middle classes' favour in Germany and Switzerland as a mediating influence against the forces of absolutism and "screaming radicalism," he was deeply worried about the effects of the bourgeois public on aesthetic values and artistic creativity. The result, Burckhardt feared, would be nothing less than the industrialization and commodification of artistic production. Art, he warned, was becoming tied to the values of the marketplace and was being forced to prove its actuality and justify its existence and purpose in social and economic terms; increasingly, its intrinsic value was being determined by its ability to fulfill the aesthetic preferences of the bourgeois public and to serve its ideological, moral, and pedagogical/didactic requirements. While this may have opened up possibilities for artists – for instance, in new forms of patronage,

22 Meier, "'Aber ist es nicht eine herrliche Sache'?", 46.
23 Meier, *Emilie Linder und Jacob Burckhardt*, 63.

sponsorship, and promotion – it posed a threat to artistic independence and integrity as both the artist and the work of art were more and more regulated by the state and "public" interests. According to critics of *Kulturpolitik*, the spirit of creativity was being sacrificed on the altar of the marketplace, since few artists could afford to offend public taste or interests if they wanted to succeed in the highly competitive art world. Not surprisingly, intense controversy existed within the art world between those who sought the general acceptance of the public (and hence were successful), and the quintessential starving artist who remained true to his or her aesthetic principles by refusing to bow to public pressure (and hence suffered relative obscurity). For Burckhardt, those who pandered to the public inevitably lowered artistic standards; the primary characteristic of contemporary popular art, he felt, was mediocrity.[24] As one artist was heard to complain, paintings, even those of artists from whom one expected only the best, had assumed the character of "fairground goods."[25]

The lowering of artistic standards and the mass production of artworks signified an important transition in artistic purpose. Members of the public now thought that the function of art was to "glorify and 'immortalize' things" simply because these were somehow important to them, whether as events or ideas. Art was supposed to be the "ever ready illustrator of themes which by chance are of objective interest to these people." The danger of such pretensions was not simply that creativity was eroded and artistic independence destroyed; more seriously, the art that was influenced and judged by the values of the market, in response to public demand, risked losing its universality and immortality. Art, then, was reduced to a response to trends, a vulgar presentism, and to symbolic expressions of the power and aspirations of the gallery-visiting, art-purchasing bourgeois. "The logic of this," Burckhardt concluded, was "that works of art become worthless and incomprehensible or even just a curiosity as soon as this objective interest has passed." Yet art, he insisted, only became eternal when it represented universal aesthetic values, when style and form existed in harmony, and when an ideal creation could emerge from a discordant world. It was subverted and trivialized when it became the subject of the "new idol: fashion."[26]

24 See his comments in JHH, 222–3, and in WB, 374–5.

25 According to the Berlin artist Wilhelm Wach in 1837, quoted in Joachim Großmann, "Verloste Kunst," 364.

26 *Aesthetik der bildenden Kunst*, 58 and 59.

The critique of aesthetic preferences of the nineteenth-century public and of *Tendenzmalerei* (trendy painting) forms a central aspect of Burckhardt's lifelong confrontation with modernity. On the one hand, he argued that the aesthetics of the age – which he felt had been reduced to mere trends – strongly reinforced, ideologically, the modern industrial society and the rising power of the middle classes. On the other hand, his confrontation with the state of contemporary art informed his understanding of aesthetics and his conception of the task of art history and gradually emerged as a *critical* voice, designed less to explain the historical evolution of art than to interpret and judge stylistic development. As a consequence, Burckhardt's art criticism provides an important context for his conservatism, his passionate longing for tradition, and his rhetoric of restoration and preservation. As with his cultural history and his general critique of modernity, his approach to the study of art can be seen as partly subversive, as constituting part of a process of demythologization and demystification of the dominant modes of art-historical and historical discourse that prefigured much of nineteenth-century thought, culture, and scholarship.

· · ·

While Burckhardt's assessment of Western culture and his theoretical and methodological approach to the study of art are increasingly well known, his attitude towards the dominant artistic trends of his own day has received less attention, in large part because he did not write extensively about contemporary art. One of his most important contributions to the history of modern art was a series of articles written in 1843, which reviewed a major exhibition of German paintings at the Royal Academy in Berlin.[27] The exhibition sparked considerable debate within the German art community. At stake, it seemed, was the future of German art, which was entering a crucial period of transition, as both artists and the general public began turning their backs on the idealism of the romantic movement, with its fatalism and ambiguity, and embraced the realism that would define the cultural language and the growing social optimism of the European bourgeoisie. Burckhardt's lengthy commentary was an important contribution to the ongoing dis-

---

27 "Bericht über die Kunstausstellung zu Berlin im Herbste 1842."

cussion; it touched upon themes that continued to preoccupy artists
and critics long after the initial debate had died down. Besides being a
valuable contemporary assessment of the state of German art during a
period of profound social and cultural change, his review also provides
insight into his later understanding of art and its purpose in the modern
world. As such, it represents a critical confrontation, not just with contemporary art, but with modernity and modern society.

The most prominent genre on display in Berlin during the autumn of
1842 was history painting. Realist historical art, whether in literature or
the visual arts, was one of the most fashionable forms of art during the
first half of the nineteenth century. The "historicization" of art – the penetration of history or "historical mindedness" into the world of artistic
creativity – was significant not just because it revealed the extent to which
cultural production was governed by a new historical consciousness, but
because it paralleled broader social and cultural transformations. On the
one hand, it reflected the transition from romanticism to historical realism. As artists sought to transform the past and the world of everyday experience into art, they became convinced that art could be made to
resemble the world of appearances; that the concrete events of the past
could be resurrected accurately and objectively; and that a realistic, essentially unmediated form of visual representation was possible. This
faith in realism, whether in history, art, or art history, reflected the prevalent spirit of optimism and progress that dominated the cultural language of Europe during the first half of the nineteenth century. This
faith, although generally speaking shaken by the events of the Revolution
of 1848, revived once again after German Unification, only to fall victim
to the growing cultural malaise that prefigured the eventual eclipse of realism in favour of impressionism towards the end of the century.

On the other hand, realist art corresponded with the rise of the new
bourgeoisie, the professional *Bildungsbürgertum,* to social prominence;
the emergence of an active public sphere in Germany; and, with the development of the notion *Kunstleben,* that synergetic mix of public creativity, patriotism, virtue, and spiritual formation and elevation. It
proved eminently suitable to governments and individuals whose goal it
was to promote nationalism and patriotism and to otherwise engage in
public political discourse. Equally important, however, realist art was
well suited to the tastes and ambitions of the bourgeoisie. Looking to
the world itself for answers – and often accepting what they encountered at face value – middle-class patrons, in an age before photography,
found in realist art the comfort and certainty of a mirrorlike form of
visual representation. Here their unpretentious tastes and values were

often flatteringly reflected, along with the security of a seemingly comprehensible, objective, and finite reality.

Realism, in short, became a central component of cultural discourse, a crucial ideological and formal underpinning for modern society. For the artists, or as Burckhardt might have said, for the business of art, the genre provided them with a unique opportunity to establish themselves as national figures catering to the aspirations and desires of the new art-buying public. Appealing to the concerns of this group and often expressing their own political voice, artists enthusiastically turned to the past for themes and motifs, especially for events of popular national interest. Along the way, they abandoned the more traditional allegorical or religious themes that had been dependent upon centuries-old cultural codes or systems of symbolism and belief, but that were now losing their relevance in the more secular, market-driven society of the nineteenth century. One result was that artists attempted to reflect in their work the progressive tendencies of the day and became involved in the major political, social, and religious controversies. History and historical mindedness – not to mention art – now intertwined with the concept of the nation and nationality became pillars of bourgeois cultural identity and literacy at a time when the middle class was struggling for full participation in political, social, and economic life. As such, historical realism became an important barometer of the tastes and aesthetic preferences of a maturing, and increasingly powerful, bourgeois public sphere.

Testimony to the renown of the history-painting genre was its prominence at numerous exhibitions throughout Germany, including the Berlin exhibition of 1842, which Burckhardt subsequently reviewed for the *Kunstblatt*, the leading journal of art history in Germany. Although the works of some of Germany's most famous artists such as Peter Cornelius, Wilhelm Kaulbach, and Alfred Rethel were conspicuous by their absence, the exhibition was considered by many to be a showcase for the very best of contemporary German art. A wide variety of genres were presented, ranging from sculpture to sketches and paintings. It was the latter, especially the many history paintings, that attracted the attention of the public and critics.[28]

From the outset, Burckhardt's review was intended to be a polemic against the dominant trends of nineteenth-century art. Like many art historians of the Restoration period, Burckhardt, for good or bad, viewed realism in general and history painting in particular as the form

---

28 For an account of the exhibition, see Schlink, *Jacob Burckhardt und die Kunsterwartung im Vormärz.*

of art most representative of the values and aesthetic preferences of the time. His assessment of contemporary German historical art, however, was unflattering in the extreme and, as was undoubtedly anticipated, generated a fair amount of controversy in German art-historical circles.

Burckhardt initially wrote the lengthy commentary with great reluctance, claiming that Franz Kugler had pressured him to do so. According to Burckhardt, Kugler did not write the review himself because he feared he might compromise his relationship with the artistic community and hurt his reputation and credibility. Quite possibly, he also feared he might compromise his position and official duties in the Prussian ministry of culture. In a letter written to Gottfried Kinkel after he had finished the reviews, but before their publication, Burckhardt explained the uncomfortable position in which Kugler had placed him. He would never have dared "to write in such a vein about the whole of contemporary art if Kugler had not coerced me with all his power into taking up the reviews, because he quite correctly wanted to shy away from making enemies of the most renowned artists. But I, as homme sans conséquences whom nobody knows, was safely able to say the truth."[29] However, although he grudgingly wrote the articles "from A to Z with a bad conscience," he felt no compelling need to paint a rosy picture of contemporary German art or to satisfy national sentiment.

The unflattering truth, Burckhardt argued, was that German artists had failed to develop a coherent, unified artistic style representative of the new historically minded age. Having explained that the fault lay not just with the individual artist's lack of "genius" and technical virtuosity, although this was certainly in evidence, he admitted, in a conciliatory gesture, that the artists were not entirely to blame for the lamentable state of German art. The principle cause of the nation's weak artistic development, he reassured his audience, was the lack of a mature, aesthetically sophisticated "public life" and their inspirationless, "fragmented times."

Burckhardt's repeated reference to the fragmented times in which they lived reflected his deep concern about the impact of mass society on artistic creativity. Culture in the modern world, he argued, was characterized by a general leveling of artistic production and expectations as the artist became subject to external pressures and the demands of an increasingly nationalistic, industrial, consumer-driven society in which the profit motive and unsophisticated mass tastes determined

29 *Briefe*, 1:223.

what was produced. As art became commodified, the artist, to no small degree, was victimized, his integrity compromised by the capricious and vague demands of the marketplace. In a similar vein, Burckhardt's more famous contemporaries, Marx and Engels, wrote in *The Communist Manifesto* that "the bourgeoisie has stripped of its halo every occupation hitherto honoured and looked up to with reverent awe. It has converted the physician, the lawyer, the priest, the poet, the man of science, into its paid wage-labourers."[30]

But as Burckhardt tried over the course of his lifetime to restore the poet's halo, he could not escape the conclusion that these alienating forces in a modern, market-driven society were causing a progressive spiritual and cultural crisis in which the unity of human nature and artistic creativity increasingly was placed under siege. In a world of possessive individualism, expressed politically and economically by liberalism and free-market capitalism, the corporate bonds of society were slowly being destroyed, while the subjects were becoming antagonistic towards one another and alienated from their true selves. Ultimately, it was this collapse of meaningful experience, brought about by the rapid social upheaval of the early nineteenth century, which produced such a profound sense of loss and spiritual division. These "fragmented times," Burckhardt concluded, had an enormous impact on art and the artist. They were what "confuse[d] and shift[ed] man's free and correct horizon, which set him on a course that is not appropriate to his inner being and muddle[d] him incessantly with dreadful spiritual and material difficulties."[31]

This crisis became a problem of art in general and history painting in particular, as artists tried to negotiate these fragmented times. The situation of the artist in the aftermath of the French Revolution of 1789 was, indeed, somewhat paradoxical. The Revolution had symbolized, among other things, the liberation of what one recent scholar has called the "binding of stylistic tradition" and had introduced, especially among the individualists of the romantic movement, an unprecedented degree of experimentation and innovation.[32] This new found artistic freedom, however, proved illusory once reactionary governments regained political ascendancy. Faced with a sullied vision of the present, the lack

30 Marx and Engels, *The Communist Manifesto* (Harmondsworth: Penguin Books 1967), 82.

31 "Bericht über die Kunstausstellung zu Berlin," 3 January 1843.

32 Waetzoldt, "Artists and Society," 41.

of a dominant cultural centre in Germany, and confessional division, many artists became disillusioned. They lost faith in the world of historical fact and certainty and turned an opportunistic eye to past masters for inspiration in an otherwise inspirationless age. But they found themselves unable to develop anything original: a notable disharmony prevailed in post-romantic art. As Burckhardt would claim elsewhere, the artist had lost his innocence and modern art its naïveté in the confusion of styles from all ages.[33]

Nowhere was this more evident than in the two most distinguished schools of painting in *Vormärz* Germany, the Düsseldorf Academy and the Nazarenes in Munich, both of which were heavily represented at the Berlin exhibition and therefore subject to most of the critics' attention. The Düsseldorf Academy, which rose to prominence through the organizational talents of its director Wilhelm von Schadow, played a major role in the transition from romanticism to realism.[34] After the Revolution of 1830, the Academy began a slow reorientation away from the overtly religious and symbolic towards more secular themes. Although von Schadow was tolerant and open towards stylistic innovation, and in fact encouraged it, he gradually lost influence over his followers and the school split into two main groups. One centred on von Schadow; the other focused largely on a prominent artist and the Academy's most distinguished student, Carl Friedrich Lessing, one of the first major German artists to embrace the new realism.

As an observant and well-versed art historian, Burckhardt was naturally well aware of the significance of the trend towards more realistic forms of visual representation in historical painting. He especially recognized the influence of history on artistic development and criticism, against which all judgments had to be made. "Our time from Winckelmann onwards is *as important* a juncture of development as the era of the Medici in that *historical* observation of art gained an influence over artists like a stroke of magic," he wrote in a short piece on one of his favourite artists, Bartolomé Esteban Murillo, a few months after the review.[35] He was consequently more than willing to give the German artists their due, if not because of the success of the particular

33 *Briefe*, 1:201; see also WB, 182.

34 Mai, "Die Düsseldorfer Malerschule und die Malerei des 19. Jahrhunderts."

35 Burckhardt, "Über Murillo," in *Die Kunst der Betrachtung: Aufsätze und Vorträge zur bildenden Kunst*, 120.

representations, then at least because of the role they played in this important transition.

Unfortunately, German artists had not yet proven themselves equal to the new challenge of historical realism. From his vantage point as a critic of contemporary aesthetic values, Burckhardt could see that Germany's most prominent artists had not changed with the times. They refused to acknowledge not only the significant transformation of the social and political context in which Romanticism had flourished, but also that their work did not reflect the values of modern society nor the preferences of the public. Instead, having failed to develop and define new artistic objectives commensurate with the changing public attitudes towards art, they remained mired in what was fast becoming an archaic and anachronistic styles. As a consequence, German art did not – indeed, could not – live up to the high expectations of the critics, whose task it was to guide and cultivate aesthetic preference and taste; or of the public, whose approval was required for artistic success.

This seemed especially clear when the German works of art were compared to two prominent Belgian paintings on display in Berlin: *The Abdication of Emperor Charles V*, by Louis Gallait; and *The Compromise of the Dutch Nobility in 1566*, by Edouard de Biefve. Although largely forgotten today, these works caused quite a sensation in Germany, sparking a debate in the pages of Germany's art journals between the proponents of the Romanicism-inspired idealist painting and those of the newer, realistic history painting.[36] Completed in 1841, just over ten years after the establishment of Belgian national independence, the two works were thought to be the most successful examples to date of the new type of history painting, foreshadowing the positive reception a few years later of Emanuel Leutze's *Washington Crossing the Delaware* (1850).

Burckhardt and other German commentators were suitably impressed by the two Belgian works, believing that both Gallait and de Biefve had managed to capture moments of great national and historical significance, thereby reflecting the pride and self-confidence of the new nation and fulfilling the criteria of successful history paintings. According to one critic, the Belgians had presented a true historical

36 They were a sensation if only because of their monumental size. The *Abdication* is 485 x 683 cm; the *Compromise*, 482 x 680 cm. Both are in the Musées Royaux des Beaux-arts, Brusells. See Jenderko-Sichelschmidt, "Die profane Historienmalerei, 1826–1860," 104.

style in which "great moments of high national interest integrated an unending quantity of important individualities into a whole."[37] Beside these works, Carl Friedrich Lessing's much celebrated painting, *Hus before the Council of Constance*, diminished in stature, not just because the Belgian paintings were colossal in size, but because Lessing's figures were stiff and the picture lacked "dramatic, historical breath." This was a problem, said Burckhardt, that characterized most of the German art on display. Stuck in the worn-out, over-emotional symbolism of the romantics, the German artists were unable to grasp the historical. They thought "more about the psychological and symbolic problem than about the dramatic act," Burckhardt complained, noting their preference for presenting "the spiritual concerns of the individual figures among themselves rather than participating in a dramatic moment, and as a consequence German historical painting deals essentially with situations."[38] This criticism was echoed by other commentators. As well, the art critic Friedrich Theodor Vischer regretted the "lack of substance" in contemporary German art, complaining about its eclectic attitude and general rootlessness and its lack of sufficient "dramatic fire."[39] Although Lessing's *Hus* was cited as one of the best German artworks because of the accuracy of its individual portraits, Burckhardt retorted that the viewer was further distracted from appreciating the whole because of the removal of the main focus from Hus, the central figure. As a result, Burckhardt felt that the "presented moment is the subordinated one and recedes completely behind the powerful characterization."[40]

Such criticism pointed to a real dilemma for artists. How exactly was one to compose a true history painting? What made history paintings historical? It was clearly not enough merely to call a painting historical for it to be so, even though German artists were apparently doing precisely that. Neither was attention to the faithful reconstruction of detail sufficient. "Many artists believe," Burckhardt declared, that "they can create historical paintings through costume, accurate portraits and individuality."[41] As an example, he referred to the painting of Sir Kenneth at the Dead Sea where, although the portrayal and lighting were excel-

37 Ibid.

38 "Bericht über die Kunstausstellung zu Berlin," 3 January 1843.

39 Quoted in Pochat, "Friedrich Theodor Vischer und die zeitgenössische Kunst," 106. On Burckhardt and Vischer, see Sitt, *Kriterien der Kunstkritik*, 83–107.

40 "Bericht über die Kunstausstellung zu Berlin," 10 January 1843.

41 Ibid., 5 January 1843.

lent, a catalogue was needed to distinguish the identity of the knight from that of other crusaders in the desert. To Burckhardt, it seemed that many artists spent more time researching than painting their subjects in order to perfect a form of visual representation accurate in both detail and historical likeness. For Burckhardt, such research, alone, did not distinguish these works from portraits, views, or even the genres of peasant and urban life. He concluded that "only the moment can make a composition historical."[42]

But what is the moment and how is it to be captured? Burckhardt defined the historical moment as the exclusive concentration on a single dramatic event, which then governs the composition of both characters and action. As Wilhelm Schlink has pointed out, the historical "moment" in this context was the articulation in art of the historicist principle of the "visualization of individuality." Schlink was also certainly correct in detecting in Burckhardt's interpretation the strong influence of his teacher, the Berlin historian Leopold von Ranke, who believed that the goal of history was to capture the individuality and uniqueness of an historical epoch.[43] In successful history paintings, then, the dramatic moment revealed and explained the particular events or actions, providing the viewer with a (visual) narrative structure. In other words, "true" history paintings were distinguished from mere "situations" because of their visual metaphors that enabled the creation of a coherent representation of the historical moment. The function of metaphor, as explained by Hayden White, is applicable in this context. Clearly, it was impossible for the artist [or the historian] to "let the facts speak for themselves." Rather, the "historian [or artist] speaks for them, speaks on their behalf, and fashions the fragments of the past into a whole whose integrity is – in its *re*presentation – a purely discursive one."[44] Burckhardt reproached the lack of "the moment" in German history painting not for the lack of a "historical" moment per se, for even a "situation," he said, could portray historical themes and motifs. What was ultimately missing was the "metaphoric" moment. It is precisely metaphor which gives reality the meaning that it does not "naturally" possess – in effect, serving as a signpost that points the way, that tells us how and why the painting should be experienced as a history painting. "The

42 Ibid.

43 Schlink, *Jacob Burckhardt und die Kunsterwartung des Vormärz*, 22–4. On the historicist principle of "individuality" or historical uniqueness, see Iggers, *The German Conception of History*, 4–5.

44 White, *Tropics of Discourse*, 125.

metaphor does not *image* the thing it seeks to characterize," White writes; "*it gives directions* for finding the set of images that are intended to be associated with that thing. It functions as a symbol, rather than a sign: which is to say that it does not give us either a *description* or an *icon* of the thing it represents, but *tells us* what images to look for in our culturally encoded experience in order to determine how we should feel about the thing represented."[45] Without a narrative or metaphoric structure – the set of directional signposts within the visual text that transmits the dramatic or historical moment to the viewer – the history paintings could not be distinguished from ordinary genre paintings. Accordingly, Burckhardt concluded that Lessing's *Hus* remained a "mere picture of a situation."

According to Burckhardt, the history paintings at the exhibition in Berlin were flawed because their representations and styles did not adequately express the symbols of their intended meanings. Instead, he declared, they reflected a critical ambiguity in visual representation because their style had no authority within the cultural language of the day. In many respects, this lack was due to problems of what we may call "cognitive style." Cognitive style refers to those tangible factors, such as artistic skill and technique, that constitute the artists' mental equipment and enable them to translate their visualizations into recognizable form. On the one hand, it is learned experience, whether in academies or workshops, and therefore takes into account the material and economic conditions of production; on the other, it is an innate experience, a reflection and unconscious absorption of prevailing attitudes and assumptions, such as taste, that dominate at any given time.

Burckhardt's criticism in the *Kunstblatt* focused on two central aspects of cognitive style: colour and perspective. To him, a fundamental weakness of the German artists, and one with important consequences, was their strangely defective use of colour, especially since colour was a major means of establishing perspective and artistic narrative. In Leonardo's system of perspective, colour occupied a subordinate position in relation, for instance, to figuration. Since Leonardo, however, colour had assumed a more sophisticated, dominant role within the system of representation, serving as a means of defining and modifying the visual experience through factors such as lighting, shading, and colour intensity. Colour, therefore, had become an indispensable stylistic element in the structure of the artwork. While Burckhardt did not hesi-

45 Ibid., 91.

tate to praise the use of colour – for example, its beauty and clarity – in specific instances, he was very critical when an obvious lack of harmony in colour distorted the perspective of a particular painting. At more than one point in his review, he observed his contemporaries' inability to master this basic technique. He complained that among even the most renowned artists, perspective was deficient and figures appeared to be "layered on one another without the proper distance, as if they were sitting flatly on a cut-out board."[46] His positive assessment of the seventeenth-century Spanish artist Bartolomé Esteban Murillo, one of the most admired and popular European artists in the nineteenth century, turned precisely on this point. Murillo's use of colour, which, according to Burckhardt, "often achieved the fire of a transparency" and was essential in establishing the proper perspective, placed him in the company of Rembrandt and Correggio. In contrast, Burckhardt saw the Düsseldorf School as being unable to master the effective use of colour – they were "so hard with colour" – and therefore unable to comprehend or bear witness to the sheer "poetry" of such compositions. As a consequence, he concluded, even the most promising of paintings at the Berlin exhibition demonstrated a "great arduousness in drawing, composition and colouring."[47]

While Burckhardt was aware of the complex technical skills involved in establishing perspective, he viewed it as much more than an instrumental or scientific phenomenon. Seen as a symbolic or metaphorical structure – as a strategy of visual and textual representation – the lack of perspective in some of the German paintings exhibited in Berlin takes on new significance: among other things, it indicates the artists' inability to express order and coherence in a subjective world and their failure to provide that world (or reality) with meaning it does not naturally possess. In other words, perspective also provides a metaphoric or narrative structure for the visual representation or text, thereby serving as the very basis of the logic of representation. In addition, perspective demands the active participation of the viewer and artist if it is to achieve its desired effect. Everything in the world of art (and history), avowed Burckhardt, was dependent upon this relationship. That he saw himself primarily in this light – as a subjective observer – cannot be overemphasized. Like an artist who was forever the outsider looking in and desiring to recreate a

46 "Bericht über die Kunstausstellung zu Berlin," 3 January 1843.
47 "Über Murillo," 110; and "Bericht über die Kunstausstellung zu Berlin," 3 January 1843.

world he could not inhabit, Burckhardt was always conscious of viewing past reality from an unbridgeable distance. His intention in his historical writing was similar to that of the artist: it was not to recreate reality, per se; rather it was to place the viewer opposite reality. As F.R. Ankersmit has written, "We can only have a concept of reality if we stand in relation to it and that requires that we are ourselves outside it. There is only reality insofar as we are standing opposite it."[48]

. . .

Although Burckhardt felt that the future of German art was bright, his optimism was overshadowed by his concern for the present state of German art. He could hardly hide his frustration and dismay at the "poverty of ideas" of most of the paintings he was forced to look at and write about. They were "weak," he complained, overly theatrical, and full of "shallow pretension"; their style was certainly not to be emulated. Totally unimpressed by German history painting, he declared at one point that "the best thing really would be to put down the palettes" altogether.[49]

While this criticism was harsh, it was his positive evaluation of the two Belgian works which sparked the most controversy. "Clearly when we consider history painting," Burckhardt summarized, "we have to admit that the French and the Belgians have rushed ahead of us in important ways. Not one single German painting in this exhibition breathes a true historical style."[50] As representations of the triumph of a new form of history painting, he continued, these paintings signal the eclipse of the two most prominent artistic schools in Germany: the Düsseldorf Academy and the Nazarenes. As a consequence, the ensuing controversy ceased to revolve around style; the issue had now become a question of national pride.

Given Burckhardt's enthusiasm for Germany at this time, it is highly doubtful that his intention was to malign German dignity. Indeed, he probably hoped that by pointing out the weaknesses of German art, he

48 Ankersmit, "Historical Representation," 219.
49 "Bericht über die Kunstausstellung zu Berlin," 12 January 1843 and 3 January 1843.
50 Ibid., 10 January 1843.

might encourage German artists to develop a style that would proudly serve the nation. Some of his readers, however, did not see his review in this light. Instead, it raised the ire of certain of the more traditionalist critics and patriotic elements of the *Kunstvereinspublikum*. For instance, Ernst Förster, the conservative co-editor of the *Kunstblatt* from Munich, quickly rose to the defence of German art. Highly sceptical about the value of historical realism in art, Förster criticized Gallait's life-like depiction of an old and ill Emperor Charles V. Identifying the lofty symbolism of the Nazarenes' idealist paintings as the true expression of the German spirit, in contrast to the crass, realistic history paintings, he said the symbolism represented the very "soul of German art and had led it to the heights of perfection." He also pointed out that contemporary German painting was universally respected and well received, especially in English and French circles, as the most successful and admired of all the "national artistic undertakings."[51]

Förster, however, fought a losing battle against public and scholarly opinion. Neither German school was as admired as he would have us believe. While the work of the Düsseldorfer Academy had potential, that of the Nazarenes in Munich, centred around Peter Cornelius and Johann Friedrich Overbeck, had an especially poor reputation. Burckhardt's criticism, then, appears to have mirrored, rather than offended, public expectations and opinion. Posterity has judged Nazarenes harshly as an artistic school, just as, in their own day, they were criticized as mediocre and somewhat anachronistic. In the words of one recent commentator, the Nazarenes "ended as one of the most sterile groups in the history of painting anywhere."[52] Representing the Catholic stream of German romanticism – the "romantic-religious stream," as Burckhardt politely wrote[53] – the Nazarenes appeared to many to be suffering from the ill effects of a type of stylistic schizophrenia. They attempted to express their Catholicism and renewed Christianity through the emulation of medieval and early Renaissance forms which, according to one

51 Ernst Förster, "Englische und französische Stimmen über deutsche Kunst," *Kunstblatt*, 2 February 1843.

52 Canaday, *Mainstreams of Modern Art*, 35.

53 Burckhardt did not think highly of Overbeck. In a written commentary that accompanied the 1841 exhibition of his painting *Triumph der Religion in der Kunst* in Frankfurt, Overbeck represented the Renaissance as the "misfortune of art history" and the deterioration and corruption of medieval traditions. Burckhardt responded angrily in "Über Murillo," 120.

contemporary critic, neither suited their material nor filled it with the necessary fervour.[54] Furthermore, while they may have experimented stylistically, their work never developed an original style and always reflected the overall contradictory, fragmented nature of early nineteenth-century German art.

Burckhardt's criticism of the Nazarenes was the result of a complex set of factors, which should be understood both within the context of the notion of *Kunstleben,* and his personal biography. On the one hand, his attack on the painter Overbeck and the Nazarene school should be seen as an extension of his earlier renunciation of Christianity and the religious piety of Basel's elite. Indeed Burckhardt's condemnation of Overbeck for his "artistic piety" was a reflection of this renunciation. But his attack takes on an even greater resonance when we learn that, despite its increasing unpopularity among the progressive, liberal middle classes, the religious art of the Nazarenes was well received in Basel's highly influential pietist circles, due in no small part to the activities of one of the public gallery's most important patrons, Emilie Linder, who incidently also enjoyed a close friendship with Overbeck. Throughout the 1840s and 1850s, Nazarene-inspired art was in vogue. Considered an important vehicle for the expression of religious experience, it was actively endorsed by the city's most prominent theologians, including Burckhardt's father, the Antistes of the cathedral, and two of his former instructors, de Wette and Karl Rudolf Hagenbach. The work of the Nazarenes clearly touched a chord among many Baslers, and a lasting monument was created when, between 1858 and 1862, the cathedral windows were decorated in the Nazarene style.[55]

When Burckhardt returned to Basel to begin his teaching career at the university as a lecturer in art history, his apostasy as well as his hostility towards the pietist art of the Munich school were generally known. During the winter of 1844–45, he began a series of public lectures on the history of painting, which were well attended despite the threat of a boycott by some of the city's leading pietists. The young man, however, scorned his opponents – "The pietists are indirectly trying to hinder me: they would have liked a more devout person than a man of the world like me"[56] – and, in his first lecture, took direct aim at the tastes of the

54 As Friedrich Theodor Vischer wrote. See Pochat, "Friedrich Theodor Vischer und die zeitgenössische Kunst," 107.

55 See especially Meier, *Emilie Linder und Jacob Burckhardt,* and Meier, "Die Basler Münsterscheiben."

56 *Briefe,* 2:183. See also Meier, *Emilie Linder und Jacob Burckhardt,* 55.

pietists, stressing that one should not just admire art that only expressed religious themes. He contended that the Nazarenes had done a great disservice to the artistic community, and, in the meantime, was forced to defend secular, non-religious art, even that of Hans Holbein the Younger, one of Basel's most famous artists, from the increasing and misguided attacks of the pietist community.

The Nazarenes' attempt to renew Christian life through art and to revitalize Christianity through religious motifs and mythical and symbolic historical paintings certainly ran counter to both Burckhardt's secularism and the secular spirit of the age. Burckhardt felt that their religious art alienated much of the general public: no longer did it speak to the public's needs or reflect society's changed attitudes. From the strictly art-historical point of view, Burckhardt, like other critics, recognized realism, not the mystical idealism of the Nazarenes, as the artistic style of the day. The values and outlook of early nineteenth-century German bourgeois society had shifted; traditional religious symbolism and piety struck a dissonant chord with an increasingly secularized, liberal public that had more pressing and mundane, if not uplifting, concerns. In short, despite pockets of pietism scattered throughout Europe, the Nazarenes seemed by and large completely oblivious to society's increasing modernization. Ironically, the artists, although part of a generation that had matured during the Wars of Liberation and sought to articulate demands for liberty, political participation, and social justice, completely misread or ignored the needs and desires of the increasingly powerful and secularized bourgeoisie during the Restoration period.

The art critic Friedrich Theodor Vischer perceived the task of the artist and the desire of the public with equal acumen when he wrote that the kind of religious art produced by the Nazarenes was outdated and that they must now rise to a new challenge, that of "secular historical" painting.[57] The modern artist must "give the *Volk* what it lacks, but vaguely feels: historical material in which appearance, action and meaning are one, in which the general is expressed in the specific, and where nature and history, the real present and the ideal, are fused together."[58] The Nazarenes' overwhelming reliance upon religious-patriotic symbolism could not compensate for the lack of "dramatical-historical" content, and, as Burckhardt was quick to argue, could not transform their work into legitimate history paintings. Although Burckhardt assessed the work

57 See Paret, *Art as History*, 20.
58 Quoted in Pochat, "Friedrich Theodor Vischer," 105.

of the Nazarene Julius Schnorr as among the best the exhibition had to offer, this was hardly a ringing endorsement of the artist and his work since, in the end, Burckhardt felt that none of the paintings of the Munich school represented a true historical style. "If we view the majority of the history paintings, we realize above all else that many paintings are categorized in the catalogue as historical but ... an impartial glance will reveal [them] as genre paintings."[59] German art had consequently failed to change with the times, he avowed; nor had it met the challenge and criteria of realist history painting. Still worse, it was not even what it claimed to be.

. . .

Burckhardt's criticism of the Nazarenes' religious work and his praise of the Belgian history paintings should not necessarily be misconstrued as a ringing endorsement of realist art in general, or of history painting in particular. Although he knew that realism and "life-like" forms of visual representation had become the most popular style of the day – a recognition of the changing function of art in society – Burckhardt had misgivings about the overall quality of nineteenth-century art. Over time he would express growing dissatisfaction with contemporary historical painting.

History painting was by no means a new genre. Renaissance Venice had developed into an important centre of such painting and, over the next centuries, it had risen to occupy pride of place alongside genre, portrait, and landscape painting. The first half of the nineteenth century saw a renewed interest in history painting – a reflection of the "historical mindedness" of the age – and the genre achieved an unprecedented level of popularity. The distinguishing feature of history painting – in contrast to other genres such as portraits or views, and even the genres of peasant and urban life, all of which also strove to reproduce the reality effect – was its story line, its narrative structure. In Burckhardt's words, through its attempt to capture the "historical moment" and to show "what had happened" (*das Geschehene*), history painting had become in fact "narrative" painting. History paintings, then, contained a narrative structure based on visual metaphors that were designed to create a coherent representation, or story, of significant past events.[60]

59 "Bericht über die Kunstausstellung zu Berlin," 5 January 1843.
60 See especially, "Über erzählende Malerei," in *Jacob Burckhardt, Vorträge*.

History painting was considered by many individuals to be the quintessential modern genre, the "most important task of art." Nineteenth-century history painting, which Burckhardt later prefered to call *erzählende Malerei* or "narrative painting," differed fundamentally from traditional history paintings in both thematic content and artistic task. Formerly, the genre had focused on the "glorification of dynasties and corporations ... with the conversion of power into allegory and mythology." Now, in a reflection of the tastes of the bourgeoisie and the spirit of the age, it told stories of the "moments from the histories of peoples and nations," events that celebrated the "fame of the particular *Volk.*" In rejecting the allegorical and the mythical, historical realism now focused primarily on facticity or actuality, a concern that captured the bourgeoisie's faith in progress and science; its general optimism and self-confidence in its broader social, economic, and political agenda; as well as its strong sense of historical mindedness and its concern for the present.[61] Historical realism was also considered to be objectively constructed and scientifically based. Artists, for example, often spent more time researching their subject matter than painting it, and they strove for a form of visual representation that was accurate in historical likeness and detail. As a result, history painting, in its detailed, "scientific," and technical virtuosity was unambiguous; it provided "instant gratification," conveying little that was abstract and, consequently, requiring minimum interpretation.

Burckhardt's enthusiastic reception of the Belgian history paintings is evidence that as a young man he regarded the genre in a positive light. Over time, however, his attitude towards history painting changed. The desire to produce a "reality effect" in art posed basic aesthetic problems for Burckhardt; indeed, history painting offended his sense of artistic purpose and his own aesthetic preferences. In catering to the "philistinism" of the new bourgeoisie, realist art, especially history painting, showed complete disregard for classical convention. One of the acknowledged aims of early nineteenth-century realist art had been to break down the barriers of neo-classicism, with its emphasis on the nobility of art and the idealized subject. True to his fundamentally conservative beliefs, Burckhardt was suspicious of this break with tradition; his conception of aesthetics reflected a desire for visual order and harmony, signifying both the continuity of artistic values and an optimistic faith in utopian perfection. He did not, however, reject realism out of hand. In fact, he admired the great Dutch genre paintings. But he admired them

61 Ibid., 250ff.

not for their attempt to create a "reality effect," but because he believed that they had managed successfully to combine convincing realism with the idealistic impulse of the artistic creation. They achieved what Burckhardt called a "blending" of idealism and realism into a unique, inspirational, and harmonious whole. Without this combination, it would not be possible, he said, to distinguish a work of art from "mere photography."[62] According to Burckhardt's classical conception of art, the value of an individual work lay in its harmonious balance between idealism and realism, its inner order and cohesion, and its search for universal truth and beauty. As one historian has noted, Burckhardt believed that great art "must represent a composite of values; no single value or concern may dominate; none is sufficient in isolation. The superior artist achieved a balance of 'values of equal weight', what Burckhardt called 'Äquivalente', or equivalents."[63]

For Burckhardt, the purpose of art was consequently not just to recreate or mimic life. Rather art, as the "second ideal creation," possessed utopian powers – both for the audience, whose imagination had to be engaged in order to realize the nature of the reconstruction, and for the artist, who strove to express what was possible. In her examination of Burckhardt's theoretical approach to the study of art, Martina Sitt refers to the continuous tension between what is and what ought to be (*Sein und Sollen*), which, for Burckhardt, represented the dynamic elements of artistic activity.[64] What was missing in modern art, with its overvaluation of realism and its goal of near-photographic representation, was precisely this tension (or harmony) between *Sein* and *Sollen*. Burckhardt placed special emphasis on this quality in his assessment of the work of the Flemish master Rubens, an artist he greatly admired. "One finds that the object of Rubens' art," he wrote in his *Recollection of Rubens*, "was the strong unity of the ideal and of a recognized part of the real world … Biblical, visionary, legendary, mythological, allegorical, pastoral, historical and even some daily life, figures as well as scenes, create a whole, and a more powerful naturalism, inspired by his own fullness of life, dares now to hold everything at the right temperature."[65] Burckhardt also stressed the critical importance of this unity in an 1877 lecture on Rembrandt, although he found it lacking, he said,

---

62 *Aesthetik der bildenden Kunst*, 171.
63 Weintraub, *Visions of Culture*, 131.
64 Sitt, *Kriterien der Kunstkritik*, 26.
65 GA, 13:394. See also "Über erzählende Kunst," in *Jacob Burckhardt, Vorträge*.

in the work of the Dutch master, ultimately judging that Rembrandt was guilty of excessive realism. Burckhardt argued that Rembrandt was so concerned with exploring his own subjectivity and the problems of artistic composition, such as light, that the subject of his art became secondary. His dedication to accuracy and detail and his desire to portray the base and the vulgar did not honour the subject: he "only searched for the ugly and barbaric in the moment and then represented it in uncouth personalities and in childishly unskillful groupings" that compromised Burckhardt's aesthetic sense and the integrity of art.[66] In stark contrast, Burckhardt felt that Rubens had succeeded not only in capturing the voluptuousness of the human form without debasing the body, but in portraying the "glorification of human beings in all their driving force and power." His work continued to astonish, said Burckhardt, because, unlike Rembrandt, Rubens presented "the fire and truth of physical and intellectual movement."[67] In other words, art existed not just to show what was (*Sein*), but also to show the ideal and the utopian, or how things should be (*Sollen*).

According to Burckhardt, the harmony of realism and idealism was the defining characteristic of the art and life of Renaissance Italy, and, to his eyes, Rubens, not Rembrandt, was heir to this tradition. The art of Florence in the late fifteenth and early sixteenth centuries, Burckhardt maintained, was characterized by the amalgamation of the "naive" idealism of the Middle Ages with the incipient realism of the era of the Medicis. He elaborated upon this theme in an essay written in 1847 while travelling in Italy, "Suggestions about the History of Christian Sculpture," which he published the following year in the *Kunstblatt*.[68] In many ways, this article was a transitional work in the development of Burckhardt's thought. Here were planted the seeds that would later germinate in his mature work on the Italian Renaissance, themes such as the development of the individual, the rise of the modern world, and the tension between idealism and realism in art.

His principal concern in this short piece was why painting had come to occupy such a prominent position in Renaissance art and how the stylistic features of painting then proceeded to transform sculpture. Moving beyond the purely artistic factors, Burckhardt examined how

---

66 "Rembrandt," in *Jacob Burckhardt, Vorträge*, 145. See also Meier, "Kunstgeschichte und Kulturgeschichte," 435ff.

67 GA, 13:391.

68 "Andeutungen zur Geschichte der christlichen Skulptur," published in the *Kunstblatt* in 1848 and reprinted in *Die Kunst der Betrachtung*, 145–62.

the functions and ideas behind specific artistic forms and genres changed and developed over time. Central to his argument was the changed outlook or "spirit of the fifteenth century," the spirit of the Renaissance, which was characterized in part by the "personal virtuosity" expressed in humanism and in a new form of realistic representation. This concern with the objective details of the world at large, in combination with an idealistic vision of humankind's spirit and potential, gave rise, he said, to the modern individual. In contrast, medieval Christian sculpture remained cloaked in the mystical veil of religious idealism. Such sculpture could not become independent or individualistic because its function was reduced to that of decoration within the context of Gothic architecture. In addition, the figurations of medieval sculpture were not based on historical forms or individuals, and artists were not concerned with accurate representations; instead, the figures and forms were idealized and symbolic and thus not expressive of personality or individuality. Only with the changed spirit, the melting of the veil, declared Burckhardt, could sculptors conceive of a need to transfer the techniques of painting and realism to their sculptures and break with the idealism of the Middle Ages. The result was the achievement of a visual harmony unique in the history of Western art.

This harmony constituted a criterion of fundamental importance for Burckhardt's judgment of aesthetic value. The balance between idealism and realism endowed an individual work of art with transcendental status and universal, eternal appeal. Burckhardt felt that much of contemporary art, especially history painting, was unable to achieve the harmony that he felt characterized the best of Renaissance art. Caught between a romantic indulgence in the medieval that was both gratuitous and anachronistic, and the incipient power of realism, contemporary German art demonstrated disharmony and lack of vision, attributed by Burckhardt to the dominant idealism. But the opposite could be true as well, he stated, if excessive realism were to reign at the expense of idealism. While Burckhardt appreciated the importance of realist art, those artists he admired, such as the Dutch genre painters, were, he felt, able to achieve "the truly (magical), compelling visualization of a situation," without sacrificing idealism.[69] However, any imbalance, such as an overriding concern with rationality in realist art, threatened the harmony of the work of art, which ultimately depended upon both the imagination and the senses. To Burckhardt's way of thinking, realism ceased to complement idealism; it now sought to replace it altogether. The mania for

69 *Aesthetik der bildenden Kunst*, 171.

details and the adamant desire to represent events and individuals as accurately as possible signified the rejection of the principles of idealism and, consequently, destroyed the possibility of artistic unity. Burckhardt contrasted this excessive desire for accuracy with earlier history paintings in which characters were presented in a very "free, conventional ideal costume, or in the wonderful costumes of their own time." Excessive detail and facticity in costumes tended to shift the focus away from the specific historical situation, and the observer became lost in a sea of detail.[70]

Contemporary history painting contradicted not only Burckhardt's particular understanding of the nature of art and aesthetics; it also contradicted his understanding of history. In his mature work, Burckhardt claimed that his goal in writing history was to capture the "recurrent, constant and typical" of any given age.[71] Unlike other genres, he argued in his lecture on aesthetics, the ultimate goal of history painting, instead of "the typical, sacred, elementary, and recurrent," was to represent "(realistically) that which has occurred once."[72] As he had pointed out in the *Kunstblatt* review, to be successful history painting had to capture the "moment." Now, having distanced himself theoretically from Ranke, Burckhardt no longer viewed the "visualization of individuality" as the objective of historical study. Because history painting concentrated on specific events or subjects of a particular time – for example, a painting of a battle – and was also overtly ideological, it could not assume any value of universal significance. It loses its "ecumenical or world character and becomes unintelligible and spiteful to large countries, confessions or parties," declared Burckhardt. Nor could such work possibly eternalize the particular, because its message was directed at specific groups and attitudes. While a painting may capture the moment and experience immediate public success, according to Burckhardt it soon lost its appeal and any socio-historical significance as understanding and ideas about the events changed. Indeed, perhaps this explains why much of nineteenth-century history painting remains obscure today. The genre, Burckhardt concluded many years after the Berlin exhibition, reflected "the general need for temporary stimulation, which reduces the half-educated people (the distinctivum of our century) to the lives of philistines."[73]

---

70 Ibid., 161 and "Über erzählende Malerei," in *Jacob Burckhardt, Vorträge,* 253.
71 WB, 227.
72 *Aesthetik der bildenden Kunst,* 158.
73 Ibid., 162–4.

While traditional history painting concentrated on particular events and personalities, it nonetheless incorporated a wide thematic range, taking as subjects Bible stories, mythology, allegories, and other themes of noble, universal content. The paintings' didactic intent was often explicit and their symbolic meaning clearly understood by the audience, which consisted more often than not of private patrons, rather than the general public. In Burckhardt's own century, however, the choice of subject matter was more restricted, even though the audience was markedly different, and artists had to satisfy a broader range of public opinion. Rather than representing universal allegories, the equivalent of the epic or tragedy in literature, artists sought to capture the attention of their audience by appealing to its tastes and by representing themes with which it could identify. As a result, history painting tended to focus on political events of national interest. The two prominent Belgian works offered the educated public moments of national historical pride designed to uplift the spirit. But they were also interpretations of the past and, as such, contained somewhat deeper ideological and political motivations, consequently becoming lessons in *Realpolitik* and losing their universal authority in the process. The advocates of realism in Germany, for example Lessing and the Düsseldorf Academy, who did not hesitate to promote secular art as a more suitable and legitimate vehicle for political and social commentary, consistently incorporated contemporary social, political, and religious themes into their work. Whether commenting on social inequities brought about by industrialization, religious intolerance, or the lack of a constitution and the need for a strong, unified national state, the artists found a sympathetic audience in the middle-class public.[74]

. . .

As we have seen, in the *Kunstblatt* review Burckhardt blamed the lamentable state of German painting in part on external factors, specifically the "fragmented times" and the lack of a public life in Germany. "It is not enough to have a history," he wrote, "in order to create historical art. One must be able to live history and to participate in public life."[75]

74 See for example, Gagel, "Die Düsseldorfer Malerschule in der politischen Situation des Vormärz und 1848."
75 "Bericht über die Kunstausstellung zu Berlin," 12 January 1843.

Given the weak social and political position of the middle classes in *Vormärz* Germany, the climate of sustained political action, and the demand for participation in civic life, this claim certainly had resonance. Nevertheless, in his review, Burckhardt did not elaborate on this important commentary on German society. Surprisingly, though, Franz Kugler did in his rebuttal of Ernst Förster's attack on Burckhardt. Kugler's arguments, in fact, went much further than his student's to include a claim for the "democratization of art." While Kugler acknowledged that German art had earned the respect of other nations, he did not see this as an excuse to stand still; rather, he urged artists to take the initiative as well as risks, because even the most "powerful and active talents will not be able to achieve anything successful following the path of the old."[76] Indeed, Kugler took Burckhardt's statement to the extreme but logical conclusion when he brashly proclaimed that art should not "remain a stranger to life. On the contrary, it must permeate life in its full, fresh immediacy ... In addition to its aristocratic element, without which our art would certainly immediately fall from its heights, there must also be a democratic element added as a necessary counterweight." Later Kugler would emphatically write, "Yes, a democratic element in the full, bold meaning of the word."[77]

What are we to make of these provocative statements, which, according to Peter Paret, echoed "through German cultural history for the next three generations?"[78] Kugler was not pleading for a socially conscious art that would represent a democratic vision of and for the people, although in France in the 1830s the call for an art *social et progressif* was being heard more and more. That new artistic vision would attempt to capture images of the conditions of the economically distressed and exploited population, while reflecting, and passing judgment on, the social and economic transformations of the day.[79] However, history painting, unlike this form of genre painting, was not what Burckhardt considered a thematically "free" genre. As others besides Burckhardt have pointed out, the best history painting consisted of elevated (aristocratic) themes that lifted the public spirit from the ordinariness of everyday life. This could not be achieved by concentrating on the mundane. History painting was therefore limited to noble, edifying themes. Thus, while the French Revolution may have widened the

76 Kugler, "Sendschreiben an Herrn Dr. Ernst Förster", *Kunstblatt*, 20 July 1843.
77 Ibid.
78 Paret, *Art as History*, 24.
79 Grew, "Picturing the People," 205.

genre's thematic range, it is unlikely that Kugler or Burckhardt would have found pictures of revolutionary masses particularly edifying. In fact, neither man was a democrat and neither necessarily wanted to look at paintings of peasants in the fields or artisans in their shops, never mind revolutionaries manning the barricades.[80]

Paret suggests that Kugler's call for more democracy in art was "a plea for greater realism in German art, for an art that renounced the idealized treatment of ceremonial and official consecrations of power, in favour of a more intense reflection of everyday life in the past as well as in the present. Such an art, to be sure, would also give new value to these commonplace and often undemocratic, even anti-aristocratic, forces in German life."[81] This seems to infer a much more democratic, reform-minded, and politically progressive stance on Kugler's part than was really the case. He was, after all, a prominent Prussian bureaucrat. Kugler certainly meant that more realism was required in terms of accuracy of historical detail, costuming, and narrative structure – that is to say, realism as a more lifelike form of visual representation – in order to provide a necessary balance to the excessive idealism of much of German artwork. Unlike his colleague Förster, Kugler believed that German art was in a state of crisis. The symbolism and romantic idealism of the Düsseldorfer and Nazarenes had run their course; the "history of art in our day is in the process of leaving one level and advancing to another."[82] From an art-historical perspective, realistic depictions of scenes from everyday life would have compromised and overstepped the parameters of history painting as it was then conceived; history painting would have been reduced to genre painting.

Instead, Kugler's statement can be seen as an endorsement and partial elaboration of Burckhardt's claim that only with a mature public life could history painting, and the arts in general, be successful in the new bourgeois age. In effect, Kugler's aim was not just to defend his young student and friend; he also used this opportunity to advocate his own

80 Likewise, the main audience for history paintings was found in the fashionable salons, not in the growing slums. As Grew argues, realist art and social commentary were often problematic. Realism often had negative consequences because a realistic portrayal of the conditions of everyday life could easily be misconstrued as criticism of the poor rather than criticism of society in general. He points out that a visual language did not yet exist for the satisfactory representation of the lower orders, and, where realism failed, artists had to develop expressionist techniques and rely on allegory if they were to successfully bring their art to the people. Ibid., 228.

81 Paret, *Art as History*, 24.

82 Kugler, "Neues aus Berlin" *Kunstblatt*, 24 June 1843.

ideas about a national art program, the prerequisite of which was a strong nation: "Only when a powerful collective consciousness prevails among the *Volk*, and when the *Volk* has a national existence, will artistic representation achieve that victorious existence that we cannot shut out of our minds."[83] But it is important to keep in mind that Kugler was not suggesting that mass or popular opinion be solicited or articulated; the basic assumption was that the true *Volk*, or nation, was the educated middle class. This class expected artists to cater to their interests and goals, document their past struggles, and lend legitimacy to their fight against absolutism. Within the context of the emerging bourgeoisie, his was less a veiled attack on Prussian absolutism than an attempt to redefine the boundaries of national public discourse through the creation of a new, more open and amenable form of artistic representation.

Burckhardt's attitude towards the relationship between public opinion and artistic creativity, which changed soon after the publication of the *Kunstblatt* reviews, would increasingly reflect his apprehension about modern society and his criticism of the "massification of all classes," who were "barbaric" because they lived in the "present, devoid of history" and "cut themselves off from their own customs and traditions."[84] In fact, once away from Berlin and out of Kugler's shadow, Burckhardt's conservatism became even more pronounced. In a number of articles he wrote while in Paris for the *Kölnische Zeitung*, Burckhardt appeared to distance himself from Kugler and his statements in the *Kunstblatt*, openly warning his German readers about the influence of the uneducated general public on cultural life.[85] That Paris was the inspiration for his criticism is not coincidental. Although a great admirer of French culture, he saw the French Revolution as not just the source of present and future crises – it was from Paris that he predicted "another explosion," soon – but as a valuable lesson about the true nature of public opinion.[86] Referring specifically to literary activity, which he considered debased because it followed the whims of the

83 Kugler, "Sendschreiben au Herrn Dr. Ernst Förster", 20 July 1843.

84 Quoted from Sigurdson, "Jacob Burckhardt's Liberal-Conservatism," 495; See also Gross, "Jacob Burckhardt and the Critique of Mass Society," 397.

85 See in particular, "Die französische Literatur und das Geld," in *Unbekannte Aufsätze Jacob Burckhardt*, 60–8.

86 *Briefe*, 2:17. Burckhardt considered the evolution and articulation of public opinion to be one of the most important developments of the French Revolution: "The great experience of 1789 was that public opinion forms and transforms the world – once the traditional powers were too weak to prevent it and once they started to make deals with individual currents in the stream of public opinion." JHH, 221.

temperamental Parisian public and bore the brunt of an often malicious French press interested only in sensational stories designed to achieve immediate success and make money, Burckhardt praised the lack of a mature public sphere in Germany. "Nothing is more reassuring and comforting than a comparable look at Germany," he wrote. "We can boldly say: none of our luminaries writes for the sake of the 'great' public, none considers hard cash to be the best form of thanks."[87]

Of course, Burckhardt was not just concerned with the impact of the public on literature. In his mature writings he developed the same theme with regard to all art. Burckhardt knew that the values of the marketplace and the requirements of the modern state were gradually transforming public values and that middle-class public opinion was exercising a tyrannical hold on the aesthetic preferences of the age. In fact, the artist now had to satisfy a broader, more influential and wealthy clientele. This had certainly not been the case during Rubens' time. In *Recollections of Rubens*, Burckhardt emphasized the lack of public influence, mass media, and the distraction of fashion in the art world, as factors that obliged artists to look deep into themselves, as well as to tradition, for inspiration:

There was no public opinion which fed on perpetual novelty; no press which served as the voice of that public opinion and which cast its net even over the art of the place and which was in a position to make artists dependent upon it. There was no novel with its programme of ceaseless invention according to the dictates of the day and dedicated to the representation of its people and events, whatever they might be, no sudden vogues to carry away the so-called "cultured" classes of the great cities, only to make way for another soon after. In a word, no public on which everything and everybody, including painting, depended, and no exhibitions in our sense of the word.[88]

Burckhardt was clearly concerned by the extent to which the public will had begun to debase and commodify the artistic enterprise. He was convinced that subject matter was being chosen not for its universal artistic value but because of the fickle demands of the general public.[89] "There is a lot to be said about the choice of lofty moments," he commented, "even if they are not always so in reality." Unfortunately, many artists were only concerned with that which offered the public immediate ex-

87 "Die französische Literatur und das Geld," 65.
88 GA, 13:393–4.
89 See also *Briefe*, 1:216–17.

citement. As a result, artists sacrificed their true task and were forced to employ exaggerated and distorted techniques – both to compensate for their misrepresentations and to create an artificial, enhanced, and usually meaningless, pathos in their work.[90]

Burckhardt disdained "official" art and tended to support the nonconformists, those artists who refused to sacrifice their vision and individuality in the face of public pressure, even if it meant obscurity and poverty. Such was the case with his friend, the painter Arnold Böcklin, who had maintained his artistic integrity and whose work seemed to encapsulate Burckhardt's understanding of the classical ideal.[91] Burckhardt clearly felt that artists, as well as poets or historians, should refuse to accommodate public pressure, which more than ever was beginning to determine the course of artistic or scholarly development. He protested that the primary concern of artists and intellectuals should be aesthetic value and the existential need for scholarship and *Bildung*. Aware of the fact that an historically conscious age would be especially receptive to historical art, Burckhardt sardonically reflected on the trendy nature of the genre, complaining that since now "the pathos of our time is politics," so naturally "the corresponding expression in painting is therefore history." Artists, he continued, in order to "get a hold of the nation," had succumbed to public pressure; as a result, he claimed, art had become the "servant of contemporary trends" (*Zeittendenzdienerin*). In a society in which the marketplace values were gaining ascendency and in which realism possessed an inflated value, the unique harmony of idealism and realism that had made Rubens and Raphael immortal no longer seemed possible. The artist who refused to capitulate to public demands would be ostracized (and presumably also impoverished) and accused of lacking a "heart for his times and people." Almost under his breath, Burckhardt added: "Fortunately, Raphael did not think like that."[92]

90 *Aesthetik der bildenden Kunst*, 161.
91 See for instance, *Briefe*, 3:139. On Burckhardt's support for Böcklin, their difficult relationship, and the controversy surrounding Böcklin's commission for paintings in Basel, see Kaegi, 7:243–8, and Meier, *Emilie Linder und Jacob Burckhardt*, 92ff.
92 *Aesthetik der bildenden Kunst*, 162.

9

The Search for an Autonomous History of Art

IN HIS 1874 INAUGURAL ADDRESS as professor of art history at the university in Basel,[1] Burckhardt announced his intention to study art from a new perspective, one that represented a departure from the established norms and practices of the discipline. This decision, the result of years of contemplation and study about the writing of art history, was consistent with his determination to chart an independent course within the academic world and to remain a dilettante. It finds an obvious parallel in his decision to write cultural history and his rejection of the underlying assumptions of conventional nineteenth-century modes of historical discourse.

Burckhardt's decision to attempt an alternative approach to the study of art was motivated by the same convictions that drew him early in his career to cultural history; namely, his mistrust of philosophical systems and his dislike of the historical positivism or *Faktenpositivismus* practised by the *viri eruditissimi*. From the outset, he was determined to avoid all discussion of philosophies of aesthetics, the most influential of which was still that of Hegel. Burckhardt declared that the philosophy of aesthetics, or beauty, which he defined as "the relationship between the (cultured) person and art," could not be systematized or theorized. At its core, it was a mysterious process that existed "in a thousand forms like the inner being of mankind and like art itself."[2] As he further emphasized in his inaugural lecture, "The connection between the artwork

---

1 "Über die Kunstgeschichte als Gegenstand eines akademischen Lehrstuhls," in GA, 13:23–8.
2 *Aesthetik der bildenden Kunst*, 35.

and the spiritual capacity of the artist and the observer will be judged by each individual in his own way."[3] Burckhardt's lecture cycle would deviate from the norms of art history in two other ways. It would be neither "the presentation of a detailed course of [artistic] development," nor a course on archaeology,[4] both of which were the traditional territory of art-historical positivists. Instead, Burckhardt proposed a much more modest agenda. He intended to introduce his students – "I do not lecture for art historians,"[5] he once claimed – to the pleasures of the contemplation of art work, to present a "short introduction to the observation of art according to eras and styles."

Burckhardt's alternative form of art-historical discourse, the basis of which was the *Betrachtung* or observation of artworks according to artistic form and style, marks an important development in the history of art, one that is still the subject of debate today. By rejecting the art historian's "teleological quest" – that is to say, by refusing to study artistic development and to indulge in purely archaeological studies – Burckhardt turned his back on chronological examinations based upon the lives of artists and artistic periods and structured his narrative topologically and typologically, according to style and function. This point of departure represented a significant redefinition of both conventional aesthetic value and the nature of the art object as historical evidence. By stressing the importance of the notion of *Kunstbetrachtung* (observation of art), which was analagous to his aestheticist principle of *Anschauung* (contemplation-observation) on which he based his approach to cultural history, Burckhardt was once more questioning the validity of scientific history. At the same time, he was undermining the fundamental principles of historicism, which provided the theoretical foundation of contemporary art-historical discourse.

. . .

Compared with the voluminous literature devoted to both Burckhardt's historical studies and his unique approach to cultural history, interest in

---

3 "Über die Kunstgeschichte," 23.
4 Ibid.
5 Kaegi, 2:505.

his art-historical work has been relatively modest.[6] This is the result of a number of factors. For scholars, as well as for the student and casual reader, Burckhardt's published work in the field of cultural history, the bulk of his output, has been more accessible than his art-historical work; as well it has maintained its relevance and interest over the decades. Moreover, most scholarly work on Burckhardt was written by historians who tended to play down, however unintentionally, his contributions to the study of art. This can perhaps best be seen in Werner Kaegi's monumental biography of Burckhardt, which has thoroughly and legitimately dominated the scholarship of the last fifty years. By no stretch of the imagination did Kaegi ignore Burckhardt's art-historical work. However, Kaegi's view of Burckhardt was based on the general assumption that, for Burckhardt, art history was subordinate to his historical work, being essentially a branch of cultural history, rather than an independent field of enquiry. The result has been a somewhat one-sided view of Burckhardt's life's work and his contributions to art history. Art historians, beginning with Burckhardt's student and successor in the chair of art history at the university in Basel, Heinrich Wölfflin, did seek to redress this imbalance and to assess his important contributions to the discipline of art history. However, despite the work of Wölfflin, Joseph Gantner, and Emil Mauer,[7] Burckhardt has remained somewhat of an elusive figure in the historiography of art history. In general studies of the discipline he has been either ignored altogether, or relegated to secondary status behind the much more prominent figures of Kugler, Karl Schnaase, Alois Riegl, or Wölfflin.[8]

Over the course of the last few years there has been a renewed interest in Burckhardt's art-historical work, a reflection not only of art historians' curiosity about the history of their discipline, but also of their belated recognition of Burckhardt's significant contribution to the development of the field.[9] Besides shedding new light on this aspect of Burckhardt's

6 This is especially true in the Anglo-Saxon world. Only a few articles on Burckhardt as art historian have been written, including Berger, "Jacob Burckhardt as an Art Historian;" Gossman, "Jacob Burckhardt as Art Historian;" and the section on Burckhardt in Weintraub, *Visions of Culture*.

7 Wölfflin, *Kunstgeschichtliche Grundbegriffe*, and "Jacob Burckhardt und die systematische Kunstgeschichte," in *Gedanken zur Kunstgeschichte*; Gantner, (ed.) *Jacob Burckhardt und Heinrich Wölfflin*, and "Der Unterricht in Kunstgeschichte an der Universität Basel, 1844–1938;" Maurer, *Jacob Burckhardt und Rubens*.

8 The major exception is Waetzoldt, *Deutsche Kunsthistoriker*.

9 See especially Siebert, *Jacob Burckhardt*; Sitt, *Kriterien der Kunstkritik*. See also the numerous articles by Meier and Schlink.

oeuvre and reminding us that he was a much respected, innovative, and influential art historian, recent studies have attempted to reconstruct his theory of art and understanding of aesthetics. In particular, scholars have focused their attention on his approach to the study of art, which he called "Kunstgeschichte nach Aufgaben und Gattungen" (art history according to function and form). Burckhardt elaborated on this approach in a series of lectures given in 1863, 1866, 1868, and 1870, and recently published by Irmgard Siebert under the title *Aesthetik der bildenden Kunst.*[10]

Despite Burckhardt's rejection of traditional modes of historical discourse, it is doubtful that "Kunstgeschichte nach Aufgaben" constituted a paradigm shift, or the formulation of an "oppositional paradigm," in the Kuhnian sense, as Irmgard Siebert has claimed.[11] Still, most scholars would agree that Burckhardt's attempt to develop a systematic study of art represented a significant re-evaluation of the tasks of both the historian and the discipline. Not everyone, however, agrees on precisely what this re-evaluation signified. One of the main issues, itself a reflection of current issues in the historiography of art history, is the relationship of "Kunstgeschichte nach Aufgaben" to art-historical contextualism and to art-historical formalism. Whereas the main objective of art-historical contextualism (also refered to as historicism or positivism) was to study art within the broader historical context (i.e., art *history*), the objective of art-historical formalism was to develop a systematic, critical theory of artistic form (i.e., *art* history). The underlying assumption of formalism, with its focus on the study of stylistic development, is that art history is an autonomous discipline and that art follows a developmental trajectory independent of external historical factors.[12]

The origins of this particular discussion can be traced back to Wölfflin, who in 1915 described Burckhardt as a "psychologist of form."[13]

10 *Ästhetik der bildenden Kunst.* The original title of Burckhardt's lectures is "Zur Einleitung in die Aesthetik der bildenden Kunst." Recent studies on Burckhardt's approach to art history also include Huse, "Anmerkungen zu Burckhardts 'Kunstgeschichte nach Aufgaben'"; Ganz, "Jacob Burckhardts *Kultur der Renaissance in Italien* und die Kunstgeschichte"; Meier, "Kunstgeschichte und Kulturgeschichte"; Karge, " 'Die Kunst ist nicht das Maaβ der Geschichte'."

11 That is, a consensual and revolutionary reordering of patterns of thought or knowledge. Siebert, Introduction to *Ästhetik der bildenden Kunst,* 25.

12 See for example Podro, *The Critical Historians of Art,* and the more recent collection of essays by Kemal and Gaskill, eds., *The Language of Art History.*

13 Wölfflin, *Kunstgeschichtliche Grundbegriffe,* 3. See also "Jacob Burckhardt und die systematische Kunstgeschichte," in Wölfflin, *Gedanken zur Kunstgeschichte,* 147–55.

According to Wölfflin, himself a pioneer historian of style and form, Burckhardt's work, especially *Die Kunst der Renaissance* (1867), signified an important step in the direction of systematic formalism. Not only did Burckhardt reject the traditional history of artists "in order to achieve the possibility of a pure treatment according to form and style," but over the course of time he came to believe that the fine arts constituted an autonomous field of enquiry, with its own language, laws, and formulas.[14] Kaegi later challenged this particular understanding of Burckhardt's approach to art history, arguing that Wölfflin was simply trying to justify his own theoretical position. In sharp contrast, Kaegi maintained that Burckhardt, whom he characterized as always more of an historian than an art historian, had continued to regard art history as a part of the general study of cultural history.[15] Burckhardt, in other words, fell within the "contextualist" camp. "History, not form, predominates here," Kaegi commented with regards to *Die Kunst der Renaissance*. Despite Burckhardt's emphasis on style and form, continued Kaegi, art clearly possessed unique qualities that required special treatment and served primarily as a source of knowledge for cultural history. He noted that Burckhardt, in the tradition of his Berlin teacher Franz Kugler, had studied art not to draw conclusions about the object of art itself, but rather because it reflected certain social, historical, and cultural truths. For Burckhardt, he said, "human beings and their will stand in the centre of his field of vision, not their work or even art. In these works human beings dominate as the subject, the eternal theme of all historical writing ... The direction Burckhardt also took in his 'most stimulating' and mature work of art history was that of cultural history."[16]

Given the general authority of Kaegi's scholarship, his interpretation carried a lot of weight. In recent years, however, as his views have come under increased scrutiny, the pendulum seems to be swinging back in Wölfflin's direction. Thus, for instance, the American art historian, Michael Ann Holly, claims in the introduction to her study of Erwin Panofsky and the development of art history that Burckhardt was uninterested "in all information extrinsic to the experience of the work (of art) on its own terms ... whether the information is biographical, historical or sociological." She concludes that "in the final analysis, the first

14 Wölfflin, "Jacob Burckhardt und die systematische Kunstgeschichte," 151.
15 Kaegi, 4:211. "Art history was for Kugler and for Burckhardt a part of cultural history."
16 Ibid., 4:208–9.

cultural historian ironically needs to be labeled a formalist as an art historian."[17] This general conclusion has also been drawn by Martina Sitt, in the most comprehensive examination to date of Burckhardt's approach to the study of art. Without specifically employing the formalist/contextualist dichotomy, Sitt nevertheless agrees that Burckhardt developed a system of evaluation – a systematic approach to art history, i.e., his *Rangsystem* – that was ordered or structured according to the principles of style and form, rather than chronology. By elevating form over context, she says, Burckhardt attempted to emancipate the study of art from its subordinate status as a subfield of general cultural history and to develop an autonomous history of art: "It is precisely the historical moment that Burckhardt as *art* historian sought from time to time to leave aside in favour of a presentation of the autonomy of eternal, timeless art." Burckhardt thought it possible, continues Sitt, "to observe the development of art free of any causal connections with political and social relationships."[18]

Perhaps the most suggestive aspect of Sitt's study, however, is her next step in the discussion. She suggests that by attempting to create an independent discipline by emancipating art from historical positivism (contextualism) and speculative philosophy of aesthetics, Burckhardt entered the relatively uncharted territory of art criticism or the critical history of art.

Sitt's classification of Burckhardt as an art critic represents an important attempt to break with the sometimes oversimplistic dichotomy between contextualism and formalism, a dichotomy still entrenched in the historiography of art history. Unfortunately, the overriding significance of Sitt's general conclusions gets lost, or at least is not fully appreciated, because she sees Burckhardt's attempt to develop a language of art criticism based on style and form – which would free the study of art from the confines of cultural history and speculative aesthetics – as inherently problematic, if not contradictory. In the end, she regards art criticism as highly subjective, resting primarily on value judgment. To a certain ex-

---

17 Holly, *Panofsky and the Foundations of Art History*, 33. Holly's interpretation is problematic for a number of reasons. In the first place, Burckhardt was not the first cultural historian. Second, she bases her conclusions on Burckhardt's cultural histories, not his work in art history. Finally, Holly, in another essay, arrives at a different conclusion when she writes that, in the *Civilization of the Renaissance in Italy*, Burckhardt "reads the great masterpieces of Renaissance art as historical documents, symptomatic of fifteenth-century cultural and social attitudes," in Holly, "Wölfflin and the Imagining of the Baroque," 1258.

18 Sitt, *Kriterien der Kunstkritik*, 68.

tent, the terms of the debate are reminiscent of the discussions about the nature of historicism and cultural history. On the one hand, art history, like historicism, "is characterized by the attempt to maintain what is deemed a scientific distance to the object [and] to eliminate to a large extent the subjectivity of the observer."[19] In other words, the primary task of the art historian is to attempt to understand art of alien cultures, produced under different systems of thought, historical circumstances, and conditions; and to explain its significance for the present in terms of historical context. For most art historians, works of art are usually treated as unique forms of historical evidence or documentation, which the historians can unearth and explain through the application of rigorous, scientific methodology. Like an event or phenomenon (or any other fact), art is seen as "a sign of the times, an index of historical, social, cultural, or individual growth, identity, change or transformation."[20] The art critic, on the other hand, is not concerned with maintaining this "scientific distance" to the object under consideration. Instead, the critic attempts to bridge this gap between subjectivity and objectivity and "emphasizes the importance of his approach to the work as a partner of the artist, especially with regard to an inevitable exercise in judgement ... The critic is interested in knowing the most inner character of artistic activity. In contrast, the art historian, conscious of the relative value of all decisions of taste, is interested in understanding and as a result recognizing the work as the 'fruit of a greater cultural historical process'."[21]

The implication, of course, is that art criticism remains subjective because it is based on judgments – the critics' tastes, likes, and dislikes, which are all inherently unscientific – and because it is allegedly divorced from the actual practice of historical research. As a result, traditional art historians often regard art criticism, like literary criticism, with a great deal of suspicion; seeing it as a form of journalism and suspect as a scholarly, scientific endeavour; hence they are ill at ease with its implications for their discipline.[22]

19 Ibid., 213.

20 Preziosi, *Rethinking Art History*, 12. This belief, argues Preziosi, is a fundamental given in the discipline.

21 Sitt, *Kriterien der Kunstkritik*, 213–14.

22 Or indeed, they regard it as a sign of crisis in (or of) the discipline. See Preziosi, *Rethinking Art History*, 21ff, who speaks of "A Crisis in, or of, Art History?" as a crisis based upon art historians' utopian "dream of scientificity," that elusive, "obscure object of desire."

These fears appear to be warranted in large part because art criticism does undermine the contextualists' reliance upon this "documentary" or "objectivist" model of knowledge, which, in the words of Dominick LaCapra, "is typically blind to its own rhetoric."[23] Said another way, traditional art-historical positivism (or contextualism) presumes an unmediated relationship between the past and the present, the author and the text. In contrast, the critical historian of art focuses primarily on the work of art itself, on its formal qualities, not the historical context in which a particular artwork was created; as well, the critical historian focuses on the exploration of a general conception of art, "those principles which governed art as a whole" and which "give us purchase on the variety of its styles and purposes."[24] In this sense, the critical historian of art, like the literary critic, is very conscious that the signs of the past in the art object are mediated in the present by the author (that this context is created by the artwork and the historian) and that they are, consequently, viewed through a distorting prism of cultural values, preconceptions, prejudices, and ideologies. Like Burckhardt's aesthetic approach to history, art criticism obliges historians to recognize the rhetorical nature of their discipline and points inexorably to the self-referentiality of language. This has been emphasized by Stephen Bann, who has argued that whereas the positivism of the traditional art historian assumes that "language is transparent to meaning, and unproblematically instrumental," art criticism implies the opposite; that is, the "self-reflexive sense of the poetic possibilities of language."[25]

This points to another important reason why critical history of art is by its very nature unsettling to traditional contextualism. Because art critics are concerned with the artwork itself, rather than the context in which it originated, they are less concerned with trying to establish the particular meaning of an artwork within a given context, or within the broader development of art and culture as a whole. Preziosi captures the assumption that meaning can be discovered and recovered in the past when he writes, "Coincident with the implicit notion that the work of art is in some way a revelation of Being or of a Truth that is already present (in the mind, in culture, and in society) is the notion that the

23 LaCapra, *History and Criticism*, 17.

24 Podro, *The Critical Historians of Art*, xx and xxi.

25 Bann, *The Inventions of History*, 223. Keith Moxey, *The Practice of Theory* 5, also writes: "Instead of believing that art history discovers the ways things really are, that its narratives map neatly onto the way in which events might actually have unfolded, art historians must appreciate how language invests their practice with the values of the present."

artwork's modus operandi is that of saying: The work reveals, expresses, re-presents some prior meaning or content."[26] But does an artwork reveal or express some prior meaning? And if it does, is this accessible to the art historian? Can it be translated into discourse? Burckhardt, after many decades of thought and study, seems to have reached the conclusion that this was impossible. As we have seen, he regarded art as a mysterious force, and the true meaning of a work of art impossible to determine: "We will never speak of the 'idea' behind a work of art."[27] His main concern was not truth and its establishment, but rather the impression left by art on the spirit and the senses. "The main objective is always the impact of the work of art on people, the sparking of an obliging imagination," he claimed in his lectures on aesthetics.[28]

For the last two centuries, contextualist assumptions have determined the way of writing the history of art. In particular, conventional art historical narrative has ascribed primacy to the mode of explanation. However, the narrative mode of explanation is based upon the hermeneutic assumption that the historian has direct or unmediated access to the phenomenal world; in other words, that the past can be constructed objectively by the historian in a value-free narrative form. The general implication is that the meaning of the past or the work of art can be grasped unmediated and in all its authenticity by the scholar. The narrative mode, then, serves a vital function in modernist historiography because it enables the historian to reconstruct causal links; this reconstruction not only creates a context in which to situate the historical evidence, it also conveys meaning. Art criticism, in contrast, regards the work of art as a text; it tends to eschew the narrative mode of explanation and is more concerned with the problems of representation and interpretation. The objective of art-critical enquiry is to engage in a dialogue with the work; concerned with form rather than content, it examines the language used to convey this to the reader. Thus, the ultimate meaning of an historical or artistic object within any given context recedes into the background.

But does art criticism really threaten to undermine the legitimacy of traditional art historical practice? Must art criticism become simply the "unmasking, or deconstruction, of the metaphysical fables manufactured by others," as Preziosi has suggested, revealing his indebtedness to

26 Preziosi, *Rethinking Art History*, 15–16.
27 "Über die Kunstgeschichte als Gegenstand eines akademischen Lehrstuhls," 23.
28 *Ästhetik der bildenden Kunst*, 35.

Derrida, in order to avoid the pitfalls of "logocentrism?" Keith Moxey has recently called for "an integration of history and theory," one that recognizes "the power of language in the construction of historical narratives [and] the concomitant awareness that the historian encounters the past only by means of linguistic representations."[29] Perhaps the most important lesson to be drawn from art criticism is the recognition that context is created by the historian, not that context and history do not exist. A final lesson, as Michael Podro has argued in his distinguished work on the German tradition of critical history of art, is that, during the nineteenth century, archaeology (or contextualism) and art criticism were not necessarily considered to be diametrically opposed, but rather complementary to the overall project of art-historical writing. Surely the fears of traditional art historians, expressed to a certain extent in Sitt's sceptical attitude towards art criticism and her insistence on maintaining a separation between art criticism and art history, derive from the failure or refusal to recognize the degree to which a form of art criticism is inherent in all art history and that, in fact, the discipline is as rhetorically based as history.

· · ·

The emergence of the study of art history as a professional academic discipline in German universities in the early nineteenth century follows a pattern similar to that of the professionalization of general history. Art historians sought to emancipate the study of art from speculative aesthetic philosophy. As well, they attempted to establish professional standards and the autonomy of the discipline within the academic community. But the initial thrust of the emancipation from philosophy resulted in only a paradoxical half-freedom: the subsumption of art history under history, as part of the general study of cultural history. A second emancipatory stage was required if art history was ever to emerge from the confines of cultural history. This process – the creation of an autonomous history of art with its own method and theory – was also profoundly paradoxical; indeed, scholars feared that it might lead to extreme formalism and, thereby, the emancipation of the history from art history.

29 Moxey, *The Practice of Theory*, 3, 6, 25.

Over the course of his professional career, Burckhardt became a pro-
ponent of an autonomous history of art. This marked a significant
change in his understanding of art. As a student and in his earlier work,
he clearly approached the study of art from a contextualist perspective.
This, as we have seen in his discussion of the Cologne cathedral, was a
reflection of the strong influence of Franz Kugler, who sought to combine art and cultural history. But just as Burckhardt distanced himself
theoretically from his mentor, Leopold von Ranke, so too he revised his
position in relation to that of Kugler. Burckhardt never became the extreme formalist that his student Wölfflin became. His later work, especially his lecture on the aesthetics of architecture, in which he
elaborated his "Kunstgeschichte nach Aufgaben," was not just an attempt to focus on the problems of artistic style and form, rather than
context; it was also an attempt to understand style and form within a
specific conception of art. In the end, he never denied the close relationship between art and history, or theory and practice, attempting instead, like Karl Schnaase, Gottfried Semper, and Alois Riegl, to strike a
judicious balance between the two.

One of the most important developments in the study of art during
the early decades of the nineteenth century was the historicization of art
scholarship. Despite the work of Johann Joachim Winkelmann (1717–
68) in the eighteenth century, connoisseurs and philosophers continued to dominate the study of art. As a consequence, the study of art remained in the shadows as a discipline. In the early nineteenth century,
as the study of art became more popular, art history began to assume its
more modern, professional form: not as an independent discipline, but
as a central element of broader universal history. Thus, the revival of interest in the study of art by non-philosophers and historians should be
seen, like the professionalization of historical studies in general, within
the context of the emerging bourgeois public sphere and the changing
social function of art. As art became more accessible, as it moved from
the private to the public sphere, it increasingly became the subject of
systematic study as scholars began to question its role in society and culture. By recognizing the fundamental differences in the art of the past
and by believing that the meaning of that art for past cultures could be
reconstructed through historical enquiry, art history was seen more and
more as a mediating force between the significance of past and present-
day art. New theories and methodological procedures adapted and developed by historians such as Ranke were applied to the study of art. Art
historians could then set broader goals in an attempt to free the disci-

pline from the narrow confines of speculative aesthetics, connoisseur-ship, and compilation, thereby recognizing its potential service to the knowledge of the general history of humankind.

This new vision was perhaps best expressed by Burckhardt's teacher Franz Kugler, whose handbooks on art played a major role in the histori-cization of art scholarship. Kugler, one of the most important figures in early nineteenth-century German art and cultural history, has been much neglected by modern scholars. Usually mentioned, as is the case here, in conjunction with Burckhardt, he was nonetheless one of the founders of the modern discipline of art history. Moreover, according to his greatest admirer, Burckhardt, he was one of its most important and innovative contributors.

Kugler was part of a generation of young scholars at the university of Berlin that rebelled against the great influence of Hegelian philosophy on modern scholarship. Early in his career he devoted much energy to the necessary compilation of raw data on cultural and artistic artifacts, actively seeking to create a greater role for art history within the general field of cultural studies. His analytical, archaeological approach, so char-acteristic of the historical positivism of the day, sought to free the study of art from the influence of speculative philosophy and fulfill the tasks of accurate historical scholarship. Although Hegel did not view art as central to his philosophical project, art nevertheless occupied an impor-tant position in his vision of the development of the spirit. According to Hegel, art was "thought-like"; consequently, the question that ultimately preoccupied him in his *Aesthetics* (1828) was how thought could be ex-pressed through art, and how art from a different age or culture could be understood in the present. Hegel derived a solution from his philos-ophy of the spirit, suggesting, in a single systematic viewpoint, that art expressed and was the embodiment of the spirit or idea.[30]

Men such as Kugler and his contemporary Gottfried Semper (1803–79) tried with varying degrees of success to tackle Hegel head on. He-gel's speculative aesthetics, they firmly believed in true historicist fash-ion, was fundamentally ahistorical because the object under consideration was deprived of its essential individuality. Moreover, they feared that, according to his aesthetic philosophy, the work of art would be enveloped by abstraction and eventually overwhelmed and smoth-ered by metaphysics. They refused to accept that the art object was in its essence a part of the contemplative, ideal realm of thought; that it could

30 See Podro, *The Critical Historians of Art*, 16ff.

simply be reduced to a symbolic representation and an embodiment of the universal spirit. Instead, they posited the notion of understanding art as part of general social life; the artwork, they stressed, could only be properly comprehended in terms of its relationship within the complex web of social and cultural phenomena. They steadfastly maintained and sought to demonstrate that art was a necessary element of human existence, one conditioned by history.

In Kugler's work, one sees the embodiment of a progressive art historical enterprise as art history passed from the compilations of energetic amateur connoisseurs; through the ahistorical, metaphysically hazy realm of speculative aesthetics in which art was reduced to a vague, symbolic representation of the universal spirit; to, finally, the concrete world of synthesis as part of the general cultural history that focused on the external relationships linking art and life. Art, for Kugler, was representative of a culture, not constitutive, and therefore lacked a history of its own. Kugler argued that the task of art history, as a subordinate branch of general cultural history, was to examine the external relationships of art to life, an attitude that was also accepted at this time by the young Burckhardt. In the 1843–44 reworking of a number of articles for the ninth edition of the Brockhaus *Konversationslexikon*, Burckhardt emphasized that art history was concerned with providing information about history in general, rather than about the works of art themselves. He essentially left unchanged the previous definition of art history as the "presentation of the origin, the development, the progress and the decline of the beautiful art form, [and which] constitutes a principal element of cultural history."[31]

The historicization of art history – the belief that art must be understood within its historical context and that, as a constitutive element of cultural history, it can represent that context – was important because it placed the study of art firmly within the realm of history and emancipated it from speculative aesthetics. In addition, this historicization significantly broadened the scope of scholarly enquiry to include not only European art but, for the first time, non-European art, as well as primitive and prehistoric art. This was possible because the historicization of art involved, indeed required, a redefinition of the nature of the artwork as a source of historical evidence. Art was not studied simply to learn about the object itself. Instead, it was viewed as reflecting social, historical, and cultural conditions; as possessing unique qualities that

---

31 *Brockhaus Conversations-Lexikon*, 9th ed., vol. 8, Leipzig, 1845, 435.

required special treatment as a source of cultural history. Even though a work of art was shaped by the inherently subjective values of the artist, it nevertheless reflected particular traditions and functions within society as a whole. It was consequently considered to be a document that could provide clues to both the object itself and, more significantly, to the broader social and cultural milieu – to those very traditions and functions – from which the work had emanated. Like a written document, therefore, a painting or a sculpture or a monument had to be understood and interpreted within a context created by the historian. Preoccupation with context and the ensuing interest in the rhetoric of the discipline did not mean that art historians were not interested in the artist or in style and form. It did mean, however, that the parameters of the discipline had changed, thus reflecting its increased maturity and sophistication, to include substantially more than the traditional biographies of artists. Indeed, in some circles these biographies were no longer considered an adequate scholarly endeavour. While it was still crucial to analyze the motivation and intention of the artist, details of the artist's life became somewhat secondary to the entire project, which was now seen as the attempt to study art from the perspective of universal history, thereby connecting the course of the development of art with external events and cultural phenomena.

· · ·

Throughout his long professional career Burckhardt was preoccupied with the complex relationship between art and history. During the first half of the nineteenth century, two main schools of thought dominated this discussion. On the one hand were those scholars perhaps represented best by Kugler, who maintained that art history was a subordinate branch of general cultural history. On the other, were scholars such as Karl Schnaase, one of the most important critical historians of art of the *Vormärz*, who sought to establish the autonomy of the study of art from general history. Burckhardt's task, albeit difficult, was to strike a balance between these two positions. He admired both men. Kugler's work he praised as the model for contextualists; his *Handbuch der Kunstgeschichte* "integrated the immense material into a great, clear presentation according to world-historical eras." Schnaase's work, although less concerned with the enumeration of works of art, he lauded as a model for the "thoughtful historical and philosophical explanation of style and periods of transition."[32]

Yet despite Burckhardt's earlier definition of art history for the Brockhaus encyclopaedia, which clearly placed him in Kugler's camp, he gradually, after returning to Basel from Berlin, distanced himself from Kugler's basic assumptions about the nature of the art-historical enterprise. As he began considering art history to be about much more than mere historical retrieval, authorship, and archaeology, he started to study art on its own terms. There is some evidence to suggest that while not rejecting the contextualist project outright, Burckhardt at least recognized its limitations as early as his 1843 *Kunstblatt* reviews. There, he raised important questions about the function of art and the aims and methodological principles of the emerging discipline, and offered an implicit and tentative critique of historicism. More concrete signs of the path Burckhardt was taking have been pointed out by Irmgard Siebert and Henrik Karge. Karge, in particular, has recently demonstrated that Burckhardt's early lectures on art history from the mid-1840s and early 1850s reveal not only Schnaase's strong influence on his ideas, but the beginnings of an independent, systematic approach to the study of art, the purpose of which was to show how the development of art followed patterns and rules independent of broader historical events and developments.[33]

The development of an alternative, systematic art-historical discourse, which Burckhardt later referred to as "Kunstgeschichte nach Aufgaben und Gattungen," resulted from a gradual transformation in his thought. His initial doubts about Kugler's understanding of art history as a form of cultural history, inspired by the work of Schnaase, as well as his increased scepticism about historicism were reinforced by his intensive study of Renaissance art and his experiences in Italy in the late 1840s. After a stressful year working on the revision of Kugler's handbooks in Berlin, he had set off for Rome eager to indulge his passion for art and his enormous capacity for study. This trip, as he fondly recalled many years later, was a period of "true meditation."[34] With Rome as inspiration and the peace of mind that comes after the completion of strenuous labours, he wrote his first major study of the Renaissance, the article "Andeutungen zur Geschichte der christlichen Skulptur." This article

32 Ibid., 436. See also Karge, "'Die Kunst ist nicht das Maaß der Geschichte'," 412.

33 See Siebert, *Jacob Burckhardt*. On Schnaase's influence, see Karge, "'Die Kunst ist nicht das Maaß der Geschichte'." Burckhardt viewed his 1842 book, *Kunstwerke der belgischen Städte*, as a sort of compendium to Schnaase's earlier work, *Niederländische Briefe*, of 1834. See GA, 1:114.

34 *Briefe*, 6:25.

signalled an important shift in his interests towards classical art. In many respects a prelude to the *Cicerone* and the *Civilization of the Renaissance*, it was a conscious effort to break away from traditional classification schemes and to focus on stylistic developments. For the first time, Burckhardt sought to clarify and verify certain basic questions concerning aesthetics and art theory as they related to historical observation and the process of contemplation. Although he remained thoroughly hostile to aesthetic philosophy – he would claim a few years later that it was necessary to "keep one's eyes shut in the face of all aesthetic theory that is now being preached"[35] – he had taken an important step: with this article no longer did he consider the study of artistic form to be a subordinate element of cultural history.

As Burckhardt's lectures reveal, by the early 1850s, unlike his mentor in Berlin, he had clearly ceased to regard art history as the handmaiden of history. In the introduction to his 1851 lecture on general art history, he proclaimed: "Art is not the measure of history; its development or decline is not an absolute witness either for or against an epoch or a nationality, but always one of the highest elements of life for a gifted people."[36] This does not mean, however, that he considered art history to be an autonomous discipline or that art could be studied independently from history. In fact, Burckhardt was still struggling to find an appropriate way of studying art. One of his main objectives at this time was to combine art history with cultural history in a project designed to bridge history and art, context and form. Always interested in those areas "where art and cultural history meet,"[37] he initially considered his work on Constantine the Great to be an example of how to combine the two.[38] Likewise, as he indicated in a letter to King Maximillian of Bavaria in 1858, he had originally planned to do the same in his book on the Italian Renaissance: "The Renaissance should be presented from the point of view that it is the mother and home of the modern man, in thought and feeling as well as in the creation of form. It *appeared* possible to treat both of these great trends as a worthwhile parallel, to blend art history and cultural history."[39] But, as Burckhardt indicates in this letter, he felt unable to fulfill his initial goal and, by the time the *Civilization of the Renaissance* appeared in print, he had abandoned these

35 Ibid., 3:161.
36 Quoted in Karge, " 'Die Kunst ist nicht das Maaβ der Geschichte'," 419. See also Siebert, *Jacob Burckhardt*, 58.
37 *Briefe*, 3:222.
38 Ibid., 3:197.
39 *Briefe*, 4:23. My emphasis.

plans.⁴⁰ By this point he was fed up with writing and now regretted "painfully this promise."⁴¹ Four years later he made up his mind to put his unpublished manuscript on Renaissance art – well over 500 pages – away forever. Only later was he pursuaded to publish it as part of the series on art history begun by Kugler before his death.⁴²

During the intervening period between the publication of *Constantine* (1852), which he viewed as an example of how to blend the two fields, and *Civilization of the Renaissance* (1860), Burckhardt decided it was no longer possible to combine art history and cultural history. One reason, no doubt, was his lack of success with this approach in *Constantine*. In the end, there was neither a presentation of artistic development nor an examination of style and form; instead, art history had been subordinated to the broader developments of cultural history and had assumed an auxiliary function.⁴³ Another important reason was the increasingly clear crystallization of his conception of "Kunstgeschichte nach Aufgaben." During the summer of 1852, a few months before his book on the age of Constantine was published, he announced to his friend Paul Heyse that his view of art had taken a "slow but complete turn." He continued: "I would never have believed that such an old, rotten cultural historian like me, who imagined that he regarded all points of view and epochs according to their value, in the end could have been so one-sided as I am. The scales have now fallen from my eyes." Feeling intellectually constricted by the scholarly norms of the day, he wrote that it was "high time for me to become free of the generally accepted, falsely objective recognition of the value of everything and become once again totally intolerant."⁴⁴

What this meant in historical terms can perhaps best be seen in *Der Cicerone*, published in 1855, which was Burckhardt's most important study of art and the first product of his reconceptualization of art history. In preparing this work from his vast collection of notes taken whilst in Italy, Burckhardt's gradually began to conceptualize art according to

40 CRI, 19.

41 *Briefe*, 4:61.

42 See ibid., 4:132. A year later he had made some revisions, but decided to put the unfinished manuscript "in his desk," this time "probably for ever." Burckhardt did not comment here on the viability of the project of the synthesis of art history and cultural history, but rather complained that he did not get enough holiday time for the long trips to Italy required to finish his research. Either way, he was happy "since I no longer study and take notes for book writing, only teaching." Ibid., 4:194.

43 See Siebert, *Jacob Burckhardt*, 93.

44 *Briefe*, 3:161.

criteria that were independent of cultural development in general. The *Cicerone* was thus an important transitional work. It marked a clear departure from the style of Franz Kugler's handbooks – despite the fact that it was dedicated to him – which were written chronologically according to world historical epochs. Instead, Burckhardt arranged his work not only according to the principles of style and form, but also according to genre, treating architecture, sculpture, and painting separately and in a manner that would anticipate his lectures on aesthetics.

In *Der Cicerone* we see "Kunstgeschichte nach Aufgaben und Gattungen" in embryonic form. As the "seed of greater research into the history of the beautiful," it was also an "affliction," which he had brought back from Italy and with which, with characteristic mistrust, he continued to wrestle. He stated that he would not be able to die in peace if he did not fulfill his destiny in this matter.[45] Indeed, Burckhardt thought he had managed to strike a balance between the two dominant approaches to art history. He announced as much in an 1851 lecture, when he stated that the art historian had two options: art history is either the "servant of history, especially cultural history and regards the beautiful as only a particular temporal element, or it proceeds from the beautiful itself and draws cultural history along only as help. Both are justified. We will have to keep to the middle."[46] By taking the middle ground with "Kunstgeschichte nach Aufgaben," Burckhardt proceeded "from the beautiful [i.e., the artwork] itself." The focus was now the work of art itself (the autonomy of the artwork), which developed according to patterns or laws different to those of history. However, at no point did this imply the rejection or subordination of history, as his much delayed volume on Renaissance art attests. History would continue to occupy a significant part of his art-historical enterprise – indeed, history remained an important element of his work particularly in the study of the "task" and the content of artworks. It would continue not as the dominant partner, but rather as essential background to artistic evolution, as a necessary partner in the art-historical project. As Siebert has concluded, just as art was "not the measure of history," so too history was not the measure of art.[47]

· · ·

45 Ibid., 3:226.
46 As quoted in Siebert, Introduction to *Ästhetik der bildenden Kunst*, 23.
47 Ibid.

It seems that, initially, Burckhardt intended "Kunstgeschichte nach Aufgaben" to be nothing more than a supplement to the traditional "history of artists" approach. While talking with Albert von Zahn, who was to edit a revised edition of *Der Cicerone* but at this time was working on his own projects, Burckhardt suggested a new format. He would present the heyday of German art history, but, rather than concentrate solely on the biographies of individual artists, he would focus instead on the artistic problems, motivating forces, and overall degree of artistic ability of each. Burckhardt maintained that this approach would dominate art history in the future, but not displace the traditional "Künstlergeschichten." He called it a valuable supplement because it would enable scholars to relate the significance of individual artists to the era.[48] That Burckhardt did not consider works on individual artists a degraded genre is demonstrated in his study of Rubens. The importance of "history of artists" was emphasized once again in his preface to an early version of the *Geschichte der Renaissance* from 1863. "The art history of the Renaissance," he wrote, "will for the greatest part always have to follow the history of artists in chronological narratives, and it has not occurred to me to want to base it on anything else. If I attempt to represent it according to artistic problem and form, that is only because I would like to add a second (systematic) element to the current narrative art history."[49] In 1875, he described what he had wanted to accomplish in the field in a letter from Rome, in which he explained that he had wished to do the type of study that would have enabled him "to reshape the study of art history to a pure history of style and form." Unfortunately for Burckhardt, he remained at least partly stuck "in the old cheese of *Künstlergeschichte*."[50]

Burckhardt's second, systematic element of art history, his "Kunstgeschichte nach Aufgaben," was designed to study the "presence" of the art objects – that is to say those extra-temporal characteristics that made the art object universal, eternal, and worthy of continued study and interest – and how this was to be recovered in the present. As with the lesson of the three powers (*Potenzenlehre*), his approach must be viewed not as a philosophy, in this case of art or aesthetics, but rather as a loose conceptualization designed to assist the viewer or historian in the process of the *Betrachtung der Kunstwerke*, or the observation of art. As one recent

48 *Briefe*, 5:55.
49 Quoted in Kaegi, 4:204.
50 *Briefe*, 6:34.

commentator has pointed out, it was a lesson about the relationship between art and observer that was grounded not in philosophical speculation, but in the historical world and, most importantly, in the world of perception and imagination.[51] The task of the student of art history was to observe and describe these vibrations and fragments of the past, in the signs from the past that remain in the work of art.

While "Kunstgeschichte nach Aufgaben" focused on style and form, it would be an exaggeration to describe it as a theory of style or as an example of pure formalism. The systematic element of Burckhardt's approach was still firmly anchored in the historical. This is especially clear when we examine Burckhardt's understanding of the term *Aufgabe*. Broadly speaking, he meant it to mean neither simply the task or purpose envisioned by the artist, nor the specific commission behind a work of art or the particular solution to problems of artistic composition. Rather, he understood the artistic *Aufgabe* as the convergence of stylistic, formal, and cultural-historical factors that would emerge as representative of the specific aesthetic needs and goals of an era and that would come together as a type of representational hegemony. During the *quattrocento*, the emergence of a particular stylistic paradigm, such as a form of sculpture or a genre of painting, would result from a different *Aufgabe* than that of the seventeenth century. Its analysis could reveal not only the more mundane things such as the *Volksgeist* or *Zeitgeist*, the cultural or social forces of an age, but, more importantly, how artists perceived their world and their culture. But its analysis could also reveal more intangible factors, such as taste, which, although often alien to us, have left enough traces behind to satisfy our "restoring capability." As Burckhardt conceived it, this approach required an understanding of art that could incorporate the relationship between the individual and art (aesthetic value) and its expression, through style.

But as the lectures on aesthetics reveal, "Kunstgeschichte nach Aufgaben" was much more than this. It was also Burckhardt's attempt to explain the motivating forces behind artistic creation – characterized by him as the *Kunsttrieb*, or artistic drive – by analyzing the historical origins and evolution of style and their individual forms over time. He sought to show how the *Kunsttrieb* was not necessarily a rational process, but rather a basic human instinct embodying the need to give expression to the beautiful and to the individual's freedom in relation to the external world. Art was the "second ideal creation", said Burckhardt, precisely

51 Meier, "Kunstgeschichte und Kulturgeschichte," 431–2.

because it recreated the world according to this relationship, thereby presenting an idealized image (a utopian vision) of what the world should be.

In a certain sense, Burckhardt's understanding of style is an expansion of Buffon's famous observation that "style is the man himself." It is not just the way one represents the world, it is the world itself. Proceeding from an aestheticist position in which no distinction is made between the aesthetic and the non-aesthetic, Burckhardt attributes metahistorical qualities to style and aesthetic value, his method was to illustrate how, like discourse, these two both encompass and inform the entire realm of human experience and how that experience is interpreted and represented. At the same time, Burckhardt averred, style and aesthetic value, like visual activity itself, are conditioned by history. They evolve over time and are responses to, and reflections of, political, socio-economic, and cultural circumstances. Burckhardt was too much of an historian to argue for the complete autonomy of art from historical developments. Indeed, his discussion of style reveals just how important he considered the historical evolution of style to be. The origins of style, its reflection of the monumental will of the artist and of the principal artistic tasks and endeavours of a given age, and the availability of material – all questions central to Burckhardt's project – could not possibly have been answered without some form of historical analysis. That Burckhardt did not consider art to be an independent power in his *Potenzenlehre*, instead subordinating it under state, religion, and culture, indicated, as well, the degree to which the development of style was influenced by historical events. Burckhardt's art-historical work consequently emphasized the integration of concrete social questions about the function of art with an analysis of the structural preconditions of social phenomena, such as language or ideology, that determined the artistic creation.

This can be seen especially in his work on the art of the Italian Renaissance, *Geschichte der Renaissance*, where Burckhardt discussed the broader cultural significance and historical context in which a style could evolve and in which a particular aesthetic value could be articulated. Themes that dominated his more famous cultural history found new expression in his work on Italian architecture. In particular, Burckhardt stressed how the individualism and ever-present quest for personal fame and glory of the *quattrocento* Italian defined the general terms of artistic production. In the new political circumstances of the Italian city-state, for example, patronage of the arts became almost obligatory, not just to express the splendour and honour of a ruler or state, but to create omnipotent symbols of political power and dynastic continuity. This required the evolution of new techniques and styles to meet the new demands; the conventional modes of artistic expression employed by medieval artists were no longer suitable. In the emerging modern world, the nature of the artistic *Aufgabe* became much more complex, reflecting changes at the political and social level. The artist was required to be much more versatile.[52]

Aesthetic value, the evolution of style, and the artistic *Aufgabe* therefore depended upon what might best be described as the general level of cultural literacy at any particular time. Burckhardt's opening statements in the "Einleitung in die Aesthetik" explicitly refer to the relationship between the cultured individual and the beautiful: "Aesthetics is the relationship of the cultured individual to art: a) to the beautiful in general; b) to artistic beauty in particular, and exists in a thousand forms like the inner nature of mankind and like art itself ... Sometimes it is mediated more, sometimes less by the study of history and by the general study of *Bildung*. The main thing is always the impact of the work of art on the individual, the arousal of an obliging imagination."[53] According to Burckhardt, what one perceived as beautiful was subject to external conditions such as the artist's skill, the level of technological development, the availability of material, or the general level of education and *Bildung* – all of which were continually in flux. The aesthetic value assigned to any particular object by the artist or the viewer was thus contingent upon external factors and accordingly firmly anchored within the historical world. Understanding the principles, or the nature of style, of any given period clearly required a thorough grounding in history, in the material conditions of artistic production, and in the attitudes and ideologies of the artists and patrons. This points to what may best be described as a post-Kantian aesthetic, one that rejects the idea of a universal, transcendant aesthetic value recognizable to all humans that "rises above the context of cultural and historical location, something that is a fixed and eternal constituent of the work of art, regardless of the circumstances in which it is placed."[54] As we have seen, Burckhardt refused to look for the "idea" behind an artwork. Art did express universal, transcendant values for him. But he located these values not in the

---

52 This work has been translated into English as *The Architecture of the Italian Renaissance*.
53 *Ästhetik der bildenden Kunst*, 35.
54 Moxey, *The Practice of Theory*, 68.

realm of beauty, but in art's utopian vision, in the instinctive desire, the elementary driving force to experience and create beauty, the *Kunsttrieb*.

Style, however, was inherently problematic for Burckhardt. Although he recognized that artistic form could not be reduced either to the material functions a given object or art was designed to fulfill, nor to the techniques employed in their production – he did not agree with his contemporary Gottfried Semper, who defined style as the "expression of the material treatment" – he was unwilling to privilege style to the same degree as the formalists. At the same time, he maintained that style could not simply be reduced to a function of history. Style is at once form and substance, he said; it is not just how the artist represents the world, but also how the artist expresses him or herself. Peter Gay has suggested that style is a centaur.[55] Half man, half beast, it is at once teasingly familiar, yet frustratingly foreign, and always mysterious. Although Burckhardt described the philosophy of history as a centaur, he too would have recognized the qualities of the centaur in the phenomenon of style. In contrast to Semper, Burckhardt maintained that style was "the means of expressing the beautiful." He described it as a language, a "language of form," or, in the context of architecture, a "structural expression ... that speaks as clearly as a language."[56] Or, one might even argue, as ambiguously as language. For Burckhardt, then, style demonstrated the ambivalence of language, its centaurian nature and metaphorical force, in its need to create analogies, to transform and modify initially mundane subject matter into something beautiful.

According to Burckhardt, the development of style was dependent upon three interrelated components: first, the "type of 'Aufgabe' the people set for itself"; second, the degree of "monumental will" the artistic task inspired in the artist; and finally, the available material and skill. These factors coalesced in the *Kunsttrieb*. Even the most primitive societies – primitive, at least, in Burckhardt's estimation – such as pre-Columbian societies of Central and South America, or Celtic society, could produce architecture that could arouse the spirit.[57] Burckhardt pointed to the artistic legacy of ancient Egypt as an outstanding example of how the monumental will of individuals and society could create a style that achieved the highest form of cultural and spiritual expression. However, the Greeks more than the Egyptians, he said, demonstrated

55 Gay, *Style in History*, 3.
56 *Ästhetik der bildenden Kunst*, 64.
57 Ibid., 35.

best how style could evolve through the principal task, or function, of the architecture. The Greek temple, built to honour the gods, became the primary form and inspiration for subsequent Greek architecture, whether houses or official buildings. As the expression of a "free monumental sense, without the slavery of symbols or tyrants," it became the purest and simplest of forms, existing in unprecedented harmony and balance as "the highest of organic styles; what is most astounding about the Greek temple is as much what is left out and avoided, than what is offered: the least and greatest in the least."[58] This form, Burckhardt argued, was not officially decreed; it had evolved and was maintained voluntarily "through free agreement … in times when one certainly could have done otherwise." Greek architecture consequently represented the highest level of "organic" style, he declared. Like Gothic architecture, which he also classified as organic, it had achieved the perfection of one specific architectural form – among the Greeks, the rectangular temple; in the Middle Ages, the multiple naved cathedral – which was logically designed to solve specific architectural problems and for specific cultural and social purposes.

In contrast to the organic style of ancient Greece and the Middle Ages, Burckhardt characterized Roman and Renaissance architecture as "spatial" in style, or *Raumstil*. Spatial style, he explained, rather than being dependent on one single "main task," was characterized by a diversity of styles and forms within the same "task," each an expression of a particular artistic school, element of cultural heritage, or artistic individuality. While spatial style did not produce original forms, it did perfect already existing forms through elaborate modification and decoration. Spatial style benefited art, Burckhardt wrote, through its versatility and diversity. Although the organic style could only achieve one particular objective, it did this to perfection.[59]

Unlike the primitive cultures, noted Burckhardt, it was possible with Greek and Roman art to penetrate more deeply the origins of the individual forms of the different styles, although this was difficult and complicated, like the study of language. It is precisely in the origins of these styles that external factors came into play. The will of the Romans or the Renaissance popes to create works of art to satisfy their lust for power and fame and symbolize their individuality, combined with the general *Kunsttrieb*, found ultimate expression in stylistic conquest, in the adapta-

58 Ibid., 39.
59 Ibid., 63–6.

tion and adoption of earlier styles and forms for new functions and purposes. For example, noted Burckhardt, the development in the Renaissance, but not in the Middle Ages, of a form of sculpture independent of architecture can be partially attributed to the changing conditions of artistic production, brought about in this particular instance by the emergence of humanism, individualism, and the rise of a class of wealthy patrons and contractors.

So even the most primitive of societies possessed an innate *Kunsttrieb*, and the level of its development and the forms it expressed were conditioned, learned, and cultivated. Burckhardt's expression of this driving force as a fiction, indeed, the "highest, most sovereign of fictions,"[60] acknowledged two fundamental elements of style. In the first place, Burckhardt recognized that style is a creative (fictional) process requiring the artist's active participation. Second, although it is a historical fact – in that it provides an understanding of the circumstances in which it evolved in any given time – style is a fiction, because it is a human construct. It is something created for its expressive purpose. It becomes, in Roland Barthes's sense of the word, a myth. Style, then, existed for Burckhardt only when a type was able to fulfill its prescribed function and gain general ascendancy, or hegemony, within a cultural sphere. When such a type formed "a general consensus on the truth and necessity of an architectural form of expression," then the style became hegemonic and established as the "truth."[61]

In other words, for Burckhardt, style can only come into being when it becomes the expression of a dominant cultural force or idea in society that possesses the power to transform the world in its image and to establish the means by which the world is read, interpreted, or experienced. But as such, style develops through its material expression a web of fictions, meanings, and myths. By focusing on the beautiful and its contingencies expressed in style, Burckhardt was going beyond the parameters of classical aesthetics, as expressed by Keats's famous line, "Beauty is truth, truth beauty." In effect, Burckhardt's primary concern was with the beautiful, rather than with the truth. "There will be no talk of the 'Idea' of the work of art," Burckhardt proclaimed, removing all doubt that, in his mind, art should work in the service of truth. He maintained that beauty in art could only be considered a vehicle of the truth insofar as its stylistic features gained general acceptance in society

60 Ibid., 67.
61 Ibid., 64.

through a sort of paradigmatic consensus. He argued that beauty in art is a myth in that this consensus changes and, like style itself, is a product of human creativity, an emplotment or grand narrative designed to order the world, but one which is always aware of its arbitrary and unnatural nature. Aesthetics, understood in this sense as the study of beauty, does not play a reconciling role between the subject and the object, between freedom and necessity, as it did for Friedrich Schiller. Burckhardt's starting point – *Anschauung* – implies, in the force of its subjective reflection, that no distinction is made between the subject and the object, between the aesthetic and the non-aesthetic. Thus if style is humankind itself, and the driving force behind style is the most sovereign of fictions, it is possible to argue that Burckhardt was in basic agreement with Nietzsche, who made no distinction between myth and truth.

. . .

There are certain problems involved in any evaluation of Burckhardt's important contributions to the study of art history, not the least of which are contextualization and the relationship of art history to cultural history in general. If we examine Burckhardt's art history within the broad parameters of his critique of modernity, it becomes clear that his attempt to develop an approach to art history that went beyond the confines of traditional contextualism represented his desire for intellectual and scholarly independence; his desire to go his own way as it were, and to remain a dilettante. More importantly, perhaps, it reflects his refusal to see art as a *fait accompli*, reduced to a confirmation of historical developments; an affirmation, in effect, of the existing social and political reality. Hence his fundamental disapproval of contemporary historical painting, which subordinated art and aesthetic value to politics, and his strong, almost instinctive desire to experience art, though "naive" observation, divorced from historical events and the inexorable processes of history.

Michael Ann Holly has suggested that Burckhardt's most famous work of art history, *Der Cicerone*, was a model of connoisseurship.[62] This is a novel interpretation. If by "connoisseurship" Holly means that the book

---

62 Holly, "Wölfflin and the Imagining of the Baroque," 1258.

is based on the scrutiny of the work of art as an object, it may be true, although this interpretation could be confused with Holly's definition of formalism. The *Cicerone,* after all, was designed as a guide book to the enjoyment of Italy's artistic treasures. On the whole, however, it is an inadequate, inaccurate characterization of this work in particular and of Burckhardt's art-historical endeavours in general. Perhaps Irmgard Siebert has a better appreciation of Burckhardt's first and most popular major work of art history when she argues that the *Cicerone* was an important transitional work for Burckhardt. With this book, she contends, Burckhardt began to distance himself from the more traditional approach practised by Kugler – which considered art history to be a branch of cultural history – and ordered the discussion more according to the work of art itself, that is according to "Aufgaben und Gattungen." In effect, Burckhardt's concern with the problems of artistic production, in addition to his analysis of the evolution of style and form, as seen in his introduction to his lecture on the aesthetics of architecture, moves him from the realm of pure connoisseurship – which he thought was often nothing more than an interest in curiosities[63] – into the more complex, varied world of formalist critical history of art.

But this interpretation is by no means unproblematic. Michael Podro has succinctly described the dilemma faced by critical historians of art in the nineteenth century: "Either the context-bound quality or the irreducibility of art may be elevated at the expense of the other. If a writer diminishes the sense of context in his concern for the irreducibility or autonomy of art, he moves towards formalism. If he diminishes the sense of the irreducibility in order to keep a firm hand on extra-artistic facts, he runs the risk of treating art as if it were the trace or symptom of those other facts. The critical historians were constantly treading a tightrope between the two."[64] The middle ground, then, was the safest place to be in this instance. Burckhardt seems to have appreciated this, as well as the difficulties that extreme formalism could present. To what extent he felt he was faced with an either/or choice between art *history* or *art* history, as Sitt's work on art criticism suggests, is not especially clear. There was much room for manoeuvre between the two poles. Burckhardt clearly envisioned a conception of art that would afford him the opportunity to examine the problems of style, but which at the same time would situate the work of art within an historical context. It might

63 "Über die Kunstgeschichte als Gegenstand eines akademischen Lehrstuhls," 26–7.
64 Podro, *The Critical Historians of Art,* xx.

be argued that Burckhardt's approach to style and form represented a crude reductionism, which holds that the style of a work of art reflects the consciousness or attitudes of an age and, therefore, eludes systematic interpretation. This could be the case if Burckhardt viewed art as a means of understanding the ideological superstructure. But Burckhardt's primary interest was always the "observation of the work of art." The art work itself remained the main object of his analysis and was not subordinated to history. In other words, in his understanding of the study of art, art was not viewed as an auxiliary to historical study, as Kugler maintained; rather art employed history as a means of gaining insight into the object of art itself. Although this approach did not lead to the complete autonomy of art, it did rescue art history from the narrow confines of both cultural history and speculative aesthetic theory.

Conclusion

PART OF THE HISTORIAN'S TASK is to seek origins and to trace influences; in short, to contextualize. Jacob Burckhardt is not a particularly easy figure to situate within the historiography or the cultural history of the nineteenth century. He was influenced by a wide range of people whose work reflected a variety of cultural traditions, trends, and circumstances. Consequently, those who attempt to sketch the origins of his work run the risk of inappropriately pigeonholing the Basel historian. How then does one define his position within nineteenth-century cultural history? On the one hand, German historians tend to place him within a broader German context, paying at worst only lip service to the fact that he was first and foremost a Basler. On the other hand, Swiss, in particular Basel, historians are faced with a paradoxical situation in that they want to acknowledge the unique influence of his Basel heritage while simultaneously preserving his position within a broader European (not exclusively German) cultural framework. They object, therefore, to an image of Burckhardt that minimizes his position in the cultural history of Basel, but they also tend to be uncomfortable with the argument that his Basel cultural heritage was unique and in any way outside the European intellectual mainstream.

This whole issue has become much more problematic since the writings of Lionel Gossman, who has consistently and persuasively portrayed the cultural elite of the Swiss city-republic as a centre of intellectual opposition to the dominant, imperialistic tendencies emanating from Berlin, the capital of the German Empire and, arguably, the major German-speaking intellectual centre in the second half of the nineteenth century. Of course, Basel shared with the rest of Europe the pains of industrialization and political modernization, but its experience of these processes was, to no uncertain degree, shaped and mitigated by the particular course of its historical development. It is, moreover, clear enough that Burckhardt did share some remarkable affinities with his compatriots Johann Jacob Bachofen; Franz Overbeck; and the sometime Basler, Friedrich Nietzsche. These thinkers did not constitute a Basel "school" of thought in the traditional sense and had, at best, only cordial relations with one another. But their shared ideals are more than coincidence; they are, in part, the result of a common cultural experience and of the particular historical circumstances in Europe and Basel in which they matured as thinkers. It is indeed possible to argue that just as Bachofen was the "anti-philologist"; Overbeck the "anti-theologian"; and Nietzsche the "anti-philosopher"; so too Burckhardt was the "anti-historian," because he rejected the dominant historiographical paradigm.

Although Burckhardt's immediate experience of political modernization in Basel may have shaped his understanding of modernity, his vision was much broader in scope, embracing the entirety of Western civilization. In this respect, Basel was a microcosm of what was transpiring in, and transforming, the nineteenth-century world as a whole. Although the particular circumstances and conditions of this social transformation may have differed from place to place, the process of political and economic modernization was a universal historical phenomenon that had an impact on every individual and which, consequently, had to be questioned and carefully analyzed. Of course, Burckhardt was not the only intellectual to view the century from the perspective of the problematic of crisis. Burckhardt's uniqueness, however, lies in the nature of his response as it emerged within the historical and cultural context in which he lived and worked.

While Burckhardt saw the beginnings of modernity in the history of Renaissance Italy, he identified its climax or crisis point as occurring during the French Revolution. Here, once and for all, the individual was cut off from the past and all restorations were more or less rendered futile. It was not just that traditional institutions and inherited world views were destroyed. For Burckhardt, the crisis ran much deeper. The French Revolution represented the ultimate victory of reason over aesthetic space: the triumph of rational, systematic thought over the sensual world of perception and instinct. The result was a concomitant collapse of meaningful experience in the present. The dynamic, but ultimately harmonious, relationship between the subject and the object that had characterized Renaissance genius was destroyed, replaced during the French Revolution by a new stance towards reality: the modern "objective consciousness." However, the ability to look at the world objectively, without preconceptions and without any sense of tradition, did not lead to the emancipation of the subject, as philosophers suggested, but to the alienation of the subject from the world of objective experience and the eventual enslavement of the subject. This can be seen at many levels. Witness, for instance, the attempt to rationalize the world of perception through the establishment of a philosophy of aesthetics; or more obviously, in the changed nature of relations of power and control in which the individual lost whatever self-control over his body he once might have had, and became increasingly managed by society. It can also be seen in the economic sphere, where the individual was abandoned to the antagonisms of market relations, and human creativity was incorporated into the price system.

Nowhere in the cultural realm was this disharmony more in evidence than in modern society's almost collective repudiation of idealism. In Burckhardt's thought, the struggle between the subjective and objective sides of human nature is perhaps best symbolized by the conflicting values represented by the dichotomous forces of realism and idealism, whether in his critique of the aesthetic preferences of the day, or in his understanding of history. The transition to realism, which began in Renaissance Italy, marked a revolution in the cultural history of the Western world, signalling the beginning of a process of rationalization that would fundamentally alter how the world was perceived. Burckhardt argued that, in contrast to Renaissance art, the art of the Middle Ages was characterized by idealism. Although the artistic "task" was relatively straightforward and sculpture and painting were employed as conventional modes of expression, Burckhardt claimed that medieval artists achieved organic perfection in their single task. As a consequence, he argued that medieval art, in its idealism, remained one of the most "beautiful witnesses" to the creative spirit of mankind. It represented art in an age of innocence and, as such, also possessed the "sweet dreams, the healthy, naive idealism of childhood."[1] In contrast, Burckhardt identified Renaissance art as characterized by the incorporation of realism, which transformed the nature of the artistic task and gave expression to the self-confidence of humanists in the present. Renaissance architecture, in a sense, became much more complicated because it "embraced several arts in the process of making prodigious advances

1 See "Über Murillo," in *Kunst der Betrachtung,* 116.

and encountering completely fresh problems."[2] For Burckhardt, idealism was never totally abandoned; in the very finest artistic achievements, it merged with realism in a glorious harmony. As Burckhardt stated, the objective and subjective sides merged in the Renaissance to form the spiritual individual.

For Burckhardt, however, realism came to dominate all forms of cultural expression in the nineteenth century. In an age of unprecedented public cultural literacy and participation, realism articulated the overwhelming confidence and optimism in reason, science and progress, practicality, and, by extension, faith in the cultural superiority of Western European civilization and its political and economic mission. This was evident not only in art and literature, both of which turned their backs on the idealism of classicism and the romantic movement, but, as we have seen, in the scholarly world as well. This last witnessed the corresponding emergence of a form of historical representation based on the goal of re-creation of "lifelike" authenticity and scientific objectivity.

Perhaps more than any other cultural artifact, the genre of history painting best articulated the aesthetic preferences of the nineteenth-century public. In its concern with factual accuracy, its desire to express great historical moments, as well as its openly didactic politicization, realism had found its most potent form of expression. However, according to Burckhardt at least, the overwhelming passion for realism came at a cost; in its name, idealism was sacrificed and the harmony that characterized the truly sublime spirit of individual creativity was lost. It is not surprising that Burckhardt characterized modern art as having lost its naïveté and its child-like innocence, and having become incapable of having a relationship to inner values.[3]

If we recognize the disunity of the modern individual, the problem becomes how to resolve this sense of crisis and re-establish the perception of unity. In effect, by doing nothing, we not only accept the state of crisis as permanent but also mystify and legitimize it. For a great number of intellectuals, the solution to the crisis of the modern individual was to be found in philosophy. In many respects, the goal of philosophy is to create a bridge between essence and experience, to overcome the ever-widening, threatening chasm between subjective and objective space. Remember, though, that Burckhardt, who as we have seen was hostile to philosophy and systematic thought in general, considered this an

2 *The Architecture of the Renaissance*, 13.
3 *Briefe*, 1:201; "Bericht über die Kunstausstellung zu Berlin," 3 January 1843.

inadequate solution because of its inherently artificial process. As he put it: in the guise of reason and logic, the ideal of philosophy was to reimpose the lost unity through theory and speculation, in effect bypassing altogether the irrational world of human instinct and perception.

Burckhardt would argue that, by their very nature, philosophy and systematic thought were unable to solve the crisis of modernity because, in creating a division between rational thought and experience (which is usually minimized or subordinated), they perpetuated still further the disunity and fragmentation of the subject and object. For him, the only effective solution, or resolution, to the crisis was to destroy all arbitrary barriers and distinctions, and to evolve a new discourse and means of looking at the world. Burckhardt achieved this by elevating the language of aesthetics – in conjunction with an ascetic lifestyle, represented in the ideal of *Bildung* – to the level of the primary structuring metaphor or narrative of existence. On the one hand, aesthetics and ascetics give Burckhardt the opportunity to "reunify" the realm of experience by denying, in effect, that anything exists outside of experience and primary perception. On the other hand, the dual forces of asceticism and aestheticism (temptation and transgression) open the way to clarification of the subject. Thus they enable Burckhardt not just to recognize the space between the subjective and the external world, but, simultaneously, to destroy this space. Mind you, to be aware of this process is in large part to become conscious of self.

Inasmuch as the poetics of the outsider and the ascetic permeated Burckhardt's life and work, it is important to note that purposeful withdrawal into a contemplative life can be as legitimate a response to crisis as rebellion, and as politically and ideologically motivated. To assume an aestheticist position is not to "de-politicize" or "de-ideologize" oneself or one's work, as Jörn Rüsen has suggested. Indeed, as Rüsen himself points out, Burckhardt's aesthetic act of historical observation and contemplation (*Anschauung*) is at its core a "process of *Bildung*" – a process of self-cultivation that is innately ideological;[4] a way of viewing and understanding the world that was conceived in practice, as in theory, as an alternative ideology to the Enlightenment ideal of practical, technical education. *Bildung*, an essentially aesthetic and ascetic understanding of the acquisition of knowledge, focused primarily on the re-establishment of meaningful experience. For Burckhardt, as for many others, this

---

4 See Rüsen, "Jacob Burckhardt: Political Standpoint and Historical Insight," and *Konfigurationen des Historismus*, 278.

highly individualistic notion of self-cultivation provided the ultimate refuge from the rationalistic ethos of the modern world.

But although Burckhardt did withdraw from active political involvement, it is questionable whether or not he withdrew from the "saeculum." As Harpham has pointed out, the learning, discipline, and culture of the secular ascetic is a highly public and civic practice. While Burckhardt may have fled to the south, he fled neither from life nor politics. Choosing to live in Basel and not Berlin – Burckhardt turned down numerous chairs of history in later life, not just in Berlin – does not mean that he somehow went underground, as Hayden White imagines. Moreover, just because he lived alone and did not publish much after 1860 does not mean he lived a secluded life and was "gratuitously medieval," even if this is some people's impression. He chose to stay in Basel because Basel was his *patria*, his home, and where he felt he belonged. That this was where his family and friends were, and that Burckhardt felt duty-bound to serve this city, its university, and its proud, independent cultural heritage, and not Berlin, the capital of a powerful, new Empire, is often ignored in the literature. That the university in Basel was struggling and the students were few in number in no way minimizes his contribution and his commitment to teaching and education, which would have been no more or less had he taught in Berlin or Göttingen. He continued to give public lectures at the university and the local academic society, which were always well attended, if not always well appreciated, well into old age, and even participated in the university administration when he was called upon to do so.

His dedication to *Bildung* and a rigid personal, spiritual, and intellectual discipline must be seen then as much as a response to crisis, as an attempt, in his own way, to confront crisis. Keeping modernity and the material world from diverting and subverting his energies and beliefs gave him the strength and the will to express in his work his dissatisfaction with the modern world, as well as his hopes for cultural renewal. In his work as both teacher and scholar, he participated in a critical dialogue with the past and the present so as to deconstruct modernity and the crisis of the modern world. Moreover, he expressed in his work a vision of history and of the world that, while in dissonance with the dominant perspectives of the nineteenth century, still celebrated life and the human spirit as embodied in human creativity and will; still attempted to overcome the spiritual alienation and fragmentation of the modern world; and still presented what might or could be. He may not have envisioned a reformist, progressive utopia, but his vision is pessimistic only from the perspective of those who hold tightly to the values he sought to expose. If the function of criticism is to demythologize the myths of modern society, then Burckhardt, from his self-imposed "Archimedean point outside events," was the arch-demythologizer who attempted to expose the unreality, conventionality, and contradictions of the bourgeois, liberal ethos. His ultimate goal was to find authentic experience (not reality), unmediated by conceptual thought and untainted by modern ideologies, as revealed directly through the sensual apparatus in all its possible initial distortions. Like someone observing the world for the first time, Burckhardt's approach to understanding the past signalled the recovery of primary irrationality. Through the phenomenon of *Anschauung* and the direct "observation of art" he hoped to demonstrate how art not only shapes but is the world.

Bibliography

BURCKHARDT: WORKS CITED

Aesthetik der bildenden Kunst. Irmgard Siebert, ed. Darmstadt: Wissenschaftliche Buchgesellschaft 1992.

The Age of Constantine the Great. New York: Dorset 1949.

"Aktenstücke zur Laufbahn Jacob Burckhardts." Paul Roth, ed. *BZfGA* 34 (1935): 5–106.

The Architecture of the Italian Renaissance. Peter Murray, ed. London: Secker and Warburg 1986.

Bemerkungen über schweizerische Kathedralen. Basel: Amerbach-Verlag 1946.

"Bericht über die Kunstaustellung zu Berlin im Herbste 1842." *Kunstblatt,* 1–4 and 20–3, (1843).

Briefe. 10 vols. Max Burckhardt, ed. Basel: Benno Schwabe 1949–86.

The Cicerone: An Art Guide to Painting in Italy. A.H.Clough, trans. New York: Charles Scribner's Sons 1908.

The Civilization of the Renaissance in Italy. Harmondsworth: Penguin Books 1990.

Ferien: Eine Herbstgabe. Basel: Benno Schwabe 1918.

Force and Freedom: Reflections on History. James Nichols, ed. New York: Pantheon Books 1943.

Gedichte. K.E. Hoffmann, ed. Basel: Benno Schwabe 1926.

Gesamtausgabe. 14 vols. Emil Dürr et al., eds. Basel: Benno Schwabe 1929–34.

The Greeks and Greek Civilization. Oswny Murray, ed., Sheila Stern, trans. New York: St. Martin's Press 1998.

Jacob Burckhardt als politischer Publizist. Emil Dürr, ed. Zürich: Fretz und Wasmuth 1937.

Jacob Burckhardt, Vorträge, 1844–1887, Emil Dürr, ed. Basel: Benno Schwabe 1918.

Jacob Burckhardts Vorlesung über die Geschichte des Revolutionszeitalters in den Nach-schriften seiner Zuhörer. Ernst Ziegler, ed. Basel: Schwabe & Co 1974.

Judgments on History and Historians. Harry Zohn, trans. Boston: Beacon Press 1958.

Die Kunst der Betrachtung: Aufsätze und Vorträge zur bildenden Kunst. Henning Ritter, ed. Cologne: Dumont 1984.

Reisebilder aus dem Süden. Werner von der Schulenburg, ed. Heidelberg: Niels Kampmann Verlag 1928.

Über das Studium der Geschichte: Der Text der Weltgeschichtlichen Betrachtungen. Peter Ganz, ed. Munich: Beck Verlag 1982.

Unbekannte Aufsätze Jacob Burckhardts aus Paris, Mailand und Rom. Josef Oswald, ed. Basel: Benno Schwabe 1922.

SECONDARY SOURCES

Angermeier, Heinz. "Ranke and Burckhardt." *AfKg* 62 (1987): 407–52.

Ankersmit, F.R. "Historical Representation." HT 27 (1988): 205–28.

– "Historiography and Postmodernism." HT 28 (1989): 137–53.

– "The Meaning of Historicism." HT 34 (1995): 143–61.

Applegate, Celia. *A Nation of Provincials: The German Idea of Heimat.* Los Angeles: University of California Press 1990.

Ashton, Rosemary. *Little Germany: German Refugees in Victorian Britain.* Oxford: Oxford University Press 1986.

Bann, Stephen. *The Clothing of Clio.* Cambridge: Cambridge University Press 1984.

– *The Inventions of History.* Manchester: Manchester University Press 1990.

Barclay, David E. *Frederick William IV and the Prussian Monarchy, 1840–1861.* Oxford: Clarendon Press 1995.

Berchtold, Alfred. *Bâle et l'Europe.* 2 vols. Lausanne: Editions Payot 1990.

Berger, Klaus. "Jacob Burckhardt as an Art Historian." In *Jacob Burckhardt and the Renaissance 100 Years After,* 38–44. Lawrence, Kans.: Miscellaneous Publications of the Museum of Art, University of Kansas 1960.

Biaudet, Jean-Charles. "Der modernen Schweiz entgegen." In *Handbuch der Schweizer Geschichte,* vol. 2, 871–986. Zürich: Verlag Berichthaus 1977.

Bietenholz, Peter G. *Basle and France in the Sixteenth Century.* Geneva: Librarie Droz 1971.

Blanke, Horst-Walter. *Historiographiegeschichte als Historik.* Stuttgart: Fromann-Holzboog 1991.

– and Dirk Fleischer, eds. *Theoretiker der deutschen Aufklärungshistorie.* 2 vols. Stuttgart: Fromann-Holzboog 1990.

– and Jörn Rüsen, eds. *Von der Aufklärung zum Historismus: Zum Strukturwandel des historischen Denkens.* Paderborn: Ferdinand Schöningh 1984.

Bödeker, Hans-Erich, Georg G. Iggers, Jonathan B. Knudson, and Peter H. Reill, eds. *Aufklärung und Geschichte: Studien zur deutschen Geschichtswissenschaft im 18. Jahrhundert.* Göttingen: Vandenhoeck & Ruprecht 1986.

Boerlin-Brodbeck, Yvonne. "Jacob Burckhardts römische Skizzenbücher." In *Jacob Burckhardt und Rom,* edited by Hans-Markus von Kaenel, 57–68. Zürich: Schweizerisches Institut in Rom 1988.

– ed. *Die Skizzenbücher Jacob Burckhardts.* (Beiträge zu Jacob Burckhardt, Bd. II). Basel: Schwabe 1994.

Bollert, Martin. *Gottfried Kinkels Kämpfe um Beruf und Weltanschauung bis zur Revolution.* Bonn: A. Marcus & E. Weber 1913.

Bonjour, Edgar. *Die Universität Basel: Von den Anfängen bis zur Gegenwart, 1460–1960.* Basel: Helbing & Lichtenhahn 1971.

Brady, Thomas A. *Turning Swiss: Cities and Empire, 1450–1550.* Cambridge (UK): Cambridge University Press 1985.

Brennan, B. "Burckhardt and Ranke on the Age of Constantine the Great." *Quaderni di Storia* 21 (1995): 53–65.

Brockhaus Conversations-Lexikon. 9ᵗʰ ed, vol 8. Leipzig, 1845.

Bruford, W.H. *The German Tradition of Self-Cultivation: Bildung from Humboldt to Thomas Mann.* Cambridge (UK): Cambridge University Press 1975.

Bucher, Erwin. *Die Geschichte des Sonderbundkrieges.* Zürich: Verlag Berichthaus 1966.

Burckhardt, Max. "Jacob Burckhardt als Zeichner." *Librarium* 20 (1977): 2–21.

– "Politische, soziale und kirchliche Spannungen in Basel um 1870." In *Franz Overbecks unerledigte Anfragen an das Christentum,* edited by R. Brändle and E.W. Stegemann, 47–66. Munich: Kaiser Verlag 1988.

– "Rom als Erlebnis und geschichtliches thema bei Jacob Burckhardt." In *Jacob Burckhardt und Rom,* edited by Hans-Markus von Kaenel. Zürich: Schweizerisches Institut in Rom 1988, 7–18.

– ed. "Rom 1848: Berichte von Jacob Burckhardt." *Corona* 9 (1939): 105–27 and 207–34.

Burckhardt, Paul. *Geschichte der Stadt Basel von der Zeit der Reformation bis zur Gegenwart.* Basel: Helbing & Lichtenhahn 1942.

Büttner, Frank. "Bildung des Volkes durch Geschichte. Zu den Anfängen öffentlicher Geschichtsmalerei in Deutschland." In *Historienmalerei in Europa,* edited by Ekkehard Mai, 77–94. Mainz: Philipp von Zabern 1990.

Canaday, John. *Mainstreams of Modern Art.* New York: Holt, Rinehard & Winston 1981.

Carrard, Philippe. *Poetics of the New History.* Baltimore: Johns Hopkins University Press 1992.

Chickering, Roger. *Karl Lamprecht: A German Academic Life (1856–1915)*. Atlantic Highlands: Humanities Press 1993.

Cornelius, Max, ed. *Heinrich von Treitschkes Briefe*. Leipzig: Hirzel 1912.

Craig, Gordon A. *The Triumph of Liberalism: Zürich in the Golden Age*. New York: Collier Books 1988.

De Jonge, Alfred R. *Gottfried Kinkel as Political and Social Thinker*. Reprint. NY: AMS Press 1966.

Dickens, Charles. *Hard Times*. Harmondsworth: Penguin Books 1969.

Dilly, Heinrich and James Ryding. "Kulturgeschichtsschreibung vor und nach der bürgerlichen Revolution von 1848." *Aesthetik und Kommunikation* 6 (1975): 15–32.

Dilthey, Wilhelm. *Gesammelte Schriften*. Leipzig: Teubner 1936.

Droysen, Johann Gustav. "Outline of the Principles of History." In *German Essays on History*, edited by Rolf Sälzer. New York: Continuum 1991.

– *Texte zur Geschichtstheorie*, edited by Günter Birtsch and Jörn Rüsen. Göttingen: Vandenhoek & Ruprecht 1972.

Dürr, Emil. "Das eidgenössische Schützenfest von 1844 in Basel in der Beurteilung Jeremias Gotthelfs, Jacob Burckhardts und Gottfried Kellers." *Neue Schweizer Rundschau* (Oct and Nov 1937): 329–49 and 411–28.

– *Freiheit und Macht bei Jacob Burckhardt*. Basel: Helbing & Lichtenhahn 1918.

Eagleton, Terry. *The Ideology of the Aesthetic*. Oxford: Basil Blackwell 1990.

Epstein, Klaus. *The Genesis of German Conservatism*. Princeton: Princeton University Press 1966.

Ermarth, Michael. "Hermeneutics and History: The Fork in Hermes' Path through the Eighteenth Century." In *Aufklärung und Geschichte: Studien zur deutschen Geschichtswissenschaft im 18. Jahrhundert*, edited by Hans-Erich Bödeker, Georg G. Iggers et al. Göttingen: Vandenhoek & Ruprecht 1986.

Flaig, Egon. *Angeschaute Geschichte: Zu Jacob Burckhardts Griechische Kulturgeschichte*. Rheinfelden: Schäuble Verlag 1987.

– "Ästhetischer Historismus? Zur Ästhetisierung der Historie bei Humboldt und Burckhardt." *Philosophisches Jahrbuch* 94 (1987): 79–95.

Förster, Ernst. "Englische und französische Stimmen über deutsche Kunst." *Kunstblatt*, 2 February 1843.

Foucault, Michel. *The Foucault Reader*, edited by Paul Rabinow. New York: Pantheon 1984.

– *The Order of Things*. New York: Vintage Books 1970.

Fuchs, Eckhardt. *Henry Thomas Buckle: Geschichtsschreibung und Positivismus in England und Deutschland*. Leipzig: Leipziger Universitätsverlag 1994.

Gagel, Hanna. "Die Düsseldorfer Malerschule in der politischen Situation des Vormärz und 1848." In *Die Düsseldorfer Malerschule*, edited by Wend von Kalnein, 68–85. Mainz: Philipp von Zabern 1979.

Gantner, Joseph. "Der Unterricht in Kunstgeschichte an der Universität Basel 1844–1938." In *Kunstwissenschaft an Schweizer Hochschulen*, 9–32. Jahrbuch: Schweizerisches Institut für Kunstwissenschaft 1972–73.

– ed. *Jacob Burckhardt und Heinrich Wölfflin: Briefwechsel und andere Dokumente ihrer Begegnung*. Basel: Benno Schwabe 1948.

Ganz, Peter. "Jacob Burckhardt und die Universität." *Oxford German Studies* 17 (1988): 51–71.

– "Jacob Burckhardt: Wissenschaft – Geschichte – Literatur." In *Umgang mit Jacob Burckhardt*, edited by Hans R. Guggisberg. 11–35. Basel: Schwabe & Co. 1994.

– "Jacob Burckhardts Kultur der Renaissance in Italien und die Kunstgeschichte." *Saeculum* 40 (1989): 193–212.

– "Jacob Burckhardts *Kultur der Renaissance in Italien*: Handwerk und Methode." DVLG (1988): 24–59.

Gass, Alfred Lukas. *Die Dichtung im Leben und Werk Jacob Burckhardts*. Bern: Franke Verlag 1967.

Gay, Peter. "Burckhardt's *Renaissance*: Between Responsibility and Power." In *The Responsibility of Power*, edited by Leonard Krieger and Fritz Stern, 198–214. New York: Doubleday 1969.

– *Style in History*. New York: Norton 1974.

Geertz, Clifford. *The Interpretation of Cultures*. New York: Basic Books 1973.

Gelzer, Urs. *Beziehungen Basels zur Innerschweiz während der Regenerationszeit 1830–1848*. Basel: Helbing & Lichtenhahn 1957.

Gilbert, Felix. *History: Politics or Culture? Reflections on Ranke and Burckhardt*. Princeton: Princeton University Press 1990.

– "Jacob Burckhardt's Student Years: The Road to Cultural History." JHI 47 (1986): 249–74.

Gilbert, William. "Burckhardt and Italy: The 'Inner Necessity'." In *Jacob Burckhardt and the Renaissance 100 Years After*, 29–36. Lawrence, Kans.: Miscellaneous Publications of the Museum of Art, University of Kansas, 1960.

Gombrich, E.H. *In Search of Cultural History*. Oxford: Clarendon Press 1969.

Gossman, Lionel. "Antimodernism in Nineteenth-Century Basel: Franz Overbeck's Antitheology and J.J. Bachofen's Antiphilology." *Interpretation* 16 (1989): 359–89.

– "Basel." In *Geneva, Zurich, Basel: History, Culture, and National Identity*, edited by Nicolas Bouvier. Princeton: Princeton University Press 1994.

– "Basle, Bachofen and the Critique of Modernity in the Second Half of the Nineteenth Century." *Journal of the Warburg and Courtauld Institutes* 47 (1984): 136–85.

– *Between History and Literature*. Cambridge, Mass.: Harvard University Press 1990.

– "The Boundaries of the City: A Nineteenth-Century Essay on 'The Limits of Historical Knowledge'." HT 25 (1986): 33–51.

- "Cultural History and Crisis: Burckhardt's *Civilization of the Renaissance in Italy.*" In *Rediscovering History: Culture, Politics, and the Psyche,* edited by Michael S. Roth. Stanford: Stanford University Press 1994.
- "Jacob Burckhardt as Art Historian." *Oxford Art Journal* 11 (1988): 25–32.
- *Orpheus Philologus: Bachofen versus Mommsen on the Study of Antiquity.* Philadelphia: Transactions of the American Philosophical Society, vol. 73, 1983.
- "The 'Two Cultures' in Nineteenth-Century Basle: between the French '*Encyclopédie*' and German Neohumanism." JES 20 (1990): 95–133.

Gothein, Eberhard. *Die Aufgaben der Culturgeschichte.* Leipzig: Duncker & Humblot 1889.

Grew, Raymond. "Picturing the People: Images of the Lower Orders in Nineteenth-Century French Art." In *Art and History,* edited by Robert I. Rotberg and Theodore K. Rabb, 203–32. Cambridge (UK): Cambridge University Press 1986.

Gross, David. "Jacob Burckhardt and the Critique of Mass Society." *European Studies Review* 8 (1978): 393–410.

Großmann, Joachim. "Verloste Kunst: Deutsche Kunstvereine im 19. Jahrhundert." *AfKg* 76 (1994): 351–64.

Gruner, Erich. "Die Schweizerische Eidgenossenschaft von der Französische Revolution bis zur Reform der Verfassung (1789 bis 1874)." In *Geschichte der Schweiz,* edited by Hans von Greyerz, Erich Gruner et al., 112–37. Munich: DTV 1987.

Guggisberg, Hans R. *Basel in the Sixteenth Century.* St. Louis: Center for Reformation Research 1982.

Habermas, Jürgen. *The Philosophical Discourse of Modernity,* translated by Frederick G. Lawrence. Cambridge, Mass.: The MIT Press 1987.

Hardtwig, Wolfgang. *Geschichtskultur und Wissenschaft.* Munich: DTV 1990.
- *Geschichtsschreibung zwischen Alteuropa und moderner Welt: Jacob Burckhardt in seiner Zeit.* Göttingen: Vandenhoek & Ruprecht 1974.

Harpham, Geoffrey Galt. *The Ascetic Imperative in Culture and Criticism.* Chicago: University of Chicago Press 1987.

Harrington, Anne. *Reenchanted Science: Holism in German Culture from Wilhelm II to Hitler.* Princeton: Princeton University Press 1996.

Hartmann, Volker. "Die deutsche Kulturgeschichtsschreibung von ihren Anfängen bis Wilhelm Heinrich Riehl." Ph.D. thesis, University of Marburg, 1971.

Heftrich, Eckhard. *Hegel und Jacob Burckhardt: Zur Krisis der geschichtlichen Bewußtseins.* Frankfurt am Main: Vittorio Klostermann 1967.

Heller, Erich. *The Disinherited Mind.* New York: Meridian Books 1959.

Herf, Jeffrey. *Reactionary Modernism: Technology, Culture, and Politics in Weimar and the Third Reich.* Cambridge: Cambridge University Press 1984.

Herkless, J.L. "Meinecke and the Ranke-Burckhardt Problem." HT 9 (1970): 290–321.

Hinde, John R. "The Development of Jacob Burckhardt's Political Thought." JHI 53 (1992): 425–36.

– "Jacob Burckhardt and Nineteenth-Century Realist Art." JES 27 (1997): 433–55.

– "Jacob Burckhardt and the Art of History." *SdS* 30 (1996): 107–23.

Hofmann, Hasso. "Jacob Burckhardt und Friedrich Nietzsche als Kritiker des Bismarckreiches." *Der Staat* 10 (1971): 433–53.

Hoffmann, K.E. *Jacob Burckhardt als Dichter.* Basel: Helbing & Lichtenhahn 1918.

Holly, Michael Ann. "Burckhardt and the Ideology of the Past." *History of the Human Sciences* 1 (1988): 47–73.

– *Panofsky and the Foundations of Art History.* Ithaca, NY: Cornell University Press 1984.

– "Wölfflin and the Imagining of the Baroque." In *Europäische Barock-Rezeption,* edited by Klaus Garber, 1255–64. Wiesbaden: Otto Harrassowitz 1991.

Hooper, John. "Changing Perceptions of Jules Michelet as Historian: History between Literature and Science, 1831–1874." JES 23 (1993): 283–98.

Howard, Thomas A. "Historicist Thought in the Shadow of Theology: W.M.L. De Wette, Jacob Burckhardt, and the Shaping of Nineteenth-Century Historical Consciousness." Ph.D. thesis, University of Virginia, 1996.

Humboldt, Wilhelm von. *Schriften zur Anthropologie und Bildungslehre,* edited by Andreas Flitner. Frankfurt am Main: Ullstein 1984.

Hurtado, Shannon H. "The Promotion of the Visual Arts in Britain, 1835–1860." *Canadian Journal of History* 28 (1993): 59–80.

Huse, Norbert. "Anmerkungen zu Burckhardts 'Kunstgeschichte nach Aufgaben'." In *Festschrift Wolfgang Braunfels,* edited by Friedrich Piel and Jörg Traeger, 157–66. Tübingen: Wasmuth 1977.

Iggers, Georg G. "Comments on F.R. Ankersmit's Paper, 'Historicism: an Attempt at Synthesis'," HT 34 (1995): 162–8.

– *The German Conception of History.* Rev. ed. Middletown, Conn.: Wesleyan University Press 1983.

– *Geschichtswissenschaft im 20. Jahrhundert.* Göttingen: Vandenhoek und Ruprecht 1993.

– "Historicism: The History and Meaning of the Term." JHI 56 (1995): 129–52.

– *New Directions in European Historiography.* Rev. ed. Middletown, Conn.: Wesleyan University Press 1984.

– "Der Programm einer Strukturgeschichte des historischen Denkens. Anmerkungen zu H. W. Blanke." In *Geschichtsdiskurs, Bd. I, Methoden der Historiographiegeschichte,* edited by Wolfgang Küttler, Jörn Rüsen and Ernst Schulin, 331–5. Frankfurt/M.: Fischer Verlag 1993.

- "The University of Göttingen, 1760–1800, and the Transformation of Historical Scholarship." *SdS* 2 (1982): 11–37

Im Hof, Ulrich. *Aufklärung in der Schweiz.* Bern: Francke Verlag 1970.

- *Isaak Iselin: Sein Leben und die Entwicklung seines Denkens bis zur Abfassung der "Geschichte der Menschheit" von 1764.* 2 vols. Basel: Benno Schwabe 1947.
- *Isaak Iselin und die Spätaufklärung, 1764–1782.* Bern: Francke Verlag 1967.

Jaeger, Friedrich. *Bürgerliche Modernisierungskrise und historische Sinnbildung: Kulturgeschichte bei Droysen, Burckhardt und Max Weber.* Göttingen: Vandenhoek & Ruprecht 1994.

Jaeger, Friedrich and Jörn Rüsen. *Geschichte des Historismus.* Munich: C.H. Beck Verlag 1992.

Jähnig, Dieter. "Jacob Burckhardts Bedeutung für die Ästhetik." DVLG 53 (1979): 173–90.

- "Kunst-Erkenntnis bei Jacob Burckhardt." DVLG 58 (1984): 16–37.

Jarausch, Konrad. "The Institutionalization of History in 18th-Century Germany." In *Aufklärung und Geschichte: Studien zur deutschen Geschichtswissenschaft im 18. Jahrhundert,* edited by Hans-Erich Bödeker, Georg G. Iggers, Jonathan B. Knudson, and Peter H. Reill, 25–48. Göttingen: Vandenhoek & Ruprecht 1986.

Jenderko-Sichelschmidt, Ingrid. "Die profane Historienmalerei, 1826–1860." In *Die Düsseldorfer Malerschule,* edited by Wend von Kalnein. Mainz: Philipp von Zabern 1979.

Jodl, Friedrich. *Die Culturgeschichtsschreibung: ihre Entwicklung und ihr Problem.* Halle, n.p. 1878.

Kaegi, Werner. *Europäische Horizonte im Denken Jacob Burckhardts.* Basel: Benno Schwabe 1961.

- *Historische Meditationen.* Zürich: Fretz & Wasmuth 1946.
- "Die Idee der Vergänglichkeit in der Jugendgeschichte Jacob Burckhardts." *BZfGA* 42 (1942): 209–43.
- *Jacob Burckhardt: Eine Biographie.* 7 vols. Basel: Benno Schwabe 1947–82.

Kahan, Alan S. *Aristocratic Liberalism: The Social and Political Thought of Jacob Burckhardt, John Stuart Mill, and Alexis de Tocqueville.* New York: Oxford University Press 1992.

Kaphahn, Fritz. "Jacob Burckhardts Neubearbeitung von Kuglers Malereigeschichte." HZ 166 (1942): 24–56.

Karge, Henrik. "'Die Kunst ist nicht das Maaß der Geschichte'." *AfKg* 78 (1996): 393–431.

Kelley, Donald R. *Foundations of Modern Historical Scholarship: Language, Law, and History in the French Renaissance.* New York: Columbia University Press 1970.

Kemal, Salim and Ivan Gaskill, eds. *The Language of Art History.* Cambridge: Cambridge University Press 1991.

Kerrigan, William and Gordon Braden. *The Idea of the Renaissance.* Baltimore: Johns Hopkins University Press 1989.

Kinkel, Gottfried. *Selbstbiographie, 1838–1848,* edited by Richard Sander Bonn: Cohen 1931.

Koschnick, Leonore. "Franz Kugler 1808–1858 als Kunstkritiker und Kulturpolitiker." Ph.D. thesis, University of Berlin, 1983.

Krieger, Leonard. *Ranke: The Meaning of History.* Chicago: University of Chicago Press 1977.

Kugler, Franz. "Der Dom zu Köln und seine Architektur." *Deutsche Vierteljahrsschrift* 1842.

– *Handbuch der Geschichte der Malerei.* Berlin: Duncker & Humblot 1837.

– *Handbuch der Kunstgeschichte.* Stuttgart: Ebner und Seubert 1848.

– *Kleine Schriften und Studien zur Kunstgeschichte.* Stuttgart: Ebner und Seubert 1853.

– "Neues aus Berlin," *Kunstblatt,* 25 July 1843.

– "Sendschreiben an Herrn Dr. Ernst Förster in München." *Kunstblatt,* 20 July 1843.

LaCapra, Dominick. *History and Criticism.* Ithaca: Cornell University Press 1985.

La Vopa, Anthony J. *Grace, Talent, and Merit.* Cambridge (UK): Cambridge University Press 1988.

Löwith, Karl. *Jacob Burckhardt: Der Mensch inmitten der Geschichte.* Lucerne: Vita Nova Verlag 1936.

– *Meaning in History.* Chicago: University of Chicago Press 1949.

Maclean, Michael J. "Johann Gustav Droysen and the Development of Historical Hermeneutics." HT 21 (1982): 347–65.

Mah, Harold. *The End of Philosophy and the Origin of "Ideology": Karl Marx and the Crisis of the Young Hegelians.* Berkeley: University of California Press 1987.

– "Suppressing the Text: The Metaphysics of Ethnographic History in Darnton's Great Cat Massacre." *History Workshop Journal* 31 (1991): 1-20.

Mai, Ekkehard. "Die Düsseldorfer Malerschule und die Malerei des 19. Jahrhunderts." In *Die Düsseldorfer Malerschule,* edited by Wend von Kalnein. Mainz: Philipp von Zabern 1979.

Maikuma, Yoshihiko. *Der Begriff der Kultur bei Warburg, Nietzsche und Burckhardt.* Königstein/Ts.: Hain bei Athenäum 1985.

Mali, Joseph. "Jacob Burckhardt: Myth, History and Mythistory." *History and Memory* 3 (1991): 86–118.

Mannheim, Karl. *Essays on the Sociology of Knowledge.* New York: Oxford University Press 1952.

Martin, Alfred von. *Nietzsche und Burckhardt: Zwei geistige Welten im Dialog.* Munich: Erasmus-Verlag, 1947.

– *Die Religion Jacob Burckhardts.* Munich: Erasmus-Verlag 1947.

Marx, Karl and Friedrich Engels. *The Communist Manifesto.* Harmondsworth: Penguin Books 1967.

Maurer, Emil. *Jacob Burckhardt und Rubens.* Basel: Birkhäuser 1951.

Megill, Allan. *Prophets of Extremity: Nietzsche, Heidegger, Foucault, Derrida.* Berkeley: University of California Press 1987.

– "Recounting the Past: 'Description', Explanation, and Narrative in Historiography." AHR 94 (1989): 627–53.

Meier, Nikolaus. "'Aber ist es nicht eine herrliche Sache, für ein Volk zu meisseln, das auch das Kühnste für wirklich hält?' Zum Italienerlebnis Jacob Burckhardts." In *Jacob Burckhardt und Rom,* edited by Hans-Markus von Kaenel, 33–56. Zürich: Schweizerisches Institut in Rom, 1988.

– "Die Basler Münsterscheiben: Zur Geschmacksgeschichte des 19. Jahrhunderts." *BZfGA* 89 (1989): 165–211.

– *Emilie Linder und Jacob Burckhardt.* Basel: Schwabe 1998.

– "Kunstgeschichte und Kulturgeschichte oder Kunstgeschichte nach Aufgaben." In *Kunst und Kunsttheorie: 1400–1900* (Wolfenbütteler Forschungen, Bd. 48), edited by Peter Ganz, Nikolaus Meier et al. Wiesbaden: Otto Harrassowitz 1991.

– "Wilhelm Lübke, Jacob Burckhardt und die Architektur der Renaissance." *BZfGA* 85 (1985): 151–212.

– "Zu Jacob Burckhardt und Friedrich Nietzsche: Ein Stück spekulativer Quellenkritik." *BZfGA* 81 (1981): 97–117.

Meinecke, Friedrich. *Werke.* Munich: Oldenbourg 1958-69.

Mommsen, Wolfgang J. "Jacob Burckhardt – Defender of Culture and Prophet of Doom." *Government and Opposition* 18 (1983): 458–75.

Moxey, Keith. *The Practice of Theory: Poststructuralism, Cultural Politics, and Art History.* Ithaca: Cornell University Press 1994.

Muhlack, Ulrich. *Geschichtswissenschaft im Humanismus und in der Aufklärung.* Munich: C.H. Beck Verlag 1991.

Mullen, Walter L. "Jacob Burckhardt, the Historian as Analyst of His Age." *Swiss American Historical Society Newsletter* 16 (1980): 6–36.

Novick, Peter. *That Noble Dream: The 'Objectivity Question' and the American Historical Profession.* Cambridge (UK): Cambridge University Press 1988.

Nurdin, Jean. "Jakob Burckhardt et le refus de la modernité." *Revue d'allemagne* 14 (1982): 88–96.

O'Brien, Charles H. "Jacob Burckhardt: The Historian as Socratic Humanist." *The Journal of Thought* 16 (1981): 51–73.

Oeri-Schenk, Heinrich and Max Burckhardt. "Aus Jacob Burckhardts Jugendzeit: Ein Nachtrag zu seiner Bildungsgeschichte." *BZfGA* 82 (1982): 97–146.

Oettinger, Klaus. "Poesie und Geschichte: Bemerkungen zur Geschichtsschreibung Jacob Burckhardts." *AfKg* 51 (1969): 160–74.

Oexle, Otto Gerhard. "Die Geschichtswissenschaft im Zeichen des Historismus," HZ 238 (1984): 17–55.

– "'Historismus:' Überlegungen zur Geschichte des Phänomens und des Begriffs," *Jahrbuch der Braunschweigische wissenschaftliche Gesellschaft* (1986): 119–55.

Paret, Peter. *Art as History: Episodes in the Culture and Politics of Nineteenth-Century Germany*. Princeton: Princeton University Press 1988.

Pochat, Götz. "Friedrich Theodor Vischer und die zeitgenössische Kunst." In *Ideengeschichte und Kunstwissenschaft im Kaiserreich*, edited by Ekkehard Mai, Stephen Waetzoldt et al., 99–131. Berlin: Mann Verlag 1983.

Podro, Michael. *The Critical Historians of Art*. New Haven: Yale University Press 1982.

Pomata, Gianna. "Versions of Narrative: Overt and Covert Narrators in Nineteenth-Century Historiography," *History Workshop Journal*, 28 (1989): 1–17.

Preziosi, Donald. *Rethinking Art History: Mediations on a Coy Science*. New Haven: Yale University Press 1989.

Ranke, Leopold von. *The Theory and Practice of History*, edited by Georg G. Iggers and Konrad von Moltke. New York: Bobbs-Merrill 1973.

Rappard, W.E. *La constitution fédérale de la Suisse, 1848–1948*. Neuchâtel: La Baconnière 1948.

Rehm, Walter. "Jacob Burckhardts Mitarbeit am Konversationslexikon." *AfKg* 30 (1940): 106–41.

– "Jacob Burckhardt und Franz Kugler." *BZfGA* 41–42 (1942–43): 151–252.

– ed. "Kunstgeschichtliche Betrachtungen von Jacob Burckhardt," *Corona* 10 (1940): 96–112 and 212–23.

Reill, Peter H. *The German Enlightenment and the Rise of Historicism*. Berkeley: University of California Press 1975.

Remak, Joachim. *A Very Civil War: The Swiss Sonderbund War of 1847*. San Francisco: Westview Press 1993.

Reszler, André. "Les premiers critiques de la modernité (Tocqueville, Proudhon, Burckhardt, Nietzsche)." *L'Europe en Formation*, 15 (1974): 18–24.

Rieke, Robert William. *Heinrich Schreiber, 1793–1872*. Freiburg im Breisgau: Verlag Eberhard Albert Universitätsbuchhandlung 1956.

Ringer, Fritz. *The Decline of the German Mandarins: The German Academic Community, 1890–1933*. Cambridge, Mass.: Harvard University Press 1969.

– *Fields of Knowledge: French Academic Culture in Comparative Perspective, 1890–1920.* Cambridge (UK): Cambridge University Press 1992.

Roth, Dorothea. *Die Politik der Liberal-Konservativen in Basel, 1875–1914.* 167. Basel: Neujahrsblatt der Gesellschaft für das Gute und Gemeinnützige 1988.

– "Zur Vorgeschichte der liberal-konservativen Partei in Basel, 1846–1874." *BZfGA* 68 (1968) 171–221.

Röthlin, Niklaus. "Burckhardts Stellung in der Kulturgeschichtsschreibung des 19. Jahrhunderts." *AfKg* 69 (1987): 389–406.

Rüsen, Jörn. "Jacob Burckhardt: Political Standpoint and Historical Insight on the Border of Post-Modernism." HT 24 (1985): 235–46.

– *Konfigurationen des Historismus: Studien zur deutschen Wissenschaftskultur.* Frankfurt am Main: Suhrkamp 1993.

– "Rhetoric and Aesthetics of History: Leopold von Ranke." HT 29 (1990): 190–204.

– *Zeit und Sinn: Strategien historischen Denkens.* Frankfurt am Main: Fischer Verlag 1990.

Sältzer, Rolf, ed. *German Essays in History.* New York: Continuum 1991.

Sarasin, Philipp. "Basel – Zur Sozialgeschichte der Stadt Bachofens." In *Johann Jakob Bachofen (1815–1887): Eine Begleitpublikation zur Ausstellung im Historischen Museum Basel 1987,* 28–40. Basel: Historisches Museum 1988.

– "Domination, Gender Difference and National Myths: The Discursive Structure of Bourgeois Identity in the Basel Pageant of 1892." *German History* 14 (1996): 141–67.

– "Sittlichkeit, Nationalgefühl und frühe Ängste vor dem Proletariat: Untersuchungen zu Politik, Weltanschauung und Ideologie des Basler Bürgertums in der Verfassungskrise von 1846/47." *BZfGA* 84 (1984): 51–126.

– *Stadt der Bürger: Struktureller Wandel und bürgerliche Lebenswelt, Basel 1870–1900.* Basel: Helbing und Lichtenhahn 1990.

Sax, Benjamin C. "Jacob Burckhardt and National History." *History of European Ideas* 15 (1992): 845–50.

– "State and Culture in the Thought of Jacob Burckhardt." *Annals of Scholarship* 3 (1985): 1–35.

Schäfer, Dietrich. *Das eigentliche Arbeitsgebiet der Geschichte.* Jena: Fischer 1888.

– *Geschichte und Culturgeschichte: Eine Erwiderung.* Jena: Fischer 1891.

Schaffner, Martin. "Geschichte des politischen Systems von 1833 bis 1905." In *Das politische System Basel-Stadt,* edited by Lukas Burckhardt, 37–53. Basel: Helbing & Lichtenhahn 1984.

Schefold, Dian. *Volkssouveränität und repräsentatvie Demokratie in der schweizerischen Regeneration, 1830–48.* Basel: Helbing & Lichtenhahn 1966.

Schieder, Theodor. "Die historischen Krisen im Geschichtsdenken Jacob Burck-hardts." In *Begegnungen mit der Geschichte.* Göttingen: Vandenhoek und Rupre-cht 1962.

– "Jacob Burckhardt und die Rheinlande." In *Begegnungen mit der Geschichte.* Göttingen: Vandenhoek und Ruprecht 1962.

Schlink, Wilhelm. "Jacob Burckhardt über den 'Genuß der Kunstwerke'." *Trierer Beiträge* 1982: 47–55.

– *Jacob Burckhardt und die Kunsterwartung im Vormärz.* Wiesbaden: Steiner 1982.

Schorn-Schütte, Luise. *Karl Lamprecht: Kulturgeschichtsschreibung zwischen Wissen-schaft und Politik.* Göttingen: Vandenhoek & Ruprecht 1984.

Schorske, Carl E. "Science as Vocation in Burckhardt's Basel." In *The University and the City,* edited by Thomas Bender, 198–209. New York: Oxford University Press 1988.

Sheehan, James J. *German History, 1770–1866.* Oxford: Oxford University Press 1989.

– *German Liberalism in the Nineteenth Century.* Chicago: University of Chicago Press 1978.

Sieber, Emil. *Basler Trennungswirren und nationale Erneuerung im Meinungsstreit der Schweizer Presse, 1830–1833.* Basel: Helbing & Lichtenhahn 1964.

Siebert, Irmgard. *Jacob Burckhardt: Studien zur Kunst- und Kulturgeschichtsschrei-bung.* Basel: Schwabe 1991.

– "Zum Problem der Kulturgeschichtsschreibung bei Jacob Burckhardt." In *Die Antike im 19. Jahrhundert in Italien und Deutschland,* edited by Karl Christ and A. Momigliano, 249–73. Berlin: Duncker & Humblot 1988.

Sigurdson, Richard F. "Jacob Burckhardt: The Cultural Historian as Political Thinker." *Review of Politics* 52 (1990): 417–40.

– "Jacob Burckhardt's Liberal-Conservatism." *History of Political Thought* 13 (1992): 487–511.

Simon, Christian. *Staat und Geschichtswissenschaft in Deutschland und Frankreich, 1871–1914.* Bern: Peter Lang 1988.

Sitt, Martina. *Kriterien der Kunstkritik: Jacob Burckhardts unveröffentlichte Ästhetik als Schlüssel seines Rangsystems.* Vienna: Böhlau Verlag 1992.

Sperber, Jonathan. *Rhineland Radicals: The Democratic Movement and the Revolution of 1848–49.* Princeton: Princeton University Press 1991.

Srbik, Heinrich Ritter von. *Geist und Geschichte vom deutschen Humanismus bis zur Gegenwart.* Munich: F. Bruckmann 1950–51.

Staehlin, Andreas. *Geschichte der Universität Basel, 1818–1835.* 3 vols. Basel: Hel-bing & Lichtenhahn 1959.

Stolz, Peter. "Stadtwirtschaft und Stadtentwicklung: Basel in den Jahrzehnten nach der Kantonstrennung (1833–1860). *Regio Basiliensis* 20 (1979): 165–87.

– "Technischer Wandel in der Wirtschaftsgeschichte Basels: Von der frühen Bandweberei bis zu den Anfängen der forschenden chemischen Industrie." *BZfAG* 81 (1981): 71–96.

Sybel, Heinrich von. "Erzbishof Conrad von Hochstaden und die Bürgerschaft von Köln." *Niederrheinisches Jahrbuch* (1843): 121–59.

Telman, D. A. Jeremy. "Clio Ascendant: The Historical Profession in Nineteenth-Century Germany." Ph.D. Thesis, Cornell University, 1993.

– Review Essay, HT 33 (1994): 249–65.

Teuteberg, René. *Basler Geschichte.* Basel: Christoph Merian Verlag 1986.

Treitschke, Heinrich von. *Die Gesellschaftswissenschaft: Ein kritischer Versuch,* edited by Erich Rothacker. Halle: Max Niemeyer Verlag 1927.

Treue, Wilhelm. "Franz Theodor Kugler: Kulturhistoriker und Kulturpolitiker." HZ 175 (1953): 483–526.

Troeltsch, Ernst. *Gesammelte Schriften.* Tübingen: Mohr 1912–25.

Turner, R. Steven. "University Reformers and Professional Scholars in Germany, 1760–1806." In *The University in Society,* 2 vols., edited by Lawrence Stone. Princeton: Princeton University Press 1974.

Wackernagel, Rudolf. *Geschichte der Stadt Basel.* 3 vols. Basel: Helbing & Lichtenhahn 1907–24.

Waetzoldt, Stephan. "Artists and Society." In *German Masters of the Nineteenth Century.* New York: Metropolitan Museum of Art 1981.

Waetzoldt, Wilhelm. *Deutsche Kunsthistoriker.* 2 vols. Leipzig: E.A. Seemann 1921.

Wandel, Lee Palmer. *Voracious Idols and Violent Hands: Iconoclasm in Reformation Zurich, Strasbourg, and Basel.* Cambridge (UK): Cambridge University Press 1995.

Warnke, Martin. "Jacob Burckhardt und Karl Marx." In *Umgang mit Jacob Burckhardt: Zwölf Studien,* edited by H.R. Guggisberg. Basel: Schwabe 1994.

Wegelin, Peter. "Jacob Burckhardt und der Begriff der Nation." *Schweizer Beiträge zur allgemeinen Geschichte* 13 (1955): 164–82.

Wehler, Hans-Ulrich, ed. *Deutsche Historiker.* Göttingen: Vandenhoek & Ruprecht 1982.

Weintraub, Karl J. *Visions of Culture.* Chicago: University of Chicago Press 1966.

Wenzel, Johannes. *Jakob Burckhardt: In der Krise seiner Zeit.* Berlin: Deutscher Verlag der Wissenschaften 1967.

West, Paul. "Jacob Burckhardt and the 'Ideal Past'." *South Atlantic Quarterly* 62 (1963): 335–46.

White, Hayden. *The Content of the Form.* Baltimore: Johns Hopkins University Press 1987.

– *Metahistory.* Baltimore: Johns Hopkins University Press 1973.
– *Tropics of Discourse.* Baltimore: Johns Hopkins University Press 1978.
Wittkau, Annette. *Historismus.* Göttingen: Vandenhoek & Ruprecht 1992.
Wölfflin, Heinrich. *Gedanken zur Kunstgeschichte.* Basel: Benno Schwabe 1940.
– *Kunstgeschichtliche Grundbegriffe: Das Problem der Stilentwicklung in der neueren Kunst.* Munich: F. Bruckmann 1915.

Index

322 *Index*

326

Index